Dictionary of Sports
and Games Terminology

ALSO BY ADRIAN ROOM
AND FROM MCFARLAND

Dictionary of Pseudonyms: 11,000 Assumed Names and Their Origins, 5th ed. (2010)

Alternate Names of Places: A Worldwide Dictionary (2009)

African Placenames: Origins and Meanings of the Names
for Natural Features, Towns, Cities, Provinces and Countries, 2d ed. (2008)

The Pronunciation of Placenames: A Worldwide Dictionary (2007)

Nicknames of Places: Origins and Meanings of the Alternate and Secondary Names,
Sobriquets, Titles, Epithets and Slogans for 4600 Places Worldwide (2006)

Placenames of the World: Origins and Meanings of the Names for 6,600 Countries,
Cities, Territories, Natural Features and Historic Sites, 2d ed. (2006)

Placenames of France: Over 4,000 Towns, Villages, Natural Features,
Regions and Departments (2004; paperback 2009)

Encyclopedia of Corporate Names Worldwide (2002; paperback 2008)

A Dictionary of Art Titles: The Origins of the
Names and Titles of 3,000 Works of Art (2000; paperback 2008)

A Dictionary of Music Titles: The Origins of the
Names and Titles of 3,500 Musical Compositions (2000; paperback 2008)

Literally Entitled: A Dictionary of the Origins of
the Titles of Over 1,300 Major Literary Works
of the Nineteenth and Twentieth Centuries (1996; paperback 2009)

Placenames of Russia and the Former Soviet Union:
Origins and Meanings of the Names for Over 2,000
Natural Features, Towns, Regions and Countries (1996)

The Naming of Animals: An Appellative Reference to Domestic,
Work and Show Animals Real and Fictional (1993)

Dictionary of Sports and Games Terminology

ADRIAN ROOM

McFarland & Company, Inc., Publishers

Jefferson, North Carolina, and London

LIBRARY OF CONGRESS CATALOGUING-IN-PUBLICATION DATA

Room, Adrian.
Dictionary of sports and games terminology / Adrian Room.
p.   cm.
Includes bibliographical references.

ISBN 978-0-7864-4226-3
softcover : 50# alkaline paper ∞

1. Sports — Terminology.
2. Games — Terminology.
I. Title.
GV567.R66   2010   796.03 — dc22   2010009227

British Library cataloguing data are available

Front cover design by Kelly Elliott

Manufactured in the United States of America

*McFarland & Company, Inc., Publishers
Box 611, Jefferson, North Carolina 28640
www.mcfarlandpub.com*

Table of Contents

Introduction

This new dictionary give the definitions of more than 8,000 terms used in sports and games. The coverage ranges alphabetically from **aikido** to **yachting** and includes such well-known sports as **American football, association football, athletics, auto racing, baseball, basketball, boxing, cricket, cycling, equestrianism, field hockey, golf, gymnastics, horse racing, ice hockey, mountaineering, rugby league, rugby union, sailing, shooting, skiing, surfing, swimming, tennis,** and **volleyball.** Less widely played sports include **archery, badminton, bowls, croquet, fencing, fives, handball, netball, parachuting, real tennis, rounders, squash, trampolining,** and **weightlifting.** Devotees of **darts** are catered for, as are enthusiasts of **billiards, judo, orienteering, pool, rodeo, skateboarding, snooker,** and **water polo.** Some sports are subsumed under a broader category, as **climbing** under **mountaineering, cross-country running** under **athletics, diving** under **swimming,** kayaking under **canoeing, mountain biking** under **cycling, rally driving** under **auto racing,** skydiving under **parachuting, speed skating** under **ice skating, Thai boxing** under **boxing.** On the other hand, **snowboarding** is regarded as distinct from **skiing, tenpin bowling** from **skittles,** and **water skiing** as not simply a variety of **skiing. Trampolining,** too, is more than just a form of **gymnastics.** (The terms **American football** and **association football, field**

hockey and **ice hockey,** are spelled out since **football** or **hockey** could apply to either.)

There are also comprehensive categories of sports, each of which has its own entry. **Aquatics** deals with sports other than (literally) "mainstream" ones such as **sailing, surfing,** and **swimming. Martial arts** embraces Japanese combative sports such as **judo, karate,** and **kendo,** each entered individually. The category **Olympics** covers terminology associated with the Games rather than individual Olympic sports, which anyway have their own specific entries, as sports existing outside the Olympics.

This is perhaps the place to point out that there are no entries for board games or card games, or for blood sports such as hunting. **Angling** qualifies for inclusion, however, as both a competitive and recreational sport, but bull-fighting does not. Nor does pigeon racing, despite its similarity to horse racing, with owners, breeders, trainers, and punters (or bettors). In the field of recreational sports, boating is also excluded, as being too general. Nor does betting appear. One must draw the line somewhere.

The language or jargon of some sports can be quite arcane. Even international sports have their exclusive terminology, and it takes a player or fan to understand it. Golf, for example, has or had its **birdie, bogey, dormy, eagle, niblick, stymie, mashie, nassau,** and **sclaff.** Tennis has its idiosyncratic scoring (**love-thirty, deuce**) and horse racing its betting terms (**ante-post, evens, nap, odds-on**). When it comes to national sports, the fog of uncertainty can thicken. For non–Americans, baseball terms such as **bunt, cut-off man, home plate, left field,** and **safety squeeze** may well remain a mystery, while across the Atlantic cricket is likely to puzzle Americans (as it even does a number of British) with its **Chinaman, doosra, golden duck, off-break, popping crease,** and **yorker**. The game's fielding positions are notoriously puzzling. Where does a player stand at **backward point, fine leg, silly mid-off,** or **third man**? Come to that, what does a **nightwatchman** do?

Boxing can baffle through its different weight categories, **bantamweight, cruiserweight,** and **welterweight** among them. What is the distinction between **flyweight, junior flyweight,** and **superflyweight**? The weights entered in the book, in kilograms and pounds, are those used in professional boxing.

Attention is particularly paid to the alternate or colloquial terms found in sporting vocabulary, such as **bailer** in cricket as an alternate term for a **full toss,** or **cabbage** in golf as a colloquial term for the **rough**. Abbreviations used in sports reports also find their place, especially where scoring is important. Cricket scores are noted for their use of **b** for **bowled** and **c** for **caught** while **lbw** (**leg before wicket**) is an abbreviation more common than the spelled-out words. Baseball, similarly, has its **ERA** and **RBI**.

It may seem strange to have entries for such common words as **ball** and even **game,** but this is often because everyday terms can have more than one meaning. A good example is **club,** which in golf alone can refer either to the implement with which the ball is struck or to the association whose members play the game. A **net,** too, can be used either to catch fish or to divide the two halves of a tennis court.

The names of sporting venues such as stadiums, golf courses, racecourses, and other sports centers are accorded their due place in the book. Among them are **Aintree, Banff Springs, Down Royal, Lake Placid, Madison Square Garden,** and **Newbury**. Racecourses are classified by type, as being either **flat** (without obstacles) or **National Hunt** (with obstacles), and there are descriptions of famous jumps, as **Becher's Brook** and the **Canal Turn** at Aintree. Entries are also provided for the various national venues of the Formula One Grand Prix in auto racing, such as the **German Grand Prix** and **Spanish Grand Prix**.

Sporting awards such as **Calcutta Cup** or **Diamond Sculls** are also represented, as are the nicknames for well-known teams, such as **Falcons** for the Atlanta Falcons American football team, and **Les Bleus** for the French national rugby union team. There are no entries for the actual teams themselves, any more than there are for individual sports players, however famous.

The names of sporting awards often coincide with the actual event for which the award is made. Thus the **Melbourne Cup** is not only an Australian horse race but the award presented to the winner, and the **Champions Trophy** is both a cricket championship and the award gained by its victors. Most names of sporting events, however, derive either from their location or from their name of their founder or commercial sponsor. In the domain of horse racing, for example, the **Derby** is thus named for its founder, the Earl of Derby, while its near-namesake, the **Kentucky Derby,** is named for the state where it is held. The names of some modern sponsored races can be extraordinarily cumbersome. Among those held at England's **Wetherby** racecourse in November 2009, for example, were the Hold Your Christmas Party Here Conditional Jockeys' Claiming Hurdle, the Book Raceday Hospitality On 01937 582035 Handicap Chase (incorporating a telephone number), and the goracing.co.uk Juvenile Maiden Hurdle (with a website). Such names are absent from the book, although their generic components (**conditional jockey**, **claiming race**, **raceday**, **handicap**, **chase**, **juvenile**, **maiden**, **hurdle**) duly feature.

All sports have a ruling or administrative body, and a selection of these also features, such as the **American Football League**, **FIFA**, **International Cricket Council**, **Jockey Club**, **National Football League**, and **Union of European Football Associations**. Many such bodies are better known by their initials than the full formal name, and a list of such abbreviations is given in the Appendix.

Definitions in the dictionary are everything. They aim to be clear and concise, so that a reader knowing little or nothing about a sport can understand the term in question. Cross-references play their important part, with each word or phrase in an entry printed in **bold** having its own entry. The definitions of individual sports are necessarily concise, and like all entries occupy a single phrase or sentence. It would clearly be impracticable if not impossible to devote a single entry to the rules of a particular individual sport, let alone summarize its history. But equally the essentials of a game or sport, however familiar, must feature as prominently as the terms it uses.

There is often an overlap in sporting terminology, so that a term associated mainly with one sport is also used in the jargon of another. Thus **rally** is a term found in at least half a dozen sports. In such cases, the names of the different sports using the term are those in which it is chiefly although not exclusively found. Clearly, it would be pointless to list all the sports in which such terms as **guard** or **penalty** are used.

Reading sports writing, one often finds a word or phrase normally associated with a particular sport used in a transferred context. A football team catching up on goals in a match may thus be said to **come from behind**, a term properly belonging to racing, while a struggling tennis player may be said to be **on the ropes**, as if in the boxing ring. Indeed, many sporting terms have entered the English language generally. Thus *across the board, down to the wire, neck and neck, stay the course* come from racing; *ballpark figure, on the ball, out in left field, step up to the plate, three strikes and you're out* from baseball; *go the distance, out for the count, roll with the punches, throw in the towel* from boxing; *can of worms, hook, line and sinker, off the hook, rise to the bait* from fishing; *he had a good inning, hit for six, keep a straight bat, off one's own bat* from cricket. *Move the goalposts* comes from soccer, *behind the eight ball* from pool, *jump the gun* from athletics, *sail close to the wind* from sailing, *go off the deep end* from swimming, and *par for the course* from golf. There are many more.

Inevitably, the entries in the book represent a only a proportion, albeit a sizable one, of sporting vocabulary overall. It would be impossible to include *all* sporting terms, to list *all* sporting awards and venues. Scores of books and encyclopedias have been devoted to the world of **sailing** alone, for example, and books on sport generally are perennially popular, especially when in the form of memoirs or biographies. The present book competes with all these. But at least it offers a substantial representation of the words, names, and phrases encountered in worldwide sports, from the familiar to the often dauntingly recondite. And that has been its objective.

Arrangement of Entries

As mentioned, the entries run in alphabetical order. The heading is followed (in brackets) by the name of the sport in which the word or phrase is used. If it is used in more than one sport (often in different senses), the names of the sports also run in alphabetical order. The label *general* in this position is applied to terms that relate to more than one sport, such as **manager** or **scorecard**. The label *sport* is used to denote entries describing a particular game or sport, as **fencing** or **hurling**.

Any word or phrase in **bold** print in an entry serves as a cross-reference to its own entry in its alphabetical place. Mention of a **game** at the beginning of an entry describing a sport refers to the sport in question. Thus the definition of **badminton** begins "a **game** for two or four people," so that the game is badminton. The same applies in entries such as **aquabobbing**, categorized as a type of **water skiing**, which begins "a form of the sport," so that the sport is water skiing. On the whole, the text of an entry aims not to repeat the name of the sport in which the word or phrase is used.

Where an entry describes an action carried out by the relevant sport's participant, the pronoun "he" is used for both sexes in the interest of brevity and simplicity. This will nine times out of ten be appropriate anyway for a male-dominated sport, such as cricket or rugby union, but for sake of consistency the usage is also applied to sports in which women are prominent participants, such as gymnastics or tennis. It would unusually pedantic to have "he or she" every time.

A number of entries append additional information or an etymology in square brackets. Thus the **badminton** entry explains how the game came to be so named, and the entry for **caddie** gives the origin of the word.

Some sports writing uses American spellings for American sports, such as baseball, and British spelling for British sports, such as cricket. But such a system presents difficulties, since one has to choose which to use for an international sport such as tennis. In the present book, the spelling generally used is American rather than British, even for predominantly British sports. In some cases, however, where both a British and an American spelling exist for a headword, the British spelling may appear as a cross-reference, so that **centre** cross-refers to **center**.

Headwords followed by an exclamation point represent a spoken command, such as **action!** in wrestling, **break!** in boxing, **easy!** in rowing, or **mush!** in sled-dog racing.

Appendix and Bibliography

The Appendix is devoted to a selection of the better-known standard abbreviations for the titles of sports ruling bodies and administrative organizations.

The Bibliography lists the books and publications consulted both for definitions of sporting terms and for the rules and origins of the sports themselves. Each title has an appended description in square brackets.

THE DICTIONARY

AAA (*athletics*) abbreviation of **Amateur Athletic Association**

abaft (*sailing*) behind the boat

A-bars (*gymnastics*) short form of **asymmetric bars**

aboard (*baseball*) another term for **on base**; (*equestrianism, horse racing*) another term for **on board**

abseil (*mountaineering*) the descent of a rock face on a fixed rope using braking and sliding mechanisms [German *Abseil*, from *ab*, "down," and *Seil*, "rope"]

abseiling (*mountaineering*) the descending of a rock face by means of an **abseil**

Abu Dhabi Grand Prix (*auto racing*) the **Formula One** international **Grand Prix** held on the Yas Marina **circuit**, Abu Dhabi

academy (*equestrianism*) a riding school

acceptor (*horse racing*) a horse that has its entry for a **race** confirmed

Accies (*association football*) nickname of the Scottish **club** Hamilton Academicals

accumulator (*horse racing*) a **bet** on four or more **races**, with the stake and winnings from each race laid on the next race, so that the **punter** either wins handsomely or loses everything

accuracy jumping (*parachuting*) a **jump** made with the aim of landing on or near the center of a **target** laid out below

ace (*baseball*) a team's best **starting pitcher**; (*golf*) a **hole in one**; (*squash, tennis*) a **serve** that the **receiver** cannot touch

acey-deucey (*horse racing*) colloquial term for a **rider** who sets his stirrups at different lengths [said to derive from *AC/DC*, "alternating current/direct current"]

acro (*skiing*) a form of **aerial** [abbreviation of *acrobatic*]

acrobat (*gymnastics*) a performer of **acrobatics**

acrobatics (*gymnastics*) a **routine** of gymnastic feats

across the board (*horse racing*) (of) a **bet** that covers all possible results in a **race**, whether a **win**, a **place** or a **show** [the board is the noticeboard on which the races and **odds** are listed]

across the flat (*horse racing*) **flat racing** under **Jockey Club** rules, as distinct from **over the sticks**

acting half-back (*rugby league*) the player, often the **hooker**, who picks the **ball** up after a **play-the-ball**

action! (*wrestling*) the command by the **referee** to start wrestling

action replay (*general*) an instant televised repeat of an important or disputed incident in a **match**, as a **goal** in **association football** or a **catch** in cricket

ad court (*tennis*) short form of **advantage court**

adaptive rowing (*rowing*) **rowing** or **sculling** in boats that have been adapted for people with physical limitations or disabilities

added money (*horse racing*) extra money added to the basic **stakes** awarded to the winner

added time (*general*) time added to the normal length of time for a **match**, as **injury time** in **association football**

Addicks (*association football*) nickname of the English **club** Charlton Athletic [corruption of *Athletic*]

additional assistant referee (*association football*) one of two extra **assistant referees** behind each **goal** who help the **referee** with decisions relating to the **goal line**, **set pieces**, and play in the **penalty area**

address the ball (*golf*) to take up a **stance** in order to strike the **ball**

Admiral's Cup (*sailing*) a biennial series of **races** off the south coast of England for national teams of three boats each, culminating in the **Fastnet Cup** [established in 1957 by the Royal Ocean Racing Club, whose admiral presents the trophy]

adolph (*trampolining*) a forward **somersault** with three and a half **twists** [so called for its similarity to a **rudolph**]

advantage (*rugby league*) a period of time allowed by the **referee** after an infringement to determine whether to award the opposing team a penalty or to allow play to continue; (*rugby union*) a period of time allowed by the **referee** after an infringement to determine whether to award the opposing team a **penalty, free kick,** or **scrum** or to allow play to continue; (*tennis*) the first **point** after **deuce**

advantage court (*tennis*) the left side of the **court,** from which the **serve** is made and received at odd-numbered **points**

advantage rule (*general*) a rule under which an infringement and its **penalty** are overlooked if this is to the advantage of the non-offending team

adventure racing (*general*) a long and arduous **race** between individuals or teams over an open, varied course, typically including a mountain or river, with progress made either on foot (or by swimming) or by a form of transport, as by bicycle, by boat, or on horseback

adventure sport (*general*) a sport played not in an enclosed area such as a **field** but pursued in an open, natural environment such as water, snow, or air and potentially hazardous, so embracing all **extreme sports** and even such conventional sports as **sailing** and **skiing**

aerial (*gymnastics*) (of) a maneuver in which a complete turn is made in the air without touching the **apparatus**; (*skateboarding*) a trick performed in mid-flight, usually by launching the **board** off a ramp; (*skiing*) a maneuver such as an **acro** carried out in mid-air

aerial contact (*general*) a contact in midair between two players, as in a **flying tackle**

aerial ping-pong (*sport*) colloquial term for **Australian Rules,** where the frequent exchanges of high kicks in the air suggest the game of **ping-pong**

aerialist (*skiing*) a skier who performs gymnastic maneuvers in midair

aero bars (*cycling*) extensions fixed to the handlebars of a **time-trial bike** or **track bike** that allow the **rider** to lean further forward and so adopt an improved aerodynamic position

aerobics (*gymnastics*) a system of rapid and strenuous exercises designed to increase fitness and improve bodyshape [term coined in 1968 by U.S. physician Kenneth H. Cooper, from *aerobic*, "requiring oxygen," with plural *-s* as in **gymnastics**]

aet (*general*) abbreviation of **after extra time**

AFC (*American football*) abbreviation of **American Football Conference**

AFL (*American football*) abbreviation of **American Football League**; (*Australian Rules*) abbreviation of **Australian Football League**

African Games (*Olympics*) regional games held since 1965 for competitors from African countries

aft (*sailing*) at or toward the rear of a boat

after extra time (*general*) (of) a **score** when **extra time** has been added to the regular time

against the darts (*darts*) (of) a **win** scored even though the opposing player had the advantage of throwing first

against the head (*rugby union*) (of) gaining the **possession** of the **ball** from a **scrum** to which the opposing team had the advantage of the **put-in**

agricultural (*cricket*) (of) a hefty or lofty **stroke,** as typically occurs in **village cricket**

aid (*equestrianism*) a prompt of the hands or legs that the rider gives a horse to make it turn, change **gait,** or the like

aid climbing (*mountaineering*) **climbing** with the assistance of special equipment such as **crampons** and **ice axes**

aikido (*sport*) a Japanese **martial art** that uses specified **moves** and **throws** [Japanese *ai,* "harmony," *ki,* "breath," and *do,* "way"]

aikidoka (*aikido*) a practitioner of **aikido**

aiming mark (*shooting*) the center spot of a **target**

Aintree (*horse racing*) the racecourse at Liverpool, England, where the **Grand National** is run

air (*basketball*) the distance between the ground and a player's feet when **shooting** or jumping for the **ball**; (*equestrianism*) a staged or rehearsed movement in **haute école**; (*snowboarding, surfing*) an airborne maneuver

air gun (*shooting*) a rifle or pistol firing lead pellets by means of compressed air

air hostess (*cricket*) colloquial term for a **ball** hit particularly high [as if able to bring down an air hostess in an airplane]

air pistol (*shooting*) a **pistol** firing lead pellets by means of compressed air

air rifle (*shooting*) a **rifle** firing lead pellets by means of compressed air

air shot (*general*) a **stroke** that fails to connect with the **ball,** as typically in **cricket** or **golf**

air sports (*general*) a category of **adventure sports,** including, among others, **gliding** and **parachuting**

airborne soccer (*sport*) a **game** similar to **association football** in which a Frisbee is substituted for the **ball**

airborne throw (*netball*) a **throw** made when a player is in the air

albatross (*golf*) a **score** of three **strokes** under **par** on a **hole** [as a "bird" greater and more impressive than an **eagle**]

Albiceleste (*association football*) nickname of the Argentine national team [blend of Spanish *albar,* "white," and *celeste,* "sky blue," the colors of the stripes on the players' shirts]

Albion (*archery*) a **round** of 36 **arrows** each for men and women at 80, 60, and 50yds (73m,

55m, and 46m); (*association football*) (1) short name of the Scottish **club** Stirling Albion; (2) short name of the English club West Bromwich Albion

alder (*angling*) an **artificial fly** that resembles the alder fly

all–American (*American football*) a **college football** player in a team made up of the best such players at each position

all–around (*gymnastics*) a competition in which the highest **score** from all **events** is combined to give an overall **champion**

All Blacks (*rugby union*) nickname of the New Zealand international team [so dubbed for their dark **strip** by British journalists at the start of their **tour** of Britain in 1905]

all–in wrestling (*wrestling*) a form of the sport with few restrictions on the permitted **holds**

All–Ireland (*Gaelic football, hurling*) (of) a **final** between teams with players drawn from both the Republic of Ireland and Northern Ireland

all–play–all (*general*) another term for a **round robin**

all–pro (*American football*) a **professional** player selected to play in the **Pro Bowl** as one of the best in his position

all–rounder (*cricket*) a player who is equally competent as **batsman** and **bowler**

all–seater stadium (*general*) a **stadium** with no accommodation for standing spectators

all–star (*baseball*) a player selected to represent his **league** in an **All–Star game**

All–Star game (*baseball*) an annual **match** between teams selected from the best players in the **National League** and the **American League**

all–ticket match (*general*) a **match** for which spectators must obtain tickets in advance

all–weather (*horse racing*) (of) a **racecourse** with a synthetic surface that allows racing to take place in any weather

All Whites (*association football*) nickname of the New Zealand national team [the color of the team's **strip**]

alley (*baseball*) a section of the **outfield** between two **fielders**; (*bowls*) the long narrow enclosure where **indoor bowls** are played; (*skittles*) the area where the **game** is played; (*tennis*) the space between the **tramlines** at the side of the **court**; (*tenpin bowling*) the long narrow enclosure where the **game** is played

alley–oop (*basketball*) a maneuver in which the **ball** is thrown up high so that another player running toward the **basket** can catch it in midair and score; (*skateboarding, snowboarding*) a **spin** made in the opposite direction to that in which the **boarder** is traveling [probably French *allez!*, "go!" and a supposed French pronunciation of

up, influenced by *Alley Oop*, a character created by U.S. cartoonist V.T. Hamlin in the 1930s]

allez! (*fencing*) the command given by the **referee** to start fencing [French *allez!*, "go!"]

Allianz Arena (*general*) a leading sports **stadium** in Munich, Germany

allowance (*horse racing*) a deduction from the **weight** that a horse carries

Alpine skiing (*skiing*) a competitive form of the sport involving **downhill** and **slalom events** [originating in countries where the Alps form part of the territory, as France and Switzerland]

also–ran (*horse racing*) a horse that ran a **race** but did not finish with a **place**

amateur (*general*) a person who takes part in sport for pleasure, as distinct from a paid **professional**

Amateur Athletic Association (*athletics*) the British national governing organization for **athletics**, founded in 1880

amble (*equestrianism*) a horse's leisurely **gait** in which the legs on one side are lifted alternately with those on the other side

American bowls (*bowling*) another name for **tenpin bowling**

American football (*sport*) a form of **football** played with an oval **ball** between teams of 11 players, **points** being scored for **touchdowns** and **goals**

American Football Conference (*American football*) one of the two **conferences** into which the **National Football League** was divided in 1969, the other being the **National Football Conference**

American Football League (*American football*) the **professional football** organization formed in 1959 to rival the **National Football League** and merging with the latter in 1970

American League (*baseball*) one of the two most prestigious North American professional **leagues**, formed in 1901 to rival the **National League**

American tournament (*general*) another term for a **round robin**

America's Cup (*sailing*) the **cup** awarded to the winner of an international series of **races** held approximately every four years between one defending vessel and one challenging vessel [first awarded by the Royal Yacht Squadron in 1851 to the U.S. schooner *America*, winner of a race around the Isle of Wight]

amidships (*sailing*) in or toward the middle of the boat

amplitude (*snowboarding*) the height of a **jump** or trick

anabolic steroids (*general*) a drug that increases muscle size, illegally taken by some **athletes** or administered to **racehorses**

Anaheim Stadium (*baseball*) the California **stadium**

that is the **home ground** of the Anaheim Angels team

anchor (*athletics*) the contestant who runs the **anchor leg**; (*cricket*) a **batsman** who can be relied on not to take risks; (*tenpin bowling*) the last **bowler** for the team, and generally the best; (*tug of war*) the person at the end of the rope, who "digs in" to steady those in front

anchor cannon (*billiards*) a **stroke** in which the two **object balls** are kept close to the **cushion** so that a series of **cannons** can be made without disturbing their position

anchor leg (*athletics*) the final **stage** of a **relay race**

anchorman (*general*) another name for an **anchor**

Anfield (*association football*) the **home ground** of the English **club** Liverpool

Angels (*baseball*) short name of the Anaheim Angels team

angle (*snooker*) to position the **cue ball** so close to the corner of the **cushion** that it is difficult to hit it in a straight line toward the **object ball**; (*squash*) a **shot** that hits one of the side walls, then the front wall, before bouncing

angle of split (*croquet*) the angle at which the **balls** diverge in a split **croquet shot**

angled shot (*table tennis*) a sharp **stroke** that sends the **ball** away at an angle

angler (*angling*) formal term for a person who fishes

angling (*sport*) the formal name for the sport or pastime of catching fish

angulate (*skiing*) to bend the body, or part of the body, away from the slope in order to maintain balance

ankle lace (*wrestling*) a **hold** in which a **wrestler** traps his opponent by the ankles, so that his back is to the **mat**

Annie's room (*darts*) a **score** of double one [from the World War I phrase "up in Annie's room" as a dismissive reply to a query regarding the whereabouts of a person or thing, the number 1 being at the top of the **dartboard**]

AN Other (*general*) a name inserted in a list of team members to represent a player yet to be announced [*another* spelled as if a personal name]

ante-post (*horse racing*) a **bet** placed before the day of the **race** [before (ante) the **runners** have their numbers posted]

apex (*auto racing*) the center point of a corner

apparatus (*gymnastics*) the equipment, or piece of equipment, on which a **gymnast** performs

appeal (*cricket*) a request from a **fielder** to the **umpire** to establish whether the **batsman** is **out** or not

appearance money (*general*) a fee paid to a famous player or performer to ensure his presence at a sporting event and so draw paying spectators

appel (*fencing*) (1) a stamp of the **front foot** in a feint; (2) a sharp blow with the **épée**, also as a feint [French *appel*, "challenge"]

apprentice (*horse racing*) shortening of **apprentice jockey**

apprentice jockey (*horse racing*) a junior **jockey** in **flat racing**, entitled to ride but receiving tuition while working for a **trainer**

approach (*golf*) shortening of **approach shot**

approach shot (*golf*) a **stroke** by which a player puts, or attempts to put, a **ball** onto the **green**; (*tennis*) a long **hit** that enables a player to move up to the **net**

approach work (*association football*) a **play** that leads in the direction of the **goal**

apron (*auto racing*) in **Indy car** and **NASCAR** racing, the paved portion of the **racetrack** that separates the racing surface from the **infield**; (*boxing*) the part of a **ring** that extends beyond the **ropes**; (*golf*) the part of the **fairway** immediately in front of the **green**

aquabatics (*aquatics*) a display of spectacular feats in or on the water [blend of Latin *aqua*, "water," and *acrobatics*]

aquaboard (*general*) a **board** for riding on the surface of the water, as in **surfing**

aquabobbing (*water skiing*) a form of the sport using a vehicle like a tricycle but with **skis** instead of wheels [the vehicle bobs or bounces on the water]

aquacade (*general*) a display of **swimming** or **diving**, usually accompanied by music [blend of Latin *aqua*, "water," and *cavalcade*]

aquadrome (*general*) a leisure facility for aquatic pursuits [blend of Latin *aqua*, "water," and **hippodrome**]

aquafit (*aquatics*) a type of **aerobics** performed in water

aqualung (*aquatics*) a self-contained **diving** apparatus with a supply of compressed air, the latter carried on the back

aquanaut (*aquatics*) another term for a **skindiver** [blend of Latin *aqua*, "water," and *astronaut*]

aquaplane (*water skiing*) another term for a **wakeboard**

aquarobics (*aquatics*) a system of exercises similar to **aerobics**, carried out to music in chest-high water [blend of Latin *aqua*, "water," and *aerobics*]

aquatic art (*swimming*) a rare alternate name for **synchronized swimming**

aquatics (*sport*) sports practiced on or in the water, such as **surfing**, **swimming**, and **water polo**

Arabs (*association football*) nickname for **supporters** of the Scottish **club** Dundee United [said to derive from the sand spread on the **pitch** in the winter of 1963 to make it playable for the **cup tie** against Albion Rovers]

Arc (*horse racing*) short name of the **Prix de l'Arc de Triomphe**

arch (*athletics*) the curve of the body of an **athlete** clearing the **bar** in the **high jump**

archer (*archery*) a person who engages in **archery**

archer's bow (*association football*) the posture of a player making a **dive**, differing from a genuine fall in that the perpetrator holds up both arms with open palms, thrusts out his chest, and bends his legs at the knee, suggesting the curve of a **bow** held by an **archer**

archery (*sport*) the art of using **bows** to shoot **arrows** at a **target**

archery darts (*archery*) a variety of the sport in which the **target** has the same arrangement as the numbers on a **dartboard**

area (*association football*) shortening of **penalty area**

arena (*general*) the area enclosed by seating in which public sporting contests take place [Latin *arena*, "sand," from the part of an ancient amphitheater that was strewn with sand for combats]

Argentinian Grand Prix (*auto racing*) the **Formula One** international **Grand Prix** held on the **circuit** at Buenos Aires, Argentina

Argonauts (*Canadian football*) short name of the Toronto Argonauts team

Argyle (*association football*) short name of the English **club** Plymouth Argyle

arm (*general*) the ability to throw

arm ball (*cricket*) a **delivery** by a **spin bowler** that travels in the direction of the **bowler**'s arm, instead of deviating from it, as is more usual

arm throw (*wrestling*) a move in which the **wrestler** throws his opponent over his shoulder while holding him by the arm

arm wrestling (*wrestling*) a form of the sport in which opponents sit facing each other at a table, firmly plant opposite elbows on the table, lock hands, and attempt to force each other's arm back and down to the surface

Armco (*auto racing*) proprietary name of the metal crash barriers on a **racetrack** formerly used to absorb the impact of cars and protect spectators [acronym of American Rolling Mill Company, the original manufacturers]

armguard (*cricket*) a form of protection worn on the forearm by a **batsman** facing the **bowler**

armhold (*wrestling*) a **hold** on an opponent's arm

armlock (*wrestling*) an **armhold** applied to an opponent's elbow to gain a **submission**

armstand (*swimming*) a **handstand** on the edge of a **diving board** held briefly before the start of a **dive**

around the horn (*baseball*) (of) a **double play** in which the **ball** is thrown from **third base** to **second base** to **first base**, putting out **runners** at the latter two [from the image of a ship rounding Cape Horn, South America]

arrow (*archery*) the thin pointed missile shot from a **bow** to land on a **target**; (*darts*) colloquial term for a **dart**; (*tenpin bowling*) one of several lines marked on the **lane** to help guide the **ball** to the **pins**

arrow-chucking (*sport*) colloquial term for **darts**

arrowman (*darts*) colloquial term for a player of the **game**

art of self-defense (*general*) a term originally applied to **boxing** but now to most of the **martial arts**

Art Ross Trophy (*ice hockey*) the **trophy** awarded to the top **point** scorer at the end of the regular **National Hockey League** season [first awarded in 1948 in honor of Art Ross, manager and coach of the Boston Bruins]

artificial fly (*angling*) a **fly** that imitates an insect, larva, or small fish

artistic gymnastics (*gymnastics*) the principal form of the sport, performed on various pieces of **apparatus**, as distinct from **rhythmic gymnastics**

artistic swimming (*swimming*) another term for **synchronized swimming**

A's (*baseball*) nickname of the Oakland Athletics team

ascender (*mountaineering*) a metal grip threaded on a rope as an aid in **climbing**

ascham (*archery*) a tall cupboard for the storage of **bows** and **arrows** [named for Sir Roger Ascham (1515–1568), author of *Toxophilus* (1545), the first English treatise on the sport]

Ascot (*horse racing*) a **flat** and **National Hunt racecourse** near Windsor, Berkshire, England, associated primarily with **Royal Ascot**

Ascot Gold Cup (*horse racing*) the most prestigious **race** at **Royal Ascot**, first run in 1807

Ashes (*cricket*) (1) a series of **test matches** between England and Australia; (2) the **trophy** awarded to the winner of the series [the trophy is in the form of a small urn, devised after the Australian victory of 1882 as a supposed receptacle of the "ashes" of English cricket but in reality said to contain the burned remains of a **bail**]

ashitori (*sumo*) a move that brings one's opponent down by the leg [Japanese *ashitori*, "leg-hold"]

Asian Games (*Olympics*) **regional games** held since 1951 for competitors from Asian countries

assist (*association football, ice hockey*) a **pass** that leads to the scoring of a **goal**; (*baseball*) a **play** that makes it possible for a **batter** or **runner** to be **put out**; (*basketball*) a **pass** that allows a **basket** to be scored; (*lacrosse*) the last **pass** made before a **goal** is scored

assistant referee (*association football*) one of the two officials on either **touchline** who help the **referee** adjudicate the **game** by using a **flag** to indicate **offsides**, **throw-ins**, and **corner kicks**

association football (*sport*) a **field game** in which two teams of 11 players compete to kick or head the **ball** into the **goal** of the opposing side [played according to the rules drawn up by the **Football Association**]

astern (*sailing*) in or toward the **stern** of a vessel

astrodome (*general*) a covered **stadium** [originally the name of the Houston Astros **baseball** team at Houston, Texas, built in 1965]

Astros (*baseball*) short name of the Houston Astros team

AstroTurf (*general*) proprietary name of an artificial surface for sports **pitches** serving as a substitute for **turf**, with a woven, grasslike pile laid on a rubber base [as installed at the Houston **Astrodome**]

asymmetric bars (*gymnastics*) the **apparatus** used by women for **artistic gymnastics**, consisting of two parallel bars at different heights [so called for distinction from the **parallel bars** used by men]

at bat (*baseball*) the turn of a player to **bat**

atemi-waza (*jujitsu*) the striking techniques that are one of the sport's five basic elements [Japanese *atemi*, "blow," and *waza*, "work"]

athlete (*general*) a person who takes part in **athletics** [from Greek *athlon*, "contest"]

athletics (*general*) (1) an overall term for sports involving contests of strength, speed, endurance, or agility; (2) such sports as now divided into **track events** and **field events**

attack (*cycling*) the sudden acceleration made by a **rider** in an attempt to break away from another rider or a group; (*general*) a collective term for the players in attacking positions, as the **forwards** in association football; (*lacrosse*) a collective term for the three players **first home, second home,** and **third home** between the **center** and the opponents' **goal**

attack line (*volleyball*) the line 3 meters from the **net** that marks the furthest point to which defending players can advance

attacker (*general*) a player whose role is mainly in attacking

attend the flag (*golf*) to hold the **flag** while another player **putts**, removing it immediately after the **ball** has been struck

attitude (*cricket*) another term for the **stance** of a **batsman**

auction race (*horse racing*) a **race** of horses bought at public auction

audible (*American football*) a tactic or **game plan** called out in coded form by the **quarterback** at the **line of scrimmage** to replace the **play** called in the **huddle** (or to execute a play without a huddle when time is short)

Augusta (*golf*) the **golf course** at the Georgia city of the same name that is the home of the **National Golf Club** and host to the **U.S. Masters**

Auld Enemy (*general*) an English team from the point of view of Scotland

Auld Mug (*sailing*) nickname of the **trophy** awarded to the winner of the **America's Cup**

Aunt Emma (*croquet*) colloquial term for an unenterprising player

Aunt Sally (*cricket*) colloquial term for a **wicketkeeper** [the **bowler** "aims" the **ball** at the wicketkeeper in the same way that balls at a fairground are aimed to smash the pipe of the wooden figure known as an Aunt Sally]

Aussie Rules (*sport*) colloquial name for **Australian Rules**

Aussies (*general*) colloquial term for an Australian sports team [abbreviation of *Australian*]

Austerity Games (*Olympics*) nickname of the **Olympic Games** held in London in 1948, when resources were still in short supply after World War II

Australian crawl (*swimming*) a fast **crawl** originating in Australia

Australian Football League (*Australian Rules*) the main governing body for the sport

Australian Grand Prix (*auto racing*) the **Formula One** international **Grand Prix** held on the **circuit** at Adelaide or Melbourne, Australia

Australian National Football (*sport*) the formal name of **Australian Rules**

Australian Open (*tennis*) the major **championship** that is the first **grand slam** competition of the year, held at Flinders Park, Melbourne, Australia

Australian Rules (*sport*) an Australian version of **rugby union** played with an oval **ball** between teams of 18 players, with **points** scored for **goals** and **behinds** [played according to rules determined by the Australian National Football Council]

Austrian Grand Prix (*auto racing*) the **Formula One** international **Grand Prix** held on the **circuit** at the A1 Ring, Spielberg, Austria

auto racing (*sport*) the racing of finely-tuned cars around a prepared or designated **circuit**

autobus (*cycling*) colloquial term for a group of lagging **riders** who stick together to help each other finish inside the time limit for a **stage** [French *autobus*, "bus"]

autocross (*auto racing*) a form of **auto racing** across country or on an unmade **track** [French *auto*, "car," and **cross-country**]

automobile racing (*sport*) the formal name of **auto racing**

autopoint (*auto racing*) a **race** over rough country in motor vehicles [the motorized equivalent of a **point-to-point**]

autres, les *see under* **les**

autumn double (*horse racing*) a **bet** on the **Cambridgeshire** and **Cesarewitch**, both **handicap races** run in the autumn

Autumn Spectacular (*golf*) colloquial name for the **World Matchplay Championship**

Avalanche (*ice hockey*) short name of the Colorado Avalanche team

avalement (*skiing*) the technique of bending then extending the legs to lessen the jolts experienced when traveling over uneven terrain [French *avaler*, "to lower"]

average (*baseball*) shortening of **batting average**; (*cricket*) (1) shortening of **batting average**; (2) shortening of **bowling average**

awasewaza (*judo*) an **ippon** made by scoring two **waza-ari** [Japanese *awase*, "combine," and *waza*, "work"]

away (*association football*) in **football pools**, a **match** won by a team playing on the **ground** of their opponents; (*general*) (1) not on one's **home ground**; (2) on the outward half of a **race**; (*golf*) (of) a player who is furthest from the **hole**

away game (*general*) a **match** played on the opponents' **ground**

away swing (*cricket*) a movement of the **ball** from the **leg side** to the **off side**

axel (*ice skating*) a **jump** from the forward **outside edge** of one **skate** to the back outside edge of the other, incorporating one and a half turns in the air [introduced by the Norwegian skater Axel Paulsen (1855–1938)]

axel lift (*ice skating*) in **pair skating**, the **lift** of a woman by her partner in which she is raised on the first element of an **axel**, supported and turned one and a half times over the man's head, then lowered on the second element

Ayr (*horse racing*) a **flat** and **National Hunt racecourse** at Ayr, southwestern Scotland

Azzurri *see* **Gli Azzurri**

b (*cricket*) abbreviation of **bowled** in scoring

b sub (*cricket*) abbreviation of **bowled by substitute** in scoring

Baa-Baas (*rugby union*) nickname of the **Barbarians**

baby split (*tenpin bowling*) a **split** in which only two **pins** are left standing

back (*archery*) the part of the **bow** handle that faces the **target** when the **archer** is shooting; (*general*) in **field games** such as **association football**, a defensive player behind the **forwards**; (*horse racing*) to place a **bet** on a horse in a **race**; (*rugby league, rugby union*) any of the seven players not in the **scrum**

back and fill (*sailing*) to trim the **sails** so that the wind alternately presses them back and fills them

back bowl (*bowls*) a **bowl** lying between the **jack** and the rear **ditch**

back crawl (*swimming*) a former term for the **backstroke**

back door (*golf*) the back or side of the **hole** when entered by the **ball**

back down (*rowing*) to move a boat backward by pushing the **oars**

back edge (*fencing*) the opposite edge of the **saber** from the **cutting edge**

back foot (*general*) the right foot, of a right-handed person, as the one further from the **target**

back four (*association football*) the four **backs** in a 4-4-2 **formation**

back full (*trampolining*) a backward **somersault** with a **full twist**

back giant (*gymnastics*) a **giant** in which the **gymnast** swings clockwise, his palms facing in the same direction as his stomach

back handspring (*gymnastics*) a **backflip** onto the hands from a standing position on one or both feet that leads to a landing upright on the **floor** or **apparatus**

back-in, full-out (*gymnastics*) a double **salto** with a **full twist** made during the second salto

back judge (*American football*) a member of the officiating team positioned **downfield** of the **line of scrimmage** at the side of the **field** who rules on whether a **pass** is fairly caught

back nine (*golf*) the last nine **holes** on a **course**

back of a length (*cricket*) a **ball** pitched short of a **length** (but not so as to be actually **short**)

back pass (*association football*) a **pass** back to one's own **goalkeeper**, who must observe the **back-pass rule**

back-pass rule (*association football*) a rule introduced in 1992 which states that a **goalkeeper** receiving a **back pass** may not handle the **ball** in the **penalty box**

back-pedal (*boxing*) to retreat from an opponent while still facing them

back pocket (*Australian Rules*) a defensive player who runs the **ball** out of **defense**

back pullover (*trampolining*) a move in which, following a **backdrop**, the legs are pulled or pushed over the head into a three-quarter **somersault** onto the feet

back row (*rugby union*) the three **forwards** (two **flankers** and the **number eight**) at the back of a **scrum**

back shot (*polo*) a **shot** played in the opposite direction to the movement of play

back straight (*athletics*) the straight part of a **track** furthest from the **finish**; (*horse racing*) the straight part of a **racecourse** furthest from the finish

back stretch (*athletics, horse racing*) anther term for the **back straight**

back swing (*gymnastics*) a backward **swing**

back the field (*horse racing*) to bet on the rest of the **runners** rather than the **favorite**

back three (*rugby union*) the **wingers** and **full back**, as the players usually furthest back in a defensive situation

back up (*angling*) to fish a pool from the bottom toward the top by making a **cast** across then walking slowly backward upstream; (*cricket*) (1) as a **fielder**, to be in readiness to stop the **ball** if it is missed by another fielder; (2) as the **batsman** at the **non-striker's** end, to start to move down the **pitch** in readiness for a possible **run** made by the **striker**; (*lacrosse*) to place a player directly behind the line of a **shot** at **goal** in order to re-sume **possession** if the shot is blocked or deflected

back walkover (*gymnastics*) a move in which a **bridge** is executed then each leg brought forward in turn via a **handstand** position

backboard (*basketball*) the board fixed behind the **basket** to deflect the **ball**; (*ice hockey*) a board fixed behind the **goal**; (*tennis*) a wall or other surface against which a player can practice **shots**

backbreaker (*wrestling*) a **hold** in which a **wrestler** presses his opponent down on his back over his knee or shoulder

backcast (*angling*) to throw a **fishing line** back before making a **cast**

backcheck (*ice hockey*) to check an opponent while skating backward toward one's own **goal**

backcourt (*tennis*) the area of the **court** between the **service line** and the **baseline**

backcourt violation (*basketball*) the **offense** of passing the **ball** back across the **center line** to a colleague

backdoor play (*lacrosse*) a **play** in which a player sends the **ball** around the back of the **defense** toward either **wing** then makes for the **goal**

backdoor slider (*baseball*) a **pitch** that appears to be beyond the outside part of the **strike zone** but that then breaks back over the **plate**

backdrop (*trampolining*) a landing made on the back

backfall (*wrestling*) a **fall** on the back

backfield (*American football*) the players who line up behind the **line of scrimmage**

backfist (*karate*) a punch with the back of the fist

backflip (*gymnastics*) a backward aerial **somersault**

backhand (*bowls*) the part of the **rink** to the left of a right-handed player, and to the right of a left-handed player; (*tennis*) (1) (of) a **stroke** with the back of the hand facing toward one's opponent; (2) the part of the **court** to the left of a right-handed player, and to the right of a left-handed player, where it often necessary to play backhand

backhand chop (*table tennis*) a **chop** made back-hand

backhand drive (*table tennis*) a **drive** made back-hand

backhand flick (*table tennis*) a **flick** made back-hand

backhand push (*table tennis*) a **push** made back-hand

backhander (*general*) a blow or **stroke** made **backhand**

backheel (*association football*) a **pass** or **shot** made with the heel

backlift (*association football*) a backward raising of the leg before the **ball** is kicked; (*cricket*) a back-ward lifting of the **bat** before the **stroke** is made

backline (*general*) a line marking the end limit of play; (*rugby union*) the players lined across the **field** behind a **scrum** or **lineout**

backmarker (*general*) (1) a contestant who starts a **race** with the least advantageous **handicap**; (2) a competitor at the back of the **field**

backpaddle (*canoeing*) to push the **paddle** back-ward in order to reverse the direction of motion

backscratcher (*skiing*) an aerial maneuver in which the **skier** touches his back with the tails of both **skis**, keeping his legs together and his knees bent under his body

backside air (*snowboarding*) an aerial maneuver executed off the **backside wall** of the **half-pipe**

backside rotation (*snowboarding*) a clockwise ro-tation for a **regular footer** or an anticlockwise ro-tation for a **goofy footer**

backside wall (*snowboarding*) the wall of the **half-pipe** behind the back of the **boarder**

backspin (*general*) a backward motion imparted to a **ball** when struck, as in **golf** or **snooker**; (*table tennis*) a backward rotation given to the **ball** ei-ther by striking it with a downward movement or by a **chop** of the **bat**

backstop (*baseball*) a screen or wall that acts as a barrier behind the **catcher**; (*cricket*) an alternate name for a **longstop**; (*rounders*) the player behind the **batter** who stops the **ball**; (*spaceball*) the frame at the end of each **court** that serves as a scoring area

backstroke (*swimming*) a **stroke** performed on the back, with alternate backward circular move-ments of the arms and scissor movements of the legs

backstroke flags (*swimming*) flags suspended above and across the pool near each end, positioned to show **backstroke swimmers** where to turn

backswing (*golf*) the movement that lifts the **club** back and away from the **ball** preparatory to striking it

backward (*swimming*) a **dive** in which the **diver** starts with his back toward the water and rotates away from the **board**

backward point (*cricket*) a **fielding** position on the **off side** similar to **point** but further out from the **batsman** and behind the line of his **wicket**

badminton (*sport*) a **game** for two or four people on a **court** with a **net** played with lightweight **rackets** and a **shuttlecock**, the object being to win more **points** than the **opposition** by preventing the shuttlecock from hitting the ground [first played in the 1870s at Badminton House, Gloucestershire, country seat of the dukes of Beaufort]

Badminton (*equestrianism*) short name of the Badminton Horse Trials, an annual **three-day event** held in the grounds of Badminton House, Gloucestershire, seat of the dukes of Beaufort

baff (*billiards*) to hit the **table** before hitting the **ball**; (*golf*) to strike the ground with the **sole** of the **club** and so send the **ball** high into the air

baffing spoon (*golf*) a former term for the **spoon** more commonly known as a **baffy**

baffy (*golf*) the former name of a 4-**wood**, a **spoon** like a **brassy** but with a slightly shorter **shaft** and a more concave face [perhaps from French *baffe*, "slap in the face"]

bag (*angling*) the amount of fish caught; (*baseball*) any **base** but **home base**; (*cricket*) (1) the total of **wickets** taken in an **innings** or **match** by a particular **bowler**; (2) shortening of **cricket bag**; (*golf*) shortening of **golf bag**

bag boy (*golf*) a male member of the **course** staff who helps place a player's **clubs** on a **cart**

bag drop (*golf*) the place where a **bag boy** or **bag girl** picks up a player's **clubs**

bag girl (*golf*) a female member of the **course** staff who helps place a player's **clubs** on a **cart**

bag tag (*golf*) the tag that identifies a particular player's **bag**

bagel (*tennis*) shortening of **bagel job**

bagel job (*tennis*) colloquial term for a **set** won in six **straight games** [from the resemblance of the loser's zero **score** to a bagel]

Baggies (*association football*) nickname of the English **club** West Bromwich Albion [from the bags in which the **stewards** carried the **gate money** along the **touchline** to their office]

baggy green (*cricket*) the baggy green cap worn by Australian **Test** players

Bahrain Grand Prix (*auto racing*) the **Formula One** international **Grand Prix** held on the **circuit** at Sakhir, Bahrain

bail (*cricket*) one of the two **bails** on the **wicket**

bail out (*golf*) to play cautiously, as in a **short game** around a **green** guarded by **bunkers**

bailer (*cricket*) another term for a **full toss** [it is aimed at the **bails**]

bails (*cricket*) the two small wooden crosspieces atop the **stumps** that form the **wicket**, which when dislodged denote that the **batsman** is **out**

Bairns (*association football*) nickname of the Scot-

tish **club** Falkirk [Scots *bairns*, "children," a local name for the townsfolk]

bait (*angling*) the food on a **hook** that attracts fish and offers them a **bite**

bait waiter (*angling*) a tray that screws into a **bank stick** to hold boxes of **bait**

baitfish (*angling*) a small fish used as **bait**

baize (*billiards, snooker*) the green woolen cloth that covers the **bed** of the **billiard table**

baker (*angling*) a type of **artificial fly** used in salmon-fishing

balance beam (*gymnastics*) a formal name for the **beam**

balestra (*fencing*) an attacking movement consisting of a **jump** forward with both feet immediately followed by a **lunge** [Italian *balestra*, "crossbow"]

balk (*baseball*) an illegal action by the **pitcher** in which he fails to deliver a **pitch** after beginning the motion to do so, thus deceiving a **baserunner**; (*billiards, snooker*) the part of the **billiard table** where play begins, marked off by the **balkline**

balkline (*athletics*) a line marking the boundary for a preliminary run when jumping; (*billiards, snooker*) a line across the bottom of the **billiard table** 29 inches (73.3cm) from the **cushion**; (*croquet*) the line at each end of the **court** from which players start

ball (*association football, rugby union*) a **pass** to a teammate; (*baseball*) a **pitch** outside the **strike zone**; (*cricket*) a **delivery** by the **bowler**; (*general*) (1) the round or oval object of varying size, shape, and composition with which a **game** or sport is played, as a **baseball**, **billiard ball**, or **football**; (2) a **game** played with a ball, as **American football** or **baseball**

ball carrier (*rugby league, rugby union*) the player carrying the **ball** at any given moment

ball court (*general*) an area such as a paved yard used for **ball games**

ball game (*general*) any **game** played with a **ball**

ball hawk (*American football*) colloquial term for a player who is quick to get **possession** of the **ball**

ball-out (*trampolining*) a one-and-a-quarter forward **somersault** executed after a **backdrop**

ball player (*association football*) a player with good **ball skills**; (*baseball*) a player of the **game**

ball skills (*association football*) the knowledge and expertise required of a **ball player**

ball tampering (*cricket*) an infringement in which the surface of the **ball** is artificially altered during a **game** to gain an advantage, as by raising its **seam** with a fingernail or applying a substance to shine it

ball up (*Australian Rules*) the procedure for starting

a **game**, in which the **umpire** bounces the **ball** in the center of the **field** and the **ruckmen** compete for **possession**

ballboy (*association football*) a boy stationed on the **sidelines** to return the **ball** for a **throw-in**, collect **corner flags** after a **match**, and the like; (*tennis*) a boy who retrieves **balls** that are out of play and returns them to the players, supplies balls to the players, and the like

ballet (*ice skating, skiing*) a movement or performance like that of a ballet dancer

ballet leg (*swimming*) a position in **synchronized swimming** in which one leg is extended perpendicular to the surface of the water

ballet leg double (*swimming*) a position in **synchronized swimming** in which both legs are extended perpendicular to the surface of the water

ballgirl (*association football*) a girl stationed on the **sidelines** to return the **ball** to the players when it goes out of play, collect the **corner flags** after a **match**, and the like; (*tennis*) a girl who retrieves **balls** that are out of play and returns them to the players, supplies balls to the players, and the like

ballkid (*tennis*) general term for a **ballboy** or **ballgirl**

Ballon d'Or (*association football*) an annual award to the player adjudged the European Footballer of the Year, first made in 1956 [French *ballon d'or*, "golden ball"]

balloon (*cricket*) to score a **duck**; (*general*) a high kick or **hit** of a **ball**

ballooning (*sport*) racing or competing in hot-air balloons, with contests of altitude, distance, duration of flight, accuracy of landing, and the like

ballpark (*baseball*) a **stadium** for **baseball**

ballwinner (*association football*) a player adept at winning the **ball**

Ballybunion (*golf*) a **golf course** at Ballybunion, Co. Kerry, Ireland

Baltimore chop (*baseball*) a **chopper** that enables the **batter** to reach **first base** before a **fielder** can catch the **ball** [originally practiced by Baltimore Orioles]

banana kick (*association football*) a sharply curving **shot** made with the inside of the boot

banana shot (*golf*) an extreme **slice** that sends the **ball** on a curving trajectory

bandbox (*baseball*) a **ballpark** smaller than average, in which it is easy to hit **home runs**

bandit (*golf*) an **amateur** player with an undeservedly high **handicap**, giving an advantage in competitions

bandy (*sport*) a **game** similar to **hockey** played on ice with curved **sticks** between teams of 11 players, the object being to score **goals** [perhaps same word as *bandy*, "to toss from one to another"]

Banff Springs (*golf*) a **golf course** at Banff, Alberta, Canada

bang-bang (*baseball*) a moment of play when a **runner** and the **ball** arrive at a **base** almost simultaneously

bank (*billiards, snooker*) another term for a **cushion**

bank shot (*basketball*) a **shot** that sends the **ball** off the **backboard** into the **basket**

bank stick (*angling*) a device that secures a **keepnet** on a river bank

banker (*association football*) a **result** forecast identically in a series of entries on a **football coupon**

Bankies (*association football*) nickname of the Scottish **club** Clydebank

banking (*cycling*) the inclined **track** surface of a **velodrome**

Bantams (*association football*) nickname of the English **club** Bradford City [from the domestic fowl, the male of which is a lively fighter]

bantamweight (*boxing*) the professional **weight** category of maximum 54kg (118lb)

banzuki (*sumo*) the official ranking list of **wrestlers** [Japanese *banzuke*, "list"]

bar (*athletics*) the crossbar to be cleared in the **high jump** or **pole vault**; (*weightlifting*) shortening of **barbell**

bar billiards (*billiards*) a scaled-down version of **billiards** played in bars

bar hop (*cycling*) in BMX, to move from the saddle to the handlebars while the **bike** is in motion

barani (*trampolining*) a forward **somersault** with a **half-twist** [apparently a proper name]

barani-in (*trampolining*) a double forward **somersault** with a **half-twist** in the first somersault

barani-out (*trampolining*) a double forward **somersault** with a **half-twist** in the second somersault

barb (*angling*) a backward-facing projection near the point of a **hook**

Barbarians (*rugby union*) an international **invitational** team with no **ground** or **clubhouse**, founded in England in 1890 [perhaps so named from the popular conception of rugby players as mindless thugs]

Barbars (*rugby union*) nickname of the **Barbarians**

barbell (*weightlifting*) a bar with attached **disk weights** and **collars** [blend of *bar* and *dumbbell*]

barber (*baseball*) (1) colloquial term for a talkative player [like the commentator "Red" Barber]; (2) a **pitcher** who fires **balls** as the head of the **batter**, so forcing him away from the **plate** [as did Sal "The Barber" Maglie]

Barça (*association football*) nickname of the Spanish **club** Barcelona

barebow (*archery*) a type of **recurve bow** but with no **sight** or **stabilizer**

barefoot skiing (*water skiing*) a form of the sport practiced without **skis**

barmaid (*tenpin bowling*) a **pin** that remains hidden behind another pin [like a barmaid behind a bar counter]

Barmy Army (*cricket*) nickname for British **supporters** of the English national team, especially when playing **test matches** abroad [so dubbed by the Australian media for their vociferous enthusiasm]

barn (*horse racing*) a collection of **loose boxes** in a **yard**

barrage (*bowls*) a cluster of **bowls** around the **jack**; (*general*) a **heat** or **round** to elect contestants or to serve as a **tie break**, as a **jump-off** in **showjumping**

barrel (*darts*) the metal part of the **dart**; (*surfing*) the hollow space beneath the curl of a breaking wave

barrier (*horse racing*) another term for the **starting gate**

bas (*hurling*) the flat blade of the **hurley**

base (*baseball*) one of the four stations around the corners of the **infield** that must be reached in turn when scoring a **run**; (*rounders*) one of the four fixed points marked by posts that must be run around to score a **rounder**

base hit (*baseball*) a **hit** that enables the **batter** to reach a **base** safely

base jumping (*sport*) a form of **parachuting** from the summit of a structure or natural height, especially a landmark, rather than from an aircraft [name devised as an acronym of *b*uilding, *a*erial, *s*pan (as a bridge), *e*arth (as a mountain), the four objects from which the **jump** is properly made, but later associated with "base" as the foot of the object where the jumper lands]

base on balls (*baseball*) the advance to **first base** awarded to a **batter** after the **pitcher** has thrown four **balls** outside the **strike zone**

base-stealer (*baseball*) a **baserunner** who advances to the next **base** when no **hit** or **error** has been made

baseball (*sport*) (1) a **game** played with **bat**, **ball**, and gloves between two teams of nine players, the object being for each **batter** to hit the ball delivered by the opponents' **pitcher** then run around a diamond-shaped circuit of four **bases** to score a **run**; (2) the hard **ball** used in **baseball**

baseball bat (*baseball*) the **bat** used in **baseball**

baseball pass (*basketball*) a long fast **pass** in which the **ball** is thrown **overarm**

baseline (*badminton, tennis*) the **backline** at each end of the **court**; (*baseball*) a line that joins two **bases**

baseliner (*tennis*) a player who plays mainly from the **baseline** and only rarely approaches the **net**

baseman (*baseball*) a **fielder** stationed near **first base** (as **first baseman**), **second base** (**second baseman**), or **third base** (**third baseman**)

baserunner (*baseball*) a **batter** who has reached **first base** safely and is now attempting to complete the circuit

bases-loaded (*baseball*) made or occurring at the moment when **baserunners** occupy **first base**, **second base**, and **third base**

basher (*skiing*) colloquial term for a fast or reckless skier

basho (*sumo*) a **tournament** comprising 15 **matches** [Japanese *ba*, "place," and *sho*, "place," the repeated meanings serving for emphasis]

basic swing (*skiing*) a **snowplow** start to a turn and a **parallel turn** to finish

basket (*basketball*) (1) the net (originally fruit basket) fixed on a ring that is used as a **goal**; (2) a scored goal; (*skiing*) the circular part of a **ski stick** near its base that prevents the pole from going too deep into the snow

basket catch (*baseball*) a **catch** made by **fielder** at waist height as the **ball** drops over his shoulder [the player's arms and hands form a "basket"]

basketball (*sport*) (1) a **game** played between teams of five players, the object being to toss the **ball** into the opponents' **basket** to score a **goal**; (2) the large inflated **ball** used in the game

bat (*baseball*) the rounded wooden implement used to strike the **ball**; (*cricket*) (1) shortening of **cricket bat**; (2) a turn at **batting**; (3) a **batsman**; (*horse racing*) a short **whip** used by a **jockey**; (*table tennis*) the small rubber-coated implement used to strike the **ball**; (*tennis*) colloquial term for a **racket**; (*trapball*) the small flat implement with which the **ball** is hit away from the **trap**

bat-pad catch (*cricket*) a **catch** taken after the **ball** has struck the **bat** of the **batsman** and then rebounded off his **pad**

Bath (*horse racing*) a flat **racecourse** at Bath, western England

batinton (*sport*) a **game** for two or four players based on **badminton** with a scoring system as in **table tennis** [blend of **bat** and *badminton*]

baton (*athletics*) the metal cylinder passed from one runner to another in a **relay race**

batsman (*cricket*) the player with a **bat** who attempts to strike the **ball** delivered by the **bowler** and score **runs**

batter (*baseball*) the player with a **bat** who attempts to strike the **ball** delivered by the **pitcher** and score a **run**; (*rounders*) the player with a **bat** who attempts to hit the **ball** delivered by the **bowler** and score a **rounder**

batter's box (*baseball*) the place where the **batter** stands to receive the **pitch**

battery (*baseball*) collective term for the **pitcher**

and **catcher** [originally the term for the pitcher alone, as the player who delivered a "battery" of **pitches**]

batting (*baseball, cricket*) playing with a **bat**, as distinct from **fielding**

batting average (*baseball*) a **score** calculated for a **batter** by dividing his total number of **hits** by his number of **at bats**; (*cricket*) a **score** calculated for a **batsman** by dividing his total number of **runs** by the number of times he has been **out**

batting order (*baseball*) the order in which a team's **batters** are **at bat**; (*cricket*) the order in which a team's **batsmen** go in to bat

batting track (*cricket*) fuller term for the **track**

baulk *see* **balk**

baulkline *see* **balkline**

BCS (*American football*) abbreviation of **Bowl Championship Series**

beach cricket (*cricket*) an informal **game** played on the beach

beach football (*association football*) an informal **game** played on the beach

beach start (*water skiing*) a start from the beach, with the **skier** sitting in the water holding the towbar of the boat

beach volleyball (*volleyball*) a form of the **game** played barefoot on an outdoor sandy **court** between teams of two players [originally played on a beach]

beach wicket (*cricket*) a slow or dry and dusty **wicket** [like one found in **beach cricket**]

beachball (*general*) a large inflatable usually colored **ball** for **games** on the beach

beachbreak (*surfing*) the point where a wave breaks on the approach to a sandy beach

beam (*gymnastics*) the raised wooden beam on which **gymnasts** perform balancing exercises

beamer (*cricket*) a fast **full toss** delivered to a **batsman** at head height

beanball (*baseball*) a **ball** pitched at the head of the **batter**; (*cricket*) another term for a **beamer** [from colloquial **bean**, "head"]

bear hug (*wrestling*) a **hold** that tightly grips an opponent's arms and upper body

Bears (*American football*) short name of the Chicago Bears team

beat (*angling*) a stretch of riverbank noted for good **fishing**; (*sailing*) to sail as close as possible to directly into the wind

beat the board (*athletics*) to thrust the foot down hard on the **board** in the **long jump**

beatout (*baseball*) a **play** in which a **batter** makes a **run** to **first base** by outrunning the **throw** of the **fielder** designed to stop him

beautiful game (*sport*) journalistic nickname for **association football** [the phrase is attributed to the Brazilian football Pelé (1940–), whose 1977

autobiography was titled *My Life and the Beautiful Game*]

Becher's Brook (*horse racing*) a difficult **jump** on the **Grand National** course at **Aintree** [named for Captain Martin Becher (1797–1864), who fell here in the first **race** in 1839]

bed (*billiards, snooker*) the flat surface of slate on the **billiard table** on which the **baize** is laid; (*darts*) one of the two narrow rings scoring a **double** or **treble** in the main segment of a **dartboard**; (*trampolining*) the area of the **trampoline** on which performers bounce and perform **routines**

bed and breakfast (*darts*) colloquial term for a **score** of 26 [from **two and six** in its general sense of "two shillings and six pence," the traditional cost of bed and breakfast at an inn]

Bees (*association football*) (1) nickname of the English **club** Barnet; (2) nickname of the English club Brentford [initial of the names, with a hint at the stinging insect]

behind (*Australian Rules*) a **goal**, worth one **point**, scored between one of the **behind posts** and the main **goalposts**

behind post (*Australian Rules*) one of the two small posts on either side of the main **goalposts**

belay (*mountaineering*) (1) the turn of a rope around a rock, especially one supplemented by anchors and braking devices, made to assist an ascending colleague; (2) the rock around which the turn is made

Belgian Grand Prix (*auto racing*) the **Formula One** international **Grand Prix** held on the **circuit** at Spa-Francorchamps, Belgium

bell lap (*athletics*) the final **lap** of a **foot race**, signaled by the sounding of a bell

bell target (*shooting*) a **target** in **air pistol** shooting that consists of a cast-iron plate with a hole in the center behind which is a bell

bellows to mend (*general*) colloquial term for shortness of breath, as in an aging **racehorse** or an unfit **boxer**

belly (*archery*) the part of the **bow** handle that faces the **archer** when shooting

belly flop (*swimming*) an inexpert **dive** in which the **diver** lands face down, flat on the water

belly putter (*golf*) a type of **putter** with a longer than usual **shaft**, the top of which is lodged in the player's midriff when making a **shot**

bellyboard (*surfing*) a short **board** which the **surfer** rides by gripping the sides and keeping the upper surface pressed to his chest, using his legs for steering

Belmont Stakes (*horse racing*) the oldest of the **Triple Crown races**, run annually at Belmont Park near New York City [named for the financier and sportsman August Belmont (1816–1890)]

belt (*boxing*) an imaginary line around the waist

below which **punches** are prohibited; (*general*) an award for achievement in a sport, as **black belt, Lonsdale Belt**

bench (*American football, association football*) a seat near the **touchline** for a team's **manager, trainer,** and **substitutes;** (*baseball*) (1) a seat for **coaches** and **reserves** at a **match;** (2) a collective term for the reserves themselves

bench press (*weightlifting*) an exercise in which the lifter lies face up on a bench with feet on the floor and raises a **barbell** from chest level to arm's length

bench-warmer (*baseball*) colloquial term for a **re-serve** [who warms the **bench** by sitting on it]

benched (*American football*) kept out of a team as a **substitute** by being retained on the **bench** for the duration of a **game** or even for several games

bend (*athletics*) (1) the curved section of the **track;** (2) the part of a **race** run around this section; (*auto racing*) another term for a **shunt**

bend the ball (*association football*) to kick the **ball** in an curving trajectory

benefit match (*general*) a **match** the proceeds of which go to a particular player or team

Bengals (*American football*) short name of the Cincinnati Bengals team

benny squad (*American football*) the special team used for the toughest **plays** with maximum physical contact [their aggression is reportedly fuelled by pre-match doses of benzedrine]

Benson & Hedges Cup (*cricket*) the **cup** awarded to the winner of the annual competition between **first-class** counties, some **minor counties,** and certain other teams, first held in 1972 and su-perseded in 2003 by the **Twenty20 Cup** [name of sponsors]

bent (*cycling*) colloquial term for a **recumbent**

berm (*cycling*) in **BMX,** a banked bend

Bermuda Race (*sailing*) a biennial **ocean race** for **yachts,** first held in 1906 and covering a **course** from Newport, Rhode Island, to Bermuda

Bermuda rig (*sailing*) a **rig** in which a large **sail** set **fore-and-aft** is fixed directly to a tall **main-mast** [originating in Bermuda]

Bernabéu (*association football*) the **home ground** in Madrid, Spain, of the Spanish **club** Real Madrid [named for a former club president, Don Santiago Bernabéu]

besom (*curling*) the broom with which the ice is swept ahead of a traveling **stone**

best of the rest (*association football*) a term for the teams that are among the best apart from those that are currently at the top

bestball (*golf*) (1) a **match** in which one player plays against two or three other players, the low-est **score** of an individual's **holes** being the one that is counted; (2) alternate name for a **fourball**

bet (*general*) a wager on the result of a sporting contest, especially in **horse racing**

betterball (*golf*) (1) a **strokeplay** between two teams of two players in which only the lower **score** of each is counted for each **hole;** (2) a **match** in which a single player competes against the best individual score of two or more players for each hole

betting shop (*greyhound racing, horse racing*) an establishment, not on a **racetrack,** licensed for the placing of **bets** and the payment of winnings

Betty (*snowboarding*) nickname for a female **boarder**

between the flags (*horse racing*) in a **point-to-point** [a **race** in which obstacles are marked by flags]

between the posts (*association football*) the playing position of a **goalkeeper**

between the sticks (*association football*) alternate term for **between the posts**

Beverley (*horse racing*) a **flat racecourse** at Bever-ley, East Yorkshire, England

BHA (*horse racing*) abbreviation of **British Horseracing Authority**

Bhoys (*association football*) nickname of the Scot-tish **club** Celtic [mock–Irish spelling of *boys*, re-lating to the club's founding in 1887 by Irish Catholics]

bias (*bowls*) (1) the bulge or greater weight on one side of a **bowl** that makes it turn to one side; (2) the actual turning that it causes

biathlete (*Olympics*) a competitor in a **biathlon**

biathlon (*Olympics*) a contest in the **Winter Olympics** combining **cross-country skiing** and **rifle shooting** [Latin *bi-*, "two," and Greek *athlon*, "contest"]

bib (*athletics, skiing*) the vest bearing their num-ber worn by competitors; (*fencing*) the padded protective part of a mask that protects the throat

bicycle (*equestrianism*) to spur a bucking horse on each side alternately

bicycle kick (*association football*) an overhead kick made with both feet off the ground and the legs moving as if pedaling a bicycle

bicycle motocross (*cycling*) formal name of **BMX**

bicycle polo (*polo*) a variety of the **game** played on bicycles instead of on horseback

biddy basketball (*basketball*) a scaled-down ver-sion of **basketball** played by young children

bidon (*cycling*) a water bottle carried on the bicy-cle during a **road race** [French]

Biellmann spin (*ice skating*) a **spin** similar to a **lay-back spin,** with the back arched and the free leg pulled up over the head [popularized by the Swiss **figure skater** Denise Biellmann (1962–)]

big air (*general*) a **freestyle** event in a sport such as **skateboarding** or **skiing** in which participants perform various tricks in the air after a **jump**

Big Eight (*American football*) a major **conference** of eight **college football** teams, comprising the universities of Colorado, Iowa State, Kansas, Kansas State, Missouri, Nebraska, Oklahoma, and Oklahoma State

Big Five (*basketball*) the teams of five institutions in the area of Philadelphia, Pennsylvania: La Salle College, the University of Pennsylvania, St. Joseph's College, Temple University, and Villanova University

Big Four (*association football*) the four English **clubs** who have dominated the **Premier League** since its formation in 1992: Arsenal, Chelsea, Liverpool, and Manchester United

big hitter (*baseball, cricket*) a player who hits the **ball** a long way

big league (*baseball*) another term for a **major league**

Big Ten (*American football*) a major **conference** of **college football** teams, comprising the universities of Illinois, Indiana, Iowa, Michigan, Michigan State, Minnesota, Northwestern, Ohio State, Purdue, and Wisconsin

Big Three (*American football*) the **college football** teams of Harvard, Princeton, and Yale universities

Big Twelve (*American football*) a major **conference** of **college football** teams, comprising the universities of Baylor, Colorado, Iowa State, Kansas, Kansas State, Missouri, Nebraska, Oklahoma, Oklahoma State, Texas, Texas A&M, and Texas Tech

bike (*cycling*) colloquial term for a bicycle [shortening of *bicycle*]; (*motorcycle racing*) colloquial term for a motorcycle [shortening of *motorbike*]

bike-o (*orienteering*) a form of **orienteering** on **mountain bikes**

Bikle's baseball (*gliding*) a contest, formally known as "distance within a prescribed area," in which pilots attempt to fly around as many designated turn points as possible [named for pilot Paul Bikle and the contour of the **course**, like that of a **baseball diamond**]

billiard ball (*billiards*) one of the three **balls** (**plain ball**, **spot white**, and **red**) used in **billiards**

billiard cloth (*billiards, snooker*) the **baize** that covers the **billiard table**

billiard cue (*billiards*) fuller term for a **cue**

billiard marker (*billiards*) the person who (or apparatus which) marks the **points** made by the players

billiard spot (*billiards*) the **spot** on the **billiard table** nearest the top **cushion** on which the **red** is placed at the beginning of a **game**

billiard table (*billiards, snooker*) the rectangular table, with **pockets** at the sides and corners, on which **billiards** and **snooker** are played

billiards (*sport*) (1) general term for a **game** played with a **cue** and **balls** on a **baize**-covered table, the aim being either to send the balls into its **pockets** or to place them in a strategically advantageous position; (2) the specific name of such a game, played with two **cue balls** (**plain ball** and **spot white**) and one **red**

Bills (*American football*) short name of the Buffalo Bills team

billy board (*surfing*) a very short **surfboard**

Billy Williams' Cabbage Patch (*rugby union*) nickname of the **ground** at Twickenham [acquired in 1907 by William "Billy" Williams and in part used as a market garden]

bind (*rugby union*) to hold on to another player, as in a **scrum**, **ruck**, or **maul**

bingo-bango-bingo (*golf*) a **bet** among players on whose **ball** will first reach the **green**, or is nearest the **hole** when all the balls are on the green, or is first into the hole

Binos (*association football*) nickname of the Scottish **club** Stirling Albion [from *Albion*]

bird (*badminton*) colloquial term for the **shuttlecock**

birdie (*golf*) a **score** of one under **par** on a **hole** [said to derive from the "bird of a shot" that U.S. golfer Ab Smith claimed he had made in an 1899 game in Atlantic City]

bird's nest (*angling*) colloquial term for a tangled **line** or **cast**

Biscuitmen (*association football*) former nickname of the English **club** Reading [from the famous biscuit (cookie) factory in the town]

Bisley (*shooting*) the village near Woking, Surrey, that is the home of the sport in Britain

Bismarck (*horse racing*) a **bet** that **bookmakers** do not expect to win [from the World War II German battleship of the name that was torpedoed although thought to be unsinkable]

bisque (*croquet*) an extra turn awarded to a weaker player in a **handicap game**; (*general*) a **point** or **stroke** allowed when regarded as an advantage

bit (*equestrianism, horse racing*) the part of the **bridle** that the horse holds in its mouth

bite (*angling*) a nibble at the **bait** by a fish

bite alarm (*angling*) a battery-operated device that indicates the movement of a fish taking a **bite**

biter (*angling*) a fish likely to take a **bite**; (*curling*) a **stone** that just touches the outer circle of the **house**

black (*snooker*) the black **ball**, worth seven **points**

Black and Whites (*association football*) (1) nickname of the Scottish **club** Elgin City; (2) nickname of the Scottish club Gretna [the colors of the teams' **strips**]

black ball game (*sport*) a name for **snooker**, as a **game** whose outcome depends on the final **potting** of the **black**

black belt (*judo, karate*) a **belt** worn to indicate attainment of the **dan** rank

Black Cats (*association football*) nickname of the Scottish **club** Sunderland [from the animal of this color, believed to bring luck]

Black Ferns (*rugby union*) nickname of the New Zealand national women's team [from the color of the team's shirts]

black flag (*auto racing*) (1) a **flag** with a car number indicating that its driver must immediately return to the **pits**; (2) a **flag** with an orange disk showing a car number indicating that the car has a mechanical fault and must immediately return to the pits

Black Jacks (*bowls*) nickname of the New Zealand national team [a pun on the white **jack**]

black line (*cycling*) another term for the **pole line**

black run (*skiing*) a **run** regarded as difficult for inexperienced skiers

black spot (*snooker*) the spot on the **billiard table** where the **black** is positioned, midway between the top **cushion** and the **pyramid** of **reds**

Blackcaps (*cricket*) nickname of the New Zealand national team [from their black caps]

Blackhawks (*ice hockey*) short name of the Chicago Blackhawks team

blade (*cricket*) (1) the long flat part of the **bat** with which the **ball** is struck; (2) the bat itself; (*golf*) a **club** that does not have a **cavity back**; (*ice skating*) the runner of a **skate**; (*rowing*) (1) the flat part of the **oar** or **scull** that enters the water during the rowing **stroke**; (2) the oar itself; (*table tennis*) the **bat** underneath its rubber covering

blader (*roller skating*) a person who uses **rollerblades**

Blades (*association football*) nickname of the British **club** Sheffield United [from the local cutlery industry]

bladework (*rowing*) the management of **oars**

blanket (*greyhound racing*) the cover worn by a greyhound during the **parade**, showing the color and number of the dog's **post** position

blanket finish (*general*) a very close **finish** to a **race** [the contestants are so close that they could be covered with a single blanket]

blast (*baseball*) colloquial term for a **home run**

blaster (*golf*) another term for a **sand wedge** [it "blasts" the **ball** out of the sand]

blazer (*general*) (1) a lightweight colored or striped jacket bearing on its breast pocket the badge of a **club** or team, worn by some **sportsmen**; (2) an sports official who wears a jacket of this type [so named from the red color of the original jackets worn by members of a St. John's College, Cambridge, boat club]

bleachers (*general*) (1) cheap open-air seats for spectators at a **sports ground**; (2) the spectators themselves [at one time the seats were "bleached" or made pale by the sun]

Bledisloe Cup (*rugby union*) the **cup** for which Australia and New Zealand have competed since 1931 [presented by Lord Bledisloe (1867–1958), governor general of New Zealand]

Bleus, Les *see under* **Les**

blind side (*rugby league*) the side of the **pitch** with less space between the **scrum** or **play-the-ball** and the **touchline** than the **open side**; (*rugby union*) the side of the **pitch** with less space between the **scrum**, **ruck** or **maul** and the **touchline** than the **open side**

blind-side flanker (*rugby union*) the **flanker** binding on the **blind side**

blind spot (*cricket*) the spot on the ground in front of a **batsman** where a **ball** pitched by the **bowler** leaves the batsman uncertain whether to **play forward** or **play back**

blinders (*horse racing*) another term for **blinkers**

blinkers (*horse racing*) a pair of sidepieces fastened to a horse's **bridle** in order to concentrate its attention on the **course** ahead

blitz (*American football*) a tactic in which a **defensive back** abandons his usual role and charges into the offensive **backfield** to anticipate a **pass**

blob (*cricket*) colloquial term for a **score** of zero [from the shape of the figure 0]

block (*American football*) the obstruction of an opposing player who does not have **possession**; (*athletics*) shortening of **starting block**; (*basketball*) the deflection of the **ball** in its upward trajectory to the **basket**; (*cricket*) (1) the spot on which the **batsman** rests the end of the **bat** when facing the **bowling**; (2) the defensive stopping of the **ball** with the bat, with no attempt to score **runs**; (*cycling*) (1) another term for the **freewheel**; (2) a tactical attempt by a **rider** to slow down a group when he does not want it to catch another rider who is in the **lead**; (*general*) the hindering of the play or action of an opponent; (*swimming*) the platform from which a **swimmer** starts the **race**; (*table tennis*) a return **shot** in which the **ball** is played immediately after it strikes the table; (*volleyball*) a barrier of arms and hands formed above the **net** with the aim of preventing a **spike** from the opposite side

block tackle (*association football*) a **tackle** made on an opposing player as he attempts to pass the **ball** or shoot at **goal**

block volley (*tennis*) a **volley** played with a stationary **racket**

blocker (*American football*) a player whose role is to obstruct opponents with a **block**; (*bowls*) a **bowl** played so that it stops short of the **head**, thus making it harder for an opponent to attack the **jack**; (*cricket*) a habitually defensive **batsman**, who makes little or no attempt to score **runs**

blocking (*boxing*) the use of the shoulders, arms, or hands to prevent an opponent's **punch** from landing cleanly

blocking back (*American football*) another term for a **quarterback**

blocks (*athletics*) shortening of **starting blocks**

blood bin (*rugby league, rugby union*) the place off the **pitch** where a player goes to have a bleeding wound attended to

blood doping (*athletics*) the injection of oxygenated blood into an **athlete** in an (illegal) attempt to enhance his performance

blood horse (*horse racing*) another term for a **thoroughbred**

blood knot (*angling*) a knot used to tie **fishing lines** of different lengths

bloodstock (*horse racing*) collective term for **thoroughbred** or **pedigree** horses

bloodwagon (*skiing*) a sled used to move injured skiers off the **slopes**

bloodworm (*angling*) a midge larva (*Chironomus*) used as **bait**

bloop (*baseball*) to hit the **ball** high beyond the reach of the **infielders**

blooper (*baseball*) (1) a **ball** hit high beyond the reach of the **infielders**; (2) a ball thrown high by the **pitcher**

blouse (*horse racing*) another term for the **silks** worn by a **jockey**

blow line (*angling*) a **line** used in **dapping** which allows the **fly** to ride on the surface of the water

blue (*general*) (1) a person chosen to represent Oxford University or Harrow School (dark blue) or Cambridge University or Eton College (light blue) in a particular sport; (2) the badge awarded for this; (*snooker*) the blue **ball**, worth five **points**

Blue Bombers (*Canadian football*) short name of the Winnipeg Blue Bombers team

Blue Brazil (*association football*) nickname of the Scottish **club** Cowdenbeath [from the color of the team's **strip** and their boast that they are on a par with the Brazilian national side]

blue day (*gliding*) a cloudless day, when the sky is altogether blue

blue flag (*auto racing*) the **flag** shown to a driver to indicate that another car is trying to overtake

Blue Jackets (*ice hockey*) short name of the Columbus Blue Jackets team

Blue Jays (*baseball*) short name of the Toronto Blue Jays team

blue jersey (*cycling*) the jersey worn by the leader of the Intergiro **sprint** competition at the halfway stage of the **Giro d'Italia** [Italian *maglia azzurra*, "blue jersey"]

blue line (*cycling*) another term for the **stayers' line**; (*ice hockey*) one of the two lines that divide the playing area into three equal parts

blue spot (*snooker*) the spot on the **billiard table** where the **blue** is positioned, midway between the top and bottom **cushions**

Bluebirds (*association football*) nickname of the Welsh **club** Cardiff City [the color of the team's **strip**]

blueliner (*ice hockey*) another term for a **defenseman**

Bluenoses (*association football*) nickname for **supporters** of the Scottish **club** Rangers [from the supposedly puritanical views of the Protestants who traditionally make up their numbers, especially when the club is playing against the rival Catholic club Celtic]

Blues (*association football*) nickname of many English **clubs**, including Birmingham City, Carlisle United, Chelsea, Chester City, Ipswich Town, Manchester City, and Rangers [the color of the teams' **strips**]; (*Australian Rules*) short name of the Carlton Blues team; (*ice hockey*) short name of the St. Louis Blues team

blunt (*skateboarding*) a move in which the tail area behind the rear **truck** is in contact with the surface face

BMX (*cycling*) a bicycle **race** over an outdoor course similar to a **motocross** course, originating in California in 1969 [abbreviation of *bicycle motocross*]

BMX bike (*cycling*) the specially modified bicycle, with smallish wheels and no gears, used in **BMX**

board (*association football*) shortening of **indicator board**; (*athletics*) the point at the end of the **runway** where the **athlete** takes off in the **long jump** and **triple jump**; (*basketball*) (1) shortening of **backboard**; (2) alternate term for a **rebound**; (*cricket*) shortening of **scoreboard**; (*darts*) shortening of **dartboard**; (*general*) short form of the formal name of the specially designed rigid platform on which a person rides in various sports, as **skateboard**, **snowboard**, **surfboard**, **wakeboard**; (*swimming*) shortening of **diving board**

boarder (*general*) a person who rides a **board** in a sport such as **snowboarding** or **surfing**

boardercross (*snowboarding*) another name for **snowboard cross**

boarding (*ice hockey*) the **offense** of pushing another player into the **boards**

boards (*ice hockey*) the wooden or plastic wall surrounding the playing area

boardsailing (*sport*) the official term for **windsurfing** [introduced because of potential problems with the proprietary status of the name *Windsurfer*]

boast (*squash*) a **shot** that hits one of the two side walls of the **court**, then the end wall, before bouncing [probably form of French *bosse*]

boast for nick (*squash*) a **boast** that lands in the **nick** and dies

boat race (*rowing*) a **race** between two or more boats

Boat Race (*rowing*) the annual **boat race** between **crews** of Oxford and Cambridge universities, held on the Thames River in London, England

boat the oars (*rowing*) to lift the **oars** out of the **rowlocks** and lay them down in the boat

boatie (*rowing*) colloquial term for a enthusiast for the sport

boating (*general*) **rowing** or **sailing** for pleasure

bob (*angling*) (1) short term for a **bobfly**; (2) a bunch of lobworms used as **bait** for eels; (*bobsledding*) short term for a **bobsled**

bob and weave (*boxing*) to make quick bodily movements up and down and from side to side in order to dodge **punches**

bob skeleton (*bobsledding*) another term for a **skeleton bob**

bobber (*angling*) a **float** attached to a **fishing line**; (*bobsledding*) a **rider** on a **bobsled**

bobfly (*angling*) a **dry fly** that bobs on the water to indicate the position of the **tail fly**

bobs (*bobsled*) the runners for a **bobsled**

bobskate (*ice skating*) an **ice skate** with two parallel blades

bobsled (*bobsledding*) the racing sled for two or more people with steering mechanism and brakes used in **bobsledding**

bobsledding (*sport*) the sport of riding or racing in a **bobsled**

bobsleigh (*bobsledding*) alternate name for a **bobsled**

bocce (*bowls*) an Italian form of the **game**, played on a narrower, shorter **green** [Italian *bocce*, plural of *boccia*, "ball"]

boccia (*bowls*) another term for **bocce**

body blow (*boxing*) a **punch** to the body

body drop (*judo*) a **throw** in which a combatant stretches out his leg and throws his opponent forward over it

body lock (*wrestling*) a **hold** in which a combatant locks his arms around his opponent's body before bringing him down to the **mat**

body swerve (*general*) a swerving movement of the body made to avoid an opponent

bodyboard (*surfing*) a short type of **surfboard** on which the **surfer** lies

bodybuilding (*general*) a form of exercising to develop the size and strength of the muscles

bodycheck (*general*) the deliberate obstruction of an opposing player's movements, permitted in **ice hockey** and (in the men's **game**) **lacrosse** but not in most other sports

bodyline bowling (*cricket*) fast, aggressive **bowling**

aimed at the body of the **batsman** and usually directed toward the **leg side** [famously practiced in England's 1932–33 **tour** of Australia]

bodysuit (*swimming*) a close-fitting one-piece costume offering little resistance to the water

bodysurfer (*surfing*) a person riding a breaking wave without a **surfboard**

bogey (*golf*) a **score** of one **stroke** over **par** for a **hole** [originally the same as par, but after 1918 as now, presumably from the idea of losing to an imaginary player, Colonel Bogey, said to be so named from "The Bogey Man," a popular song of the 1890s]

bogu (*kendo*) the armor worn by a **kendoka** [Japanese]

boil (*angling*) a swirling disturbance on the surface of the water made by a fish coming to a **fly**

Boks (*rugby union*) short form of the nickname **Springboks**

Bolivarian Games (*Olympics*) **regional games** held since 1938 for competitors from South American countries [named for the South American revolutionary leader Simón Bolívar (1783–1830)]

bolo (*boxing*) a long sweeping **uppercut** [said to resemble a slash with a bolo knife]

bolt (*horse racing*) to run out of control, as a horse may do at the **start** of a **race**

bomb (*American football*) a long looping forward **pass**; (*basketball*) a long **shot** into the **basket**

Bombers (*Australian Rules*) short name of the Essendon Bombers team

bonification (*cycling*) a time bonus given to **riders** in the **Tour de France** who achieve a **place** at the end of a **stage** [French *bonification*, "bonus"]

bonk (*cycling*) sudden fatigue in a **race**, often due to lack of food [imitative of the sensation]

bonk bag (*cycling*) colloquial term for a **musette**

bonspiel (*curling*) a combined **tournament** and social gathering lasting two or three days [said to derive from French *bon*, "good," and Dutch or Flemish *spel*, "game"]

boobird (*general*) colloquial term for a **supporter** who boos his team when they play poorly

boogie board (*surfing*) colloquial term for a **bodyboard**

book (*association football*) to administer a **booking**

bookie (*horse racing*) colloquial shortening of **bookmaker**

booking (*association football*) the entering of a player's name in a notebook by the **referee** as the record of an **offense**, signaled by the showing of a **yellow card** to the offender

bookmaker (*general*) a person who accepts **bets** in a sport such as **horse racing** and pays out the winnings

bookmakers (*greyhound racing, horse racing*) another term for a **betting shop**

boom (*sailing*) a pole that controls the position of a **sail**

Boomers (*basketball*) colloquial name of the Australian national men's team [from *boomer*, a male kangaroo, Australia's national animal]

boost (*swimming*) a rapid headfirst rise out of the water in **synchronized swimming**

boot (*general*) colloquial term for a kick

Boot Hill (*cricket*) colloquial name for the hazardous **short leg** position [from the nickname of the cemetery in Dodge City, Kansas, where many 19th-century gunfighters were buried after they "died with their boots on"]

boot money (*rugby union*) money formerly paid to **amateur** players by manufacturers of sports equipment as an inducement to wear their brand of boots for televised matches

boot one (*baseball*) to make an error

bootleg (*American football*) a **play** in which a **quarterback** simulates a **pass** to another player but then runs in the opposite direction concealing the **ball** near his hip [from the term for smuggled goods]

Borderers (*association football*) nickname of the Scottish **club** Berwick Rangers [based near the border with England]

Borders (*association football*) nickname of the Scottish **club** Gretna [based near the border with England]

bore (*athletics, horse racing*) to push other competitors out of the way to gain advantage in a **race**

Boro (*association football*) nickname of the English **clubs** Middlesbrough and Scarborough [shortened form of the placenames]

borrow (*golf*) the allowance made for a slope or the wind on a **green**, usually by putting the **ball** uphill of the **hole**

bos (*hurling*) another spelling of **bas**

bosie (*cricket*) less common term for a **googly** [a specialty of the English **bowler** B.J.T. Bosanquet (1877–1936)]

Bosman ruling (*association football*) a ruling that a **footballer** whose contract has expired may be given a free **transfer** to another **club** inside the European Union [the result of a 1995 case brought by the Belgian player Jean-Marc Bosman (1964–)]

boss (*association football*) colloquial term for a **manager**

bossaball (*sport*) a **game** invented in Belgium in 2005 that combines **association football**, **volleyball**, **trampolining**, and capoeira (a Brazilian **martial art** and dance combination), played on an inflatable **court**

Boston crab (*wrestling*) a **hold** in which a combatant sits on the buttocks of a prone opponent and pulls upward on the latter's legs [so they are bent like those of a crab]

Boston Marathon (*athletics*) an annual **marathon** in Boston, Massachusetts, first run in 1897

bottom (*baseball*) the second part of an **inning**, during which the **home** team bats

bottom edge (*cricket*) (1) the lower edge of a **bat** as held by the **batsman**; (2) a (usually inadvertent) **stroke** off this part

bottom fishing (*angling*) **fishing** for fish that live near the bottom of the sea, usually done from the shore or a pier

bottom order (*cricket*) the **batsmen** who come last in the **batting order**

bottom pocket (*billiards, snooker*) one of the two **pockets** in the **balk** area of the **billiard table**, where play begins

bouldering (*mountaineering*) a form of **rock climbing** in which climbers attempt to negotiate large boulders without the use of ropes

boules (*sport*) a French form of **bowls** played on rough ground with metal **bowls** that are thrown at a smaller target **ball** [French *boules*, "bowls"]

bounce (*Gaelic football*) a downward throw of the **ball** so that it rebounds to the hand of the thrower, as a way of retaining **possession** and gaining ground; (*general*) a rebound of the **ball** when thrown, dropped, or hit; (*golf*) the projection at the bottom of the back of a **wedge**; (*trampolining*) a rebound made on the **bed** of the **trampoline**

bounce-out (*darts*) the landing of a dart on the wire of a **dartboard** so that it falls to the ground

bounce pass (*general*) a **pass** in which a player sends the **ball** to a teammate by bouncing it

bouncer (*archery*) an **arrow** that rebounds from the **target**; (*cricket*) a fast **delivery** that sends the **ball** up sharply from the **pitch** so that it reaches the **batsman** at chest or head height

boundary (*cricket*) (1) the outer limit of the playing area, traditionally marked with a rope or white line; (2) a **hit** by a **batsman** that clears the boundary to score a **four** or a **six**

boundary line (*general*) a line around the playing area beyond which the **ball** is **out of play**

bout (*boxing, fencing, judo, wrestling*) a contest

bow [rhyming with "hoe"] (*archery*) the curved piece of flexible plastic or other material (originally wood), bent by means of a cord stretched between its ends, that is used for shooting **arrows**

bow [rhyming with "how"] (*horse racing*) a horse's debut in a **race**; (*rowing*) (1) the front of the boat; (2) the **rower** who sits in it; (*sailing*) the forepart of the boat

bow-hand (*archery*) the hand in which the **bow** is held, normally the left

bowl (*American football*) (1) a bowlshaped **stadium** in which **college football** is played; (2) the **game**

itself; (3) a **postseason** game between specially invited teams; (*bowls*) (1) the heavy **ball** with a **bias** that is rolled toward the **jack**; (2) the **delivery** of the bowl; (3) a turn at **bowls**; (*cricket*) (1) a **delivery** of the **ball** to the **batsman** by the **bowler**; (2) to **dismiss** a batsman with such a delivery

Bowl Championship Series (*American football*) the **championship** series, held in one of five **bowls**, that determines which top two college teams will meet in competition

bowl game (*American football*) an established **postseason game** held at a named **bowl**

bowl-in (*polo*) another term for a **throw-in**

bowled (*cricket*) (of) a **batsman** who is **out** because a **ball** delivered by the **bowler** has struck the **stumps** and dislodged one or both of the **bails**

bowler (*bowls*) a player of the **game**; (*cricket*) the player who delivers the **ball** to the **batsman**

bowler's wicket (*cricket*) a **pitch** that favors **bowlers**

bowling (*bowls*) the playing of the **game**; (*cricket*) the action of delivering the **ball** by the **bowler**; (*sport*) alternate name for **tenpin bowling**

bowling alley (*bowls*) the **alley** where **indoor bowls** are played; (*skittles, tenpin bowling*) the **alley** where the **game** is played

bowling analysis (*cricket*) the performance record of a **bowler**, giving figures for **overs** and **maiden overs** bowled, **runs** conceded, **wickets** taken, and the like, from which his **bowling average** can be calculated

bowling average (*cricket*) a **score** calculated for a **bowler** by dividing the number of **runs** scored off his bowling by the number of **wickets** he takes

bowling crease (*cricket*) the **crease** from behind which the **bowler** delivers the **ball**

bowling green (*bowls*) the **green** where the **game** is played

bowling machine (*cricket*) a machine that delivers **balls** to a **batsman** when practicing in the **nets**

bowls (*sport*) a **game** played between individuals or teams in which **bowls** are rolled toward a **jack** on a **green**, the aim being to place as many of one's bowls as possible closer to the jack than the nearest bowl of one's opponent or opponents

bowman (*archery*) an **archer**, who wields a **bow**; (*rowing*) fuller term for the **bow**

bowshot (*archery*) the distance to which an **arrow** can be shot from a **bow**

bowside (*rowing*) the left side of the boat from the point of view of the **rowers**, as the side on which the **bow** sits

bowsight (*archery*) a **sight** attached to the **bow** to help the **archer** aim

bowstring (*archery*) the cord of a **bow**

box (*association football*) shortening of **penalty box**; (*athletics*) the support in which an **athlete** plants the base of the **pole** when making a **vault**; (*baseball*) the place where the **batter** stands; (*cricket*) (1) a padded shield for the genitals worn inside the trousers by **batsmen** and **wicketkeepers**; (2) alternate term for the **gully**; (*horse racing*) shortening of **loose box**; (*rugby union*) the area behind the **scrum** or **line-out**

box kick (*rugby union*) a high kick, usually by the **scrum-half**, into the **box**

box lacrosse (*lacrosse*) formal name of **boxla**

box out (*basketball*) to take up a position between an opponent and the **basket** so as to be well placed for a **rebound**

box score (*baseball*) the tabulated results of a **game**

boxed in (*athletics*) trapped by other competitors against the inside of the **track** and so unable to overtake

boxer (*boxing*) a person who boxes or is skilled in the sport

boxing (*sport*) a **combat sport** in which two competitors trade **punches** with fists enclosed in **boxing gloves**

boxing gloves (*boxing*) the special padded gloves worn by **boxers**

boxing match (*boxing*) a **match** or contest between two **boxers**

boxing ring (*boxing*) fuller term for a **ring**

boxing weight (*boxing*) the particular **weight** category at which **boxers** are matched

boxla (*lacrosse*) an indoor version of the **game**, played in an **ice hockey rink** with the ice removed or covered

brace (*association football*) two **goals** scored by the same player in a **match**; (*canoeing*) a recovery **stroke** made to prevent the **canoe** from overturning; (*cricket*) a **duck** scored by the same **batsman** in two **innings**; (*sailing*) a rope attached to the **yard** of a **square-rigged** vessel for the purpose of trimming the **sail**

bracket (*ice skating*) a **half-turn** that takes the skater from one edge of the **skate** to the opposite edge

Braemar Gathering (*general*) the best-known annual **Highland games**, held at the village of Braemar, Scotland, and traditionally attended by royalty

brakeman (*bobsledding*) the person who sits at the back of the **bobsled** and applies the brakes

braking zone (*auto racing*) the part of the **track** before a corner where drivers apply the brakes

brandling (*angling*) a type of red worm used as **bait**

Brands Hatch (*auto racing*) a **circuit** in Kent, England, that was formerly the site of the **British Grand Prix**

brassie (*golf*) another spelling of **brassy**

brassy (*golf*) the former name of a 2-**wood** [so called because it had a brass **sole**]

Bravehearts (*rugby league*) nickname of the Scottish national team [from Braveheart, the name given to the Scottish patriot William Wallace (*c.*1270–1305), who defeated the English at Stirling in 1297 and ravaged the northern counties of England]

Braves (*baseball*) short name of the Atlanta Braves team

Brazilian Grand Prix (*auto racing*) the **Formula One** international **Grand Prix** held on the **circuit** at either São Paolo or Interlagos, Rio de Janeiro

break (*athletics*) a move by a **runner** away from a **lane** toward the inside of the **track**; (*billiards, pool, snooker*) (1) the **shot** made by a player to **break the balls**; (2) a consecutive series of **pots**; (3) the **score** at the end of such a series; (*cricket*) the change of direction of a **ball** delivered by the **bowler**; (*croquet*) a turn in which more than one **point** is scored in consecutive **shots**; (*cycling*) a move made by a **rider** or group of riders away from a larger group or from the **peloton**; (*golf*) another term for a **borrow**; (*horse racing*) the **start** of a **race**; (*surfing*) an area of water where the waves are suitable for riding; (*tennis*) a **win** gained by a player able to **break service**

break! (*boxing*) a command by the **referee** to the **boxers** in a **clinch** to separate

break back (*tennis*) to win an opponent's **service game** immediately after losing one's own such game

break-back (*cricket*) a **ball** that turns sharply from the **off side** on pitching

break-fall (*martial arts*) a controlled **fall** in which the impact is absorbed by the arms and legs

break one's duck (*cricket*) to score one's first **run** as a **batsman**, so that one's **score** will not be a **duck**

break point (*tennis*) a **point** that gives a player a chance to **break service**

break service (*tennis*) to win a **game** in which one's opponent is serving

break the balls (*billiards*) to open the **game** by striking the **red ball** or giving a **miss**; (*snooker*) to open the **game** by striking one of the **red balls**

break the throw (*darts*) to win a **leg** in which one's opponent made the first **throw**

break the wicket (*cricket*) to dislodge the **bails** of a **wicket** and thus **stump** or **run out** the batsman

breakaway (*cycling*) another term for a **break**; (*general*) a sudden attack or forward movement; (*rugby football*) an outside **forward** in the **back row**

breakdown (*rugby union*) the ending of a **run**, causing competition for the **ball**, usually after a **tackle**

breakfast (*darts*) shortening of **bed and breakfast**

breaking ball (*baseball*) a **pitch** that changes direction in flight, as a **curveball** or **slider**

breast the tape (*athletics*) to come first in a **foot race** by breaking the **tape** with one's chest

breaststroke (*swimming*) a **stroke** made breastdown, with circling movements of the arms and frog-like kicks of the legs between the arm movements

breeder (*horse racing*) a person who breeds horses, and especially **thoroughbreds**

Breeders' Cup (*horse racing*) the **cup** awarded to the winner of a **flat race** founded in 1984 at Hollywood Park, Texas, and administered by **breeders** in a series of promotional **races** with thoroughbreds

breeze-up sale (*horse racing*) a sale in which prospective purchasers can watch young or untried horses go through their paces

breezing (*horse racing*) moving at a brisk **pace** but under some restraint from the **jockey**

Brewers (*baseball*) short name of the Milwaukee Brewers team

brick (*basketball*) colloquial term for a poor **shot**

Brickyard (*auto racing*) nickname of the **circuit** on which the **Indianapolis 500** is held [so named for the millions of bricks laid in 1909 to build a new and firmer surface]

bricole (*billiards*) a rebound of the **ball** from a **cushion**; (*real tennis*) a rebound of the **ball** from a side wall [French *bricole*, "trifle"]

bridge (*billiards, snooker*) (1) a support for the **cue** made by placing one's fingers on the **billiard table** and raising the thumb; (2) a metal support at the end of a **rest**, serving the same purpose; (*gymnastics*) an arched position of the body; (*wrestling*) an arched position formed with one's back facing the **mat**, adopted to avoid a **fall**

bridge out (*wrestling*) to escape from an opponent's move by rolling over from a **bridge** onto one's stomach

bridle (*equestrianism*) the gear on a horse's head that controls and guides it

Brighton (*horse racing*) a **flat racecourse** at Brighton, East Sussex, England

Britannia Cup (*rowing*) the **cup** first presented in 1969 to the winners of a **race** for coxed fours at Henley; (*sailing*) a **cup** first presented in 1951 to the winners of a **race** for small **yachts** from any country

British and Irish Lions (*rugby union*) formal name of the **Lions**

British Grand Prix (*auto racing*) the **Formula One**

international **Grand Prix** held on the **circuit** at **Silverstone**

British Horseracing Authority (*horse racing*) the organization that regulates the sport in Britain [known as the British Horseracing Board until 2007, when it took over the regulatory powers of the **Jockey Club**]

British Lions (*rugby union*) former name of the **Lions**

British Open (*golf*) formal name of the **Open Championship**

broad jump (*athletics*) another term for the **long jump**

broadsiding (*motorcycle racing*) another term for **powersliding**

broken field (*American football*) the area beyond the **line of scrimmage** where the **defense** is relatively scattered

bronc-riding (*rodeo*) the riding by a competing **cowboy** of a **bronco**

bronco (*rodeo*) a wildly bucking horse ridden by a competing **cowboy**

Broncos (*American football*) short name of the Denver Broncos team; (*rugby league*) short name of the English **club** London Broncos

Bronx Bombers (*baseball*) nickname of the New York Yankees team [their **stadium** is in the Bronx, New York City]

bronze (*Olympics*) shortening of **bronze medal**

bronze duck (*cricket*) a **duck** scored by a **batsman** on his third ball [from **bronze** as a third award]

bronze medal (*Olympics*) the medal awarded as third **prize** [bronze is a less valuable metal than gold or silver]

broodmare (*horse racing*) a **mare** kept for breeding

Brooklands (*auto racing*) a former **circuit** near Weybridge, Surrey, England, closed in 1939 on the outbreak of World War II and never reopened

broom (*curling*) the implement used to sweep the ice ahead of a moving **stone**

broom wagon (*cycling*) the support vehicle that picks up **riders** who abandon a **stage race** or fall too far behind [French *voiture balai*, "broom wagon"]

broomball (*sport*) a game similar to **ice hockey** in which a **volleyball** is propelled over the ice with brooms

broomhandle putter (*golf*) a type of **putter** with a long **shaft**, held at the top in one hand at chest height and lower down in the other hand at waist height, like a broomhandle

brown (*snooker*) the brown **ball**, worth four **points**

brown belt (*judo, karate*) a **belt** worn to indicate the highest attainment in the **kyu** rank

brown spot (*snooker*) the spot on the **billiard table** where the **brown** is positioned, midway on the **balkline**

Browns (*American football*) short name of the Cleveland Browns team

Bruins (*ice hockey*) short name of the Boston Bruins team

Brumbies (*rugby union*) a **Super 14** team based in Canberra, Australia, formed in 1996 [from the brumbies, wild horses native to Australia]

brushback (*baseball*) a **pitch** aimed deliberately at the head of the **batter** to force him to retreat off **home plate**

bubble float (*angling*) a round plastic **float** containing water

Buccaneers (*American football*) short name of the Tampa Bay Buccaneers team

buck (*equestrianism*) a vertical **jump** by a horse, with the back arched and the feet bunched together

bucket (*basketball*) colloquial term for a **basket**; (*rowing*) an abrupt forward movement of the body

Bucks (*basketball*) short name of the Milwaukee Bucks team

Bucs (*American football*) colloquial short name of the **Buccaneers**

Buddies (*association football*) nickname of the Scottish **club** St. Mirren [plural of a Scots form of *body*, "person"]

budo (*sport*) another term for the **martial arts** [Japanese *budo*, "way of the warrior"]

bug (*horse racing*) the **weight** allowance given to an **apprentice** as **jockey** [an apprentice is denoted in a **race** program by an asterisk (*), a symbol known to printers as a bug]

bug boy (*horse racing*) an **apprentice** as **jockey** [he has been given a **bug**]

buggy (*auto racing*) a small, sturdy vehicle used in **off-roading**, as a beach buggy or dune buggy

bulger (*golf*) a former type of wooden **club** with a concave face

bull (*archery, shooting*) (1) the center spot of the **target**; (2) a **shot** that hits this spot; (*darts*) (1) the small red (or black) circle at the center of the **dartboard**, worth 50 **points**; (2) a **dart** that hits this spot

bull-dogging (*rodeo*) another term for **steer-wrestling**

bull-riding (*rodeo*) the competitive bareback riding of a Brahma bull

Bulldogs (*Australian Rules*) short name of the Western Bulldogs team; (*rugby league*) short name of the English **club** Batley Bulldogs

bullet (*American football*) colloquial term for a fast, accurate **pass**

bullet race (*horse racing*) a **sprint** of less than five **furlongs** on the **flat**

bullpen (*baseball*) (1) the part of the **ground** just off the **diamond** where **pitchers** warm up; (2) collective term for the **relief pitchers** of a team

Bulls (*basketball*) short name of the Chicago Bulls team; (*rugby league*) short name of the English **club** Bradford Bulls

bullseye (*archery, darts, shooting*) formal name of a **bull**

bully (*Eton wall game*) a **scrimmage**; (*field hockey*) the opening move, in which one player from each team taps the ground and an opponent's **stick** alternately three times, then tries to be first to hit the **ball** lying between them

bully-off (*field hockey*) formal name of a **bully**

Bully Wee (*association football*) nickname of the Scottish **club** Clyde [Scots *bully*, "excellent," and *wee*, "small," as the team was long weaker than other Glasgow teams]

bum (*general*) an obsessive devotee of a sport

bump (*rowing*) the act of bumping in a **bumping race**

bump and run (*American football*) a tactic in which a **cornerback** deliberately bumps into the **receiver** and runs with him to block a **pass**; (*golf*) an **approach shot** played so that the **ball** travels a long way after it lands

bump ball (*cricket*) a **ball** that bounces just in front of a **fielder** attempting a **catch**

bump supper (*rowing*) a celebratory dinner held at Oxford or Cambridge university after the **bumping races**, hosted by the college that finished **Head of the River**

bumper (*cricket*) another term for a **bouncer**; (*horse racing*) shortening of **bumper race**

bumper race (*horse racing*) a **flat race** for young **National Hunt** horses that have not yet raced over **hurdles** or in **steeplechases** and that have not run under the rules of flat racing

bumping race (*rowing*) a **race**, rowed between college **eights** at Oxford and Cambridge universities, in which the boats, starting at fixed intervals, each aim to "bump" (touch) the one in front before being "bumped" by that behind, dropping out when this happens

bumps (*rowing*) colloquial short name for **bumping races**

bunch (*cycling*) another term for the **peloton**

bunch sprint (*cycling*) a **sprint** for the **finishing line** made by the **bunch** at the end of a **race** or **stage**

bung (*angling*) a type of **float** used when **fishing** for pike

bunker (*golf*) a **hazard** in the form of a sand-filled hollow

bunny (*cricket*) another term for a **rabbit**

bunsen (*cricket*) colloquial term for a **pitch** favorable to **spin bowlers** [rhyming slang, *Bunsen burner* giving **turner**]

bunt (*baseball*) a blocking of the **ball** with the **bat** so that it does not travel far, usually done to let a **baserunner** advance

burger (*skateboarding*) colloquial term for a bad bruise

Burghley (*equestrianism*) short name of the Burghley Horse Trials, an annual **three-day event** held in the grounds of Burghley House near Stamford, Lincolnshire, England

burnout (*auto racing*) in **drag racing**, the procedure of spinning the rear tires in water to heat and clean them before a **race**

Busby Babes (*association football*) former nickname of the English **club** Manchester United [from Sir Matt Busby (1909–1994), **manager** of the youthful team in the 1950s]

bush league (*baseball*) colloquial term for a **minor league**

bust (*darts*) to exceed the required **score**

butt (*archery*) the mound of earth behind the **target**; (*snooker*) the thicker end of the **cue**

butt-ending (*ice hockey*) an **offense** committed by jabbing an opponent with the end of the handle of the **stick**

butterfly (*swimming*) a breast-down **stroke** with the arms extended and moving together in a circular motion while the legs perform a **dolphin kick**

buttock (*wrestling*) a **throw** using the buttocks or hip

button (*curling*) another term for a **tee**; (*fencing*) the soft covering over the point of a **foil** or épée; (*rowing*) a fitting fastened on an **oar** to stop it slipping through the **rowlock**

buttonhook (*American football*) a type of **pass** in which the intended **receiver** runs straight toward a defensive **back** then stops and doubles back to the passer

butts (*shooting*) a **range** for **target** practice

buzzard (*golf*) a **score** of two **strokes** over **par** for a **hole** [as distinct from an **eagle**]

buzzbait (*angling*) an artificial **bait** with small blades that stir the water

buzzer-beater (*basketball*) colloquial term for a **basket** scored just before the end of play

by (*horse racing*) born to a named **sire** [often coupled with **out of** to name the **dam**]

bycatch (*angling*) fish inadvertently caught with the intended **catch**, especially when immature or of a protected species

bye (*cricket*) a **run** made from a **ball** that passes the **batsman** without being struck or touched by him, the run being credited to the team rather than to the **score** of the batsman; (*general*) the position of a player or team against whom no opponent has been drawn and who proceeds to the next **round** uncontested; (*golf*) a **hole** or holes remaining to be played when a **match** is decided

byline (*association football*) another term for the **touchline**

c (*cricket*) abbreviation of **caught** in scoring

c and b (*cricket*) abbreviation of **caught and bowled** in scoring

cabbage (*golf*) colloquial term for the **rough**

caber (*athletics*) the heavy pole, usually the trimmed trunk of a tree, used in the sport of **tossing the caber** at **Highland games**

caddie (*golf*) the person who assists a **golfer** during a **round** by carrying the **clubs**, advising on the choice of club, and using his knowledge of the **course** to **read the green** [Scots form of French *cadet*, originally "youngest son"]

caddie car (*golf*) a small motorized vehicle for transporting players and equipment around a **course**

caddie cart (*golf*) a light trolley for carrying a bag of **golf clubs** around a **course**

caddy (*golf*) another spelling of **caddie**

cadence (*cycling*) the rate at which a **rider** is pedaling

cage (*baseball*) an enclosed area for batting practice; (*ice hockey*) colloquial term for the **goal**

Calcutta Cup (*rugby union*) the **cup** for which England and Scotland have competed since 1879 [so called as made from the silver rupees remaining in the funds of the Calcutta Football Club, India, when it was disbanded in 1877]

Calder Memorial Trophy (*ice hockey*) the **trophy** awarded for the **rookie** of the year [named for Frank Calder, president of the **National Hockey League** from 1917 to 1943]

Caley Jags (*association football*) nickname of the Scottish **club** Inverness Caledonian Thistle ["Caley" from *Caledonian*, "Jags" as a colloquial term for the jagged leaves of a thistle, the Scottish national emblem]

calf-roping (*rodeo*) an **event** in which a mounted competitor chases a calf, lassoes it, dismounts, throws the calf to the ground by hand, then ties up three of its feet with a short rope

Calgary Stampede (*rodeo*) an annual **event** and stampede in Calgary, Alberta, Canada, founded in 1912

call (*cricket*) a shouted direction by a **batsman** to his partner whether to run ("Yes!") or to remain in the **crease** ("No!"); (*tennis*) a decision by the **umpire** or a **line judge** on the status of a **shot**

call a cab (*horse racing*) to wave one arm as a **jockey** in order to retain balance when taking a **fence**

call one's shot (*billiards, snooker*) to say which **ball** one intends for which **pocket**

callisthenics (*gymnastics*) special exercises designed to achieve strength, fitness, and grace of movement

calx (*Eton wall game*) the area behind the **goal line**, defined by a white line [Latin *calx*, "lime"]

cam (*mountaineering*) a mechanical device that grips into a crack in the rock

caman (*hurling, shinty*) the slim curved **stick** used in the **game**

Camanachd Cup (*shinty*) a **cup** involving 16 teams, first competed for in 1896 [Gaelic *camanachd*, "shinty"]

Cambridgeshire (*horse racing*) an annual **handicap** at **Newmarket**, first run in 1839 [name of the county in which it was originally located]

camel spin (*ice skating*) a **spin** on one foot, with the back arched and the non-skating leg extended horizontally behind [the pose suggests the humped back of a camel]

camogie (*hurling*) a modified form of the **game** played by women [played with a **stick** called a *camog*, a Gaelic word related to **caman**]

campaign (*horse racing*) to prepare a horse for a **race**

can (*golf*) colloquial term for the **hole**

Can-Am (*auto racing*) short name of the Canadian-American Grand Challenge Cup, an annual series of **races**, six in the U.S. and two in Canada, first held in 1866

can of corn (*baseball*) colloquial term for an easy **catch** for a **fielder** [said to derive from the can on a stack in a grocery that a sales clerk would knock down with a stick and catch]

Canada Cup (*golf*) former name of the **World Cup**

Canadian canoe (*canoeing*) a long narrow **canoe** propelled by a single-bladed **paddle**

Canadian football (*sport*) a **game** similar to **American football** but with 12 players a **side** and a longer field of play

Canadian Grand Prix (*auto racing*) the **Formula One** international **Grand Prix** held on the Gilles Villeneuve **circuit** at Montreal, Canada

Canadiens (*ice hockey*) short name of the Montreal Canadiens team

Canal Turn (*horse racing*) a difficult **jump** on the **Grand National** course at **Aintree**

Canaries (*association football*) nickname of the English **club** Norwich City [either from the local former breeding and exhibition of canaries, or from the city's mustard-making industry, with the associated color represented in the yellow shirts of the players]

cannon (*billiards*) the striking of both the **red** and one's opponent's **ball** in a single **shot**; (*croquet*) a **croquet shot** and **roquet** made in a single **stroke**; (*snooker*) a **shot** in which the **cue ball** deflects from the **object ball** into another **ball** [altered form of **carom**]

cannon game (*billiards*) another term for **carom billiards**

cannon-off (*bowls*) a **delivery** in which one **bowl** rebounds at an angle from another

cannonball (*tennis*) colloquial term for a fast **serve**

canoe (*canoeing*) the light, narrow, flat-bottomed boat, propelled by one or more **paddles**, that is used for the sport

canoe polo (*water polo*) a form of the **game** in which the participants are in short **canoes** using double **paddles**

canoeing (*sport*) (1) a contest between **canoeists**; (2) the pastime of traveling in **canoes**

canoeist (*canoeing*) (1) a competitor in **canoeing**; (2) a person who travels in a **canoe**

canopy (*parachuting*) the overhead, expanding part of a **parachute**

canopy formation (*parachuting*) the stacked formation adopted by **skydivers** once their **canopies** have opened

canter (*equestrianism*) a horse's **gait**, slower than a **gallop** but faster than a **trot**, in which three legs are off the ground at the same time [shortening of *Canterbury gallop*, from the easy **pace** at which medieval pilgrims rode to Canterbury]

Canucks (*ice hockey*) short name of the Vancouver Canucks team

canvas (*boxing*) the floor of a **ring**; (*rowing*) a term used to describe the measure of **lead** between two boats in a close **race**, fixed as the length between the **bow** and the first **oarsman** [properly the covering over the ends of the boat, originally made of canvas]

canyoning (*sport*) an **extreme sport** in which participants jump into a fast-flowing mountain stream or waterfall and allow themselves to be swept rapidly downstream

cap (*association football*) (1) a commemorative cap given to a national player each time he plays in an international **match**; (2) an appearance by a national player at international level; (*general*) a distinguishing cap worn by a player or participant in a particular sport

Capitals (*ice hockey*) short name of the Washington Capitals team

capriole (*equestrianism*) an element of **dressage** in which the horse leaps up with all four feet off the ground and kicks its back legs at the height of the **jump** [Old French *capriole*, "leap"]

captain (*general*) the leader of a sports team or **club**

Captain Armstrong (*horse racing*) a **jockey** who holds his horse back with a "strong arm" in order to stop it drawing ahead

captain's pick (*general*) (1) a player selected for a team by its **captain**; (2) an outstanding player

carabiner (*mountaineering*) a steel link with a spring clip in one side through which a rope can be threaded in **abseiling** [German *Karabinerhaken*, "spring hook"]

carambole (*billiards*) the formal name of a **carom**

card (*golf*) shortening of **scorecard**; (*horse racing*) shortening of **racecard**

Cardinals (*American football*) short name of the Arizona Cardinals team; (*baseball*) short name of the St. Louis Cardinals team

cardio (*general*) exercises to tone the circulatory system, carried out in a **gymnasium** and typically involving equipment such as the **treadmill** or **exercise bike** and **cross-training** [abbreviation of *cardiovascular exercises*]

Carling Cup (*association football*) the **cup** for which teams in the **Football League** compete [to 1982 called the League Cup, a name still popularly current, and after that date successively the Milk Cup, Littlewoods Cup, Rumbelows Cup, Coca Cola Cup, and Worthington Cup, eventually adopting its present sponsored name in 2003]

Carlisle (*horse racing*) a **flat** and **National Hunt** racecourse at Carlisle, Cumbria, England

Carnoustie (*golf*) the **course** near Dundee, Scotland, that until 1975 hosted the **Open Championship**

carom (*billiards*) another term for a **cannon** [shortening of *carambole*, from French *carombole*, from Spanish *carambola*, "the red ball in billiards"]

carom ball (*cricket*) a ball bowled by a **spin bowler** with a flick of his middle finger [named after *carom* as an Indian board game in which disks are flicked onto the table]

carom billiards (*billiards*) a form of **billiards** played on a **table** with no **pockets** and thus consisting in making a series of **cannons**

carpet (*bowls*) the surface on which **indoor bowls** is played; (*cricket*) the surface of the **pitch** and the **outfield**; (*golf*) (1) colloquial term for the **fairway**; (2) colloquial term for the **putting green**

carriage driving (*equestrianism*) a **discipline** in which a two- or four-wheeled carriage with one or more horses competes in **dressage**, a **cross-country time trial**, and the negotiation of a winding course marked out by **cones**

carrot (*croquet*) the part of the **hoop** below the ground

carry (*golf*) the distance a **ball** travels through the air before touching the ground at or near its destination; (*ice hockey*) to advance the **puck** down the ice by controlling it with one's **stick**

carry one's bat (*cricket*) to remain **not out** after batting throughout an **innings**

cart (*golf*) shortening of **golf cart**

CART Championship (*auto racing*) former name of the ChampCar Championship [acronym of Championship Autoracing Teams]

Cartmel (*horse racing*) a **National Hunt** racecourse at Cartmel, Cumbria, England

cartwheel (*bowls*) a **bowl** delivered with a marked

bias; (*gymnastics*) a sideways **somersault** with arms and legs extended

carving (*skiing*) a technique of making fast turns by turning the **skis** so that the edges cut into the snow; (*snowboarding*) a technique of making fast turns by turning the **board** so that the edge cuts into the snow; (*surfing*) the execution of large smooth turns on a wave

carving skis (*skiing*) **skis** specifically designed for **carving**

Cas (*rugby league*) short name of the English **club** Castleford Tigers

cast (*angling*) the throwing of a **fishing line** or **net**; (*trampolining*) a sideways movement across the **bed**

castle (*cricket*) colloquial term for the **wicket** defended by the **batsman**

casual water (*golf*) a pool of water caused by rain or flooding, from where a **ball** can be repositioned without penalty

cat (*sailing*) shortening of **catamaran**

cat stance (*karate*) a position in which the **front foot** is raised ready to kick

cat-twist back drop (*trampolining*) a **full twist** to a **back drop**

catamaran (*sailing*) a boat with two **hulls**

catch (*angling*) (1) the capture of a fish; (2) the amount of fish caught; (*baseball*) the catching by a **fielder** of the **ball** hit by the **batter** before it touches the ground, so that he is **out**; (*bowls*) a **bowl** that prevents another from passing; (*cricket*) the catching by a **fielder** of the **ball** hit by the **batsman** before it touches the ground, so that he is **out**; (*general*) a simple **game**, popular among children, in which a **ball** is thrown and caught in turn; (*rowing*) the moment when the **blade** enters the water at the beginning of the **stroke**

catch a crab (*rowing*) to sink the **oar** too deep (or not deep enough) in the water, causing the **rower** to fall back and the boat to be jolted and even halted [as if the oar had been caught by a crab]

catch and kick (*Gaelic football*) to catch the **ball** and instantly kick it as a **pass**

catch and release (*angling*) the practice of releasing a fish after it has been caught and weighed

catch-as-catch-can (*wrestling*) a form of the sport in which any **hold** is allowed

catch-waist camel spin (*ice skating*) in **pair skating**, a **camel spin** with the free legs pointing in opposite directions and each partner's arms around the other's waist

catcher (*baseball*) the **fielder** positioned behind the **batter**

catenaccio (*association football*) a rigidly defensive system of **play** introduced in the 1960s by the Italian **club** Inter Milan, comprising four **defenders**, three **midfielders**, and three **attackers** [Italian *catenaccio*, "bolt"]

Cats (*Australian Rules*) short name of the Geelong Cats team

cats on the counter (*darts*) the winning of a **game** [said to derive from the "cats" or large drinking pots that the losers were obliged to line up on the counter before the next game]

Catterick (*horse racing*) a **flat** and **National Hunt** racecourse at Catterick Bridge, North Yorkshire, England

catworm (*angling*) a worm (*Nephthys hombergi*) commonly used as **bait**

caught (*cricket*) (of) a **batsman** whose **stroke** resulted in a **catch**, so that he is **out**

caught and bowled (*cricket*) (of) a **batsman** whose **stroke** gave a **catch** to the **bowler**

caught behind (*cricket*) (of) a **batsman** whose **stroke** gave a **catch** to the **wicketkeeper** (who is behind the **wicket**)

Caulfield Cup (*horse racing*) the **cup** awarded to the winner of an annual **race** at Caulfield, Melbourne, Australia, first run in 1879

cauliflower ear (*boxing*) an ear permanently swollen and disfigured by repeated blows [in appearance resembling the clumped shape of a cauliflower]

caution (*association football*) another term for a **booking**; (*boxing*) a reprimand given to a **boxer** by the **referee** following an infringement, three such reprimands usually resulting in a **warning**

Cavaliers (*basketball*) short name of the Cleveland Cavaliers team

caver (*caving*) a person who explores caves

caving (*sport*) the exploration of caves

cavity back (*golf*) a **clubhead** with a depression on the back

Celtic League (*rugby union*) a contest between major Irish, Welsh, and Scottish teams, introduced in 2001 [the teams come from the Celtic countries of the British Isles]

Celtics (*basketball*) short name of the Boston Celtics team

center (*American football*) the player in the center of the offensive line who begins the **play** with a **snap** of the **ball** to a player in the **backfield**; (*archery, shooting*) the area of the **target** between the **bull** and the **outer**; (*association football*) a kick from either of the **wings** to the center of the **pitch**; (*Australian Rules*) a player in **midfield**; (*basketball*) the position of a player immediately under the **basket**; (*field hockey*) a **pass** from either of the **wings** to the center of the **pitch**; (*lacrosse*) a **midfield** player who competes in the **draw** and links play between **defense** and attack; (*netball*) a player who can operate anywhere on the **court** except in the **shooting circle**; (*rugby league, rugby union*) one of the two **three-quarters** in the center of the **pitch**

center back (*association football*) a player in the middle of the **defense**

center bounce (*Australian Rules*) another term for a **ball up**

center circle (*association football*) the circle painted on the middle of the pitch, at the center of which is the **center spot**

center field (*baseball*) the part of the **outfield** directly behind **second base** as viewed from **home plate**

center fielder (*baseball*) the **fielder** positioned in **center field**

center forward (*association football, field hockey*) the central player in the line of **forwards**

center half (*association football, field hockey*) the central player behind the **center forward**

center halfback (*Australian Rules*) a defensive player operating near the middle of the **50-meter arc**

center half-forward (*Australian Rules*) an attacking player operating behind the **full forward**

center line (*ice hockey*) another term for the **red line**

center pass (*field hockey*) the **pass** that starts the game, made by a **center** from the **center spot** to a teammate; (*netball*) the **throw** from the center of the **court** that starts the game

center service line (*tennis*) the line parallel to the **tramlines** that divides the right and left **service courts**

center spot (*association football*) the painted spot in the center of the **pitch** from which the **kick-off** is made at the start of each **half** and after the scoring of a **goal**; (*billiards*) the **spot** on the **billiard table** midway between the two middle **pockets**, corresponding to the **blue spot** in **snooker**

center square (*Australian Rules*) the square marked in the center of the **oval**

center three-quarter (*rugby union*) one of the two middle players in the line of **three-quarters**

centerboard (*sailing*) a retractable **keel** or fin

centerman (*ice hockey*) the **forward** playing between two **wingers**

Central American and Caribbean Games (*Olympics*) **regional games** held since 1926 for competitors from the countries of Central America and the Caribbean

Central American Games (*Olympics*) the name to 1935 of the **Central American and Caribbean Games**

central circle (*wrestling*) the inner circle of the **mat**

central contract (*cricket*) the contracting of a player to his national team as well as to his county or state team

central fire (*shooting*) (of) a cartridge with its fulminate in the center of the base

central wrestling area (*wrestling*) the circle on the mat between the **passivity zone** and the **central circle**

centre (*general*) another spelling of **center**

Centre Court (*tennis*) the central and most important **court** at **Wimbledon**, where the **final** of the **championships** is played

centurion (*cricket*) a **batsman** who scores a **century**

Centurions (*rugby league*) short name of the English **club** Leigh Centurions

century (*cricket*) a **score** of 100 **runs** by a **batsman**; (*snooker*) a **break** of 100 or more **points**

Cesarewitch (*horse racing*) an annual **handicap** at **Newmarket**, first run in 1839 [inaugurated by the tsesarevich, the heir to the Russian throne who became Alexander II (1818–1881)]

chain gang (*American football*) the members of the officiating team who measure the 10 yards needed to gain a new set of **downs**

chainring (*cycling*) the gear wheel that drives the chain

chains (*American football*) a method employed by the officiating team to measure the **yardage** needed to gain a new set of **downs**

chainwheel (*cycling*) another term for the **chainring**

Chair (*horse racing*) a **jump** on the **Grand National** course at **Aintree**

Chairboys (*association football*) nickname of the English **club** Wycombe Wanderers [from the furniture-making industry in the town of High Wycombe]

chairlift (*skiing*) a set of seats suspended on cables used to transport skiers uphill

chairman (*wrestling*) one of the three officials in charge of a **bout**, the others being the **judge** and the **referee**

chalk (*snooker*) the small cube of colored chalk rubbed on the tip of the **cue** to give a good contact when striking the **cue ball**; (*weightlifting*) the magnesium carbonate powder (not actually chalk) applied by **weightlifters** to their hands to help them grip the **barbell**

chalk eater (*horse racing*) colloquial term for a **punter** who bets only on the **favorite** [he follows the **bookmaker** as he writes up the latest **odds** in chalk]

challenge (*general*) an invitation to take part in a sporting contest, especially to a reigning **champion**

Challenge Cup (*rugby league*) the leading British cup competition, first held in 1929

challenge match (*general*) a **match** held as a **challenge**

challenger (*general*) a person who takes up a **challenge**, especially to a reigning **champion**

champ (*general*) colloquial shortening of **champion**

champagne breakfast (*darts*) a **score** in a single **throw** of treble 20, treble 5, and treble 1, bettering a **breakfast**

ChampCar (*auto racing*) a finely tuned car, but with a smaller engine than a **Formula One** car, that takes part in the annual **championship** of this name [short for Championship Car]

champion (*general*) a competitor who has excelled all others, especially in **boxing**

Champion Hurdle (*horse racing*) an annual **race** at **Cheltenham**, first run in 1927

Champion Jockey (*horse racing*) the title of the **jockey** who rides the most **winners** in a particular season, in both **flat racing** and **National Hunt**

Champions' Dinner (*golf*) popular name for the **Masters Club**

Champions League (*association football*) informal name of the **UEFA Champions League**

Champions Trophy (*cricket*) an annual **one-day international tournament** first held in 1998, regarded as the most important of its kind after the **World Cup**; (*field hockey*) an annual **tournament** first held in 1978

Championship (*association football*) the group of teams that replaced **Division** 1 in 2004; (*general*) short title of a particular **championship**, as the **Open Championship** in **golf**

championship (*general*) (1) a contest held to determine who will be **champion**; (2) the **title** awarded to the winner of such a contest

chance (*general*) an opportunity of achieving a positive result during a **match**, such as **dismissing** a **batsman** in **cricket** or scoring a **goal** in **association football**

change (*cricket*) the substitution of one **bowler** (or type of **bowling**) for another during a **match**; (*horse racing*) the fractions of a second taken to declare the time of the first four horses in a **race**

change bowler (*cricket*) a **bowler** who relieves the regular bowlers in a **match**

change ends (*general*) to switch from occupying one half of an area of play, as a **pitch** or **court**, to the other, so changing the direction of play

change-foot spin (*ice skating*) a **spin** in which a **jump** is made from one foot to the other

change-up (*baseball*) an unexpectedly slow **pitch** intended to deceive the **batter**

changeover (*athletics*) the handing over of the **baton** by one runner to another in a **relay race**; (*general*) the point in a **game** or match at which the two sides **change ends**

changing room (*general*) a room or premises at a **sports ground** where players change their clothes before and after a **game** and discuss tactics

Chanticleers (*rugby league*) the English name for the French national Tricolores team [from Chanticleer as a name for the domestic cock, the symbolic bird of France]

chap and lie (*bowls*) to deliver a **bowl** so that it hits another and takes its place; (*curling*) to deliver a **stone** so that it hits another and takes its place

charge (*golf*) to play a **round** aggressively

charge down (*rugby league, rugby union*) to run toward a kicked **ball** and block it with the hands or body

Chargers (*American football*) short name of the San Diego Chargers team

charging (*basketball*) the **offense** of running into a stationary **defender** while in **possession** of the **ball**

charity event (*general*) an amateur contest, such as a **race** or **match**, organized to raise money for charity

charity stripe (*basketball*) colloquial term for the **foul line**

charity toss (*basketball*) colloquial term for a **free throw**

chase (*real tennis*) the second impact of an unreturned **ball**, for which the player scores unless his opponent betters it by a similar impact nearer the end wall; (*horse racing*) shortening of **steeplechase**

chase track (*horse racing*) a **racetrack** with **fences** (for a **steeplechase**)

chaser (*cycling*) a **rider** who is trying to catch up with a **break**; (*horse racing*) a horse that competes in **steeplechases**

chassé (*ice skating*) a sequence in which the foot that is not in contact with the ice moves up next to the skating foot without passing it and replaces it as the skating foot [French *chassé*, "chase"]

cheap (*cricket*) (of) a **wicket** taken after the **batsman** has scored only a few **runs**

check (*ice hockey*) the (legitimate) blocking of an opponent's forward progress with one's shoulder or hip

check side (*snooker*) a **side** that causes the **cue ball** to rebound off the **cushion** at less of an angle than in a normally struck **shot**

checkdown (*American football*) a short **pass** to a **running back** as a final option when the **wide receivers** are covered

checkered flag (*auto racing*) another spelling of **chequered flag**

checking (*trampolining*) the technique of absorbing the recoil from the **bed** by flexing the body at the hips, knees, and ankles

checkmark (*athletics*) the indicator on the **track** that tells the incoming runner in a **relay race** when he should start to accelerate

checkout (*darts*) a **score** that wins a **game** in one turn

cheekpieces (*horse racing*) strips of sheepskin sewn onto each side of a horse's **bridle** to help it concentrate its attention on the **course** ahead, much in the manner of **blinkers**

cheer squad (*general*) volunteer **supporters** drafted in to empty spectator seats in a **stadium**

cheerleader (*general*) one of a team of uniformly dressed young women who spur on a sports team with coordinated shouts, cheers, and chanting

cheese (*skittles*) the heavy wooden **ball** used to knock down the **skittles**

cheesecake (*tenpin bowling*) a **lane** in which it is easy to make high **scores**

chef de mission (*Olympics*) the person who supports, promotes, and generally guides a national team [French *chef de mission*, "mission leader"]

chef d'équipe (*general*) the person generally responsible for a team's practical arrangements, especially when they are traveling [French *chef d'équipe*, "team leader"]

Cheltenham (*horse racing*) a **flat** and **National Hunt** **racecourse** at Cheltenham, Gloucestershire, England, the location of the **Cheltenham Gold Cup**

Cheltenham & Gloucester Trophy (*cricket*) the **trophy** awarded to the winners of an annual one-day competition of 60 **overs** per side, first held in 1963 [originally the Gillette Cup but renamed in 2001 for new sponsors]

Cheltenham Gold Cup (*horse racing*) the **cup** awarded to the winner of an annual **steeplechase** at **Cheltenham**, first run in 1924 and now regarded as the greatest **prize** of the **National Hunt**

Chepstow (*horse racing*) a **flat** and **National Hunt** **racecourse** at Chepstow, Gwent, Wales

chequered flag (*auto racing*) the black-and-white **flag** indicating the end of a **race**, shown to the winner and to each subsequent car that crosses the **finishing line**

cherries (*greyhound racing*) colloquial term for the **racetrack** [rhyming slang for **dogs**, from Cockney *cherry hogs*, "cherry pits"]

Cherries (*association football*) nickname of the English **club** Bournemouth [from the red shirts of the players]

cherry (*cricket*) colloquial term for a **new ball** [from its color and its "virginity"]

chest (*association football*) to hit or direct the **ball** with the chest

chest pass (*basketball*) a **pass** in which the player holds the **ball** at chest level then passes it to a teammate without bouncing it

chest trap (*association football*) control of the **ball** using the chest

Chester (*horse racing*) a **flat racecourse** at Chester, Cheshire, England

chewy on your boot! (*Australian Rules*) a call to a player to discourage him from performing well in a particular **play** [as if chewing gum were on his boot]

Chicago Stadium (*basketball*) the **home ground** of the Chicago Bulls team, Chicago

chicane (*auto racing*) a sharp double bend on a **track** [French *chicane* "quibble at law"]

Chiefs (*American football*) short name of the Kansas City Chiefs team

chili dip (*golf*) a weak **loft** following a **mishit** [like scooping up a mouthful of chili with a taco]

chimney (*mountaineering*) a cleft in a rock face just wide enough to admit a climber to enter

chin (*boxing*) the ability to withstand **punches**; (*gymnastics*) to pull oneself up so that one's chin reaches the **horizontal bar**

chin music (*baseball*) colloquial term for a **pitch** that passes close to the head of the **batter**; (*cricket*) colloquial term for a **bouncer** that flies up close to the head of the **batsman** [originally a punch on the jaw]

chin-up (*gymnastics*) an exercise in which the **gymnast** uses his arms to lift his chin over the **horizontal bar**

chinaman (*cricket*) an **off break** or **googly** bowled by a left-arm **bowler** to a right-handed **batsman** [said to have been introduced by a West Indian bowler of Chinese descent]

Chinese cut (*cricket*) a **mishit** in the form of an **outside edge** that sends the **ball** behind the **wicket** [perhaps so called because it is "devious," from racial stereotyping]

Chinese Grand Prix (*auto racing*) the **Formula One** international **Grand Prix** held on the **circuit** at Shanghai, China

Chinese snooker (*snooker*) a situation where the **cue ball** is awkwardly placed, close to or touching another **ball**, but without actually being a **snooker**

chip (*general*) a **hit** or kick that sends a **ball** high into the air over a short distance; (*golf*) shortening of **chip shot**

chip in (*golf*) to put the **ball** in the **hole** directly from a **chip shot**

chip shot (*golf*) a **shot**, usually close to the **green**, that sends the **ball** in a low trajectory, so that it runs forward on landing

chip the winner (*curling*) to cast a **stone** that "chips" the edge of another stone

Chipolopolo (*association football*) nickname of the Zambian national team [local *chipolopolo*, "copper bullets," for the copper important in the national eonomy and the deadly speed of the players]

chockstone (*mountaineering*) a stone jammed in a crack, **chimney**, or crevice

choctaw (*ice skating*) a turn from either edge of the **skate** to the other edge on the other foot in the opposite direction [as distinct from a **mohawk**]

choke (*golf*) (1) to shorten the swinging length of the **club** by gripping it lower down the **shaft**; (2) to crack or lose one's nerve when in an apparently winning position

choke hold (*judo, wrestling*) a move to restrain one's opponent by encircling his neck with one's arm or legs

chop (*general*) a short, sharp downward blow or **stroke**

chop block (*American football*) an illegal **block** below the knees

chop volley (*tennis*) a **volley** hit at waist height close to the **net**

chopper (*baseball*) a **ball** that bounces high after being hit down to the ground

christiania (*skiing*) formal term for a **christie**

christie (*skiing*) a method of stopping short when descending at speed, executed by turning with the **skis** parallel [from Christiania, former name of Oslo, Norway, where introduced]

Christmas tree (*auto racing*) colloquial term in **drag racing** for the array of yellow, green, and red lights used to start a **race**

christy (*skiing*) another spelling of **christie**

chuck (*cricket*) a **delivery** taken to be a **throw**, and so illegal

chuck and chance it (*angling*) to fish without knowing whether a fish lies where the **cast** is made

chucker (*cricket*) a **bowler** whose **delivery** is regarded as a **throw**, and so illegal

chui (*judo*) a **penalty** awarded for a serious violation [Japanese *chui*, "warning," "caution"]

chukka (*polo*) one of the six periods into which a **game** is divided [Hindi *chakkar*, "wheel," "circle"]

chukker (*polo*) another spelling of **chukka**

chum (*angling*) a **groundbait** of chopped fish [origin uncertain]

Churchill Downs (*horse racing*) the **racetrack** at Louisville, Kentucky, where the **Kentucky Derby** is held

chute (*canoeing*) a narrowing part of a river that causes an increase in speed; (*horse racing*) an extension to a **straight** in an oval **racecourse**, used in special **races**; (*parachuting*) shortening of **parachute**

Cincinnati Reds (*baseball*) short name of the Cincinnati Red Stockings team

circle (*athletics*) the area within which an **athlete** must remain when throwing the **hammer**, discus, or **shot**; (*general*) a circular or semicircular area marked on a playing area such as a **field**, **court**, or **rink**

circuit (*athletics*) a single tour of a running **track**; (*auto racing*) the specially designed looping road or **track** on which **races** are held; (*general*) (1) a designated **cross-country** route, as in **motocross**; (2) the **venues** visited in turn by sports competitors; (3) any circular route

circuit slugger (*baseball*) a regular **slugger** who has to run the **circuit** of the **bases** every time he hits a **home run**

circuit training (*general*) a form of athletic training using a series of different exercises [the series forms a "circuit" or round of exercises]

circus (*general*) a team or group of players traveling together to compete in different places

cite (*rugby union*) to make an official complaint about a player after a **game**

Citizens (*association football*) short name of the English **club** Manchester City

City (*association football*) short name of a British **club** with "City" in its name, as Brechin City, Bristol City, Chester City, Elgin City, Manchester City, Norwich City

claimer (*horse racing*) another term for a **claiming race**

claiming race (*horse racing*) a **race** in which any horse that has taken part may be bought ("claimed") at a previously fixed price by anyone who has entered a horse at the same **race meeting**

clap skates (*ice skating*) in **speed skating**, **skates** with a blade hinged at the front so that it can be separated from the heel of the skate and thus stay longer in contact with the ice

Claret Jug (*golf*) popular name of the **trophy** awarded at the **Open Championship** [from its original design in 1873 in the style of a silver jug used to serve red wine]

Clarets (*association football*) nickname of the English **club** Burnley [from the dark red shirts of the players]

clash of the ash (*sport*) descriptive nickname of **hurling** [the **hurley** is traditionally made from the wood of the ash tree]

clash of the titans (*general*) nickname for a key **match** or contest, especially between national or major teams

classic bow (*archery*) another name for the **recurve bow**

classic race (*horse racing*) one of the five **English classics**

classic technique (*skiing*) the traditional racing technique in **Nordic skiing**, using a diagonal stride with the **skis** parallel

classics (*horse racing*) short name of the **English classics**

claw (*bowls*) a **delivery** grip in which the **bowl** is held in the palm with the three middle fingers on the playing surface and the thumb and pinkie stretched either side

clay (*shooting*) colloquial shortening of **clay pigeon**

clay court (*tennis*) (1) a **court** with a clay surface; (2) alternate term for a **hard court**

clay pigeon (*shooting*) the saucer-shaped disk of baked clay shot at as a substitute game bird in **trapshooting**

clay-pigeon shooting (*shooting*) a form of **trapshooting** using a **clay pigeon**

clean (*angling*) without a **catch**; (*weightlifting*) the first phase of the **clean and jerk** movement in which the **weightlifter** lifts the **barbell** from the floor to shoulder height and holds it there with arms bent in preparation for the **jerk**

clean and jerk (*weightlifting*) a **lift** in two parts in which the **clean** is followed by the **jerk**

clean bowled (*cricket*) (of) a **batsman** who has been **bowled** by a **ball** that hit his **stumps** without first hitting his **bat** or **pad**

clean round (*equestrianism*) another term for a **clear round**

clean sheet (*association football*) a **match** in which no **goals** are conceded

clean-up hitter (*baseball*) the **hitter** who bats fourth for the batting **side**, whose **hits** are thought likely to enable a **baserunner** to score

clear (*badminton*) an overhead **shot** that sends the **shuttlecock** from one **baseline** to the other

clear hip circle (*gymnastics*) a variant of the **hip circle** in which the **gymnast** does not touch the bar with his hips

clear round (*equestrianism*) in **showjumping**, a **round** ridden without any **faults** or **penalties**

clear the boundary ropes (*cricket*) fuller term for **clear the ropes**

clear the ropes (*cricket*) to hit the **ball** clear over the **ropes** that mark the **boundary**, so scoring a **six**

clear the table (*snooker*) to play a **break** that clears all **balls** from the **billiard table**

clearance (*association football*) a defensive kick away from a dangerous attacking position; (*field hockey*) a defensive **hit** away from a dangerous attacking position

cleat (*cycling*) a device attached to the bottom of a cycling shoe that engages with the mechanism on a **clipless pedal** and locks the **rider** to his bicycle

cleek (*golf*) an old-fashioned narrow-faced iron-headed **club**, corresponding to a **2-iron**

clerk of the course (*auto racing, horse racing*) an official in charge of administration

clerk of the scales (*horse racing*) the official whose responsibility is to **weigh in** the **jockeys**

clew (*sailing*) the lower corner of a **sail**

climb (*cycling*) a section of a **race** or **stage** that takes **riders** up a long hill or mountain

climb the ladder (*American football*) to jump very high in order to catch the **ball**

climber (*cycling*) a **rider** who specializes in **climbs**

climbing (*mountaineering*) the activity of ascending natural heights such as rocks, cliffs, or mountains, either for its own sake or as an integral part of the sport

climbing rope (*mountaineering*) a rope serving as an essential aid in **climbing**

climbing wall (*mountaineering*) a specially constructed wall with handholds and footholds, used for practicing techniques in **rock climbing** or **mountaineering** generally

clinch (*boxing*) the holding of one's opponent in such a way that he cannot throw **punches**

clip (*American football*) an illegal **block** below the waist from behind; (*cricket*) a sharp **stroke** of the **ball**

clipless pedals (*cycling*) **pedals** that lock the **rider** to his bicycle by means of **cleats** on the soles of his shoes [so called because they avoid the need for **toeclips**]

Clippers (*basketball*) short name of the Los Angeles Clippers team

clipping (*ice hockey*) the **offense** of delivering a **check** below an opponent's knees

clips (*cycling*) shortening of **toeclips**

clock golf (*golf*) a form of **putting** on a **green** marked like a clock dial, in which players putt from each hour figure in turn to a central **hole**

clocker (*horse racing*) a person such as a **racing** correspondent who times the training runs of horses in order to get a guide to their **form**

clogger (*association football*) colloquial term for a player whose **tackles** are often **fouls**

Clonmel (*horse racing*) a **flat** and **National Hunt racecourse** at Clonmel, Co. Tipperary, Ireland

close down (*association football*) to deny one's opponents room to maneuver

close finish (*general*) a **finish** that is only narrowly won or gained

close-hauled (*sailing*) with **sails** trimmed as closely as possible to the direction the wind is coming from

close season (*angling*) a set time of the year when it is illegal to catch fish; (*general*) a period or **season** when a sport is not normally played, as winter for **cricket** in Britain

close the card (*horse racing*) to be the final **race** in a **race meeting**

closer (*baseball*) a **pitcher** whose specialty is defending a **lead** late in the **game**

clothesline (*American football*) a **foul** in which a player jabs his forearm into the throat of an oncoming opponent; (*wrestling*) the striking of a moving opponent across the face or in the windpipe with one's outstretched arm [the effect is like running into a clothesline]

clout (*archery*) in long-distance shooting, a special large **target** in the form of a flat surface on the ground divided into concentric circles

club (*general*) (1) the implement used for striking the **ball** in various **games**, as a golf club; (2) an association of people with common social, sporting, or other interests; (3) a formal association of players of a named sport, as a **football club** or **golf club**

club call (*rugby league*) the right of a **club** to select their opponents in a **semifinal**

club linesman (*association football*) an official who assists the **referee** in **matches** where there is no **assistant referee**, as in many local **games**

clubface (*golf*) the striking surface of a **club**

clubhead (*golf*) the part of the **club** that strikes the **ball**

clubhouse (*golf*) the premises attached to a **golf course**

clutch team (*general*) a tough team that battles on when in a poor position [they are "in the clutch" or in a critical situation]

coach (*general*) a professional **trainer**, typically in **athletics** or **rowing**

coaming (*canoeing*) the raised rim of a **cockpit**

coarse fish (*angling*) any freshwater fish other than those of the salmon family, as distinct from a **game fish**

Cobblers (*association football*) nickname of the English **club** Northampton Town [from the local footwear industry]

cock-a-bondy (*angling*) a type of **dry fly** [corruption of Welsh *coch a bon ddu*, "red with a black stem"]

cocked hat (*snooker*) a **shot** in which the **object ball** rebounds off three **cushions** toward a middle **pocket** [the trajectory resembles the outline of a three-cornered cocked hat]

cockpit (*auto racing*) the place where the driver sits in the car; (*canoeing*) the space in the deck of a **kayak** in which the **kayaker** sits [originally the pit where cockfights were held]

cocktail (*horse racing*) a horse that is not a **thoroughbbred** [properly a horse with a cocked tail]

codriver (*auto racing*) in rally driving, the person who takes turns in driving the vehicle and who assists the main driver by carrying out organizational and administrative work

coffee grinder (*gymnastics*) a movement in which the **gymnast**, in a squatting position, circles his leg while keeping both hands on the floor

coffin (*cricket*) colloquial term for the case used to carry a player's equipment and clothing

coffin corner (*American football*) the angle between the **goal line** and the **sideline** [a **punt** is often aimed here so that it may go out of bounds and become a **dead ball**]

collapse (*general*) the sudden failure or breakdown of a player or team during a contest; (*rugby union*) the breakdown of a **scrum**, especially when deliberately caused by a set of **forwards** so that the two **front rows** fall toward each other

collar (*rowing*) another term for a **button**; (*weightlifting*) the device that secures the **disk weights** to the **barbell**; (*wrestling*) a move in which the opponent is tackled by the neck

collar the bowling (*cricket*) to hit the **balls** delivered by the **bowler** all over the **field**

college football (*American football*) the sport as played by teams of students at universities, colleges, and military academies

Colliers (*association football*) nickname of the English **club** Barnsley [from the local coal-mining industry]

color (*snooker*) any of the six colored **balls** which are played after a **red**

colors (*general*) the distinctive colors worn by a participant in a sport to show membership of a team, **club**, college, or the like, or the identity of an owner or sponsor

colt (*cricket*) a player during his first **season**; (*general*) (1) a young, inexperienced player; (2) a member of a junior team; (*horse racing*) a male horse under four years old

Colts (*American football*) short name of the Indianapolis Colts team

combat sport (*general*) a one-to-one sport in which each combatant continually attacks the other and protects himself from him, as **wrestling** or one of the **martial arts**

combination (*boxing*) a series of **punches** thrown in quick succession

combination bat (*table tennis*) a **bat** with different types of rubber on each side, used for different **shots**

combined event (*skiing*) a downhill **run** followed by two **slalom** runs

combined spin (*swimming*) in **synchronized swimming**, a descending **spin** through at least 360 degrees followed immediately by an ascending spin in the same direction

come about (*sailing*) to change direction

come again (*angling*) to rise or take the **bait** a second time; (*horse racing*) to regain speed

come from behind (*general*) to progress from the rear of a group of contestants or from a losing position into a winning position

come home (*general*) to complete a **course**

come in (*cricket*) to start an **innings**; (*fencing*) to get within the **guard** of one's opponent; (*general*) to take a specified place in a **race**

come off (*cricket*) to cease **bowling**

come on (*cricket*) to begin to **bowl**

comebacker (*baseball*) a **ball** hit directly back along the ground by the **batter** to the **pitcher**

comma position (*skiing*) a position in which the body is curved to one side, like a comma

Commonwealth Games (*general*) a quadrennial sports contest between countries of the Commonwealth, first held (as the British Empire Games) in Hamilton, Ontario, in 1930

complete (*American football*) (of) a **pass** that is successfully caught by a **receiver**

complete game (*baseball*) a **game** in which a **pitcher** records all 27 **outs** without being replaced by a **relief pitcher**

compound bow (*archery*) a **bow** equipped with a system of pulleys and cables that allows the **archer** to pull back the **bowstring** more easily

compression (*golf*) the measure of the resilience of a **ball**

compulsory (*gymnastics*) a **routine** that contains obligatory moves

con (*general*) abbreviation of **conversion** in sports reports

concours hippique (*equestrianism*) another term for **showjumping** [French *concours hippique*, literally "hippic contest"]

conditional (*horse racing*) shortening of **conditional jockey**

conditional jockey (*horse racing*) a **jockey** who may claim an **allowance**

conditional race (*horse racing*) a **race** in which only **conditional jockeys** may ride

conditions race (*horse racing*) the highest grade of **flat race**, divided into **pattern races** and **listed races** [the races are governed by a condition or set of conditions]

condor (*golf*) a (rare) **score** of four **strokes** under **par** on a **hole** [as a "bird" greater and more impressive than an **albatross** or an **eagle**]

cones (*equestrianism*) a **discipline** in **carriage driving**, in which the horse and carriage are maneuvered through a path of cones with balls balanced atop, the dislodging of which incurs **penalty points**

conference (*general*) an association of sports teams that play each other, especially those representing educational institutions

Conn Smythe Trophy (*ice hockey*) the **trophy** first donated in 1965 that is presented to the outstanding performer in the **Stanley Cup playoffs** [named for the Canadian player Conn Smythe (1895–1980), founder of the Toronto Maple Leafs]

connections (*horse racing*) the people associated with a particular horse, such as the **owner** and **trainer**

conquest (*mountaineering*) the successful ascent of a mountain

consolation match (*general*) a **match** for contestants who have been unsuccessful or have not won

consolation prize (*general*) a **prize** awarded to a contestant who was unsuccessful or just failed to win

consolation race (*general*) a **race** for contestants who have been unsuccessful or have not won

contact (*baseball*) the touching of a **baserunner** by a **fielder** who holds the **ball**

contact sport (*general*) a sport involving bodily contact between players

Continental Cup (*ice hockey*) the chief European **club championship**

continuation stroke (*croquet*) the bonus **stroke** taken either after a player has **run a hoop** or (as a second bonus stroke) after a **roquet**

continuous spin (*swimming*) in **synchronized swimming**, a descending **spin** through at least 720 degrees

contre-la-montre (*cycling*) another term for a **time trial** [French *contre la montre*, "against the watch"]

control point (*orienteering*) one of the checkpoints marked on a map that competitors must visit en route to their destination

conversion (*American football*) the scoring of an extra **point** after a **touchdown** by kicking the **ball** over the **crossbar**; (*rugby league*, *rugby union*) the scoring of two extra **points** after a **try** by kicking the **ball** over the **crossbar**

Copa America (*association football*) a biennial **championship** for South American countries, first officially held in Montevideo, Uruguay, in 1917 [Spanish *Copa América*, "America Cup"]

Copa del Rey (*association football*) an annual Spanish **championship** founded in 1902 [Spanish *Copa del Rey*, "King's Cup," named for Alfonso XIII (1886–1941)]

Copa Libertadores (*association football*) an annual **championship** for South American countries, first played in 1960 [Spanish *Copa Libertadores de América*, "Liberators of America Cup"]

Corbett (*mountaineering*) a Scottish mountain peak between 2,500 and 3,000 ft in height with a reascent of 500ft on all sides [first listed by J.R. Corbett (1876–1949)]

Cork (*horse racing*) a **flat** and **National Hunt** racecourse at Mallow, Co. Cork, Ireland

corkscrew (*boxing*) a **punch** thrown with the elbow out and a twisting motion of the wrist

corkscrew back drop (*trampolining*) one and a half **twists** to a **back drop**

corner (*association football*) shortening of **corner kick**; (*boxing*) (1) one of the diagonally opposite angles of the **ring**, where a **boxer** sits between **rounds** and is attended by a **second**; (2) another term for the second himself

corner flag (*association football*) one of the four flags that mark the corners of the **pitch** where the **touchline** meets the **goal line**

corner forward (*hurling*) a player in an attacking position on the **wing**

corner hit (*field hockey*) another term for a **long corner**

corner kick (*association football*) a kick awarded to the attacking team at one of the four corners of the **pitch** when a defending player puts the **ball** out of play beyond the **goal line**

corner man (*boxing*) another term for a **second**

cornerback (*American football*) a **defensive back**, usually covering an opposing **wide receiver**

Coronation Cup (*horse racing*) a **race** run the day after the **Derby**

Coronation Stakes (*horse racing*) a **race** run during **Royal Ascot**

corps à corps (*fencing*) bodily contact between two **fencers** [French *corps à corps*, "body to body"]

corridor of uncertainty (*cricket*) the area just outside the **off stump** of a **batsman**, where he is unsure what kind of **stroke** to play or whether to play one at all

Cottagers (*association football*) nickname of the English **club** Fulham [from their **home ground** at **Craven Cottage**]

Cotton Bowl (*American football*) an annual **college football** game played since 1937 in Dallas, Texas, matching teams from the **Big Twelve Conference** and Southeastern Conference

Cougars (*rugby league*) short name of the English **club** Keighley Cougars

count (*baseball*) a tally of the number of **balls** and **strikes** that have been thrown during an **at bat**; (*boxing*) the counting up to ten seconds by the **referee** when a **boxer** is down on the **canvas**, after which a win to his opponent by a **knockout** is declared

countback (*general*) a method of determining a winner in a contest when two competitors have an equal **score** by taking their overall performance into account

counter (*boxing*) an attack made immediately after an opponent throws a **punch**; (*curling*) a **stone** in the **house** that could be worth a **point** at the completion of the **end**; (*fencing*) a **parry** in which one **foil** immediately follows the other; (*ice skating*) a **figure** in which the body is revolved in a direction opposite to that in which it was previously being revolved

counter play (*American football*) an offensive **play** in which the player carrying the **ball** moves in the opposite direction to the other players

counterpunch (*boxing*) fuller term for a **counter**

country (*cricket*) another term for the **outfield**

country club (*general*) a **club** in a rural area with facilities for sports such as **golf**, **swimming**, and **tennis**, as well as leisure and social activities

County (*association football*) (1) short name of the English **clubs** Notts County and Stockport County; (2) short name of the Scottish club Ross County

County Championship (*cricket*) an annual contest by **county cricket** teams, first officially held in 1890

county cricket (*cricket*) the sport as played between **first-class** teams representing the 18 historical British counties of Derbyshire, Durham, Essex, Glamorgan, Gloucestershire, Hampshire, Kent, Lancashire, Leicestershire, Middlesex, Northamptonshire, Nottinghamshire, Somerset, Surrey, Sussex, Warwickshire, Worcestershire, and Yorkshire

county ground (*cricket*) the **home ground** of a **club** of **county cricket** players

county match (*cricket*) a **match** between **county cricket** teams

coup (*billiards*) the act of striking a **ball** so that it goes into a **pocket** without hitting another ball [French *coup*, "blow"]

Coupe Aéronautique Gordon Bennett (*ballooning*) the sport's most prestigious **trophy**, named for the U.S. newspaper editor James Gordon Bennett, Jr. (1841–1918) and awarded since 1906 for the furthest distance traveled from the launch site [French *Coupe Aéronautique*, "Aeronautical Cup"]

coupon (*general*) a printed betting form on which to enter forecasts of sports results, as especially a **football coupon**

course (*general*) the ground or area over which a **race** is run or a **game** played, as a **golf course**; (*horse racing*) shortening of **racecourse**

course and distance (*horse racing*) (of) a measure for calculating a horse's performance on a particular **course** and in a **race** over the same distance

course management (*golf*) the manner in which a player adapts his **game** to the demands of a particular **course**

course specialist (*horse racing*) a **trainer** or **jockey** with a good record in **races** at a named **racecourse**

court (*general*) a walled or marked-off area in which a sport is played, as a **squash court** or **tennis court**

court game (*general*) a game played in a walled **court**, such as **fives**, **squash**, or **real tennis**

court player (*handball*) a player other than the **goalkeeper**

court tennis (*sport*) another term for **real tennis** [so named for distinction from **lawn tennis**]

cover (*cricket*) shortening of **cover point**; (*horse racing*) of a **stallion**, to copulate with a **mare**

cover drive (*cricket*) a **drive** by a **batsman** that goes through the **cover** area

cover point (*cricket*) a **fielding** position on the **off side** between **point** and **mid-on**; (*lacrosse*) a defensive player just in front of **point** whose role is to mark the opponents' **second home**

cover shot (*darts*) a **throw** at another high number when the treble 20 **bed** is obscured by a **dart** or darts already thrown

cover tackle (*rugby union*) a **tackle** by a player running across the **field** behind his teammates on a player who has broken through the defensive line

covers (*cricket*) a comprehensive term for **cover point** and **extra cover**; (*general*) a waterproof covering spread over a playing area such as a **cricket pitch** or **tennis court** to protect it from rain

cow corner (*cricket*) colloquial term for the area of the **field** near the **boundary** on the **leg side** between **deep midwicket** and **long-on** [an area where **fielders** are rarely positioned and so where cows can graze during a **game** of **village cricket**]

cow shot (*cricket*) colloquial term for a **slog** to the **leg side** in the direction of **cow corner**

cowabunga! (*surfing*) a **surfer**'s cry of exhilaration when riding the crest of a wave [a meaningless exclamation originating on *The Howdy Doody* TV show in the 1950s]

cowboy (*rodeo*) a performer in the sport

Cowboys (*American football*) short name of the Dallas Cowboys team

Cowes Week (*sailing*) a week of competitive **racing** held annually at Cowes, Isle of Wight, England, since 1826

cox (*rowing*) the steersman who sits opposite **stroke** and gives instructions during a **race** [shortening of **coxswain**]

coxed four (*rowing*) a boat with four **rowers** and a **cox**

coxed pair (*rowing*) a boat with two **rowers** and a **cox**

coxless four (*rowing*) a boat with four **rowers** and no **cox**, the steering being done by the **bowman** with rudder lines attached to his shoes

coxless pair (*rowing*) a boat with two **rowers** and no **cox**

coxswain (*rowing*) formal term for a **cox** [from *cock*, "boat," and *swain*, "servant"]

Coyotes (*ice hockey*) short name of the Phoenix Coyotes team

crackback (*American football*) an illegal **tackle** in which a **receiver** blocks a **linebacker** or defensive **back** by crashing into him at knee level

cradle (*bowls*) a **delivery** grip in which the **bowl** is held in the palm with the fingers close together and the thumb just below the disk on the side of the **bowl**; (*cricket*) a device for practicing close **fielding** in the form of a bowl-shaped structure that deflects a **ball** thrown into it; (*lacrosse*) a gentle rocking action that keeps the **ball** near the edge of the netting in the **crosse** as the player runs with it

cradle back drop (*trampolining*) a **half-twist** to a **back drop**

crampon (*mountaineering*) a spiked metal attachment on a climbing boot that provides a grip on snow and ice

crash and dash (*skiing*) a timed **run** between two points on a **piste**

crash ball (*rugby union*) the taking or making of a **pass** by a player at the moment he receives a **tackle** from the front

crash dive (*trampolining*) a three-quarter forward **somersault** with the body fully extended during its descent to the **bed**

crash mat (*athletics, gymnastics*) a thick mattress used to absorb the impact of landing after a **jump** or other aerial maneuver

crash out (*general*) to be eliminated unexpectedly or dramatically from a contest [as literally in **auto racing**]

crash tackle (*association football*) a vigorous **tackle**

Craven Cottage (*association football*) the **home ground** of Fulham **football club**, London

crawl (*swimming*) a high-speed **stroke** with alternate rotation of the arms from the shoulder and rapid kicks of the legs

crazy golf (*golf*) a form of **putting** in which the **ball** has to be maneuvered over or through a range of obstacles to reach the central **hole**

cream-puff hitter (*baseball*) colloquial term for a weak or ineffective **batter**

crease (*cricket*) a line that regulates the positions of the **bowler** and **batsman** at the **wicket**; (*ice hockey, lacrosse*) an area marked out in front of the **goal**

creeper (*cricket*) a **ball** that travels low along the ground after being delivered by the **bowler** [it does not bounce up as expected but "creeps" beneath the **bat**]

crew (*general*) a team of people giving technical support to a competitor, as in **rally driving**; (*rowing*) the **oarsmen** (and **cox**, where appropriate) in a racing boat; (*sailing*) the body of people (or the sole person) manning a boat or **yacht**

cricket (*sport*) a **game** played with **bat** and **ball** by two teams of 11 players on a marked-out **pitch**, the object of the **batsmen** being to score as many

runs as possible and that of the **bowler** and **fielders** to **dismiss** the batsmen as soon as possible

cricket bag (*cricket*) a type of long bag for carrying a player's **bat** and other equipment

cricket ball (*cricket*) the hard, red **ball** covered in polished leather that is delivered by the **bowler** to the **batsman** and caught or retrieved by the **fielders**

cricket bat (*cricket*) the long, flat-sided, wooden implement with which the **batsman** strikes the **ball**

cricket club (*cricket*) an established **club** of **cricketers** [typically in the names of **county cricket** teams, as Surrey Cricket Club]

cricket ground (*cricket*) the **field** with a central **pitch** where **cricket** is played

cricket match (*cricket*) a **match** between two teams

cricket pads (*cricket*) the **pads** worn by **batsmen**

cricket pitch (*cricket*) the central **pitch** on the **field** where the **game** is played

cricket stumps (*cricket*) the three **stumps** (with **bails**) that form the **wicket**

cricketana (*cricket*) publications or other items concerned with **cricket**

cricketer (*cricket*) a person who plays **cricket**, whether for pleasure or professionally

criterium (*cycling*) a **race** consisting of a series of **laps** over public roads [French *critérium*, "test"]

critical area (*lacrosse*) the area immediately in front of the **goal**

critical point (*skiing*) another name for the **k point**

Crocodiles (*handball*) popular name of Australia's national men's team [from the reptile native to the country]

Croke Park (*Gaelic football*) the **stadium** in Dublin, Ireland, that is the **venue** for the **All-Ireland finals** and other important **matches**

Croker (*Gaelic football*) local nickname for **Croke Park**

crooked number (*baseball*) colloquial term for any number other than 0 or 1 on the **scoreboard** [all such numbers have more complex figures]

croquet (*croquet*) a **shot** in which the **striker** places his **ball** in contact with the ball that it struck in a **roquet** and now strikes it so that it drives the other ball away; (*sport*) a **game** on a lawn for two or four players who compete to hit **balls** with **mallets** though **hoops** to a central **peg** [said to be dialect form of French *crochet*, from *croche*, "hook"]

croquet ball (*croquet*) one of the colored wooden **balls** with which **croquet** is played

croquet hoop (*croquet*) one of the six **hoops** through which **balls** are driven

croquet lawn (*croquet*) a lawn on which **croquet** is played

croquet shot (*croquet*) fuller term for a **croquet**

cross (*association football*) a transverse **pass**, especially when made to the area in front of the opponents' **goal**; (*boxing*) a straight **punch** delivered from the side; (*gymnastics*) a position on the **rings** in which the body is held rigid and the arms extended horizontally

cross-batted (*cricket*) (of) a **shot** played with the **bat** horizontal

cross-body ride (*wrestling*) another term for a **grapevine**

cross-buttock (*wrestling*) a **throw** in which the hip is used to throw the opponent off his balance

cross-country (*equestrianism*) an **event** that simulates riding through open country, including **jumps**; (*general*) the crossing of open country, avoiding roads, either for exercise or as a competitive **race**

cross-country running (*athletics*) a **foot race** across sections of countryside, with obstacles such as hedges, ditches, and stiles

cross-country skiing (*skiing*) a **race** across sections of countryside, as in **Nordic skiing**

cross-court (*table tennis*) (of) a **shot** hit diagonally from one corner of the table to the other; (*tennis*) (of) a **shot** hit diagonally across the **court**

cross-fire (*shooting*) firing at a rival's **target** in error

cross-foot spin (*ice skating*) a **spin** performed on the flat of the **blades** with the legs crossed

cross-handed grip (*golf*) a grip with the right hand below the left (for a right-handed player)

cross-training (*general*) (1) training in different sports in order to improve one's skills and performance in one's main sport; (2) a form of fitness training that alternates in a single session between exercises using **gymnasium** equipment and **aerobics**

crossbar (*general*) the horizontal bar across a pair of **goal posts**

crosscheck (*ice hockey, lacrosse*) an **offense** in which a player holds up his **stick** with both hands and pushes it across an opponent's body

crosse (*lacrosse*) the playing **stick**, with a pocket at the top end for catching, carrying, and throwing the **ball**

crossfield (*association football*) (of) a long **pass** made sideways

crossing (*rugby union*) an illegal move in which a player crosses in front of the player carrying the **ball**, thus preventing the defensive team from making a **tackle**

crosskick (*association football*) a **kick** of the **ball** across the **field**

crossline (*angling*) a **fishing line** stretched across a stream with a number of **hooks** attached

crossover (*ice skating*) a basic move in which one **skate** is crossed over the other when turning a corner and increasing speed

crossover dribble (*basketball*) a **dribble** made first with one hand then the other

crouch (*athletics*) shortening of **crouch start**

crouch start (*athletics*) a position adopted with the knees bent at the **start** of a **race**

crown (*general*) a reward or honor accorded the winner of a **championship** or other contest

crown bowls (*bowls*) **bowls** played on a **crown green**

crown green (*bowls*) a **green** that is larger than that used for **lawn bowls** and that slopes gently upward from the sides to a central "crown"

Crows (*Australian Rules*) short name of the Adelaide Crows team

Crucible (*snooker*) the theater in Sheffield, England, where the world **championship** is held

crucifix (*gymnastics*) another name for the **cross**

cruiser (*boxing*) a **cruiserweight** boxer

cruiserweight (*boxing*) the professional **weight** category of maximum 86kg (190lb)

crush stroke (*croquet*) an illegal **stroke** made when a **mallet** touches a **ball** that is in contact with a **peg** or **hoop**, other than playing it away

Cruyff turn (*association football*) a move to lose a tracking opponent in which the player pretends to pass the **ball** but instead drags it back, turns his body, and runs in the opposite direction [introduced by the Dutch player Johann Cruyff (1947–)]

Cubs (*baseball*) short name of the Chicago Cubs team

cue (*billiards, snooker*) a long tapered wooden rod with a leather tip, used to strike the **ball** [French *queue*, "tail"]

cue ball (*billiards, snooker*) the **ball** struck by the **cue** so that it in turn strikes the **object ball**

cue extension (*billiards, snooker*) a shaft extension attached to a **cue**, used when a **shot** with a standard-length cue is not possible

cue tip (*billiards, snooker*) the leather tip of a **cue**

cuervo (*gymnastics*) a **vault** in the form of a **handspring** off the **springboard**, then a **half-twist** followed by a backward **salto** off the **horse** [introduced by the Cuban **gymnast** Jorge Cuervo in 1973]

Cultural Olympics (*Olympics*) an arts festival staged to complement the **Olympic Games**, first held at the 2000 Sydney Olympics and evolving from an educational enterprise initiated in 1929 by U.S. art patron and civic leader Samuel S. Fleisher (1871–1944)

Cumbrians (*association football*) nickname of the English **club** Carlisle United [from the county of Cumbria in which they are based]

cup (*general*) the **trophy** in the form of an ornamental cup awarded to a winner or **champion**; (*golf*) the plastic or metal casing lining a **hole**

Cup (*association football*) shortening of **Cup Final**

cup final (*general*) the final and deciding **match** in a competition for a **cup**

Cup Final (*association football*) the **match** between the winners of the **final** of the **FA Cup**, held at **Wembley**

cup of coffee (*baseball*) colloquial term for a spell in the **majors** by a player who then returns to the **minors**

cup tie (*general*) one of a series of **matches** to decide the winner of a **cup**

cup-tied (*association football*) (of) a player ineligible to play for his **club** in a **cup tie** because he played for another club earlier in the competition; (*general*) (of) a player unable to play in a **cup tie** because he is injured or otherwise disallowed

cup winner (*general*) the winner of a **cup**, especially in a **final**

Cuppers (*field hockey, rugby union*) colloquial term for the annual intercollegiate matches at Oxford University, played for a **cup** [*cup* with the Oxford slang suffix *-er*]

cuppy (*golf*) (of) a **ball** in a "cup" or shallow depression in the ground

curl (*American football*) a pattern of play in which two **receivers** cross each other; (*cricket*) a **ball** delivered by a **bowler** that curves before or after pitching; (*surfing*) the part of a hollow wave that loops over as it breaks

curl pattern (*American football*) the route taken by a **receiver** when he runs up the **field** then turns back toward the **line of scrimmage**

curler (*curling*) a player of the sport

curling (*sport*) a game, played mainly in Scotland, in which each team slides a series of **stones** over the ice toward a **target** circle while aiming to dislodge the other team's stones already in the circle

Curragh (*horse racing*) the center of the Irish horse-breeding industry in Co. Kildare, Ireland, with a **course** that hosts many important **flat races**, including the **Irish Derby**

Currie Cup (*cricket, rugby union*) the **cup** awarded to the winner of a series of **matches** between provincial teams in South Africa [presented in 1890 by Sir Donald Currie (1825–1909)]

Curtis Cup (*golf*) the **cup** awarded to the winner of the biennial **tournament** between **amateur** women's teams from the U.S. and the U.K and Ireland [donated in 1932 by the former U.S. amateur **champions** Harriot and Margaret Curtis]

curve (*baseball*) shortening of **curveball**

curveball (*baseball*) a **ball** thrown by the **pitcher** with a **spin** that gives it an arcing trajectory

curvet (*equestrianism*) an element of **dressage** in which the horse rears up then leaps forward on its hindlegs before its forelegs are lowered [Italian *corvetta*, "little curve"]

cush (*billiards, snooker*) colloquial shortening of **cushion**

cushion (*billiards, snooker*) the padded lining of the inner side of the **billiard table**, from which the **balls** rebound

cusp (*ice skating*) the point in a turn when the skater moves from one edge of the **skate** to the other

custodian (*association football*) colloquial term for a **goalkeeper**

cut (*American football*) the regular sackings during **pre-season** practice of players deemed not fit enough to make the grade; (*cricket*) a **shot** on the **off side**, between **cover** and **third man**, made with the **bat** almost horizontal; (*fencing*) a **stroke** with the edge of the weapon rather than the point; (*golf*) (1) a **stroke** that deliberately makes the **ball** move from left to right in the air (for a right-handed player); (2) a reduction of the **field** in a **tournament** after a set number of **rounds**, so that only players with the better **scores** qualify to play in the final round; (*tennis*) a downward **stroke**, usually involving **spin**

cut and thrust (*fencing*) the use of both the edge and the point of the weapon

cut back (*association football*) to kick back sharply

cut fastball (*baseball*) another term for a **cutter**

cut in the ground (*horse racing*) (of) a **course** where the **going** is **soft** or **yielding** [so that the horse's hooves imprint the **turf**]

cut line (*squash*) another term for the **service line**

cut-off man (*baseball*) a **fielder** who goes out to a long **throw** from the **outfield** before it reaches the **infield**

cut-over (*fencing*) an offensive **disengage** made over the opponent's blade

cutback (*surfing*) a maneuver to change direction and head back toward the breaking part of the wave

cutter (*baseball*) a **fastball** with a late veer to one side; (*cricket*) a **ball** that turns sharply after pitching

cutting edge (*fencing*) the sharp edge of a **saber**

Cy Young Award (*baseball*) a **trophy** awarded to the outstanding **pitcher** in the **major leagues**, inaugurated in 1956 [commemorating the U.S. player Cy Young (1867–1955)]

cycle (*baseball*) a **single, double, triple,** and **home run** hit by a **batter** in a single **game**; (*cycling*) a bicycle

cycle race (*cycling*) a **race** of **cyclists**, as individuals or in teams

cycleball (*sport*) a modified form of **association football** in which the players, mounted on bicycles, maneuver the **ball** with their front wheels

cycling (*sport*) (1) the sport of racing on bicycles; (2) the riding of a bicycle for exercise or pleasure

cyclist (*cycling*) a participant in a **cycle race**

cyclo-cross (*sport*) **cross-country** racing on bicycles

D (*association football*) the semicircular area at the edge of the **penalty box** outside which players must stand when a **penalty** is being taken; (*billiards, snooker*) the semicircular area that adjoins the **balk line** at the bottom end of the **billiard table**; (*field hockey*) another name for the **shooting circle** [the areas have the shape of a capital "D"]

dab (*cricket*) a gentle deflection of the **ball** by the **batsman** to the **off side**

daffy (*skiing*) a maneuver in which an air-borne **skier** extends one leg forward and the other back

daily double (*horse racing*) a **bet** on the winners of two different **races** on one day of a **meeting**, with the stake and winnings from the first placed on the second

daisycutter (*cricket*) a **ball** bowled along the ground, or one that stays low after pitching

Dakar rally (*auto racing*) short name of the **Paris-Dakar rally**

Dale (*association football*) short name of the English **club** Rochdale

dam (*greyhound racing*) the mother of a greyhound; (*horse racing*) the mother of a **foal**

dan (*martial arts*) a grade of **black belt** [Japanese *dan*, "grade," "step"]

dance floor (*golf*) colloquial term for the **green** [it is flat and smooth]

dancing (*ice skating*) shortening of **ice dancing**

dandy line (*angling*) a weighted **fishing line** with crosspieces at short intervals, each with a **hook** at either end

danger (*horse racing*) a horse seen as a possible threat to a likely winner

danger line (*athletics*) the distance a runner must go before overtaking a rival and winning a **race**

danger man (*general*) a player seen as posing a particular threat

danger position (*wrestling*) a position that places an opponent's back at less than a right angle to the **mat**

dangerous play (*association football*) any **play** which is likely to injure another player, such as raising one's leg to kick the **ball** from an opponent as he is running up for a **header**

dap (*angling*) to fish with a **fly** that bounces gently on the surface of the water

Dark Blues (*association football*) nickname of the Scottish **club** Dundee [from the color of the team's shirts]

dark horse (*horse racing*) a horse whose **racing form** is not known

dart (*darts*) the small pointed missile thrown in **darts**

dartboard (*darts*) the circular **target** at which **darts** are thrown, with a **bull** worth 50 **points** and 20 numbered segments, each containing two **beds**

dartist (*darts*) a player of the **game** [perhaps a deliberate suggestion of *artist*]

dartitis (*darts*) colloquial term for the syndrome in which a player is unable to throw a **dart** properly or even at all

dartman (*darts*) a player of the **game**

darts (*sport*) an indoor **game** in which players take turns to throw three **darts** each at a **dartboard** with the aim of achieving a particular **score**

dash (*athletics*) former term for a **sprint**

Davis Cup (*tennis*) the **cup** awarded to the winner of an international **tournament** for men's teams first held in 1900 as a **challenge match** between Britain and the U.S. [donated by the U.S. player Dwight F. Davis (1879–1945)]

dead (*general*) (of) a **ball** that is not in play or temporarily inactive, either because it has gone outside the playing area or because a particular rule comes into effect; (*golf*) (of) a **ball** that is so close to the **hole** that a **putt** is regarded as unmissable; (*table tennis*) (of) a **ball** hit with no **spin**

dead ball (*association football*) a stationary **ball** ready to be played, as in a **free kick** or a **corner**; (*cricket*) a **ball** that is **dead** because it is in the hands of the **wicketkeeper** or **bowler**, it has been hit for a **boundary** by the **batsman**, or the batsman who hit it is **out**; (*real tennis*) a **ball** that is **dead** after a **point** is won or lost

dead-ball line (*rugby league, rugby union*) the line behind the **goal line** beyond which the **ball** is out of play

dead bat (*cricket*) a **bat** held by the **batsman** in such a way that the **ball** drops straight down on striking it

dead cert (*horse racing*) a horse regarded as certain to win a **race**

dead draw (*bowls*) a **draw** played with **dead weight**

dead end (*bowls*) an **end** that has to be replayed when the **jack** is hit off the **rink**

dead fish (*baseball*) a **hit** that at first travels fast but that then hits the ground and comes to a standstill

dead heat (*general*) an exact **tie** in a **race**

dead lift (*weightlifting*) a controlled raising of the **barbell** from the floor until the lifter is standing upright

dead weight (*bowls*) the **delivery** of a **bowl** that puts it right next to the **jack** or another bowl

dead wood (*tenpin bowling*) **pins** that have been knocked down and that lie in front of those still standing

deadbait (*angling*) a dead fish used as **bait**

Deaflympics (*Olympics*) short name of the World Games for the Deaf, a series of sporting **events** for deaf competitors on the lines of the **Olympics** [blend of **deaf** and *Olympics*]

death spiral (*ice skating*) in **pair skating**, a move in which the man spins the woman around him in a circle as she skates on one foot with her body almost horizontal to the ice

decathlete (*Olympics*) a competitor in a **decathlon**

decathlon (*Olympics*) a men's **event** consisting of 10 separate contests held on two consecutive days: **100 meters, long jump, shot put, high jump, and 400 meters** on day one, **110-meter hurdles, discus, pole vault, javelin, and 1,500 meters** on day two [Greek *deka*, "ten," and *athlon*, "contest"].

decider (*general*) (1) a move or action in a **game** that proves decisive, as a **goal** in **association football**; (2) a final **match** or race in a series that determines the outcome

decision (*boxing*) the awarding of a fight in which there has been no **knockout** to the **boxer** with the greater number of **points**

deck (*skateboarding*) another term for a **skateboard**; (*surfing*) the top surface of the **surfboard**

deck cricket (*cricket*) a version of the **game** formerly played on shipboard in an area enclosed by netting

deck game (*general*) a **game** played in modified form on the deck of a passenger liner or other ship, as **deck golf, deck quoits,** or **deck tennis**

deck golf (*golf*) a form of the **game** played on deck

deck quoits (*quoits*) a form of the **game** played on deck

deck tennis (*tennis*) a form of the **game** played on deck

declaration (*cricket*) the action taken by the **captain** when he decides to **declare**

declare (*cricket*) to end an **innings** voluntarily before all 10 **wickets** have fallen, usually because the **captain** considers his **batsmen** have made enough **runs**; (*horse racing*) to notify the authorities that a **trainer** intends to enter a horse in a particular **race**

dedans (*real tennis*) (1) the open **gallery** at the end of the **service side** of the **court**; (2) the spectators who generally view the action through this [French *dedans*, "inside"]

dedicated matchday (*association football*) a day on which the players in a **match** donate a day's wages to a named charity, their **supporters** also being encouraged to contribute

Dee (*association football*) short name of the Scottish **club** Dundee

deep (*association football*) well behind one's teammates; (*cricket*) not close to the **wickets**

deep-water start (*water skiing*) a **start** in which the skier is pulled up out of the water by the boat while holding on to the handle of the tow rope

defender (*general*) (1) a player whose role is mainly defensive; (2) a reigning **champion** who seeks to maintain his **title**

defense (*American football*) the team that does not have **possession** of the **ball** at the start of a **play**; (*boxing*) an attempt by a reigning **champion** to defend his **title** in a contest; (*general*) the members of a team whose main role is to prevent the opposing team from scoring

defenseman (*ice hockey, lacrosse*) a player whose prime role is defensive

defensive back (*American football*) a player who begins the play away from the **line of scrimmage** and whose main role is to defend against **passes**

defensive end (*American football*) a defensive player who lines up at the end of the **line of scrimmage**

defensive wall (*association football*) fuller term for a **wall**

degree of difficulty (*swimming*) a measure, based on a mathematical formula, that indicates the difficulty of a **dive**

deke (*ice hockey*) a maneuver to deceive an opponent and so draw him out of his defensive position [Canadian shortening of *decoy*]

delivery (*general*) the throwing or **bowling** of a **ball**, as in **cricket** or **bowls**

demolition derby (*auto racing*) a **race** in which cars are deliberately crashed into one another, the winner being the last car left running

Demons (*Australian Rules*) short name of the Melbourne Demons team

demonstration sport (*general*) a sport staged at the **Olympics** or **Commonwealth Games** purely for demonstration purposes but subsequently often gaining official recognition, as **basketball** at the1904 Olympics (included from 1936), **baseball** at the 1912 Olympics (included from 1978), and **kabaddi** at the 2010 Commonwealth Games

deny (*association football*) to prevent an opposing player or team from scoring a **goal**

derby (*general*) a **race** or sporting contest of any kind, especially when keen and held between neighboring teams, as a **match** between Manchester City and Manchester United in **association football** [in a general sense so called from the **Derby**, but in the narrower sense said by some to come from a contest between two parish teams in Derby itself]

Derby (*greyhound racing*) short name of the **Greyhound Derby**; (*horse racing*) (1) an annual **race** for three-year-old **colts** and **fillies** run at **Epsom** since 1780 [founded by Edward Stanley, 12th Earl of Derby (1752–1834)]; (2) short name of the **Kentucky Derby**

descender (*mountaineering*) a device for controlling a descent on a rope

desi (*baseball*) colloquial shortening of **designated hitter**

designated hitter (*baseball*) a tenth player named in the **lineup** to bat anywhere in the **batting order** instead of the **pitcher**

deuce (*tennis*) a level **score** of three **points** each (as if "forty-all"), when one of the sides must win two successive points to win the **game** [Old French *deus* (modern *deux*), "two"]

deuce court (*tennis*) the right side of the **court**, from which the **serve** is made and received at even-numbered **points**

deuce game (*tennis*) a **game** in which the **score** is level at **deuce**

Devil Rays (*baseball*) short name of the Tampa Bay Devil Rays team

devil-take-the-hindmost (*cycling*) a **track race** in which after a given number of **laps** the last to cross the **finishing line** drops out until only two are left to contest the final **sprint**

Devils (*ice hockey*) short name of the New Jersey Devils team

devil's number (*cricket*) a **score** of 87 **runs**, regarded as unlucky by Australian **cricketers** [the number is 13 short of a **century**]

devil's own (*darts*) a **score** of 88 [from "Devil's Own," nickname of the Connaught Rangers (88th Foot), a British army regiment noted for their bravery in the Peninsular War]

Devizes-to-Westminster Race (*canoeing*) an annual **race** of 125 miles along the Kennet and Avon Canal and Thames River from Devizes, Wiltshire, to Westminster, London

Devon (*angling*) shortening of **Devon minnow**

Devon minnow (*angling*) an **artificial fly** that imitates a swimming minnow

Dewar Cup (*shooting*) the **cup** awarded to the winner of a **rifle shooting** contest between the United States and Britain, first held in 1909 [presented by Thomas Robert Dewar, 1st Baron Dewar (1864–1930)]

diamond (*association football*) a diamond-shaped formation of four central **midfielders** behind two **strikers**; (*baseball*) (1) the diamond-shaped part of the **field**, marked off by the **baselines**; (2) the field itself; (*pool*) one of the diamond-shaped inlays on the top surfaces of **cushions**, used as reference points when playing **doubles**

diamond duck (*cricket*) a **duck** scored by a **batsman** who is **out** on the first **ball** of a **match**

Diamond League (*athletics*) a series of international athletic meetings first held in 2010

Diamond Sculls (*rowing*) the **trophy** first presented in 1844 to the winner of a **race** for single **sculls** at **Henley Royal Regatta**

Diamondbacks (*baseball*) short name of the Arizona Diamondbacks team

Diamonds (*association football*) (1) nickname of the Scottish **club** Airdrie United [from the red and white diamond shape on the team's **strip**]; (2) short name of the Scottish **club** Rushden and Diamonds

dibble (*angling*) to dip the **bait** lightly in and out of the water

dibbly-dobbler (*cricket*) a slow **ball** with imparted **spin**

did not finish (*auto racing*) failed to complete the **course**

die (*general*) to flag or lag in a contest, especially one involving great effort, such as **cycling**

dig (*cricket*) colloquial term for an **innings**; (*volleyball*) a **shot** made with the hands clasped and the arms extended so that the **ball** is kept up in the air

dig pass (*volleyball*) a **pass** made with a **dig**

Dilscoop (*cricket*) a **stroke** in which the **batsman** goes down on one knee and "scoops" the **ball** over the head of the **wicketkeeper** to send it straight to the **boundary** [introduced in 2009 by the Sri Lankan batsman Tillakaratne Dilshan]

dime defense (*American football*) a defensive formation involving six **defensive backs** [so called as it has more players than a **nickel defense**]

dimple (*golf*) one of the small depressions on a **golf ball**

ding (*surfing*) a hole in the bottom of a **surfboard**

dinged (*American football*) suffering concussion after being hit on the head in a **tackle**

dinger (*baseball*) colloquial term for a **home run**

dinghy (*sailing*) any small open boat

dink (*general*) to send the **ball** a short distance in a gentle arc

dip (*athletics*) a lunge for the **finishing line** in a race

dip-net (*angling*) a long-handled **net** for lifting up fish from the water

direct free kick (*association football*) a **free kick**, awarded after a **foul** or an **offside**, from which a **goal** can be scored without the **ball** being touched by another player (as distinct from an **indirect free kick**)

directeur sportif (*cycling*) the **manager** of a professional team [French *directeur sportif*, "sporting director"]

dirt (*horse racing*) shortening of **dirt track**

dirt bike (*motorcycle racing*) a motorcycle designed for riding on **dirt tracks**

dirt jumping (*cycling*) a **discipline** in BMX in which **riders** take off from dirt ramps and perform aerial tricks

dirt track (*horse racing*) a **racetrack** with an earth surface; (*motorcycle racing*) a **racetrack** with a surface of rolled cinders, brickdust, and the like

dirty air (*auto racing*) turbulent air from a car in front of another

discipline (*general*) a branch of sport, or an **event** in a sports contest

discus (*athletics*) (1) a heavy thick-centered disk thrown for throwing; (2) the **field event** in which it is thrown

disengage (*fencing*) to pass one's sword over or under the opponent's sword in order to change the line of attack

disgorger (*angling*) a device for extracting a **hook** from the throat of a fish

dish (*baseball*) another term for the **plate**; (*basketball*) to pass the **ball**

disk weight (*weightlifting*) one of the two rubber-coated metal disks of differing weight that are secured on the ends of a **barbell** to make it heavier

disk wheel (*cycling*) a wheel composed of a solid disk (rather than spokes) used in **time trials** and some **track races**

dismiss (*cricket*) to end the **innings** of a **batsman** or side so that he or they are **out**

dismount (*gymnastics*) the ending of a **routine** by leaving a piece of **apparatus**

disobedience (*equestrianism*) the misbehavior of a horse in an **event**, such as a **refusal**

disqualification (*boxing*) the elimination of a **boxer** from a contest because he has received three **warnings** from the **referee**

distance (*boxing*) (1) the range within which a **boxer** can strike his opponent; (2) the scheduled duration of a **match**; (*fencing*) the interval of space that must be kept between the two combatants; (*horse racing*) (1) the length of a **race**, measured in **miles** and **furlongs**; (2) a point 240 yards (220m) back from the **winning post**, which a horse must have reached when the winner finishes in order to run in a subsequent **heat**

distance jumping (*water skiing*) an **event** in which the skier is towed up and off a specially prepared ramp then travels through the air as far as possible

distance post (*horse racing*) a post marking the **distance** to the **winning post**

distance runner (*athletics*) an **athlete** who competes in **middle-distance running** or **long-distance running**

ditch (*bowls*) the shallow trough around a **green** or, in **indoor bowls**, at either end of the **carpet**

ditcher (*bowls*) a **bowl** that runs off or is knocked off the **green** into the **ditch**

dive (*aquatics*) an underwater exploration made with an **aqualung** or similar apparatus; (*association football*) a **play** in which a player throws himself to the ground in an **archer's bow** position in an attempt to deceive the **referee** into believing he was tripped in an illegal **tackle** and should thus be awarded a **penalty** or **free kick**;

(*boxing*) a feigned **knockout** as a tactical move; (*swimming*) a swift, usually head-first, descent into the water

diver (*aquatics, association football, swimming*) a person who executes a **dive**

dividend (*association football*) a share in the payout from a **football pool**

diving (*aquatics, swimming*) the carrying out of **dives**

diving board (*swimming*) the **springboard** or **platform** from which a **dive** is made

division (*association football*) a group of teams within a **league** between which **fixtures** are arranged [in 2004 Division 1 became the **Championship** and Divisions 2 and 3 became Leagues 1 and 2]; (*cricket*) one of the two groups of nine teams introduced in the **Pro40 League** in1999 and the **County Championships** in 2000; (*general*) a group of teams that compete in a contest, as between college **eights** in a **bumping race**

divot (*golf*) (1) a small piece of turf dug up by the **head** of a **golf club** during a **stroke**; (2) the hole left where the turf has been dug up in this way [apparently of Scottish origin]

DNF (*auto racing*) abbreviation of **did not finish**

dobbler (*cricket*) shortening of **dibbly-dobbler**

dock start (*water skiing*) a start in which the skier is pulled onto the water by the boat while standing or sitting on a dock or pontoon

Dockers (*Australian Rules*) short name of the Fremantle Dockers team

doctor (*angling*) a type of hackled **dry fly**

dodgeball (*sport*) a **game** in which players form a circle and try to hit their opponents with a large **ball**, which they try to dodge

Dodgers (*baseball*) short name of the Los Angeles Dodgers team

dog (*horse racing*) a horse that is slow or difficult to handle

dog paddle (*swimming*) a simple **stroke** with alternate arm movements [like the front legs of a swimming dog]

dog racing (*sport*) another name for **greyhound racing**

dogfall (*wrestling*) a **fall** in which both **wrestlers** touch the ground together

Doggett's Coat and Badge (*rowing*) the **trophy** awarded to the winner of an annual **sculling race** between newly qualified watermen on the Thames in London [founded in 1715 by Thomas Doggett, an Irish actor, who donated an orange-colored coat with a silver badge]

dogleg (*golf*) a **hole** with a bending **fairway** [in the shape of a dog's leg]

dogs (*sport*) colloquial term for **greyhound racing**, especially as a betting sport

dogsled (*sled dog racing*) a **sled** pulled by a team of dogs

dohyo (*sumo*) the **ring** or marked area in which the **wrestlers** compete [Japanese *dohyo*, "sumo ring"]

doigté (*fencing*) the use of the fingers to manipulate the sword [French *doigté*, "fingered"]

dojo (*martial arts*) (1) a room or hall where instruction is given in various arts of **self-defense**; (2) an area of padded mats for this purpose [Japanese *do*, "way," and *jo*, "place"]

doll (*horse racing*) a **hurdle** used as a barrier on a **racecourse** to exclude certain areas from use by **riders** [perhaps a form of *dool*, "boundary mark"]

dolly (*cricket*) a slow easy **catch** [from *doll*, as it is "child's play"]

dolphin kick (*swimming*) an element of the **butterfly** in which the legs are held together and moved up and down by bending and straightening them at the knee

Dolphins (*American football*) short name of the Miami Dolphins team

dome (*general*) shortening of **astrodome**

domestic (*general*) (of) a contest between teams in their native country, not **international**

domestique (*cycling*) a **rider** who accompanies and supports a professional team in a **road race** [French *domestique*, "servant"]

Donald (*mountaineering*) a Scottish Lowland hill of 2,000ft or more [first listed by Percy Donald]

Doncaster (*horse racing*) a **flat** and **National Hunt** **racecourse** at Doncaster, South Yorkshire, England, the location of the **St. Leger**

donkey derby (*general*) a series of **races** by contestants mounted on donkeys

donkey drop (*cricket*) a slow **ball** bowled or hit so that it travels in a high arc

Dons (*association football*) (1) nickname of the Scottish **club** Aberdeen [perhaps shortening of *Aberdonians*, name of townsfolk]; (2) short name of the English **club** Milton Keynes Dons; (3) nickname of the English **club** Wimbledon [shortened form of the placename]

donut (*auto racing*) to spin a car by pulling on the handbrake [from the circular motion]; (*parachuting*) in skydiving, a **free fall** formation in which team members form a hollow circle with linked arms; (*tennis*) colloquial term for a **game** score 6–0

Doonhamers (*association football*) nickname of the Scottish **club** Queen of the South [based in Dumfries, whose inhabitants talk of their home town as *doon hame*, "down (at) home"]

door (*real tennis*) the third **gallery** from the end of the **service side** or the second from the end of the **hazard side** [both galleries formerly had doors]

doosra (*cricket*) a **leg break** bowled with an apparent **off-break** action by a right-arm **bowler** [Hindi *doosra*, "the other one"]

dope (*general*) a drug illegally administered to an **athlete** or a **racehorse**

dope sheet (*horse racing*) a daily bulletin with details of the horses entered for a **race** and information on their past **form**

dormie (*golf*) a situation in **matchplay** in which a player is as many **holes** ahead of an opponent as there are holes left to play [perhaps related to Latin *dormire*, "to sleep," as the player cannot lose even by going to sleep]

dormy (*golf*) another spelling of **dormie**

dorothy (*cricket*) colloquial term for a **six** [rhyming slang, from *Dorothy Dix*, the name adopted by the popular U.S. journalist Elizabeth Meriwether Gilmer (1861–1951)]

dot ball (*cricket*) a **delivery** from which no **runs** are scored [conventionally recorded by the **scorer** as a dot]

dot down (*rugby league, rugby union*) to make a perfunctory **touchdown** of the **ball**

double (*association football*) the winning of the **Premiership** and **FA Cup** in one **season**; (*baseball*) a **hit** that allows the **batter** to reach **second base**; (*darts*) a **score** of twice the usual amount, obtained when the **dart** lands in the outer **bed** of the **dartboard**; (*horse racing*) shortening of **daily double**; (*pool, snooker*) a **shot** in which the **object ball** rebounds off a **cushion** into the opposite **pocket**; (*tennis*) shortening of **double fault**; (*trampolining*) a double **somersault**

double axel (*ice skating*) an **axel** that incorporates two and a half turns in the air

double back (*gymnastics*) a move with two successive **backflips**

double blue (*general*) (1) a person who has twice won a **blue**; (2) the awards themselves

double bogey (*golf*) a **score** of two **strokes** over **par** for a **hole**, double that of a **bogey**

double century (*cricket*) a **score** of 200 **runs** by a **batsman**, double that of a **century**

double double (*basketball*) the feat of recording double figures in two categories in a **game**

double dribble (*basketball*) a **dribble** made with two hands or after stopping, both illegal

double eagle (*golf*) another term for an **albatross**

double fault (*tennis*) two successive **faults** in a **service**, causing the loss of a **point**

double full (*trampolining*) a backward **somersault** with **double twist**

double header (*general*) two **games** or **matches** played on the same day

double-leg tackle (*wrestling*) a move in which a **wrestler** grasps his opponent's legs to bring him down

double play (*baseball*) a **play** that **puts out** two **runners**

double poling (*skiing*) using both **ski poles** at the same time, especially at a **start**

double pump (*basketball*) a feint in which a player attempts to deceive an opponent by pretending to shoot in mid-air before taking a **shot**

double scull (*rowing*) a two-manned boat in which each **rower** has a pair of **sculls**

double spare (*skittles, tenpin bowling*) the knocking down of all of the **pins** with one's first **ball** [twice as good as a **spare**]

double steal (*baseball*) a **play** in which two **baserunners** each make a **steal**

double takeout (*curling*) a **takeout** that removes two **stones** from play

double team (*basketball*) the strategy of assigning two **defenders** to one **attacker**

double top (*darts*) a **score** of 40 made by a **throw** into the **double** ring of the segment numbered 20 at the top of the **dartboard**

double trap (*shooting*) in **trapshooting**, the simultaneous release of two **targets** at different heights and angles

double-wake cut (*water skiing*) an approach for a **jump** in which the skier gathers speed by twice crossing the wake of the boat

double wing (*American football*) an offensive **backfield** formation with two **halfbacks** located close to the **line of scrimmage** and just outside the **ends**

doubles (*general*) a **game** between two pairs of players, as typically in **tennis**

doughnut (*auto racing, parachuting*) another spelling of **donut**

down (*American football*) one of four consecutive periods of play during which a team must score or advance the **ball** 10 yards in order to retain **possession**; (*boxing*) (1) beaten because a part of the body other than the feet is touching the **canvas**; (2) beaten because helpless on the **ropes**; (3) beaten because judged unfit by the **referee** to continue

down-and-out (*American football*) a **pass** pattern executed by running **downfield** then making a 90-degree turn and running toward one of the **sidelines**

Down Royal (*horse racing*) a **flat** and **National Hunt** racecourse in Co. Antrim, Northern Ireland

down the line (*association football*) (of) a **shot** traveling parallel to and close to the side of the **pitch**; (*shooting*) another term for **trapshooting**; (*tennis*) (of) a **shot** traveling parallel to and close to the side of the **court**

down to the wire (*horse racing*) as far as the **finishing post**

downfield (*general*) in or toward the end of the field nearest the **goal** of the opposing team

downhill (*skiing*) a downhill **race**

Downpatrick (*horse racing*) a flat and **National Hunt** racecourse at Downpatrick, Co. Down, Northern Ireland

downstream gate (*canoeing*) on a **slalom** course, a **gate** to be negotiated following the direction of the current

downswing (*golf*) the part of the **swing** in which the **club** is moving down toward the **ball**

downtown (*basketball*) colloquial term for the area beyond the **three-point line**

Doyenne, La (*cycling*) nickname of the **Liège-Bastogne-Liège road race** [French *la doyenne*, "the senior," as the oldest of the one-day top-class races]

drabbling (*angling*) a manner of **fishing** for barbel with a **rod** and long **line** passed through a piece of lead

draft (*auto racing, cycling*) another term for **slipstream**

drag (*snooker*) the slightly delayed motion of the **cue ball**, caused by **backspin**, when struck just under the center

drag racing (*auto racing*) a **race** held over a straight quarter-mile as a test in acceleration, usually between two cars at a time

drag strip (*auto racing*) a **course** specially built or modified for **drag racing**

Dragon (*sailing*) a **yacht** of the International Dragon class, 8.88m (29.2ft) long

Dragons (*rugby league*) short name of the English **clubs** Catalans Dragons and Doncaster Dragons

dragshot (*snooker*) a **shot** that imparts **drag** to the **ball**

dragster (*auto racing*) a car specially built or modified for use in **drag racing**

dragway (*auto racing*) (1) a road or **course** used for **drag racing**; (2) the paved area of a **drag strip**

drail (*angling*) a piece of lead around the shank of the **hook**

drain (*basketball*) colloquial term for a clean **shot** through the **basket**

drain a putt (*golf*) another term for **sink a putt**

draw (*American football*) a running **play** disguised as a passing play; (*archery*) to pull back the **bowstring** and **arrow** ready to shoot; (*bowls*) a gentle **delivery** that makes the **bowl** curve toward the point aimed for; (*canoeing*) a method of turning the **canoe** by making a **stroke** at right angles to the direction of travel; (*cricket*) another term for an **inside edge**; (*curling*) (1) the degree of curve in the trajectory of a **stone**; (2) a **shot** sufficiently weighty to reach the **house**; (*general*) (1) a **game** that ends with an equal **score**; (2) the random process used to assign opponents

in a **game** or starting positions in a **race**; (*golf*) a **stroke** that purposely makes the **ball** move in the air from right to left (of a right-handed player) or from left to right (of a left-handed player); (*horse racing*) in **flat racing**, the randomly allocated position of a horse in the **starting stalls**; (*lacrosse*) the method of starting the women's **game** in which the two **centers** balance the **ball** on the backs of their horizontally held **sticks** then toss it in the air as they pull the sticks up and away; (*snooker*) a **stroke** that makes the **cue ball** recoil after hitting another **ball**

draw stumps (*cricket*) to end a **game** by removing the **wickets**

draw weight (*archery*) the force required to pull back the **bowstring** to its maximum

drawn game (*general*) a **game** that ends in a **draw**

dream team (*general*) a perfect or ideally matched team

Dream Team (*basketball*) nickname of the U.S. national team that won **gold** at the 1992 **Olympics** in Barcelona

dress (*angling*) to prepare a **fly** for use on a **hook**

dressage (*equestrianism*) the performance of a horse in particular **gaits** and maneuvers in response to signals from the **rider** [French *dressage*, "training"]

dressing room (*general*) a **changing room** as a place where a team can discuss the **game** or the selection of players, be addressed by their **manager** or **coach**, and the like

dribble (*general*) a closely controlled gradual advancing of the **ball** by means of repeated movements of the hand or foot, as appropriate

dries (*auto racing*) tires, especially **slicks**, designed for use in dry-weather conditions

drift (*auto racing*) a controlled skid, used to negotiate bends

drill (*association football*) to kick the **ball** hard and straight, especially into the **net**

drive (*American football*) a sequence of **plays** by a team without losing **possession**; (*badminton*) a hard low **shot** over the **net** made with the **racket** horizontal; (*basketball*) a forceful advance toward the **basket**; (*bowls*) a fast, straight **delivery** that eliminates the **bias**; (*cricket*) a **shot** played with the **bat** held vertically so that the **ball** travels along the ground in front of the **batsman**; (*golf*) a powerful **shot** from the **tee** using a **driver**; (*lacrosse*) a fast, direct run for **goal**; (*rowing*) the action of pulling the **oar** through the water; (*rugby union*) a team's pushing forward of a **maul**; (*table tennis, tennis*) a fast, straight **return** delivered **underarm**

drive off (*golf*) to hit the **ball** from the **tee**

drive the green (*golf*) to hit the **ball** from a **tee** onto the **green**

drive-through penalty (*auto racing*) a **penalty** in which a driver must enter the **pit lane**, drive through it at the prescribed speed, then rejoin the **race**

driver (*golf*) a wooden-headed **club** used to hit the **ball** a long way, especially from the **tee**

driving iron (*golf*) an **iron** with an enlarged head used for **tee shots** when accuracy is required

driving range (*golf*) a place for **golfers** to practice their **drives**

drop (*golf*) the act of repositioning the **ball** from an unplayable position by letting it fall from one's outstretched arm; (*rugby league, rugby union*) (1) shortening of **drop goal**; (2) shortening of **drop kick**

drop ball (*association football*) the dropping of the **ball** by the **referee** to restart play at the point where a **game** was temporarily suspended

drop fly (*angling*) an **artificial fly** attached to a **leader** above the **tail fly**

drop goal (*rugby league, rugby union*) a **goal** scored by means of a **drop kick**

drop in (*skateboarding*) to enter a **half-pipe** or obstacle from the top; (*surfing*) (1) to obstruct another **surfer** by starting to surf in his path; (2) to slide down the face of a wave immediately after **takeoff**

drop kick (*rugby league, rugby union*) a kick of the **ball** when it bounces from the ground after being dropped from the kicker's hand; (*wrestling*) a kick made with both feet while jumping in the air

drop-knee (*surfing*) a turn with both knees bent and the trail leg crossed behind the lead leg

drop line (*angling*) a weighted **line** for **fishing** near the bottom of a river

drop one's hands (*horse racing*) to relax one's hold on the reins and allow the horse to coast home, an **offense** if done by miscalculation when crossing the **finishing line**

drop shot (*badminton*) a gentle **shot** from the **baseline** at the back of the **court** that just clears the **net**; (*table tennis*) a **shot** that falls just over the opponent's side of the **net**; (*tennis*) a delicate **shot** that just clears the **net** and lands the other side of it

drop stroke (*general*) another term for a **drop shot**

drop volley (*tennis*) a gentle **volley** that just clears the **net**

dropout (*rugby league*) a **drop kick** to restart play after the **ball** has gone dead, taken from the center of the **twenty-meter line**; (*rugby union*) a **drop kick** to restart play after the **ball** has gone dead, taken from the center of the **twenty-two meter line**

dropped goal (*rugby league, rugby union*) another term for a **drop goal**

dropper (*angling*) another term for a **drop fly**

drops (*cycling*) the lower sections of the curved handlebars on a **road bike**

dry bob (*cricket*) a boy at Eton College who plays **cricket** in the summer term, as distinct from a **wet bob** [*bob* perhaps the personal name *Bob*]

dry fly (*angling*) an **artificial fly** that does not sink in the water but floats on the surface

dry leaf (*association football*) a **free kick** with an unpredictable trajectory, as distinct from a **falling leaf**

dry slope (*skiing*) a slope with an artificial surface, used for training or out-of-season practice

dual mogul (*skiing*) a head-to-head **race** between two skiers down a **mogul**

dual slalom (*skiing, snowboarding*) another term for a **parallel slalom**

dub (*angling*) to **dress** a **fly**

duck (*cricket*) a **score** of no **runs** by a **batsman** [originally *duck's egg*, from the egg-shaped "0" on the **scoreboard**]

duck dive (*surfing*) a maneuver in which the **board** is "ducked" under an oncoming wave

duck hook (*golf*) a **mishit** that veers sharply to the left (for a right-handed player)

Ducks (*ice hockey*) short name of the Anaheim Ducks team

Duckworth-Lewis method (*cricket*) a mathematical system used to calculate the total required for a team batting second in a one-day **game** interrupted by rain [devised in 1997 by statisticians Frank Duckworth and Tony Lewis]

duet (*swimming*) in **synchronized swimming**, a **routine** performed by two contestants

duff (*golf*) a **mishit** that occurs when a player's **club** hits the ground behind the **ball**

dugout (*general*) a sunken shelter or covered bench area beside a sports **pitch** with seating for a team's **manager** or **trainer** and for those players not in the current **game**

duke (*boxing*) the verdict in a **match** [from the practice of raising the winner's arm, from the slang term for a fist, from rhyming slang *duke of Yorks*, "forks," slang for the hands]

dummy (*association football, rugby league, rugby union*) a feint of passing the **ball** in order to mislead an opponent and run past him

dummy half (*rugby league*) another term for an **acting half-back**

dummy scissors (*rugby union*) a feigned **scissors** move

dump (*volleyball*) a feigned **spike** that sends the **ball** just over the **net** or a **block**

dumper (*surfing*) a wave that crashes down with great force, causing **surfers** to fall

dun (*angling*) an **artificial fly** that imitates the **mayfly** before hatching [*dun*, "dull brown"]

Dundalk (*horse racing*) a **flat** and **National Hunt racecourse** at Dundalk, Co. Louth, Ireland

dunk (*basketball*) a **shot** made by jumping up and pushing the **ball** down through the **basket**

dunker (*basketball*) a player who shoots a **dunk**

duster (*baseball*) a **pitch** aimed high in the direction of the **batter**

Dutch Grand Prix (*auto racing*) the **Formula One** international **Grand Prix** held on the **circuit** at Zandfoort, Netherlands

Dutch 200 (*tenpin bowling*) colloquial term for a **score** of 200 **points**, achieved by bowling alternate **strikes** and **spares**

dyno (*mountaineering*) colloquial term for a vigorous leap for a distant hold [shortening of *dynamic*]

each way (*horse racing*) a **bet** for a **win** and a **place**

eagle (*golf*) a **score** of two **strokes** under **par** on a **hole** [a "bird" twice as impressive as a simple **birdie**]

Eagles (*American football*) short name of the Philadelphia Eagles team; (*association football*) nickname of the English **club** Crystal Palace [it can both "soar" and "swoop"]; (*Australian Rules*) short name of the West Coast Eagles team; (*rugby league*) short name of the English **club** Sheffield Eagles

early bath (*rugby league*) colloquial term for an order to a player to leave the **field** after an infringement [he takes a bath in the **changing room** before the rest of the team]

earned run (*baseball*) a **run** conceded by a **pitcher** without the intervention of an **error**

earned run average (*baseball*) the number of **earned runs** conceded by a **pitcher** per nine **innings** pitched

earthworm (*angling*) the common worm used as **bait**

easy! (*rowing*) a command to stop rowing

easy all! (*rowing*) fuller form of **easy!**

Ebor (*horse racing*) an annual **handicap** run at **York** since 1843 [abbreviation of *Eboracum*, the Roman name of York]

ECB (*cricket*) abbreviation of **England and Wales Cricket Board**

echelon (*cycling*) a **paceline** in which the **cyclists** are arranged in a stepped formation to gain a **slipstream** effect [French *échelon*, from *échelle*, "ladder"]

eclectic (*golf*) a contest comprising a number of **rounds** played under **strokeplay** conditions, with each player selecting his lowest **score** at each **hole**

Eclipse Stakes (*horse racing*) an annual **race** run at **Sandown Park** since 1886 [named for the famous **racehorse** Eclipse (1764–1789)]

ecothon (*general*) a **cross-country endurance race** incorporating elements of **running, mountain biking, kayaking, swimming,** and **abseiling** [combination of *eco-*, denoting concern for the environment, and *-thon*, from **marathon**]

Edgbaston (*cricket*) the **home ground** of Warwickshire **county cricket club**, Birmingham

edge (*cricket*) to give a slight touch to the **ball** with the edge of the **bat**; (*general*) the edge of the **board** in a sport such as **wakeboarding**

edging (*skiing*) the technique of tilting the **skis** so that the edges dig into the snow, thus giving a better grip

egg position (*skiing*) another term for the **tuck position**

eggbeater (*swimming*) in **synchronized swimming**, a technique of treading water by rotating the legs, so keeping the body upright and the hands free

eggplant (*snowboarding*) a one-handed **handplant** through 180 degrees with the front hand planted on the lip of the wall and **backside rotation**

eight (*rowing*) a **crew** of eight **rowers** and a **cox**

eight-ball pool (*pool*) a form of the **game** played with 15 numbered **object balls** and a **cue ball** in which the **black**, numbered 8, is the last to be **potted**

eight-count (*boxing*) a **count** of eight seconds by the **referee** that a **boxer** who is **down** must take while the referee decides whether or not to continue the **bout**

800 meters (*athletics*) a **foot race** of the stated distance

eighteen (*Australian Rules*) a team of 18 players

eighteen-hole (*golf*) (of) a **course** having 18 **holes** (as is the norm)

eighteen-yard box (*association football*) another name for the **penalty area** [its extent in front of the **goal**]

eights (*rowing*) a **race** between **eights**, especially those at Oxford University in **Eights Week**

Eights Week (*rowing*) the annual week in which **bumping races** between college **eights** are held at Oxford University

eightsman (*rowing*) a **rower** in an **eight**

Eisenhower Trophy (*golf*) the **trophy** awarded to the winner of a biennial international competition first held in 1958 [named for U.S. president Dwight D. Eisenhower (1890–1969)]

eisschiessen (*sport*) a German form of **curling** [German *Eis*, "ice," and *schiessen*, "to shoot"]

elapsed time (*auto racing*) in **drag racing**, the time taken to cover the **course** from **starting line** to **finishing line**

elbow (*horse racing*) a slight bend in a **racecourse**

element (*gymnastics*) a move or maneuver in a **routine**

elevator (*wrestling*) a move in which a combatant

places his leg behind one of his opponent's legs and raises it to throw him off balance

eleven (*association football*) a team of 11 players; (*cricket*) a team of 11 players

eligible receiver (*American football*) an offensive player, usually a **back** or a player on the end of the **line of scrimmage**, who is legally empowered to catch a **pass**

eliminator (*general*) a contest in which a competitor is eliminated, as from a **bout** in **boxing**

elite cyclist (*cycling*) a competent **cyclist**, especially one riding in a sponsored team

Elliott (*sailing*) a class of **keelboat** sailed by a crew of three [named for its New Zealand designer Greg Elliott]

Embassy Championship (*darts*) an annual **championship** first held in 1978 at Nottingham, now at Frimley Green, Surrey [name of sponsor]

Emirates Stadium (*association football*) the **home ground** of Arsenal **football club**, London [name of sponsors]

Empire Pool (*swimming*) a former **swimming pool** at **Wembley**, opened in 1934 for the Empire Games (the present **Commonwealth Games**) but closed after the 1948 **Olympics**

enclosure (*horse racing*) an area marked off for (specified) spectators at **races**, such as the **Members' Enclosure** or the **silver ring**

end (*American football*) a player positioned at the extremity of the **line of scrimmage**; (*archery*) a group of (usually three) **arrows** shot in a single sequence [from one end of the **range**]; (*bowls*) a complete sequence of play in one direction [the **bowls** are delivered from one end of the **green**]; (*curling*) the completion of 16 **stones** [delivered from one end of the **rink**]; (*general*) one of the two halves of a playing area such as a **court** or **field**

end around (*American football*) an offensive **play** in which an **end** runs behind the **line of scrimmage**, is handed the **ball**, then continues running to the opposite side of the **field**

end run (*American football*) an attempt to run wide with the **ball** round the end of a defensive line rather than try to break through it

end zone (*American football*) the area behind the **goal line** into which the offensive team attempts to take the **ball** to score a **touchdown**

endo (*gymnastics*) a **stalder** in a forward position on the **horizontal bar** and **asymmetric bars** [introduced by the Japanese **gymnast** Yukio Endo (1937–2009)]; (*motorcycle racing*) a crash in which the **rider** and his **bike** flip end over end

endurance race (*general*) a **race** over a long-distance **cross-country course**

endurance riding (*equestrianism*) a test of a horse's stamina over a long-distance **cross-country course**

enduro (*auto racing, motorcycle racing*) a long-distance **cross-country race** that tests the endurance of the vehicles rather than their speed [short form of *endurance*]

enforcer (*ice hockey*) an aggressive team player whose main role is not to score **goals** but to intimidate the **opposition**

en garde! (*fencing*) a command to **fencers** before a **bout** to assume a position from which they can either attack or defend [French *en garde!*, "on guard!"]

England and Wales Cricket Board (*cricket*) the administrative body of the **game**, both professional and recreational, in England and Wales

English (*snooker*) another term for **side**

English classics (*horse racing*) the five oldest and most important British **flat races**: the **Two Thousand Guineas, One Thousand Guineas, Oaks, Derby**, and **St. Leger**

English League (*association football*) another term for the **Football League**, distinguishing it from the **Scottish League**

En-Tout-Cas (*tennis*) proprietary name of a hard **tennis court** that can be used in all weathers [French *en tout cas*, "in any case"]

entry (*swimming*) the end point of a **dive**, when the **swimmer** enters the water

entry fee (*horse racing*) the fee paid to enter a horse in a **race**

épée (*fencing*) a narrow-bladed, sharp-pointed sword formerly used for dueling, now having a **button** on the end [French *épée*, "sword"]

Epsom (*horse racing*) a **flat racecourse** at Epsom Downs, near Epsom, Surrey, England, the location of the **Derby, Oaks**, and **Coronation Cup**

equalizer (*association football*) a **goal** that levels the **score**

equestrianism (*sport*) the riding and control of horses, involving such **disciplines** as **dressage, showjumping**, the **three-day event, carriage driving**, and **endurance riding**

équipe (*general*) a team and its equipment, especially in **auto racing** [French *équipe*, "team"]

Equitrack (*horse racing*) proprietary name of a type of **all-weather** surface on a **racecourse** [perhaps blend of *equi-*, "equal," and *equine*, "relating to horses," with **track**]

ERA (*baseball*) abbreviation of **earned run average**

ergo (*rowing*) shortening of **ergometer**

ergometer (*rowing*) a land-based machine on which **rowers** can train and test themselves

error (*baseball*) an instance of a **fielder** failing to record an **out**

escape road (*auto racing*) a slip road off a **circuit** into which a car can be driven when failing to negotiate a bend or otherwise running out of control

Eskimo roll (*canoeing*) a technique of using the **paddle** against the water to right a **canoe** or **kayak** that has tipped or rolled over [said to be the method used by Eskimos in kayaks]

Eskimoes (*Canadian football*) short name of the Edmonton Eskimoes team

ET (*auto racing*) abbreviation of **elapsed time**

Eton field game (*sport*) a form of **association football** played at Eton College [played in the **field**, as distinct from the **Eton wall game**]

Eton fives (*fives*) a form of **fives** played between **doubles** in a three-walled **court** [originally played between the buttresses of the chapel at Eton College]

Eton wall game (*sport*) a form of **association football** played against a wall at Eton College [played at a wall, as distinct from the **Eton field game**]

étrier (*mountaineering*) a small rope ladder used as a climbing aid [French *étrier*, "stirrup"]

Europa League (*association football*) the **knock-out competition** that in 2009 replaced the **UEFA Cup** as a contest between European **clubs** finishing near the top of their domestic **league**

European Champions' Cup (*association football*) the **cup** awarded to the **champions** in an annual competition played among European **clubs** since 1956

European Championship (*association football*) a **championship** competition played every four years among European **clubs** since 1960

European Cup (*association football*) short name of the **European Champions' Cup**

European Cup Winners' Cup (*association football*) the **cup** awarded to the winners of the main European domestic **club** competitions, first played in 1961 but discontinued in 1999, after which cup winners competed in an expanded **UEFA Cup**

European Grand Prix (*auto racing*) the **Formula One** international **Grand Prix** held on the **circuit** at Valencia, Spain [so named for distinction from the **Spanish Grand Prix**]

European Super Cup (*association football*) the **cup** awarded to the winners of the **Europa League** and the **European Champions' Cup**

European Tour (*golf*) an annual series of **tournaments** in European countries, now widened to include countries far outside Europe, as South Africa and Malaysia

evening rise (*angling*) the increased **rise** of trout to **bait** on a summer evening

evens (*horse racing*) a **bet** in which the amount staked is equal to the amount won if the horse wins

event (*equestrianism*) shortening of **three-day event**; (*general*) an item in a sporting contest

eventing (*equestrianism*) participation in a **three-day event** or equestrian **events** generally

Everest of the sea (*sailing*) nickname of the **Vendée Globe**

exacta (*horse racing*) alternate name for a **perfecta** [American Spanish *quiniela exacta*, "exact **quinella**"]

execution (*gymnastics*) the technical performance of an **element** or **routine**

exercise bike (*general*) a machine like a bicycle used for exercise in a **gymnasium** or in the home

Exeter (*horse racing*) a **National Hunt racecourse** at Kennford, near Exeter, Devon, England

exhibition game (*general*) a **game** played for instruction purposes or public entertainment

Exiles (*rugby union*) nickname of the **club** London Irish [formed in London as a club for Irishmen in 1898, following the earlier London Scottish (1878) and London Welsh (1885)]

expansion bolt (*mountaineering*) a bolt that expands inside a hole or crack in a rock face to provide a firm support

expansion club (*American football, basketball*) a **club** that has bought a **franchise** from a professional **league** so that it can now start to buy players from other teams

expedite rule (*table tennis*) a rule, applied in a long **game**, that obliges the **server** to win each **rally** within a given number of **strokes** or else forfeit the **point** to the **receiver**

explosion shot (*golf*) a **shot** that sends the **ball** in a high trajectory out of a **bunker** by striking the sand behind the ball with a strong swing of the **club**

explosive ability (*American football*) the ability of a **running back** to use strength, speed, and agility to dodge or ram through the defensive line in order to gain a **touchdown**

Expos (*baseball*) short name of the Montreal Expos team

exposed (*horse racing*) having a well-known **racing form**, unlike a **dark horse**

exposing (*wrestling*) a scoring variant in which **points** are won for exposing an opponent's back to the **mat** at an angle of 90 degrees or more

exposure (*mountaineering*) the insecurity or precariousness of a position taken by a **climber**

extension (*horse racing*) the lengthening of a horse's **stride** at a particular **pace**; (*snooker*) a section added to the end of a **cue** or inserted in the middle (of a two-piece cue) to increase its length when a **shot** with a standard cue is impossible

extra (*cricket*) a **run** scored from a **bye**, **leg bye**, **wide** or **no-ball** rather than by hitting the **ball** and then running

extra cover (*cricket*) a **fielding** position on the **off side** between **cover** and **mid-off**

extra innings (*baseball*) additional **innings** played to decide the winner if a **game** is tied after nine innings

extra point (*American football*) a **point** scored after a **touchdown** by **snapping** the **ball** from the two-yard line and kicking it through the **goalposts**

extra time (*general*) time added at the end of a **game** or **match** to produce a decisive result when there is a **tie** at the normal finishing time

extreme fighting (*sport*) another name for **ultimate fighting**

extreme sport (*general*) an unconventional sport, often a variant of a conventional one, that potentially exposes participants to danger, such as **free running** (from **running**)

f (*horse racing*) abbreviation of **furlong** (or *furlongs*) in **racing** reports

FA (*association football*) abbreviation of **Football Association**

FA Cup (*association football*) the **cup** awarded to the winners of the **knockout competition** for professional English **clubs**, inaugurated by the **Football Association** in 1871

face-off (*ice hockey*) the procedure for starting or restarting play in which a **linesman** drops the **puck** between two opposing players; (*lacrosse*) the procedure for starting or restarting play in the men's **game** by which the **ball** is placed between the **crosses** of the players as they squat down, the aim being to capture it or fling it to a player on the same side

fade (*golf*) a **stroke** that deliberately causes the **ball** to move from left to right in the air (for a right-handed player) or from right to left (for a left-handed player)

fadeaway (*basketball*) a **shot** taken while leaning or falling away from the **basket**

fail (*athletics*) to be unsuccessful in clearing the **bar** at a given height in the **high jump** or **pole vault**

fair ball (*baseball*) a **ball** hit between the **baselines** into the field of play

fair catch (*American football*) an unopposed **catch** by a member of the team receiving a **punt** or **kickoff**

fair goal (*American football*) a **score** of three **points** gained by kicking the **ball** through the **goalposts** of the opposing team

fair play (*general*) the principle of playing or participating in a sport according to the rules

faire Fanny (*pétanque*) to lose a **game** 13–0 [French *faire Fanny*, "to do a Fanny," from a legend that a French barmaid named Fanny allowed members of the losing team to kiss her as a **consolation prize**]

fairway (*golf*) the closely mown area of turf between the **tee** and the **green**, as distinct from the uncut **rough** or **hazards**

fairway wood (*golf*) a **wood** other than a **driver**, used for **shots** from the **fairway**

Fairyhouse (*horse racing*) a **flat** and **National Hunt** racecourse in Co. Meath, Ireland, the location of the **Irish Grand National**

fake (*general*) a misleading movement to trick an opponent

Fakenham (*horse racing*) a **National Hunt** racecourse at Fakenham, Norfolk, England

fakie (*skateboarding, snowboarding, water skiing*) a move in which the **boarder** rides backwards [origin uncertain]

Falcons (*American football*) short name of the Atlanta Falcons team; (*rugby union*) short name of the English **club** Newcastle Falcons

fall (*cricket*) the loss of a **wicket**; (*wrestling*) (1) another term for a **bout**; (2) a **throw** that keeps an opponent on the **mat** for a particular time

Fall Classic (*baseball*) colloquial term for the **World Series**

fall guy (*association football*) jocular name for a player executing a **dive**

fall line (*skiing*) the natural line of a route down a slope; (*surfing*) the line of fastest descent to the base of a wave [a term borrowed from geography, where it denotes the zone of falls and rapids between an upland region and a plain]

faller (*horse racing*) a horse that falls at a **fence** or **hurdle** and fails to complete the **race**

falling leaf (*association football*) a long-range **shot** that sends the **ball** into a curving aerial trajectory

false start (*general*) a **start** to a **race** made ahead of the official signal and therefore invalid

fan (*baseball*) another term for **strike out** [the batter ineffectually "fans" his **bat** at a **ball**]

fancy (*horse racing*) to select a horse as the likely winner of a **race**; (*general*) a dated term for enthusiasts of a particular sport, especially originally **boxing** or **horse racing** [the word *fancier* is still current for a breeder of distinctive varieties, as of cats or pigeons]

fanny dipper (*surfing*) a **surfer**'s nickname for an ordinary **swimmer** [who merely "dips his fanny" in the water]

fantasy cricket (*cricket*) a competition on the lines of **fantasy football** but with **cricketers** instead of **footballers**

fantasy football (*association football*) a competition in which entrants select an ideal team of real players from different **clubs** and score **points** according to the actual performance of those players for their respective clubs

Far Eastern Games (*Olympics*) **regional games** held from 1913 to 1950 for competitors from China, Japan, and the Philippines

far post (*association football*) the **goalpost** that is farthest from the **ball** at a given moment

farm (*cricket*) to contrive, as a **batsman**, to receive most of the **bowling**

farm team (*baseball*) a **minor league** team that provides players as needed to a **major league** team

fartlek (*athletics*) a method of training for **marathons** and **long-distance running** in which bursts of fast running alternate with slower spells [Swedish *fart*, "speed," and *lek*, "play"]

fast bowler (*cricket*) a **bowler** who usually bowls at a fast **pace**

fast break (*basketball*) an attempt to score by moving the **ball** forward quickly after gaining **possession**

fast leg theory (*cricket*) another name for **bodyline bowling**

fast side (*association football*) the shortest distance, as the **goalkeeper** sees it, for the **ball** to travel from a player toward or into the **net**

fast suit (*swimming*) another term for a **bodysuit**

fastball (*baseball*) a **delivery** from the **pitcher** thrown at maximum speed

Fastnet Cup (*sailing*) the **cup** awarded to the winner of a biennial **race** from Cowes, Isle of Wight, to the Fastnet Rock, off the southwest coast of Ireland, and back to Plymouth.

fat (*golf*) striking the ground before the **ball**, so that it does not travel far

fault (*billiards, snooker*) a failure to hit the correct **ball**, incurring a **penalty point**; (*equestrianism*) in **showjumping**, an error in performance, such as **disobedience**, that incurs a **penalty point**; (*tennis*) a **serve** that fails to land the **ball** within the **service court**

fault line (*real tennis*) the line parallel to the **main wall** in the **hazard** end which, with the **service line** at right angles to it, marks the area into which the **server** must send the **ball**

favorite (*horse racing*) the horse expected to win a **race** and which thus attracts the most **bets**

FC (*association football*) abbreviation of **football club**, as in the names of such **clubs**

feather (*angling*) a crudely made **artificial fly** resembling a small fish; (*boxing*) shortening of **featherweight**; (*cricket*) to strike the **ball** lightly with the edge of the **bat**; (*rowing*) to turn the **oars** parallel to the water when swinging them forward in order to reduce wind resistance; (*snooker*) (1) to run the **cue** back and forth across the **bridge** between finger and thumb while preparing a **shot**; (2) to touch the **cue ball** unintentionally while doing this

feather fishing (*angling*) a method of **fishing** from a drifting boat with weighted **tackle** to which **feathers** are attached

feathered paddle (*canoeing*) in **kayaking**, a **paddle** with blades at right angles to each other

featherweight (*boxing*) the professional **weight** category of maximum 57kg (126lb); (*horse racing*) the lightest **weight** that may be carried by a horse

feature race (*horse racing*) a **steeplechase** that prepares horses for a **championship race**

Fed Cup (*tennis*) the **cup** awarded to the winners of an international women's team **championship** held from 1963 [inaugurated by the International Lawn Tennis Federation]

Federation Cup (*tennis*) former name of the **Fed Cup**

feed (*general*) in **field games**, to pass the **ball** to another player; (*rugby league, rugby union*) another term for a **put-in**

feeding station (*cycling*) a point in a **road race** where **riders** can pick up food and drink

feet (*field hockey*) the infringement that occurs when the **ball** comes into contact with the player's foot

feint (*boxing*) the faking of a **punch** with the intention of disorientating one's opponent; (*fencing*) a deceptive movement made to trick one's opponent into changing his tactics

fence (*equestrianism, horse racing*) a structure (of varying design) for a horse to jump

fencer (*horse racing*) a horse trained to jump **fences**

fencing (*sport*) (1) the sport of attack and defense with a sword; (2) this sport as an **element** of the **modern pentathlon** in the **Olympics**

Fenway Park (*baseball*) the **home ground** of the Boston Red Sox team in Boston, Massachusetts

ferret (*cricket*) colloquial term for a poor **batsman** [he is sent in after a **rabbit**]

fevvers (*darts*) a **score** of 33 [said to derive from "Firty-free fahsand fevvers on a frush's froat," a Cockney pronunciation of "Thirty-three thousand feathers on a thrush's throat"]

Ffos Las (*horse racing*) a **National Hunt** racecourse in southwestern Wales

field (*athletics*) shortening of **field events**; (*baseball, cricket*) (1) the arrangement of the **fielders**; (2) collective term for the **fielders** themselves; (*cycling*) another term for a **peloton**; (*general*) (1) an enclosed area of grass or other ground marked out for playing a **field game**; (2) all the competitors or participants in a contest or sport; (3) all such competitors except a specified one; (*horse racing*) collective term for the horses in a **race**

field archery (*archery*) a form of the sport in which competitors move along a path aiming at **targets** (sometimes designed to look like animals), as distinct from **target archery**

field event (*athletics*) any **event** other than a race, such as the **high jump**, **shot put**, or **discus**

field game (*general*) a **game** played on a **field** or **pitch**. such as **association football**, **field hockey**, or **rugby union**

field general (*American football*) another term for a **quarterback**

field goal (*American football*) a **score** of three **points** made by kicking the **ball** through the **goalposts**, usually on the fourth **down**; (*basketball*) a **goal** scored from normal play, rather than from a **free throw**; (*rugby league*) another term for a **drop goal**

field hockey (*sport*) a **field game** played between teams of 11 players each who use **sticks** to hit the **ball** toward (and into) the **goal** of their opponents [as distinct from **ice hockey**]

field judge (*American football*) a member of the officiating team, positioned **downfield** of the **line of scrimmage**

field player (*field hockey*) a player other than the **goalkeeper**

field sports (*general*) outdoor pursuits traditionally associated with the English aristocracy and involving animals, such as hunting, shooting, and **fishing** [*field* in the sense "rural"]

fielder (*baseball, cricket*) a player who catches or stops (and returns) the **ball**, as a member of the side that is not batting; (*horse racing*) a person who backs the **field** against the **favorite**

fielder's choice (*baseball*) a **play** in which a **fielder** allows a **batter** to reach **first base** but a **baserunner** ahead is **put out**

· **fielding** (*baseball, cricket*) playing in the **field**, as distinct from **batting**

fieldsman (*baseball, cricket*) a dated alternate name for a **fielder**

Fiesta Bowl (*American football*) the **bowl** in Phoenix, Arizona, where a **college football** national **championship** is contested

FIFA (*association football*) the world governing body of **association football**, formed in 1904 [abbreviation of French *Fédération Internationale de Football Association*, "International Federation of Association Football"]

Fifers (*association football*) nickname of the Scottish **club** East Fife

fifteen (*rugby union*) a team of 15 players

fifteen-all (*tennis*) a level **score** of one **point** each

1,500 meters (*athletics*) a **foot race** of the stated distance

fifteen-love (*tennis*) a **score** of one **point** to nil to the **server**

50-meter arc (*Australian Rules*) a semicircular line around the **goal** at each end of the **pitch**

fight-off (*fencing*) a contest to decide a **tie**

fighting weight (*boxing*) the specified **weight** or weight range within which a **boxer** must come to be eligible to fight in a particular class

figure (*ice skating*) a movement or set of movements that follow a prescribed pattern and that often begin and end at the same point

figure eight (*equestrianism*) a **dressage** exercise in which the horse traces two connected circles, one clockwise, the other anticlockwise

figure floating (*swimming*) the forming of set patterns by **swimmers** floating in the water

figure of eight (*general*) the tracing of the outline of a figure "8," as by a skater in **ice skating**

figure skater (*ice skating*) a skater who executes **figures**

figure skating (*ice skating*) the execution of **figures**

Filberts (*association football*) nickname of the English **club** Leicester City [from the team's **home ground**, Filbert Street, Leicester]

fill the bases (*baseball*) alternate term for **load the bases**

filly (*horse racing*) a female horse under the age of four

final (*general*) the deciding **heat** or **game** in a contest

final whistle (*association foootball*) the **whistle** that ends the **game**, usually at **full time**

find the back of the net (*association football*) to score an accurate **goal**

find the net (*association football*) to score a **goal**

find the open man (*basketball*) to pass the **ball** to a player who is unmarked and so in a better position to receive it than others

find water (*golf*) to hit the **ball** into a water **hazard**, obliging the player to take a **drop**

fine leg (*cricket*) a **fielding** position on the **leg side** boundary at a more acute angle to the **batsman** than **long leg**

finesse (*croquet*) a strategic move in which a player apparently wastes a turn in order to gain a future advantage

finger tab (*archery*) a piece of leather worn on the finger to prevent injury when releasing an **arrow**

finish (*general*) (1) the end of a sporting contest; (2) the point where a **race** ends; (*rowing*) the final stage of a **stroke**, when the **blade** is brought out of the water

finish line (*athletics*) alternate form of **finishing line**

finish straight (*auto racing*) the straight section of **track** where the **grid** is and where **races** end

finisher (*cricket*) a **middle order batsman** whose tactical skills help his side score a winning **innings**

finishing line (*general*) the line marking the end of a **race**

finishing post (*horse racing*) the post marking the end of a **race**

Finn (*sailing*) a class of single-handed **dinghy** [originated in Helsinki, Finland, in 1952]

fins (*surfing*) small vertical projections on the underside of the **surfboard** that aid stability; (*water skiing*) small projections located on the underside of some **skis** that aid stability and help the skier make sharp turns

fire (*bowls*) to make a fast direct **shot** aimed simply to displace the **bowls** of one's opponent; (*cricket*) the tendency of a bowled **ball** to fly up erratically

firing line (*shooting*) the line from which competitors shoot

firm (*association football*) a group of militant **supporters**, especially of a team in a **derby**; (*horse racing*) a category of **going**

first base (*baseball*) the first of the **bases** to which a **batter** must run, situated on the right side of the **infield** as viewed from **home plate**

first baseman (*baseball*) the **fielder** positioned near **first base**

first change (*cricket*) the third **bowler** brought on in an **innings** after one of the original two is changed

first-class (*cricket*) played between **county cricket** teams

first cut (*golf*) the area of **rough** with quite short grass bordering the **fairway**

first down (*American football*) the first in a series of four **downs** which a team must make to retain **possession** of the **ball**

first eleven (*cricket*) the best **eleven** to represent a school, college, or the like

first half (*general*) the half of a **game** or **match** before **half time**

first home (*lacrosse*) the first of the three **homes** positioned near the **goal** of the opposing team and usually acting as the main **goalscorer**

first pitch (*baseball*) a ceremonial opening **pitch** made at the start of a **season** or **game** and often thrown by an honored guest, as traditionally by the U.S. president currently in office.

first service (*tennis*) the first **service** of the two allowed at the start of a **game**

first slip (*cricket*) the nearest of the **slips** to the **wicketkeeper**

first touch (*association football*) a player's initial contact with a **pass** or **cross**

fish and globe (*darts*) a **score** of 45 [said to derive from a fairground game in which a score of 45 would win the player a goldfish in a jar]

fish the water (*angling*) to place a **fly** in a likely spot for a **bite** or **catch** rather than make a **cast** to a particular fish

fisherman (*angling*) an everyday term for an **angler**

fishing (*sport*) the everyday term for **angling**

fishing line (*angling*) the fine strong nylon filament used in a **fishing rod**

fishing net (*angling*) a net used for catching fish or lifting them out of the water when caught

fishing rod (*angling*) a long slender rod to which a **line** is fastened for catching fish

fishing tackle (*angling*) the equipment such as **rods**, **lines**, and **nets** used for catching fish

fistiana (*boxing*) colloquial term for anecdotes about **boxers** and the sport in general

fisticuffs (*boxing*) facetious term for the sport

fitness walker (*athletics*) a person who walks for exercise or pleasure (or both)

five (*basketball*) a team of five players

five-a-side (*association football*) a form of the **game** played, usually indoors and with a smaller **pitch** than usual, between teams of five players on each side [created in Uruguay in 1930 and now more popular than the traditional 11-a-side game]

five-eighth (*rugby league*) alternate term in Australia and New Zealand for a **standoff** [positioned between the **scrum half** (as if "four-eighth") and the **center three-quarter** (as if "six-eighth")]

five-fer (*cricket*) the taking of five **wickets** by a **bowler** for a given number of **runs** [respelling of *five for* (so many runs), based punningly on the name of the U.S. movie actress Michelle Pfeiffer (1958–)]

five-love (*tennis*) colloquial shortening of **fifteen-love**

five-meter line (*rugby union*) the line five meters in from the **touchline** behind which the **lineout** forms

Five Nations (*rugby union*) name of the **Six Nations** until 2000, when Italy joined

501 (*darts*) a popular form of the **game** in which players start at this figure and deduct all **scores** from it, aiming to reduce the starting score to exactly zero

5,000 meters (*athletics*) a **long-distance race** of the stated length run over 12.5 **laps**

five-yard line (*rugby union*) another term for the **five-meter line**

fives (*sport*) a **game** similar to **squash** played with a gloved hand in a walled **court** [said to refer to the five fingers of the hand but really of uncertain origin]

fivesome (*golf*) a **game** for five players

fixed odds (*horse racing*) a **bet** with **odds** that are predetermined, as distinct from the **starting price**

fixed rope (*mountaineering*) a rope anchored to a route by the **lead** climber and left for those following

fixed-wheel (*cycling*) (of) a rear wheel with no **freewheel** so that the wheel and pedals turn together

fixture (*general*) a date fixed for a sporting event such as a **match** or **race**

fizzer (*cricket*) a fast and possibly wayward **ball** delivered by the **bowler**

flag (*American football*) a marker thrown by a member of the officiating team to denote the occurrence of an infringement; (*general*) a flag deployed by an official to convey immediate information, as the **start** of a race, an **offside** in **association football**, or a **shot** in **shooting**; (*golf*) a flag marking the location of a **hole**

flagman (*polo*) an official who signals a **goal** by waving a **flag**

flagstick (*golf*) another term for a **flag**

flair (*gymnastics*) a move performed on the **pommel horse** or **floor** in which the **gymnast** swings his open legs in front of or behind his arms, with only his hands touching the horse or floor

Flames (*ice hockey*) short name of the Calgary Flames team

flamingo (*swimming*) in **synchronized swimming**, a position in which one leg is extended perpendicular to the surface while the other is drawn up to the chest

flamme rouge (*cycling*) a red **flag** marking the point 1km from the **finish** of a **road race** or **stage** [French *flamme rouge*, "red flame"]

flanconade (*fencing*) a **thrust** in the side [French *flanconade*, from *flanc*, "side"]

flank (*general*) another term for the **wing**

flank back (*rugby union*) another term for a **flanker**

flank forward (*rugby union*) another term for a **flanker**

flanker (*American football*) a player who lines up in a position on the **end**; (*rugby union*) one of the two players loosely bound on either side of the **scrum**

flannels (*cricket*) the white (properly flannel) trousers traditionally worn by **cricketers**

flapping (*greyhound racing*) a form of **racing** not registered under the National Greyhound Racing Club; (*horse racing*) a form of **racing** not subject to **Jockey Club** or **National Hunt** regulations

flapping meeting (*greyhound racing, horse racing*) a **meeting** for **flapping**

flapping track (*greyhound racing*) a **racetrack** for **flapping**

flaptrack (*greyhound racing*) another term for a **flapping track**

flare (*American football*) shortening of **flare pass**

flare pass (*American football*) a quick **pass** out to a **back**

flash the leather (*baseball*) to make a good defensive **play** [with the **leather**]

flashcard (*general*) one of a set of large colored cards held up by a spectator in a **stadium** and with other such cards forming a picture or message

flasher (*cricket*) a **batsman** who plays forcefully at **balls** delivered outside the **off stump**

flat (*horse racing*) (1) the level ground, without

jumps, over which **flat races** are run; (2) shortening of **flat racing** [in this sense often spelled with a capital letter, as "the Flat"]

flat race (*horse racing*) a **race** over the **flat**

flat racing (*horse racing*) **racing** over the **flat**

flatwater (*canoeing*) calm water, as on a lake

flea flicker (*American football*) a deceptive **play** in which a **runner** or **receiver** pitches the **ball** back to a teammate who then attempts to advance it

flèche (*fencing*) a running attack [French *flèche*, "arrow"]

Flèche Wallonne (*cycling*) a **race** from Liège to Charleroi, Belgium [French *Flèche Wallonne*, "Walloon Arrow," for its location in Wallonia, southern Belgium]

fleet race (*sailing*) a **race** for several single boats over the same **course**

fletching (*archery*) the feathers of an **arrow** [French *flèche*, "arrow"]

flic-flac (*gymnastics*) another term for a **back handspring** [French *flic-flac*, imitating the sounds of the hands and feet as they make contact with the **floor** or **apparatus**]

flick (*field hockey*) another term for a **scoop**; (*general*) a **stroke** made with a quick turn of the wrist, as when throwing or playing a **ball**

flick-on (*association football*) a light forward **header** of the **ball** to a teammate

flier (*cricket, golf*) an alternate spelling of **flyer**

flight (*archery*) the feathered or plastic attachment at the end of an **arrow** that stabilizes its trajectory; (*athletics, horse racing*) a series of **hurdles** on a **racetrack**; (*badminton*) one of the feathered or plastic attachments that stabilize the trajectory of a **shuttlecock**; (*darts*) the feathered or plastic attachment at the end of a **dart** that stabilizes its trajectory; (*general*) the trajectory of a **ball** through the air

flip (*gymnastics*) another term for a **somersault**

flip-flop (*gymnastics*) a backward **somersault**

flip jump (*ice skating*) another term for a **toe jump**

flipper (*cricket*) a **ball** delivered with a backward **spin** by a **leg-spin bowler** with an extra flip of the fingers, causing it to skid off the **pitch**

float (*angling*) a buoyant object made of cork or other material on the end of a **fishing line** that by its movement indicates a **bite**

float-fishing (*angling*) **fishing** while floating down a river

floatboard (*windsurfing*) a simple **sailboard** sometimes used by beginners in the sport

floater (*surfing*) a maneuver in which the **surfer** rides the very top of the wave

floor (*gymnastics*) the matted ground area in an **arena** where exercises and **routines** are performed

floor exercises (*gymnastics*) a **routine** of exercises such as **acrobatics** and **tumbling** performed on the **floor**, as distinct from on **apparatus**

floorman (*horse racing*) an assistant to a **tick-tack man**

flop (*golf*) shortening of **flop shot**

flop shot (*golf*) a short **pitch shot** with a very high trajectory

flopper (*skittles*) a **throw** that knocks down all nine **skittles**

flub (*golf*) another term for a **fluff**

fluff (*general*) a misplayed **shot** or **stroke**

fluke (*snooker*) a fortuitous **pot**, typically resulting from an unintended collision of **balls** or a random rebound from a **cushion**

flushgate (*skiing*) a series of three or more **slalom gates** on a slope

Flushing Meadows (*tennis*) the site in Queens, New York, of the **U.S. Open**

flutter kick (*swimming*) an element of a **stroke** such as the **crawl** in which the legs are held straight and moved alternately up and down

fly (*American football*) a specific **pass** pattern in which the **receiver** runs straight down the **field**; (*angling*) a **hook** dressed to look like a fly for use as **bait**; (*swimming*) shortening of **butterfly**

fly ball (*baseball*) a **ball** hit high in the air, as distinct from a **ground ball**

fly fishing (*angling*) the catching of fish with **flies** as **bait**

fly hack (*rugby union*) a kick of a **ball** lying loose on the ground

fly half (*rugby union*) another term for a **standoff half**

fly hook (*angling*) a **hook** baited with a **fly**

fly kick (*rugby union*) a kick of the **ball** while it is in the air

fly line (*angling*) a **fishing line** with an **artificial fly**

fly out (*baseball*) to be **put out** by a **fielder** catching a **fly ball**

fly rod (*angling*) a **rod** with an **artificial fly**

fly slip (*cricket*) a **fielding** position between the **slips** and the **boundary**

fly-tying (*angling*) the art or act of dressing a **hook** to represent a **fly** and serve as **bait**

flyaway (*gymnastics*) a move on the **horizontal bar** and **asymmetric bars** in which the **gymnast** swings down, releases his hold, and lands, usually via a **backflip**

flybook (*angling*) a case like a book for holding **flies**

flybox (*angling*) a small compartmented box for holding **flies**

flyer (*cricket*) a **ball** pitched short that flies up from the **pitch**; (*golf*) a mishit **ball** that travels further than intended

Flyers (*ice hockey*) short name of the Philadelphia Flyers team

flying camel (*ice skating*) a combination of a **jump** and a **spin** that ends in a **camel spin**

flying change (*equestrianism*) a move in which the leading leg in the **canter** position is changed while the horse is in the air

Flying Dutchman (*sailing*) a class of double-handed **dinghy** [named for the ghostly Dutch ship condemned to sweep the seas around the Cape of Good Hope for ever]

flying finish (*auto racing*) in **rally driving**, the crossing of the **finishing line** at speed at the end of a **stage**

Flying Finn (*auto racing*) in **rally driving**, a nickname for a fast Finnish **rally driver** [Finns are famed for their speed and the nickname was current for the **long-distance runner** Paavo Nurmi (1897–1973) before it was applied to the **champion** rally driver Hannu Mikkola (1942–)]

flying horse (*wrestling*) a **throw** similar to a **flying mare**

flying machine (*horse racing*) colloquial term for a fast **racehorse**

flying mare (*wrestling*) a **throw** in which one **wrestler** heaves another over his back using his opponent's arm as a lever

flying rings (*gymnastics*) an **apparatus** consisting of rings suspended in pairs from wire cables

flying sit spin (*ice skating*) a combination of **jump** and **spin** that ends in a **sit spin**

flying start (*general*) a **start** in which the contestants pass the **starting line** at full speed

flying tackle (*association football, rugby league, rugby union*) a **tackle** made while running or jumping

flyweight (*boxing*) the professional **weight** category of maximum 51kg (112lb)

foal (*horse racing*) a young horse up to the age of 12 months

foible (*fencing*) the part of a **foil** blade between the middle and the point [Old French *foible*, "weak"]

foil (*fencing*) a light blunt-edge sword with a **button**; (*wrestling*) an incomplete **fall**

Folkestone (*horse racing*) a **flat racecourse** at Westenhanger, near Folkestone, Kent, England

follow (*general*) to support a team or an individual in a particular sport; (*horse racing*) to **back** a particular horse whenever it runs in a **race**

follow on (*cricket*) to start a second **innings** immediately after the first after failing to reach a **score** a predetermined number of **runs** fewer than that of the opposing team's first innings

follow through (*cricket*) (1) to complete the action of a **stroke** after the **ball** has been struck by the **batsman**; (2) to complete the action of a **delivery** after the ball has been released by the **bowler**; (*golf*) to complete the action of a **stroke**

after the ball has been struck by the player; (*snooker*) to continue to move the **cue** forward after the **cue ball** has been struck

following stroke (*billiards*) a **stroke** designed to spin the **ball** forward by striking it above the center

following wind (*athletics*) a tail wind that assists an **athlete** to run or jump further

Fontwell Park (*horse racing*) a **National Hunt racecourse** at Fontwell, near Arundel, West Sussex, England

foot (*motorcycle racing*) to touch the ground with one's foot in a **trial** and so incur a **penalty**

foot-o (*orienteering*) the basic form of **orienteering** on foot

foot-over-foot (*ice hockey*) fast forward movement on a direct but narrow path

foot race (*athletics*) a **race** run on foot

foot spot (*pool*) in **nine-ball pool**, the spot on the table on which the number 1 **ball** is positioned

footbag (*general*) the **ball** used in **Hacky Sack** and similar sports, typically having a crocheted exterior and filled with sand or plastic beads

football (*American football*) (1) the large inflated **ball** with which the **game** is played; (2) the common name of the **game** in the U.S.; (*association football*) (1) the large inflated ball with which the **game** is played; (2) the common name of the **game** in the U.K.

football academy (*association football*) a training center for student players of the **game**

Football Association (*association football*) the ruling body of the **game** in the U.K., formed in London in 1863

football club (*association football*) a **club** for professional players of the **game**

football coupon (*association football*) a coupon used for an entry in the **football pools**

football ground (*association football*) a **pitch** where the **game** is played, with accommodation for spectators

Football League (*association football*) a competition in the **game** on a **points** system, inaugurated in 1888 for professional **clubs**

Football League Cup (*association football*) former name of the **Carling Cup**

football match (*association football*) a **match** between rival teams

football pitch (*association football*) a **pitch** or **ground** where the **game** is played

football pools (*association football*) a commercially organized competition, introduced in England in 1923, in which **bets** are placed on the results of weekly **football matches**

football special (*association football*) a specially chartered train taking **supporters** to **matches**

footballer (*association football*) a **professional** or **amateur** player of **football**

footer (*bowls*) a round **mat** on which a player of **crown bowls** stands when delivering the **bowl**; (*sport*) colloquial term for **association football**

footfault (*tennis*) a **fault** committed by stepping over the **baseline** when serving

foothold (*mountaineering*) a place to fix one's foot in while climbing

footie (*sport*) colloquial term for **association football**

footwork (*association football*) skillful use of the feet in maneuvering the **ball**

footy (*sport*) another spelling of **footie**

foozle (*golf*) another term for a **mishit** [German dialect *fuseln*, "to work badly"]

force (*billiards*) a **stroke** in which the **cue ball** is struck off-center so that it stops or goes off at an angle; (*real tennis*) a powerful **shot** aimed at the **dedans**; (*tennis*) a powerful **stroke** played with the aim of forcing an error from one's opponent

force the game (*cricket*) to take risks in order to increase the rate of scoring

force the pace (*general*) to adopt a fast **pace** in a **race** in order to tire one's rival or rivals

forceout (*baseball*) the putting out of a **baserunner** by obliging him to advance to the next **base** when it is not safe to do so

fore! (*golf*) a warning cry to anyone in danger of being hit by the **ball** [probably from *before*]

fore-and-aft (*sailing*) lengthwise [of any **sail** not set on **yards**]

fore-and-after (*sailing*) a ship with a **fore-and-aft rig**

fore caddie (*golf*) a **caddie** formerly posted ahead to see where the **ball** went

forearm pass (*volleyball*) another term for a **dig**

forecheck (*ice hockey*) a **check** made to an opponent in his own defensive area

forecourt (*tennis*) the part of the **court** between the **service line** and the **net**

forehand (*badminton, table tennis, tennis*) a **stroke** made with the arm extended away from the body and the palm of the hand facing one's opponent; (*bowls*) the right side of the **rink** (for a right-handed **bowler**), where the **bowl** is delivered to the right and curves back to the left; (*polo*) a **stroke** of the **ball** forward or sideways to a teammate

forehand chop (*table tennis*) a **chop** made as a **forehand**

forehand drive (*table tennis*) a **drive** made as a **forehand**

foremast (*sailing*) the mast nearest to the **bow** of a boat

Forest (*association football*) short name of the English **club** Nottingham Forest

forkball (*baseball*) a **pitch** in which the **ball** is delivered with the thumb, forefinger, and middle finger spread apart, so that it falls down sharply or is otherwise unpredictable

form (*general*) (1) the condition of training and physical fitness of a competitor, especially a **racehorse** or **athlete**; (2) a record of a competitor's past performance

form book (*horse racing*) a record of a horse's **form**

form horse (*horse racing*) another term for the **favorite**

form sheet (*horse racing*) another term for a **form book**

formation (*association football*) the arrangement of the players (aside from the **goalkeeper**) into a particular disposition on the field, such as 4-4-2, denoting four **defenders**, four **midfielders**, and two **attackers**

formation lap (*auto racing*) a **lap** made before the **race** so the cars can warm up their tires

formula (*general*) a numerically ranked set of technical specifications for racing vehicles, especially in **auto racing** and **motorcycle racing**

Formula One (*general*) the top-ranking **formula** for vehicles entered in **Grand Prix** racing [so named as built according to an evolving formula established after World War I by the Fédération Internationale de l'Automobile]

forte (*fencing*) the thicker, stronger half of a **foil** blade [French *fort*, "strong"]

forty-fifteen (*tennis*) a **score** to the **server** of three **points** to one

forty-five (*tennis*) colloquial term for **forty-fifteen**

45-meter kick (*Gaelic football*) a **free kick** awarded to an attacking team when the **ball** goes out of play beyond the **goal line** off a **defender**

forty-love (*tennis*) a **score** to the **server** of three **points** to nil

40-meter line (*rugby league*) a line marked across the **pitch** 40 meters from the **try line** at each end

49er (*sailing*) a class of double-handed **dinghy** [named for its length of 4.99m]

49ers (*American football*) short name of the San Francisco 49ers team

40–20 rule (*rugby league*) a rule stating that if a player kicks the **ball** from inside his own **40-meter line**, and it goes on the bounce into **touch** between the **20-meter line** of the **opposition** and the **try line**, his side are awarded the **put-in** at the **scrum**

forward (*basketball*) a player who operates mainly in the area around the **basket**, unlike a **guard**; (*general*) in **field games** such as **association football**, an attacking player such as a **center forward** or a **winger**; (*rugby league, rugby union*) any of the players in the **scrum**; (*sailing*) at or toward the front of a boat

forward pass (*rugby league, rugby union*) an illegal **pass** in which the **ball** is thrown forward

forward pocket (*Australian Rules*) a player operating in the **50-meter arc** near the **goal**

Fosbury (*athletics*) shortening of **Fosbury flop**

Fosbury flop (*athletics*) a style of **high jump** in which the **athlete** clears the **bar** headfirst with body extended face-up and lands on his back [introduced at the 1968 **Olympic Games** by the U.S. athlete Dick Fosbury (1947–)]

foul (*general*) an infringement of the rules, resulting in a **penalty** such as the award of a **direct free kick** to the opposing team in **association football**

foul ball (*baseball*) a **ball** struck behind the **baselines** that counts as a **strike** unless there are already two strikes against the **batter**

foul circle (*basketball*) the circular area marked behind the **foul line**, inside which a player taking a **free throw** stands

foul lane (*basketball*) the area between the **basket** and the **foul line**, outside which other players must stand when a **free throw** is attempted

foul line (*basketball*) a line 15ft (4.6m) from the **backboard**, from which **free throws** are taken

foul out (*basketball*) to be dismissed from the **game** for committing more than the permitted number of **personal fouls**

foul play (*general*) a **foul** of any kind, whether penalized or not

foul pole (*baseball*) one of the two structures marking the division between the edge of the **outfield** and **foul territory**

foul territory (*baseball*) any part of the **ground** that is outside the field of play

foul throw (*association football*) an improperly made **throw-in**

foul tip (*baseball*) a **ball** barely deflected by the **bat**

four (*cricket*) a **score** of four **runs** gained by hitting the **ball** over the **boundary**; (*rowing*) a boat with four **oars** worked by four **rowers**

four-cross (*cycling*) downhill **BMX** for four **riders** on **mountain bikes**

four-figure form (*horse racing*) the four-digit code in a **racing form** that denotes a horse's performance in the previous four **races**, so that 1320 means won, third, second, **unplaced**

400 meters (*athletics*) a **sprint** or **hurdle race** of the stated distance

four-meter line (*handball*) a mark 4 meters in front of the **goal** where the **goalkeeper** stands during a **seven-meter throw** but which he cannot cross

four-minute mile (*athletics*) a **foot race** over a **mile** run in four minutes or less, long an unbroken **record** [first broken in 1954 by the British **athlete** Roger Bannister]

Four Nations Championship (*rugby league*) an annual **championship** contested by the national teams of England, Australia, New Zealand, and France, founded in 1999 as the Tri-Series and known until 2009, when France was included, as the Tri-Nations Series

four-point landing (*skiing*) a landing from a **jump** with both **poles** planted in the snow

470 (*sailing*) a class of double-handed **dinghy** [named for its length of 4.70m]

fourball (*cricket*) a poorly bowled **ball** with which the **batsman** can easily score a **four**; (*golf*) a **match** between two pairs of players, in which only the lower **score** of each pair for the **hole** is counted

foursome (*golf*) a **match** between two pairs of players, in which each pair plays only one **ball**, players taking alternate **strokes**

fourth official (*association football*) an official who assists the **referee** and **assistant referees** from the **technical area**

fourth umpire (*cricket*) an official who assists in international **matches** and who takes the place of the **third umpire** if the latter has to stand in for one of the regular **umpires**

Foxes (*association football*) nickname of the English **club** Leicester City [from the reputation of Leicestershire for fox hunting]

foxtrot (*equestrianism*) a horse's **pace** with short steps, as in changing from **trotting** to **walking**

frame (*snooker*) (1) the triangular form in which the **balls** are grouped for the **break**; (2) the balls themselves so grouped; (3) a single **game**

franchise (*American football*) an organization that operates a team in the **National Football League**

franchise player (*American football*) a player paid at a premium rate and not eligible to be signed by other teams

free (*Australian Rules*) shortening of **free kick**

free agent (*general*) a player not under contract to any professional team or **club** [the term gained currency in 1976, when a U.S. Court of Appeals ruled against the "reserve clause" that bound a professional **baseball** player to a particular team]

free ball (*snooker*) (1) the nomination of any **ball** as the **object ball** as a right granted after being **snookered** by a **foul**; (2) the ball itself so nominated

free bounce (*trampolining*) a straight **bounce** with no movement made while in the air

free climbing (*mountaineering*) **climbing** with the use of ropes but without any other aids

free drop (*golf*) a rule allowing a player to lift a **ball** from its resting place and drop it elsewhere without **penalty**

free fall (*parachuting*) the part of a descent before the **parachute** opens, especially in **skydiving**

free flying (*parachuting*) the adoption of different positions while making a descent

free-for-all (*general*) a contest open to anyone

free gate (*canoeing*) a **gate** that can be entered from either direction

free hit (*field hockey*) a **shot** taken when an **offense** has been committed outside the **shooting circle** or by an **attacker** inside the **23-meter line** of the **opposition**

free kick (*association football*) a kick, awarded after a **foul** or **offside**, which the opposing side is not allowed to hinder or block

free pass (*netball*) a **pass** awarded after an infringement

free pistol (*shooting*) a **pistol shooting** competition in which the pistol does not have to conform to the specifications required for other competition pistols

free program (*ice skating*) a **routine** in which the skaters perform movements of their own choosing, as distinct from a **short program**

free running (*sport*) an **extreme sport** in which participants use techniques from **gymnastics**, **martial arts**, and **climbing** to negotiate obstacles in an urban setting

free shot (*netball*) another term for a **penalty shot**

free skating (*ice skating*) a form of competitive **figure skating** in which the skater selects items from an officially approved list of moves and maneuvers such as **jumps** and **spins**

free throw (*basketball*) an unrestricted **throw** to the **basket**, awarded as a **penalty** against the opposing side after an infringement; (*handball*) a **throw** awarded for various types of **foul**

free-throw lane (*basketball*) another name for the **foul lane**

free-throw line (*basketball*) another name for the **foul line**; (*handball*) another name for the **nine-meter line**

freediver (*aquatics*) another term for a **skindiver**

freediving (*aquatics*) another term for **skindiving**

freeride (*skiing*) shortening of **freeride skiing**; (*snowboarding*) a type of **board** which can be used both on and off **piste**

freeride skiing (*skiing*) an extreme form of the sport in which participants attempt difficult **jumps** and turns

freeriding (*cycling*) a type of competition in **mountain biking** in which **riders** negotiate a **track** with demanding obstacles

freeski (*skiing*) shortening of **freestyle skiing**

freestyle (*general*) a style or method of performance that the competitor is free to choose; (*swimming*) another term for the **front crawl** [popularly chosen as the fastest **stroke**]; (*wrestling*) another term for **all-in wrestling**

freestyle skiing (*skiing*) a form of the sport in

which competitors choose their events, the most popular being **aerials** and **moguls**

freewheel (*cycling*) the mechanism that can temporarily disconnect the rear wheel from the driving gear so that it continues to turn freely when the **rider** is not pedaling

freeze (*curling*) a **draw** in which a **stone** stops near another stone; (*ice hockey*) to try to regain control of the **puck** by holding it against an area of the **boards** or even by falling on it, in the process stopping play

French billiards (*billiards*) another term for **carom billiards**

French blinkers (*horse racing*) colloquial term for **cheekpieces**

French cricket (*cricket*) a simplified form of the game, popular among children, in which the **batsman** is **out** if struck by the **ball** on the legs below the knee

French drive (*cricket*) a fortuitous **snick** off the **bat** through the **slips**

French Grand Prix (*auto racing*) the **Formula One** international **Grand Prix** held on the Magny Cours **circuit** at Dijon, France

French Open (*tennis*) the international **championship tournament** held annually since 1891 on the **clay courts** of the Stade Roland-Garros, Paris

fresh (*horse racing*) not having raced recently

fried egg (*golf*) colloquial term for the hollow created by a **ball** that has landed in soft sand in a **bunker**

friendly (*association football*) a **match** arranged outside normal competition

fringe (*golf*) the area bordering the **green**, where the grass is slightly longer

fringe sports (*general*) sports regarded as less important or popular

Frisbee golf (*sport*) a game similar to **golf** but played with a Frisbee instead of a **golf ball** and **clubs**

frog hair (*golf*) the well-cut grass between the **fairway** and the **green**, in length somewhere between the two

front (*trampolining*) a forward **somersault**

front crawl (*swimming*) the **crawl** performed face down

front five (*rugby union*) another term for the **tight five**

front foot (*general*) the left foot (of a right-handed person), as the one nearer the **target**

front four (*American football*) the two **ends** and two **tackles** in a team's defensive line

front giant (*gymnastics*) a **giant** in which the gymnast swings counterclockwise, his palms facing in the same direction as his back

front handspring (*gymnastics*) a **handspring** that starts with a forward **flip**

front nine (*golf*) the first nine **holes** on a **course**

front row (*rugby league, rugby union*) the three **forwards**, comprising the two **props** and the **hooker**, in the front row of the **scrum**

front-row union (*rugby league, rugby union*) informal name for the **front row** [as a union of players of similar physique and temperament]

front walkover (*gymnastics*) a **handstand** performed with the legs split and then one foot brought over to be followed by the other foot into an upright position

frontenis (*sport*) a Latin-American **ball game** similar to **handball** and essentially consisting of **jai alai** or **pelota** played with **tennis rackets** [blend of **fronton** and Spanish *tenis*, "tennis"]

frontman (*general*) another term for a **forward**

fronton (*pelota*) the wall against which the **game** is played [Spanish *frontón*]

frontrunner (*general*) (1) a (human or animal) contestant who runs best when in the **lead** or who can set a fast pace; (2) a leading contestant

frontside air (*snowboarding*) an **air** performed off the **frontside wall**

frontside wall (*snowboarding*) the wall of the **halfpipe** in front of the **boarder**

frosh (*general*) colloquial term for a member of a freshman sports team [perhaps from German *Frosch*, "grammar-school pupil"]

frozen rope (*baseball*) colloquial term for a **ball** that travels on a fast, level trajectory

fuel load (*auto racing*) the amount of fuel on board a car

full (*trampolining*) a **full twist** executed in a somersault

full ball (*snooker*) a **stroke** that sends the **cue ball** against the full face of the **object ball**

full-bore (*shooting*) (of) a larger caliber than **smallbore**

full count (*baseball*) a situation in which the **pitcher** has thrown three **balls** and two **strikes** to the **batter**

full-court press (*basketball*) a tactic in which the defensive team challenges opponents in all areas of the **court**, not just in their own area

full forward (*Australian Rules*) an attacking player operating near the opponents' **goal**

full-in, back-out (*gymnastics*) a double **salto** with a **full twist** in the first salto

full nelson (*wrestling*) fuller term for a **nelson**

full pitch (*cricket*) another term for a **full toss**

full roll (*croquet*) the distance traveled by a struck **ball** when equal to that of the ball that struck it

full time (*general*) the end of a **match**, when the time allotted for it has expired

full toss (*cricket*) a **ball** delivered by the **bowler** that does not pitch before reaching the **batsman**

full twist (*gymnastics*) a complete **twist**

fullback (*American football*) an offensive player

who lines up behind the **quarterback** and **halfback** and who is used primarily for **line plunges** and **blocks**; (*association football, field hockey*) a defensive player positioned near the **goal**; (*rugby league, rugby union*) the player who normally stands furthest back on the **pitch** in a defensive position

fumble (*American football*) to lose hold of the **ball** when in **possession** of it

fun run (*athletics*) a **long-distance race** usually less than a **marathon** in length staged either for amusement or to raise funds for charity rather than as a serious athletic competition

funboard (*windsurfing*) a **board** specially designed to give greater speed

fungo (*baseball*) a **ball** struck high in the air for **fielders** to practice catching [origin uncertain]

fungo bat (*baseball*) a special lightweight **bat** for striking **fungos**

funny car (*auto racing*) in **drag racing**, a car with a fiberglass body built to resemble an ordinary car

furlong (*horse racing*) a standard distance equal to one-eighth of a **mile**

furlong marker (*horse racing*) a post by a **racecourse** showing the number of **furlongs** to the **winning post** [the word "furlong" may be omitted in reports, as "Notre Pere fell five out when returning to action at Down Royal" (*The Times*, November 21, 2009)]

futsal (*association football*) an indoor version of the **game** between teams of five players. [blend of Spanish *fútbol*, "football," and *sala*, "room"]

futurity race (*horse racing*) a **race** for two-year-olds nominated even before they are foaled

Gable Endies (*association football*) nickname of the Scottish **club** Montrose [local people are so nicknamed for the Flemish architecture of some town houses with gable ends]

Gaelic football (*sport*) a **game** somewhat similar to **rugby union** played in Ireland by teams of 15 a side with a round **ball** that can be kicked, bounced, or punched but not thrown or run with, the aim being to score **goals** and **points**

gaff (*angling*) a **hook** used to catch large fish; (*sailing*) a **spar** to which the head of a **fore-and-aft sail** is fastened

gaffer (*general*) colloquial term for a **manager** or **coach**

gag (*angling*) a device for keeping the jaws of a newly caught fish open while the **hook** is extracted

gain (*trampolining*) a movement along the **bed** in the opposite direction to that of the **element** being performed

gain line (*rugby league*) an imaginary line on which a **play-the-ball** or **scrum** has taken place, as a defining point beyond which a player or team

may take the **ball**; (*rugby union*) an imaginary line on which a **set piece**, **ruck**, or **maul** has taken place, as a defining point beyond which a player or team may take the **ball**

gait (*equestrianism*) the rhythm and sequence of leg movements in which a horse moves

galáctico (*association football*) a top-ranking signed **footballer** [Spanish *galáctico*, "superstar," a term originally used for a player signed for Real Madrid]

gallery (*golf*) the spectators at a **tournament**; (*real tennis*) one of the eight openings in the side **penthouses** of the **court**, **shots** into which count as **chases**

gallery hit (*cricket*) a good **shot** appreciated and applauded by the spectators

gallop (*equestrianism*) a horse's fastest **gait**, at each **stride** of which all four feet are off the ground; (*horse racing*) a **track** where horses are exercised at a **gallop**

Galway (*horse racing*) a flat and **National Hunt racecourse** in Co. Galway, Ireland

game (*general*) (1) a competitive sport with established rules; (2) an episode or period of play, at the end of which there is usually a **result** or **score**; (*sport*) a byname of **association football** (as "the game")

game ball (*general*) another term for a **game point**

game breaker (*American football*) a player who determines the outcome of a **game**

game fish (*angling*) any freshwater fish of the salmon family except the grayling, as distinct from a **coarse fish**

game of two halves (*association football*) a **match** in which the **second half** noticeably differs from the **first half**, for example in the style of play

game on! (*darts*) traditional call of the announcer to signal the beginning of a **game**

game plan (*American football*) a winning strategy worked out in advance

game point (*general*) a stage in a **game** at which the next **point** wins

game, set, and match (*tennis*) a complete and decisive victory, achieved by a player who has won a **game**, then a **set**, and finally the **match**

game shot (*darts*) the **shot** that wins a **leg** of the **game**

games (*general*) a session of competitive **games**

Games (*Olympics*) shortening of **Olympic Games** [often preceded by the name of an **Olympic city** to refer to a specific contest, as London Games, Moscow Games]

gamesmanship (*general*) the art of defeating an opponent by purely psychological means [from the title of a humorous book by Stephen Potter, *The Theory and Practice of Gamesmanship, or the Art of Winning Games Without Actually Cheating* (1947)]

gap (*baseball*) another term for an **alley**

gaper (*cricket*) colloquial term for an easy **catch** [anything that "gapes" offers easy access]

gapper (*baseball*) a **ball** hit into an **alley**

garbage (*general*) colloquial term for an easy **shot** or scoring opportunity

gardening (*cricket*) colloquial term for the tamping down of a loose area of turf on the **pitch**, as carried out by a **batsman** with his **bat**

garland (*skiing*) alternate left and right turns across a slope

garryowen (*rugby union*) another term for an **up-and-under** [popularized by the Garryowen **club** in Limerick, Ireland]

gate (*canoeing*) an obstacle in the form of two free-hanging poles on a **slalom** course, which participants must pass between without touching them; (*cricket*) the gap between the **pad** and **bat** of a **batsman** as he plays a **ball**; (*equestrianism*) a high, narrow **fence**; (*general*) collective term for the people who pay to see a **game** or **match** [they pay at the gate]; (*horse racing, motorcycle racing, skiing*) shortening of **starting gate**; (*rowing*) the U-shaped attachment at the outer end of the **outrigger** that holds the **oar** at the point where it pivots; (*skiing*) the two flagged poles between which a skier must pass in a **slalom** event

gate money (*general*) payment collected from a **gate**

gather (*baseball, rugby football*) to catch a **ball** as it moves through the air; (*cricket*) to pick up a rolling **ball**

Gatorade (*athletics*) proprietary name of a soft drink containing ingredients that include glucose, citric acid, sodium bicarbonate, and potassium chloride, drunk by **athletes** instead of water to replenish rapidly lost body fluids and salts [so named as an "aid to the Gators," nickname of the University of Florida **college football** team]

Gaylord flip (*gymnastics*) a **routine** on the **horizontal bar** comprising a front **giant** and a one-and-a-half front **salto** over the bar followed by a regrasp of the bar [introduced in 1978 by the U.S. **gymnast** Mitch Gaylord (1961–)]

gazunder (*cricket*) colloquial term for a low **ball** [which *goes under*]

GB&I (*golf*) abbreviation of Great Britain and Ireland as a **professional** or **amateur** team in an international contest

gee-gees (*horse racing*) colloquial term for the horses in a **race** as the object of a **bet** [from *gee-gee*, a child's word for a horse]

gelding (*horse racing*) a castrated male horse

general classification (*cycling*) the positions of **riders** in a **race** based on overall time

general impression (*equestrianism*) an aspect of **dressage** for which **points** are awarded

genoa (*sailing*) a large **jib** that overlaps the **mainsail**

gentle (*angling*) a soft maggot used as **bait**

gentle art (*sport*) another term for **angling**

Gentlemen v. Players (*cricket*) an annual **match** between a team of **amateurs** ("Gentlemen") and a team of **professionals** ("Players"), first staged at **Lord's** in 1906 but discontinued from 1962, when amateur status was abolished

genuine (*greyhound racing, horse racing*) relied on to perform well in a **race**

German Grand Prix (*auto racing*) the **Formula One** international **Grand Prix** held on the Nürburgring **circuit** near Bonn, Germany

Gers (*association football*) short name of the Scottish **club** Rangers

get (*squash, tennis*) colloquial term for a difficult **shot** successfully reached and returned

get down (*golf*) to manage to get the **ball** in the hole

get the trip (*horse racing*) to stay the **distance** of a **race**

get up (*horse racing*) to win a **race** by a close margin

ghillie (*angling*) another spelling of **gillie**

ghost goal (*association football*) (1) a **goal** generally judged to be fair but disallowed by the **referee**; (2) a goal judged to be fair by the referee but in reality not valid

gi (*martial arts*) another spelling of **gie**

giant (*gymnastics*) a move on the **asymmetric bars**, **rings**, **parallel bars**, or **horizontal bar** in which the **gymnast**, from a **handstand** position, describes a 360-degree circle by swinging down past the ground then right up into a handstand again

giant slalom (*skiing, snowboarding*) an **event** similar to the **slalom**, but over a longer **course** and with greater intervals between the **gates**

giantkiller (*general*) an individual or team that defeats a far superior opponent

Giants (*American football*) short name of the New York Giants team; (*baseball*) short name of the San Francisco Giants team; (*rugby league*) short name of the English **club** Huddersfield Giants

gie (*martial arts*) a **judo** or **karate** costume [Japanese *ki*, "clothing"]

Gienger (*gymnastics*) a **routine** on the **horizontal bar** and **asymmetric bars** comprising a **flyaway** with a **half-twist** followed by a regrasp of the bar [introduced in 1978 by the German **gymnast** Eberhard Gienger (1951–)]

gill net (*angling*) a type of **fishing net** in which fish are caught by their gills

Gillette Cup (*cricket*) original name of the **Cheltenham & Gloucester Trophy**

gillie (*angling*) a hired guide and adviser to an **angler**, mainly in Scotland and Ireland, performing much the same role as a **caddie** to a **golfer** [Gaelic *gille*, "lad"]

Gills (*association football*) nickname of the English **club** Gillingham

gimme (*golf*) a short **putt** that an opponent is excused from playing as it is virtually unmissable [respelling of *give me*]

gimp (*angling*) a **fishing line** bound with wire

girls (*rugby union*) a nickname used by **forwards** for **backs**

Giro d'Italia (*cycling*) an annual **stage race** held in Italy since 1909 and modeled on the **Tour de France** [Italian *Giro d'Italia*, "Tour of Italy"]

give a horse its head (*horse racing*) to let a horse go freely

give a miss (*billiards*) to allow an opponent to score by deliberately failing to hit the **object ball**

give a ten (*rowing*) to row flat out for ten **strokes**

give-and-go (*association football*) another term for a **one-two** [the player passes the **ball** ("gives") then runs ("goes")]

give way! (*rowing*) the spoken instruction to begin rowing

glance (*cricket*) a **stroke** by the **batsman** that deviates the **ball** only slightly from its line of flight as delivered by the **bowler**

glass (*basketball*) colloquial term for the **backboard** [it deflects the **ball** as a mirror reflects an image]

glass arm (*baseball*) colloquial term for a sore arm resulting from tendons damaged by throwing or pitching **balls**

Glaziers (*association football*) former nickname for the English **club** Crystal Palace, now known as the **Eagles** [from the club's original location at the Crystal Palace, London, a huge glass conservatory built for the 1851 Great Exhibition]

Gleneagles (*golf*) a noted **golf course** in the grounds of a hotel near Perth, Scotland

Gli Azzurri (*association football*) nickname for the Italian national team [Italian *gli azzurri*, "the blues," from the color of their **strip**]

glide (*cricket*) another term for a **glance**; (*skiing*) a smooth downhill **run**

glide wax (*skiing*) a substance applied to **skis** in order to decrease their friction against the snow

glider (*gliding*) the engineless aircraft used in **gliding**; (*hang-gliding*) shortening of **hang-glider**

gliding (*sport*) the competitive sport of flying in **gliders**, which are towed to a high altitude by a powered aircraft then released, leaving the pilot to use **thermals** to maintain altitude or soar even higher

glissade (*mountaineering*) the act of sliding down a slope in a standing or squatting position, often using an **ice ax** for braking

Globetrotters (*basketball*) short name of the Harlem Globetrotters team

Glorious Goodwood (*horse racing*) traditional epithet for the annual **races** at **Goodwood**

glove (*baseball*) a player regarded in terms of his ability, like a **bat** in **cricket**; (*cricket*) to strike the **ball**, as a **batsman**, with one's glove rather than the **bat**

gloveman (*cricket*) colloquial term for a **wicketkeeper** [who wears large gloves]

Glovers (*association football*) nickname for the English **club** Yeovil Town [from the local glove-making industry]

gloves (*boxing*) shortening of **boxing gloves**; (*general*) the special gloves worn in various **ball games**, as by the **goalkeeper** in **association football** or the **wicketkeeper** in **cricket**

glovework (*cricket*) colloquial term for the skills of the **gloveman**

go about (*sailing*) to change **course**

go close (*horse racing*) to finish in second or third place [a term often used as a prediction of a horse's chances in a **race**]

go down (*general*) to be defeated in a contest; (*horse racing*) to go from the **paddock** to the **start** of a race

go in (*cricket*) to begin an **innings**

go-kart (*auto racing*) a low racing vehicle consisting basically of a frame with wheels, engine, and steering gear but now often closer in design and form to a light **racecar**

go on (*cricket*) to begin **bowling**

go one better (*horse racing*) to finish a **race** in a higher position than previously, especially when this was a **place**

go the distance (*boxing*) to complete the scheduled duration of a fight

go the route (*baseball*) to **pitch** for the entire game

go yard (*baseball*) to hit a **home run**

goal (*general*) (1) in **association football** and many other **games**, the pair of **posts** with a **crossbar** into or over which the **ball** is kicked, hit, or carried to make a **score**; (2) a corresponding structure in other sports, as a **basket** in **basketball** or a **net** in **netball**; (3) the score itself

goal area (*general*) the area in front of the **goal**

goal-area line (*general*) a line parallel to the **goal line**

goal attack (*netball*) an attacking player restricted to the **shooting circle**, attacking **third**, and center third

goal average (*association football*) a method, replaced in 1976 by the **goal difference**, of deciding the **league** position of two or more **clubs** with the same total of **points**, in which the number of **goals** scored by a club was divided by the number scored against them

goal celebration (*association football*) an exuberant

or extravagant display of triumph by a player who has just scored a **goal**

goal circle (*field hockey, netball*) another name for the **shooting circle**

goal crease (*lacrosse*) the circle around the **goal** which only defensive players may enter

goal defense (*netball*) a defensive player restricted to the **shooting circle**, defending **third**, and center third

goal difference (*association football*) a method, replacing the **goal average** in 1976, of deciding the **league** position of two or more **clubs** with the same total of **points**, in which the number of **goals** scored against a club is deducted from the number it has itself scored

goal hit (*shinty*) the method of bringing the **ball** back into play after it has gone over the **goal line**

goal kick (*association football*) a **free kick** awarded to the defending team in the **six-yard area** of the **penalty box** when the opposing team puts the **ball** behind the **goal line** (but not between the **goalposts** to score a **goal**)

goal line (*American football, association football, field hockey, ice hockey*) the line marking the end of the **pitch**, on which the **goals** stand; (*rugby league, rugby union*) another term for the **try line**

goal shooter (*netball*) an attacking player restricted to the **shooting circle** and attacking **third**

goal square (*Australian Rules*) a square marked in front of the **goal**

goalball (*sport*) a **game** designed specifically for the blind, played on an indoor **court** with a **ball** containing a bell, the aim being to roll the ball past the opposing team into their **goal**

goalhanger (*association football*) a player who spends much of the **game** lurking near the **goal** of the opponents for an opportunity to score

goalie (*association football*) colloquial shortening of **goalkeeper**

goalkeeper (*general*) the player who defends the **goal** in a **game** such as **association football**

goalless draw (*general*) a **draw** with a **score** of 0–0, no **goals** having been scored by either team

goalminder (*ice hockey*) another term for the **goaltender**

goalmouth (*association football*) the area immediately in front of the **goal**

goalposts (*general*) the **posts** that form the **goal**

goalscorer (*general*) a player who regularly or reliably scores **goals**

goaltender (*ice hockey*) a player whose role is to stop the **puck** from entering the **net**

goaltending (*basketball*) the illegal touching of the **ball** as it comes down toward the **basket**

gobble (*golf*) colloquial term for a **putt** played so powerfully that if the **ball** had not gone into the

hole it would have gone far beyond it [the hole "gobbled" it up]

goer (*horse racing*) a horse that runs fast

gofer (*baseball*) a **pitch** that can be hit for a **run**, especially a **home run** [the **batter** can *go for* it]

goff (*golf*) an archaic spelling of **golf**, reflecting the word's old-fashioned pronunciation

going (*horse racing*) the condition of the ground at a **racecourse** in terms of its moisture and "give," conventionally divided into *heavy* (very wet and soft), *yielding, soft, good-to-soft, good, good-to-firm, firm, standard*, and *hard* [parts of the **course** may be placed in a subsidiary category, giving a formula such as "good (good-to-firm in places)"]

gold (*Olympics*) shortening of **gold medal**

Gold Cup (*horse racing*) shortening of **Ascot Gold Cup, Cheltenham Gold Cup, Hennessy Gold Cup**, or any similarly named **trophy**

gold glove (*baseball*) an annual award made to the outstanding **fielder** in the **league** at each position

gold medal (*Olympics*) the medal awarded as first **prize** [gold is a more valuable metal than silver or bronze]

Golden Boot (*association football*) the name until 1991 of the **Golden Shoe**

golden duck (*cricket*) a **duck** scored by a **batsman** who is **out** first **ball** [from **gold** as the first award]

golden girl (*Olympics*) journalistic epithet for a female winner, or potential winner, of a **gold medal**, especially if fair-haired and good-looking

Golden Globe Race (*sailing*) a quadrennial single-handed round-the-world **race** first held in 1968 [name of the **trophy** awarded]

Golden Gloves (*boxing*) an **amateur** competition originating in 1927 as a U.S. intercities **tournament**, the winner receiving a gold medal and a pair of miniature golden gloves

golden goal (*association football*) the first **goal** scored in **extra time**, as a method of settling a **draw** [introduced in 1996 but abandoned in 2004, like the **silver goal**, in favor of the **penalty shoot-out**]

Golden Shoe (*association football*) an annual award made to the player scoring the most **goals** in **league matches** from the top **division** of every European national league [formerly known, under different and less stringent rules, as the **Golden Boot**]

golden sombrero (*baseball*) a notional award given to a **batter** who **strikes out** four times in a **game** [a feat cynically regarded as greater than a **hat trick**]

Goldie (*rowing*) the reserve **eight** of Cambridge University, who race their Oxford counterpart,

Isis, immediately before the **Boat Race** [named for a Cambridge boatman]

golf (*sport*) a **game** played with a **club** used to propel a **ball** into each **hole** on a **course** [perhaps from Dutch *kolf*, "club"]

golf bag (*golf*) a bag for carrying **golf clubs**

golf ball (*golf*) the small rubber-cored **ball** with which **golf** is played

golf cart (*golf*) a small motorized vehicle used to drive around a **golf course**

golf club (*golf*) (1) a long-handled metal-faced (formerly wooden-faced) **club** with which the **ball** is struck; (2) an association of players with its own **golf course** and **clubhouse**

golf course (*golf*) the area of specially prepared ground with **fairways** and **hazards** on which **golf** is played

golf croquet (*croquet*) a shorter and faster form of the **game** in which each turn consists of a single **stroke**

golf links (*golf*) another term for a **golf course**, properly one on low ground by the sea [not from *link*, "ring in a chain," but an Old English word meaning "bank"]

golf widow (*golf*) a woman whose husband spends a good deal of time playing **golf**

golfer (*golf*) a player of **golf**

golfiana (*golf*) a collector's term for items of **golfing** interest

golfing (*golf*) the sport of playing **golf**

good (*golf, tennis*) (of) a **shot** made accurately; (*horse racing*) a category of **going**; (*wrestling*) (of) a **lift** approved by the majority of the three **judges**

good areas (*cricket*) colloquial term for those parts of a **pitch** where a **ball** delivered by the **bowler** makes it difficult for the **batsman** to score easily

good ball (*rugby union*) a **ball** whose **possession** has potential for scoring a **try** or at least a good run up the **field**

Goodwood (*horse racing*) a flat **racecourse** at Goodwood Park, near Chichester, West Sussex, England, the picturesque setting of **Glorious Goodwood**

Goodwood Revival (*auto racing*) an annual **race** of classic (period) cars held from 1998 on the former **Formula One racetrack** at **Goodwood**

goofy footer (*snowboarding*) a **boarder** who rides with the right foot in front of the left, as distinct from a **regular footer**; (*surfing*) a **surfer** who rides with the right foot in front of the left, as distinct from a **natural footer**

googly (*cricket*) an **off break** bowled with an apparent **leg-break** action by a right-arm **bowler** to a right-handed **batsman** (or the converse) [origin uncertain]

goon squad (*ice hockey*) a group of specially selected players whose role is to intimidate the **opposition**

Gooners (*association football*) another spelling of **Gunners**

goose egg (*general*) a zero **score** [from the egg-shaped figure 0 for zero]

goose step (*rugby union*) a **hitch-kick** action performed by a player while running so that he seems to be slowing down although is really speeding up [from the military march step]

gopher (*baseball*) another spelling of **gofer**

gore (*parachuting*) the sector-like section of a **canopy**

gorge (*angling*) a **bait** intended to be swallowed by the fish

GP (*auto racing*) abbreviation of **Grand Prix**

Grace Road (*cricket*) the **home ground** of Leicestershire **county cricket club**, Leicester

grade cricket (*cricket*) a form of the **game** in Australia in which **clubs** compete in grades

graduation race (*horse racing*) a **race** designed to develop inexperienced horses

Graham (*mountaineering*) a Scottish mountain peak between 2,000 and 2,400 feet in height with a reascent of 500 feet on all sides [named for Fiona Torbet, née Graham, who published a list of them in 1992]

grand amplitude (*wrestling*) a **throw** in which the combatant's center of gravity is lower than that of his opponent

Grand Challenge Cup (*rowing*) the **cup** awarded to the winner of a **race** for **eights** at **Henley Royal Regatta**, inaugurated in 1839

Grand Final (*rugby league*) a system of **play-offs** introduced to the **Super League** in 1996 to replace the earlier **premiership** system

Grand National (*horse racing*) Britain's most famous **steeplechase**, run annually at **Aintree** since 1839

Grand Prix (*auto racing*) an international **race** for **Formula One** cars first held in France in 1906 and now staged on a number of **circuits** around the world [name originally used for the **Grand Prix de Paris**]; (*general*) a title for any major contest or **championship**, as the MotoGP

Grand Prix de Paris (*horse racing*) an international **race** for **three-year-olds** run annually at **Longchamp** since 1863 [French *Grand Prix de Paris*, "chief **prize** of Paris"]

grand prix freestyle (*equestrianism*) the final **round** of a **grand prix dressage** competition, in which horse and **rider** perform a series of maneuvers to music

grand salami (*baseball*) colloquial alteration of **grand slam**

grand slam (*association football*) the winning of

the domestic **league**, all domestic **cups**, and the **European Champions' Cup**; (*baseball*) a **home run** hit when there is a **baserunner** at each **base**; (*cycling*) the winning of the **Tour de France**, **Giro d'Italia**, and **Vuelta d'España** in the same **season**; (*equestrianism*) the winning of the **Kentucky Three-Day Event** and the equivalent contests in England at **Badminton** and **Burghley**; (*golf*) the winning of the four **Majors**; (*rugby union*) the winning of all **matches** in the **Six Nations**; (*tennis*) the winning of the **Australian Open**, **French Open**, **Wimbledon**, and the **U.S. Open** [a term from card playing, as the winning of every trick in a game, with *slam* of unknown origin but popularly associated with the sense "bang"]

Grande Boucle (*cycling*) (1) an annual **stage race** for female **cyclists** equating to the **Tour de France**; (2) a nickname for the Tour de France [French *Grande Boucle*, "Great Loop"]

grandstand (*general*) an elevated structure for spectators at a **racecourse** or other **venue**

grandstand finish (*general*) a close and exciting **finish** to a **race** or other contest

granny gear (*cycling*) colloquial term for a very low gear

grapevine (*ice skating*) a **figure** in which the **skates** trace interlacing lines on the ice; (*wrestling*) a **hold** in **all-in wrestling** in which a combatant uses his legs to turn his opponent

grass (*angling*) to bring a fish to the bank; (*cricket*), to drop a **catch**; (*rugby league, rugby union*) to knock an opponent to the ground

grass court (*tennis*) a **court** with a grass surface, as distinct from a **hard court**

grass hockey (*sport*) another name for **field hockey**

grass skis (*skiing*) **skis** similar to **roller skates** that are used for skiing down grassy slopes

grass-track racing (*motorcycle racing*) a form of **speedway** over grass **tracks**

grasshopper (*angling*) the live insect used as **bait**

Grasstex (*tennis*) proprietary name of an artificial surface for **tennis courts** consisting of a composition base with a top layer of natural fibers reinforced by emulsified asphalt [blend of *grass* and *texture*]

gravel trap (*auto racing*) an area of gravel near a corner, used to slow cars down if they run off the **track**

gray race (*horse racing*) an annual **race** at **Newmarket** for gray horses only

great game (*sport*) an epithet for **golf**

Great North Run (*athletics*) an annual **half marathon** run through Newcastle and Gateshead, northeastern England [name perhaps suggested by the *Great North Road*, a historic highway running north to this region from London]

Great South Run (*athletics*) an annual **half marathon** run in and around Portsmouth, Hampshire, as the southern equivalent of the **Great North Run**

Grecians (*association football*) nickname of the English **club** Exeter City [said to derive from a local reenactment of the Trojan War, in which the Greeks besieged the city of Troy]

Greco-Roman (*wrestling*) a type of **wrestling** in which only the upper body and arms, not the legs, may be used for moves and **holds** [from the supposed classical form of the sport]

green (*bowls*) the area of closely mown grass on which the **game** is played; (*golf*) the area of closely mown grass around the **hole** where **putting** takes place; (*snooker*) the green **ball**, worth three **points**

green card (*field hockey*) a card shown by the **referee** as a warning to a player after a relatively minor infringement

green cloth (*billiards, snooker*) a term for the **billiard table** [shortening of *board of green cloth*, for its **baize** covering]

green flag (*auto racing*) a **flag** shown to a driver to indicate that a hazard has been cleared and that cars can return to normal racing speed

green horse (*equestrianism, horse racing*) a horse that has not yet been trained, or that has only just begun training

green jacket (*golf*) the jacket presented to the winner of the **Masters** by the winner from the previous year

green jersey (*cycling*) (1) the jersey worn by the winner of the **points competition** in the **Tour de France** [French *maillot vert*, "green jersey"]; (2) the jersey awarded to the **King of the Mountains** in the **Giro d'Italia** [Italian *maglia verde*, "green jersey"]

green spot (*snooker*) the spot on the **billiard table** where the **green** is positioned, in the left corner of the **D** as viewed from the **balk** end

greenback (*surfing*) a wave before it breaks

greenie (*surfing*) another term for a **greenback**

greenkeeper (*bowls*) the person who has the care of the **green**; (*golf*) the person who has the care of the **course**

greensome (*golf*) a type of **fourball** play in which all players drive, then each pair selects the **ball** with which they aim to complete the **hole** [blend of **green** and **foursome**]

gremlin (*surfing*) (1) colloquial term for a young **surfer**; (2) colloquial term for a troublemaker who frequents the beach but is not a surfer [probably alteration of *goblin*]

gremmy (*surfing*) colloquial shortening of **gremlin**

Grey Cup (*Canadian football*) the **cup** awarded

annually to the **champion** team of the Canadian Football League [donated in 1909 by Earl Grey (1851–1917), governor general of Canada]

Greyhound Derby (*greyhound racing*) the sport's top **race** in Britain, first held in 1927 [named after the **Derby**]

greyhound racing (*sport*) a sport in which (usually) six greyhounds pursue a **lure** around a circular or oval **track**, the first dog to finish being the winner

grid (*American football*) shortening of **gridiron**; (*auto racing*) a pattern of lines painted on the **racetrack** to indicate the positions of the cars at the **start**

gridder (*American football*) a player of the **game**

gridiron (*American football*) the **field** on which the **game** is played, with lines marked across every five yards; (*sport*) a byname of **American football**

grille (*real tennis*) a square opening in a corner of the end wall of the **court**, a **shot** into which scores a **point**

grind (*skateboarding*) a move in which one of the **trucks** is scraped along the **grind rail** or other surface

grind rail (*skateboarding*) a long narrow bar on which stunts can be performed

grip (*general*) the manner in which a player holds a **cricket bat**, **golf club**, **tennis racket**, or the like

griptape (*skateboarding*) a tough adhesive tape used on the **board** to provide extra grip for the feet

gripwax (*skiing*) a substance applied to **skis** to increase friction and thus also traction

Grizzlies (*basketball*) short name of the Vancouver Grizzlies team

grommet (*general*) colloquial term for any sort of young **boarder** [perhaps from *grummet*, "ship's boy," influenced by **gremlin**]

groom (*equestrianism*) an assistant and adviser to the driver in **carriage driving**

gross (*horse racing*) (of) a horse that is naturally large-girthed, as distinct from overweight

ground (*cricket*) the area behind the **popping crease** with which the **batsman** must be physically in contact to avoid being **stumped** or **run out**; (*general*) the area on which a **game** is regular played

ground angling (*angling*) **fishing** without a **float**, with a weight placed close to the **hook**

ground ball (*baseball*) a **ball** hit along the ground, as distinct from a **fly ball**

ground fielding (*cricket*) catching or stopping a **ball** near the ground

ground line (*equestrianism*) in **show jumping**, the line along the base of a **fence**, used to judge the point of a horse's **takeoff**

ground out (*baseball*) to hit a **ground ball** and be **put out** by not reaching **first base** before the **throw** from a **fielder**

ground shot (*tennis*) another term for a **ground stroke**

ground staff (*cricket*) a paid staff of promising young players kept by a **club**; (*general*) a group of people who look after a **sports ground** or **playing field**

ground stroke (*tennis*) a **stroke** played after the **ball** has bounced, especially one made from the **baseline**

ground under repair (*golf*) an area of the **course** that is being repaired and therefore not valid for play

groundbait (*angling*) **bait** dropped to the bottom of a stream or river to attract fish there

grounder (*baseball*, *cricket*) a batted **ball** that rolls along the ground instead of flying through the air

groundhopper (*association football*) a **supporter** who travels to different **grounds** to see as many **matches** as possible

groundman (*general*) another spelling of **groundsman**

groundsman (*general*) a person who takes care of a **sports ground** or **playing field**

group (*horse racing*) one of the categories of **pattern races**, group 1 including the **English classics** and other important international races; group 2 the less important international races, and group 3 mainly **domestic** races; (*shooting*) a cluster of **hits** on a **target**

group race (*horse racing*) another term for a **pattern race**

grovet (*wrestling*) a **hold** in which a combatant grips his opponent's head between his chest and forearm, forcing his rival's shoulders to the **mat** with his other arm [origin uncertain]

grub (*cricket*) a **ball** that runs flat along the ground after leaving the hand of the **bowler**

grub kick (*rugby league*, *rugby union*) a **ball** dropped from the hand and kicked along the ground

grubber (*cricket*) another term for a **grub**; (*rugby league*, *rugby union*) shortening of **grub kick**

grudgeby (*rugby union*) colloquial term for the keenly contested annual **varsity match** between Oxford and Cambridge universities, first held in 1872 [blend of *grudge match*, "contest aiming to settle longstanding rivalry," and *rugby*]

grummet (*general*) another spelling of **grommet**

gruppetto (*cycling*) another term for an **autobus** [Italian *gruppetto*, "little group"]

guard (*American football*) a **lineman** positioned immediately to the left or right of the **center**; (*basketball*) a player who mainly operates away from the **basket**, unlike a **forward**; (*bowls*) a delivery of the **bowl** that blocks an opponent's path to the **jack** or to another bowl; (*boxing*) a defensive stance, with the gloves raised to protect the face; (*cricket*) the position of the **bat** taken by the **batsman** in front of the **wicket** when he is ready to receive a **ball**; (*curling*) a **stone** played into a position where it can protect another stone from being hit; (*fencing*) the metal cup at the end of the **hilt** that protects the hand from being hit

guernsey (*Australian Rules*) a type of sleeveless shirt worn by team players

guide runner (*athletics*) a person who accompanies a visually impaired **track athlete**

Guineas (*horse racing*) shortening of **One Thousand Guineas** or **Two Thousand Guineas**

gulley (*octopush*) the long tray that serves as a **goal**

Gulls (*association football*) nickname of the English **club** Torquay United [from the seagulls that frequent the coastal town]

gully (*cricket*) a **fielding** position on the **off side**, between **point** and **slips** [from *gully* in its basic sense "channel," referring to the gap between the named positions]

gumshield (*boxing*) another term for a **mouthpiece**

gun (*surfing*) a large heavy **surfboard** used for riding big waves

Gunners (*association football*) nickname of the English **club** Arsenal [from the workers at the Royal Arsenal, London, who founded the club in 1886]

gunwale (*rowing*) the top section on the sides of a **shell**, to which the **outriggers** are fixed

gutters (*tenpin bowling*) the gulleys that run the length of the **lane** and to either side of it

gut wrench (*wrestling*) a move in which a combatant rolls his opponent onto his back while in a **bridge** position

gutty (*golf*) an old-fashioned type of **golf ball** [made from *gutta percha*]

gybe (*sailing*) to swing a **sail** from one side of the boat to the other in order to alter course

gybe mark (*sailing*) a mark showing where **yachts** must **gybe** in an **ocean race**

gym (*gymnastics*) familiar shortening of **gymnasium** or **gymnastics**

gym rat (*general*) a person who regularly attends a **gym**

gymkhana (*auto racing*) an **autocross** contest; (*equestrianism*) a contest between amateur or young **riders** in various equestrian sports [Hindi *gend khana*, "ball house," influenced by **gym**]

gymnasium (*general*) a place, hall, or building for **gymnastics** or indoor sports [originally, in ancient Greece, a public place where youths exercised, from Greek *gymnos*, "naked"]

gymnast (*general*) a person who performs or practices **gymnastics**

gymnastics (*sport*) a range of moves or exercises performed on the **floor** or on **apparatus**, either competitively or to tone the body and improve agility and coordination

gyoji (*sumo*) the **referee** [Japanese *gyoji*, "referee"]

hack (*curling*) footholds of metal or rubber at each end of the **rink** from which players can push off; (*general*) to kick the shins of another player (illegally); (*rugby union*) shortening of **fly hack**

hacker (*golf, tennis*) colloquial term for a poor player [who hacks at the **ball**]

hacking (*sport*) the riding of a horse in the countryside for recreation

hackle (*angling*) an **artificial fly** made of a cock's hackle or neck feather

Hacky Sack (*sport*) proprietary name of a **game** of U.S. origin in which players attempt to kick a **footbag** without letting it touch the ground [from **hack**, "kick," and **sack**]

hail (*shinty*) (1) a **goal**; (2) a **score** [apparently from *hail!*, the shout with which the player scored a goal]

hail Mary (*American football*) colloquial term for a high **pass** thrown into the **end zone** at the very end of a **game** [a desperate move for which a prayer is needed]

hailkeeper (*shinty*) a **goalkeeper**

hairdryer treatment (*association football*) a berating by a **manager** of his team for their poor play [his scolding hits them like a blast of hot air]

hairpin (*auto racing*) a sharp double bend on the **track** [shaped like a hairgrip or bobby pin]; (*skiing*) two successive **vertical gates** on a **slalom** course

hairy Mary (*angling*) a kind of **artificial fly** [from its appearance]

hajime (*judo*) the command with which the referee starts a **bout** [Japanese *hajime*, "beginning"]

haka (*rugby union*) the Maori war dance performed by the **All Blacks** before the start of a **match** [Maori *haka*, "dance"]

half (*American football*) shortening of **half time**; (*general*) (1) one of the two periods of equal length into which a **game** is divided; (2) one of the two parts of the field of play either side of the **halfway** line; (3) shortening of **center half**, **left half**, **right half**, or **halfback**

half ball (*snooker*) a **stroke** that sends the **cue ball** against the edge of the **object ball**

half bisque (*croquet*) a restricted **bisque** in which no **point** can be scored

half blue (*general*) a person who is second choice for a **blue** or who is chosen to play in a minor sport such as **badminton** or **lacrosse**

half butt (*snooker*) a **cue** longer than the standard cue, usually used with a **rest**

half century (*cricket*) a **score** of 50 **runs**; (*snooker*) a **break** of 50 **points**

half cock (*cricket*) a **stroke** made by a **batsman** that plays the **ball** neither forward nor back

half-court line (*squash*) a line on the floor of the **court** that divides the back of the court into two

half-forward flank (*Australian Rules*) an attacking player who plays on the **flank** near the **50-meter arc**

half gainer (*swimming*) a **dive** in which a **backflip** is followed by a head-first plunge into the water facing the **board**

half-in, half-out (*gymnastics*) a move comprising a double **salto** with a **half twist** on each salto

half marathon (*athletics*) a **foot race** just over half the length of a **marathon** (13 miles 352 yards, 21.243km)

half mile (*athletics*) the former equivalent of the **800 meters**

half miler (*athletics*) a **runner** specializing in the former **half mile** or present **800 meters**

half nelson (*wrestling*) a **nelson** applied on one side only, with one of the combatant's arms under one of his opponent's arms

half-one (*golf*) a **handicap** of one **stroke** every second **hole**

half pass (*equestrianism*) in **dressage**, a sideways and forward movement in which the horse crosses its legs

half-pipe (*skateboarding*) a U-shaped structure made of concrete from which **boarders** launch the **board** to perform aerial maneuvers; (*snowboarding*) a U-shaped channel cut into the snow from which **boarders** launch the **board** to perform aerial maneuvers

half pirouette (*equestrianism*) a half-circle turn by the horse with its inside hind foot as a pivot

half roll (*croquet*) a **croquet** in which the opposing **ball**, when struck, travels two or three times as far as the **striker's ball**

half shot (*golf*) a **shot** played with about half the usual **swing**

half strike (*tenpin bowling*) alternate term for a **spare**

half time (*general*) the interval between the first **half** of a **game** and the second

half twist (*gymnastics*) a half-rotation of the body around the spine

half volley (*association football*) a kick in which the player's boot makes contact with the **ball** as it begins to bounce up off the ground; (*cricket*) a **stroke** by the **batsman** of a **ball** as it starts to rise after pitching; (*tennis*) a **shot** of the ball immediately after it bounces

halfback (*American football*) a **running back** positioned between the **quarterback** and **fullback**; (*rugby league*) either of the players **scrum half** and **standoff half**; (*rugby union*) either of the

players **scrum half** and **fly half**, providing a link between the **forwards** and the **three quarters**

halfback flank (*Australian Rules*) a running **defender** who plays on the **flank**

halfway line (*association football, rugby league, rugby union*) the line that separates the two equal **halves** of the **pitch**

halieutics (*angling*) a formal term for the art of **fishing**, especially as the title of a treatise [Greek *halieutes*, "fisher," from *hals*, "sea"]

Hall of Fame (*general*) an institution that honors outstanding figures in the history of a particular sport, as the **Baseball** Hall of Fame, Cooperstown, New York, the **Golf** Hall of Fame, St. Augustine, Florida, and the **Pro Football** Hall of Fame, Canton, Ohio

halt! (*fencing*) a command to stop fencing

halve (*golf*) to play a **hole** or **match** in the same number of **strokes** as one's opponent

halyard (*sailing*) a rope used for raising or lowering a **sail**

ham (*boxing*) an incompetent **boxer**

Hambletonian (*horse racing*) an annual **harness race** for **trotters**, first held in 1926 at Syracuse, New York, but now at the Meadowlands **racetrack**, New Jersey [named for Hambletonian (foaled 1849), the ancestor of most harness racers]

Hamilton Park (*horse racing*) a **flat racecourse** at Hamilton, central Scotland

hammer (*athletics*) (1) a heavy metal **ball** attached to a long flexible wire which is thrown by being swung around the thrower's head and then released; (2) the **field event** in which it is thrown

hammerlock (*wrestling*) a **hold** in which the opponent's arm is twisted up behind his back

Hammers (*association football*) nickname of the English **club** West Ham United [not directly from the placename but from the shipbuilding department of the Thames Ironworks, London, where workers formed the club in 1895]

Hampden Park (*association football*) the **home ground** in Glasgow, Scotland, of both the Scottish **club** Queens Park and the national team

Hampden roar (*association football*) traditional term describing the vociferous support for the home or national team at **matches** at **Hampden Park**

hand (*general*) a **round** or **innings**

hand line (*angling*) a **fishing line** without a **rod**

handbags (*association football, rugby union*) colloquial term used by radio and TV commentators for a confrontation between players [from the concept of a woman's handbag used to belabor a rival or opponent]

handball (*association football*) the **offense** of touching or striking the **ball** with one's hand; (*Aus-*

tralian Rules) the act of passing the **ball** by holding it in one hand and striking it with the fist of the other; (*sport*) (1) a **game** with seven players a side played on an indoor **court** between **goals** in which the **ball** is struck with the palm of the hand; (2) a game similar to **fives** in which a ball is struck with the gloved hand against a wall

handcycle (*cycling*) a hand-cranked tricycle used in **races** by disabled **riders**

handhold (*mountaineering*) a projection or other feature that one can grasp while climbing

handicap (*general*) a **race** or competition in which an inferior competitor's chances are improved by some means, as being given a **head start**; (*golf*) the number of **strokes** by which a player's average **score** exceeds **par** for the **course**, this number being subtracted from the player's score in **strokeplay** competitions; (*horse racing*) a **race** in which each horse carries a **weight** determined by its **handicap mark** in order to equalize its chances against other **runners**; (*polo*) a value assigned to each player based on previous performances [apparently from *hand i' cap* ("hand in the cap"), from a game of chance in which a hand drawn out of a cap holds either something or nothing]

handicap mark (*horse racing*) the assessment of a horse's **form**, expressed as a figure between 0 and 140 and used as the basis for calculating the **weight** it carries in a **handicap**

handicap race (*horse racing*) a **race** run as a **handicap**

handicapper (*horse racing*) (1) an official who assigns a **handicap** to a horse; (2) a horse running in a **handicap race**

handin (*badminton, real tennis, squash*) the player whose side has the **service**

handle (*association football*) to commit the **offense** of **handball**; (*horse racing*) the total takings from **bets** placed on a **race**

handled the ball (*cricket*) the **offense** committed by a **batsman** who deliberately touches the **ball** with a hand not holding the **bat**, as a result of which he is **out**

handler (*boxing*) a person who trains and acts as a **second** to a **boxer**; (*horse racing*) another term for a **trainer**

handling game (*rugby union*) play in which the **ball** is primarily advanced by being handled, as against a **kicking game**

handoff (*American football*) the passing of the **ball** from the **quarterback** to a **running back**; (*rugby league, rugby union*) a {legal} move in which a player with the **ball** pushes away an opponent

handout (*badminton, real tennis, squash*) (1) the player whose side is receiving the **service**; (2) the situation when the first player on the serving side loses his service

handover (*athletics*) the passing of the **baton** from one runner to another in a **relay race**; (*rugby league*) the change in **possession** after the **sixth tackle**

handpass (*Australian Rules*) another term for a **handball**

handplant (*snowboarding*) a move in which a **boarder** plants one or both hands on the rim of the **halfpipe** to pivot into a turn

hands (*association football*) alternate term for **handball**

hands and heels (*horse racing*) riding without the use of a whip [using the hands and heels only to direct and encourage the horse]

handsling (*cycling*) a method used to change places in the **madison**, by which teammates grip hands, then release the grip, so that one **rider** can propel the other forward

handspring (*gymnastics*) a movement in which the **gymnast** moves forward or backward onto his hands from a standing position, then completes a **somersault**, landing on his feet.

handstand (*gymnastics*) a move in which the **gymnast** supports his body vertically on his hands in an upside-down position

handy (*horse racing*) in a prominent position in a **race**

hang (*horse racing*) to veer to one side while running

hang a left (*skiing*) to turn to the left

hang a right (*skiing*) to turn to the right

hang five (*surfing*) to have the five toes of one foot projecting over the nose of the **board**, usually to gain speed

hang-glider (*hang-gliding*) the light engineless aircraft used in **hang-gliding**

hang-gliding (*sport*) a sport in which the participant glides from a height such as a clifftop hanging in a harness from a **hang-glider**, which he controls by shifting his body weight in opposition to the control frame

hang ten (*surfing*) to have the ten toes of both feet projecting over the nose of the **board**, usually to gain speed

hang up one's boots (*association football*) to retire from the sport

hang up one's gloves (*boxing*) to retire from the sport

hanging lie (*golf*) the position of the **ball** when it is resting on a slope

hangtime (*American football*) the time that a kicked **ball** remains in the air; (*basketball*) the time a player is able to remain in the air when shooting or jumping for the **ball**

Har-Tru (*tennis*) proprietary name of an artificial surface for **tennis courts**, made from crushed greenstone [combination of *hard* and *true*]

harbor race (*sailing*) a race around a course marked out by buoys, often in several **laps**

hard (*horse racing*) a category of **going**

hard court (*tennis*) a **court** laid with clay, cement, or the like, as distinct from a **grass court**

hardball (*sport*) another term for **baseball** [as against **softball**]

hare (*athletics*) another term for a **pacemaker** [he sets the pace, like the artificial hare or **lure** in **greyhound racing**]

hare and hounds (*general*) a **race** in which a **runner** with a **head start** (the hare) leaves a trail for the others (the hounds) to follow; (*motorcycle racing*) a form of **enduro** with no checkpoints

harl (*angling*) a type of **artificial fly** [made from a *harl*, the barb of a feather]

Harmsworth Cup (*powerboat racing*) the **cup** awarded to the winner of an international **race** for boats under 40ft (12m) in length [presented in 1903 by Sir Alfred Harmsworth (1865–1922), later Lord Northcliffe]

harness race (*horse racing*) a **race** between **trotters** or **pacers** harnessed to **sulkies**

harness racing (*horse racing*) the staging of **harness races** as a sporting contest

harriers (*athletics*) in **cross-country running**, a group or **club** of participants in the sport [with Harriers often part of their name]

Harriers (*association football*) short name of the English **club** Kidderminster Harriers

Harrow drive (*cricket*) another term for a **Chinese cut** [presumably from Harrow School]

Harry Sunderland Trophy (*rugby league*) the **trophy** awarded since 1965 to the **man of the match** in the **Super League Grand Final** [named in commemoration of Australian tour manager Harry Sunderland (1890–1964)]

Harry Wraggs (*association football*) nickname of the Scottish **club** Partick Thistle [rhyming slang for the more common nickname **Jags**, from the English **jockey** Harry Wragg (1902–1985)]

Hart Memorial Trophy (*ice hockey*) the **trophy** awarded annually to the **Most Valuable Player** [named for Cecil Hart, manager of the Montreal Canadiens 1926–39]

hash marks (*American football*) the marks at intervals of one yard that run the length of the **field**, the two sets of such marks on the **gridiron** marking the furthest distance from the center of the field at which the **ball** can be placed to restart play [so called from their resemblance to *hash marks*, "military service stripes"]

hat trick (*association football*) the scoring of three **goals** by the same player in a single **match**; (*cricket*) the feat of taking three **wickets** with consecutive **balls**; (*general*) three successes of any kind in any sport [so called as deserving the award of a new hat]

Hatters (*association football*) nicknames of the English **clubs** Luton Town and Stockport County [from the hat-manufacturing industry in each town]

haul (*cricket*) a good number of **wickets** taken by a **bowler** in a **match** [as if loot in a robbery]

haute école (*equestrianism*) a group term for the more difficult feats of **horsemanship** [French *haute école*, "high school"]

have the mount (*horse racing*) to ride a particular horse in a **race**

Hawk-Eye (*general*) proprietary name of a computer program that uses high-speed video cameras around a **tennis court** or **cricket ground** to create a 3D image of the **ball** as it moves and calculate the path it would have taken [invented by Paul Hawkins as an aid to radio and TV commentators]

Hawks (*Australian Rules*) short name of the Hawthorn Hawks team; (*basketball*) short name of the Atlanta Hawks team; (*rugby league*) short name of the English **club** Hunslet Hawks

Haydock Park (*horse racing*) a **flat** and **National Hunt racecourse** near Ashton-in-Makerfield, northwestern England

haymaker (*boxing*) colloquial term for a wild swinging **punch**; (*cricket*) colloquial term for a sweeping **stroke** with the **bat** [suggestive of a sweeping scythe in haymaking]

hazard (*billiards, snooker*) a **stroke** in which one of the **balls** goes into a **pocket** as either a **winning hazard** or a **lozing hazard**; (*fives*) a feature of a **court** that affects the behavior of a **ball** played on to it, as the **pepperbox** in **Eton fives**; (*golf*) an obstacle in the form of a **bunker** or **water hazard**; (*real tennis*) any of the openings or **galleries** around the **court** that are not **winning openings**

hazard side (*real tennis*) the half of the **court** into which the **ball** is served

head (*bowls*) the grouping of **bowls** around the **jack**; (*greyhound racing*) the length of a greyhound's head, used to describe the distance between two dogs at the **finish**; (*horse racing*) the length of a horse's head, used to describe the distance between two **runners** at the **finish**

Head of the River (*rowing*) the title given the **crew** finishing first in the **bumping races** at Oxford and Cambridge

Head of the River Race (*rowing*) an annual **race** for **eights** over the reverse **Boat Race** course, first held in 1926

head pin (*tenpin bowling*) the frontmost **pin** in the triangular arrangement

head start (*general*) an advantage given to a contestant at the **start** of a **race** [in **horse racing** that of a horse in front of others by the length of a **head**]

head string (*pool*) a line a quarter the length of the **table** from the top, behind which a player must make any **break**

header (*association football*) a **pass** or **shot** at **goal** made by directing the **ball** with the head

headhunter (*baseball*) colloquial term for a **pitcher** who throws **bean balls**; (*ice hockey*) a player who by physical means in this **contact sport** aims with others to remove star **opposition** players from the **game**

Headingley (*cricket*) the **home ground** of Yorkshire **county cricket club**, Leeds

headless spin (*ice skating*) a **spin** like the **upright spin** but with the head tilted away

headlock (*wrestling*) a **hold** in which a combatant puts his arms around his opponent's head and tightens his grip by interlocking the fingers of both hands

Headquarters (*horse racing*) another term for **Newmarket** as the center of English **racing**

headwork (*association football*) the directing of the **ball** by means of **headers**; (*cycling*) smart tactical riding at the **start** of a **sprint race**

Hearts (*association football*) short name of the Scottish **club** Heart of Midlothian

heat (*general*) (1) a single eliminating **round** in a **race**; (2) a division of a contest in which the winner goes on to a final test [so called because it is intense or "burning"]

Heat (*basketball*) short name of the Miami Heat team

heater (*baseball*) colloquial term for a fast **ball**

heavy (*horse racing*) a category of **going**

heavy artillery (*golf*) colloquial term for the **driver**

heavyweight (*boxing*) the professional **weight** category of maximum 91kg (201lb)

hecht (*gymnastics*) a **dismount** from the **horizontal bar** or **asymmetric bars** in which the **gymnast** releases the bar at the height of a **back swing**, sails forward with arms outstretched, and lands upright on the feet [presumably introduced by a gymnast named Hecht]

heel (*golf*) the lowest part of the **clubhead**; (*rugby league, rugby union*) to send the **ball** out at the back of the **scrum** with the heel

Heineken Cup (*rugby union*) the **cup** awarded annually since 1996 to the winner of a competition for major European **clubs** and provincial teams [name of sponsor]

Heisman Trophy (*American football*) the **trophy** awarded annually since 1935 to the outstanding player in **college football** [named in honor of U.S. collegiate football coach John Heisman (1869–1936)]

helicopter (*skiing*) an upright aerial **spin** of 360 degrees

heliskiing (*sport*) an **extreme sport** in which a **skier** is dropped by helicopter at the top of a mountain, then skis down to the treeline

Hell of the North (*cycling*) nickname of the **Paris-Roubaix race** [French *l'enfer du nord*, "hell of the north," from the devastated World War I landscape through which the **course** formerly ran]

helmsman (*sailing*) the steersman

Henley (*rowing*) short name of **Henley Royal Regatta**

Henley Royal Regatta (*rowing*) Britain's oldest **regatta**, with many prestigious **trophies**, held annually at Henley-on-Thames, Oxfordshire, since 1839

Hennessy (*horse racing*) short name of the **Hennessy Gold Cup**

Hennessy Gold Cup (*horse racing*) the **cup** awarded to the winner of an annual **race** at **Newbury**, first contested in 1957 [name of sponsor]

heptathlete (*Olympics*) a competitor in a **heptathlon**

heptathlon (*Olympics*) a women's **event** consisting of seven separate contests held on two consecutive days: **100-meter hurdles**, **shot put**, **high jump**, and **200 meters** on day one, **long jump**, **javelin**, and **800 meters** on day two [Greek *hepta*, "seven," and *athlon*, "contest"]

Hereford (*archery*) a **round** of 72 **arrows** at 80yds (73m), 48 at 60 (55m), and 24 at 50 (46m); (*horse racing*) a **National Hunt racecourse** near Hereford, Herefordshire, England

herringboning (*skiing*) a technique for climbing a slope in **cross-country skiing** by which the tips of the **skis** are angled outward [they make a herringbone-like pattern in the snow]

hesitation dribble (*basketball*) a **dribble** in which a player feints to stop before continuing to take the **ball** forward [based on *hesitation dance*, which has pauses at intervals]

Hexham (*horse racing*) a **National Hunt racecourse** at Hexham, Northumberland, England

Hibees (*association football*) nickname of the Scottish **club** Hibernian

Hibs (*association football*) short name of the Scottish **club** Hibernian

Hickstead (*equestrianism*) the location in West Sussex, England, of many **showjumping** events

high bar (*gymnastics*) (1) the higher of the two **asymmetric bars**; (2) another term for the **horizontal bar**

high cheese (*baseball*) colloquial term for a **fastball** thrown at the top of or above the **strike zone**

high dive (*swimming*) a **dive** from a high **diving board**

high house (*shooting*) the higher **trap** in **skeet**

high hurdles (*athletics*) a **race** in which the **hurdles** are 107cm (42in) high

high jump (*athletics*) a **field event** consisting of a **jump** over a high **bar**

high post (*basketball*) an offensive position on the **court** near the **foul circle**

high-sticking (*ice hockey*) an **offense** in which a player touches an opponent with the **stick** above shoulder level

high tackle (*association football*) a **tackle** in which the player's foot is dangerously high, resulting in a **foul**

high-toss serve (*table tennis*) a **serve** in which the **ball** is tossed high in the air

highboard (*swimming*) (of) a high **diving board**

Highland games (*general*) an annual contest held in the Scottish Highlands with competitions in sports (including **tossing the caber** and **tug of war**), piping, and traditional dancing

hiking (*sailing*) a maneuver to keep the boat flat in the water by which the **helmsman** balances between the middle of the boat and the side or sits on the edge of the boat, sometimes leaning far out

hilt (*fencing*) the handle of the sword, including the **guard**

Hindenburg (*kitesurfing*) an accident in which the **kite** stalls and crashes into an onshore structure [after the disastrous crash in 1937 of the German dirigible *Hindenburg*]

hip circle (*gymnastics*) a move on the **horizontal bar** or **asymmetric bars** in which the **gymnast** executes a circle with his hips touching the bar

hiplock (*wrestling*) a form of **cross-buttock**

hit (*baseball*) a **stroke** that sends the **ball** into the field of play, allowing the **batter** to reach **first base** safely; (*fencing*) an accurate contact of the sword with the **target**; (*general*) a **stroke** or **shot** that sends a **ball** or other missile (as an **arrow** in **archery** or a **round** in **shooting**) to a **target** or simply through the air; (*rugby union*) another term for a **tackle**

hit and giggle (*cricket*) derisory name for **one-day cricket** [pun on *slap and tickle*, a euphemism for amorous frolicking, by comparison with a dedicated five-day **test match**]

hit-and-run (*baseball*) a maneuver in which the **baserunner** at **first base** begins to run as soon as the **pitcher** begins to throw the **ball**, expecting the **batter** to put the ball into play, thus giving the baserunner more time to advance safely and force the **infielders** to move out of position

hit-in (*polo*) the hitting of the **ball** into the field of play

hit-out (*field hockey*) a **pass** awarded to a defending team to restart play after the **ball** has been sent over the **goal line** (without a **goal** being scored) by the attacking team

hit the ball twice (*cricket*) a (possibly inadvertent) **stroke** by the **batsman** in which he hits the **ball** twice and so is **out**

hit the post (*association football*) to kick or head the **ball** against one of the **goalposts**

hit the wall (*athletics*) to lose energy suddenly in **long-distance** running, such as a **marathon**, so that it is a physical and psychological struggle to complete the **course**

hit wicket (*cricket*) a **stroke** by a **batsman** in which he hits the **wicket** with his **bat** or a part of his body and dislodges the **bails**, so that he is **out**

hitch and kick (*athletics*) another term for a **hitch kick**

hitch kick (*athletics*) a style of **long jump** in which the jumper makes two or more strides in the air before landing feet together

Hitler's Games (*Olympics*) a byname for the 1936 **Olympic Games**, held in Berlin, Germany, where they were turned to advantage by Hitler as a showcase to demonstrate his theory of the superiority of the Arian races

hitter (*baseball*) another term for the **batter**

hockey (*sport*) general name in British use for **field hockey** or in North American use for **ice hockey**

hockey ball (*field hockey*) the hard white **ball** with which the **game** is played

hockey mom (*ice hockey*) colloquial term for a mother who dedicates many hours to driving her children to organized sports activities, especially **hockey games**, and to supporting their participation in these, often with a greater degree of commitment than a **soccer mom**

hockey stick (*field hockey*) the long wooden stick with a curved end with which the **ball** is struck; (*ice hockey*) the long (formerly wooden) stick with an angled blade with which the **puck** is struck

Hockeyroos (*field hockey*) nickname for the Australian national women's team [blend of **hockey** and **Kangaroos**]

hodad (*surfing*) colloquial term for a person who hangs around surfing beaches but does not surf [origin uncertain]

hog (*curling*) a **stone** that fails to reach the **hog line**

hog line (*curling*) a line drawn across each end of the **rink**, 10m (33ft) from the **hack** and 6.4m (21ft) from the **tee**, which a **stone** must cross to count

hog score (*curling*) another term for the **hog line**

hoist (*ice hockey*) an illegal trapping of an opponent by two players

hold (*boxing*) a grip of the opponent that prevents him from throwing **punches**; (*judo, wrestling*) a particular manner of gripping and immobiliz-ing the opponent; (*mountaineering*) shortening of **handhold** or **foothold**

hold-down (*judo*) a grip in which the opponent is held down on the ground

hold serve (*tennis*) to win one's own **service game**

hold service (*tennis*) alternate form of **hold serve**

hold the throw (*darts*) to win a **leg** in which one threw first

hold up (*horse racing*) the keep a horse toward the rear of the **field** in a **race**

holding (*American football*) the act of illegally grasping an opponent with the hands; (*ice hockey*) the act of illegally grasping an opponent with the hands or **stick**

hole (*association football*) colloquial term for the space between the **midfielders** and the **attack-ers** where the attacking midfielders play; (*base-ball*) colloquial term for the area of the **infield** between **shortstop** and **third base**; (*golf*) (1) the cylindrical hollow 4¼ inches in diameter in the center of the **green** into which the **ball** is played; (2) the distance, or the part of the **game**, between the **tee** and the hole; (3) the **score** for playing a ball into the hole in the fewest **strokes**

hole in one (*golf*) a **shot** from the **tee** that sends the **ball** straight into the **hole**

hole out (*cricket*) to be **caught** by a **fielder** and so **out**; (*golf*) to play the **ball** into the **hole**

home (*association football*) in **football pools**, a **match** won by a team playing on their **home ground**; (*baseball*) shortening of **home plate**; (*general*) (1) an area where a player is free from attack; (2) another term for the **goal**; (3) arrived at the **finish** of a **race**; (*golf*) on the second nine **holes** of the **course**; (*lacrosse*) one of the three players **first home**, **second home**, and **third home**

home advantage (*general*) the means used by the **hosts** of a sporting contest to gain a tactical ad-vantage over the **visitors**, as by giving **athletes** advance access to **venues**, arranging competi-tion schedules to suit domestic participants, and block-booking seats near the **finish line** to cre-ate a vociferous concentration of **supporters**

home base (*baseball*) another term for the **home plate**

home brew (*Canadian football*) a player who is a native of the city for which his team is named

home game (*general*) a **game** played on a team's **home ground**

home ground (*general*) the **ground** where a team is normally based

home gym (*gymnastics*) an installation of gymnas-tic equipment in a person's private home

home plate (*baseball*) the **plate** over which the

pitcher aims the **ball** and to which the **batter** must return to score a **run**

home run (*baseball*) a **hit** that goes far enough to enable the **batter** to make a complete circuit of all four **bases**

home straight (*horse racing*) the final stretch of a **racecourse**, leading to the **finish**

home stretch (*horse racing*) another term for the **home straight**

home thrust (*fencing*) a **thrust** that reaches the point where it is aimed

homer (*baseball*) colloquial term for a **home run**

Honest Men (*association football*) nickname of the Scottish **club** Ayr United [from Robert Burns's description of the town in "Tam o' Shanter": "Auld Ayr, wham ne'er a town surpasses / For honest men and bonnie lasses"]

honest player (*ice hockey*) colloquial term for a player who is equally effective as **attacker** and **defender**

honk (*cycling*) to pedal while standing up out of the **saddle**, as a way to gain greater power or to rest the legs while making an ascent [perhaps from *honk*, "to sound a horn," as of a driver seek-ing to power ahead]

honor (*golf*) the right to play first from the **tee**

hook (*angling*) the barbed piece of wire that is at-tached to the **fishing line** to carry the **bait**; (*as-sociation football*) a kick of the **ball** from the angle of the ankle and boot; (*boxing*) a swinging blow with the elbow bent; (*cricket*) a **stroke** played with a horizontal or rising **bat** that sweeps the **ball** to the **leg side** behind the **wicket**; (*gen-eral*) the curve of a **ball** in flight; (*golf*) a mishit of the **ball** that sends it through the air from right to left (for a right-handed player) or the converse; (*rugby league, rugby union*) to obtain **possession** of the **ball** in the **scrum** by using the foot to kick it backward; (*surfing*) the top part of a wave

hook shot (*basketball*) a **shot** made by a player side-on to the **basket** by curving up the arm far-ther away from it

hooker (*rugby league, rugby union*) the **forward** who **binds** between the two **props** in a **scrum** and who **hooks** the **ball** back

hooking (*ice hockey*) the **offense** of using a **stick** as a hook to hinder an opponent

hoop (*basketball*) the hard circular part of the **bas-ket** from which a net is suspended; (*croquet*) one of the metal arches through which the **ball** must pass; (*horse racing*) one of the bands in contrast-ing colors on the **silks** of a **jockey**

hoops (*sport*) colloquial term for **basketball**

Hoops (*association football*) nickname of the En-glish **club** Queens Park Rangers [from the team's blue and white hooped shirts]

hop (*athletics*) the first stage of the **triple jump**

hop, skip, and jump (*athletics*) a former term for the **triple jump**

hop, step, and jump (*athletics*) a former term for the **triple jump**

horizontal bar (*gymnastics*) a steel bar, suspended on a frame above the ground, used in men's competition for the rhythmic execution of various swinging and turning movements

Hornets (*association football*) nickname of the English **club** Watford [from the team's black shirts with yellow and red trim]; (*basketball*) short name of the Charlotte Hornets team; (*rugby league*) short name of the English **club** Rochdale Hornets

horse (*gymnastics*) a leather-covered wooden block used for **vaulting** (lengthwise by men, widthwise by women) [its use suggests the feat of mounting a horse by leaping onto it]

Horse of the Year Show (*equestrianism*) an annual competitive **event** presented by the British Show Jumping Association, first held in 1949 and currently staged at the National Exhibition Centre, Birmingham

horse race (*horse racing*) a **race** between horses with (usually professional) **riders**, especially as a **spectator sport** intimately associated with money and the placing of **bets**

horse racing (*sport*) the conducting of **horse races** as a competitive sport

horse trials (*equestrianism*) a general term for a **three-day event**

horsebox (*horse racing*) a road trailer or railcar designed to transport one or more horses

horseman (*equestrianism*) a person skilled in **horsemanship**

horsemanship (*equestrianism*) the art of riding, training, and managing horses

horsewoman (*equestrianism*) a woman who rides horses and is knowledgeable about them

hosel (*golf*) the socket for the **shaft** in the **clubhead**

hospital ball (*association football*) colloquial term for a poorly executed **pass**, so placing the recipient (typically a **defender** or the **goalkeeper**) in a risky situation

hosts (*general*) the team who arrange and manage a **match** with rivals on their **home ground**

hot corner (*baseball*) colloquial term for **third base**, where the **fielder** has little time to react to **balls** hit in his direction

hot dog (*surfing*) (1) a **surfboard** of above-average size; (2) a **surfer** who performs showy maneuvers on such a **board**

hot-rod racing (*auto racing*) the racing of hot rods, as cars specially modified to give added power and speed

hotpot (*horse racing*) colloquial term for a horse that has been heavily backed

hotshot (*baseball*) a player renowned for making accurate **shots** at the **basket**

house (*curling*) the **target** for the **stones**, as a set of three concentric rings on the ice with the **tee** in the center

how's that? (*cricket*) the **appeal** of the **fielding** side to the **umpire** to declare that the **batsman** is **out**

howzat? (*cricket*) an alternate spelling of **how's that?** [a representation of the spoken form]

huddle (*American football*) the gathering together of a team behind their **line of scrimmage** to receive instructions before the next **play**

hull (*sailing*) the frame or body of a boat

Hull KR (*rugby league*) short name of the English **club** Hull Kingston Rovers

hundred (*cricket*) a **score** of 100 **runs**

Hungarian Grand Prix (*auto racing*) the **Formula One** international **Grand Prix** held on the Hungaroring **circuit** near Budapest, Hungary

Huns (*association football*) a (derogatory) nickname for the Scottish **club** Rangers

hunter (*horse racing*) a horse used for hunting

hunter chase (*horse racing*) a **steeplechase** for amateur **riders** on **hunters**

Huntingdon (*horse racing*) a **National Hunt racecourse** at Brampton, near Huntingdon, Cambridgeshire, England

hurdle (*athletics*) one of the barriers which contestants jump in **hurdling**; (*horse racing*) (1) one of the barriers (lighter and lower than a **fence**) which horses jump in a **steeplechase**; (2) a **race** with these

hurdler (*athletics*) an **athlete** good at **hurdles**; (*horse racing*) a **racehorse** good at **hurdles**

hurdles (*athletics, horse racing*) a **race** over **hurdles**

hurley (*hurling*) the wooden broad-bladed **stick** used both to hit and to carry the **ball**

hurling (*sport*) an Irish **game** similar to **field hockey** played between teams of 15 using **hurleys** and a hide-covered cork **ball** [from *hurl*, "fling violently"]

Hurlingham Club (*polo*) the organization responsible for governing **polo**, first played at this London sporting club in 1874

Hurricanes (*ice hockey*) short name of the Carolina Hurricanes team

hurry-up offense (*American football*) an offensive strategy in which the minimum time is taken to **huddle** and line up between **plays**

hutch (*cricket*) colloquial term for the **pavilion** [as the place where the players eat and drink, with an implied pun on **rabbit**]

hybrid (*golf*) another term for a **utility club**

I-formation (*American football*) an offensive formation in which two **backs** line up behind the

quarterback [the formation is I-shaped, perpendicular to the **line of scrimmage**]

ICC (*cricket*) abbreviation of **International Cricket Council**

ice ax (*mountaineering*) an ax used by climbers to cut footholds in ice or compacted snow

ice dance (*ice skating*) an alternate term for **ice dancing**

ice dancing (*ice skating*) a form of **ice skating** based on the movements of ballroom dancing

ice diving (*aquatics*) **scuba** diving below the surface of frozen water

ice hockey (*sport*) an evolution of **field hockey**, played between teams of six on a **rink**, in which players equipped with **skates** and **sticks** try to send a **puck** into the **goal** of their opponents

ice rink (*ice hockey, ice skating*) a **rink** with a prepared layer of ice

ice skates (*ice hockey, ice skating*) **skates** mounted on **blades** for moving over ice

ice skating (*sport*) a sport in which competitors, either singly or in pairs, execute **figures** on a **rink**

ice the puck (*ice hockey*) to shoot the **puck** from a team's own side of the **red line** to beyond the opposing team's **goal line**, as a result of which play is stopped and a **face-off** takes place in the offending team's zone on the face-off spot nearest to where they last touched the puck

ice track (*ice skating*) a frozen track used in **speed skating**

ice yacht (*sailing*) a lightly built boat with runners and a **sail**, used in **ice yachting**

ice yachting (*sailing*) the sport of traveling over ice in an **ice yacht**

icing (*ice hockey*) the action of a player who **ices the puck**

Iditarod Race (*sled dog racing*) an annual **dogsled race** run from Anchorage to Nome, Alaska [named for the village on the historic trail followed by the race]

IM (*swimming*) abbreviation of **individual medley**

impost (*horse racing*) the **weight** carried by a horse in a **handicap**

Imps (*association football*) nickname of the English club Lincoln City [from the "Lincoln Imp," a grotesque carving of a gnome-like figure in the city's cathedral]

in chancery (*boxing, wrestling*) (of) a combatant's head held under his opponent's arm

in front (*general*) ahead in scoring

in-goal (*rugby league, rugby union*) the area between the **goal line** and the **dead-ball line**, in which a **try** may be scored

in hand (*billiards*) (of) a **ball** that has to be played from the **D**; (*croquet*) (of) a **ball** after a **roquet** has been made and until **croquet** has been taken

in-lap (*auto racing*) the **lap** made before a **pit stop**

in-off (*billiards, snooker*) a **stroke**, also known as a **losing hazard**, in which a player's own **ball** goes into a **pocket** after striking another ball

in the hole (*baseball*) (of) a **batter** due to bat in two places after the current batter

in the money (*horse racing*) among the winners, whether as **runners** or **bettors**

Ina Bauer (*ice skating*) a move similar to a **spread eagle** but executed with one knee bent and the other leg stretched out behind [invented by the German skater Ina Bauer (1941–)]

inbounds (*general*) the central, usually marked-out area of a **field** or **court**

incomplete (*American football*) (of) a **pass** that is not caught by a **receiver**

Indian dribble (*field hockey*) a **dribble** technique in which a player drives the **ball** repeatedly from right to left and left to right while moving over the **pitch** [introduced by the national team of India at the 1956 **Olympics**]

Indian wrestling (*wrestling*) (1) a form of the sport in which opponents lie on their backs side by side, head to toe, interlock one arm and leg, and attempt to force each other's leg down; (2) a form of the sport in which opponents stand face to face, interlock one arm, brace the outsides of corresponding feet against each other, and attempt to unbalance each other; (3) another term for **arm wrestling**

Indianapolis 500 (*auto racing*) a **race** of 500 miles (200 **laps**) held annually since 1911 at the Indianapolis Motor Speedway, Indiana

Indians (*baseball*) short name of the Cleveland Indians team

indicator board (*association football*) the electronic number board held up by the **fourth official** to indicate the amount of **added time** to be played or the identity of a **substitute**

indirect free kick (*association football*) a **free kick**, awarded after a **foul**, from which a **goal** cannot be scored unless the **ball** is touched by another player first (as distinct from a **direct free kick**)

individual medley (*swimming*) a **medley** raced between individual **swimmers**

individual pursuit (*cycling*) a **track race** ridden by two **riders** head-to-head

indoor bowls (*bowls*) a form of the **game** played indoors on a **carpet** with a single **rink**

indoor cricket (*cricket*) a form of the sport adapted for play indoors

indoor football (*association football*) a form of the **game** played indoors, usually as **five-a-side**

indoor hockey (*field hockey*) a form of the **game** adapted for play indoors, with up to seven players a side

indoor target archery (*archery*) a form of **target archery** staged indoors

indoor volleyball (*volleyball*) the original indoor form of the sport, as distinct from **beach volleyball**

Indy car (*auto racing*) the low-slung, fenderless (open-wheel) **racecar** that competes in the **Indianapolis 500**

Indy 500 (*auto racing*) colloquial name of the **Indianapolis 500**

infield (*auto racing, horse racing*) the area enclosed by the **racetrack**; (*baseball*) the area enclosed within the **baselines**; (*cricket*) the part of the **field** near the **wicket**

infielder (*baseball*) any player positioned around the **infield**

infighting (*boxing*) engaging at very close quarters, so that it is impossible to throw full-length **punches**

injury time (*association football*) **stoppage time** that is added on to the regulation 90 minutes of a **match** to make up for time lost because of injuries

inline skates (*roller skating*) another term for **rollerblades**

inner (*archery, shooting*) the part of the **target** next to the **bull**

inning (*baseball*) a turn at **batting** for each team

innings (*cricket*) a turn at **batting** for a **batsman** or for a whole team

·**inquiry** (*horse racing*) shortening of **stewards' inquiry**

inrun (*skiing*) the portion of a **ski jump** during which the skier travels down the ramp

inside center (*rugby union*) the **center** who plays between the **fly half** and the **outside center**

inside edge (*cricket*) a deflection of the **ball** from the inner edge of the **bat**; (*ice skating*) the inner of the two edges of the **blade** of a **skate**

inside left (*association football, field hockey*) an attacking position on the left side toward the center of the **field**

inside right (*association football, field hockey*) an attacking position on the right side toward the center of the **field**

inside-the-park home run (*baseball*) a **home run** scored without the **ball** going beyond the field of play

inside track (*general*) the inner **track** of a **racetrack** or **racecourse**, which is shorter because of a curve and therefore advantageous

inspection (*horse racing*) an examination of the **course** by **stewards** before a **race** or **meeting** when **racing** is in doubt because of bad weather

instant replay (*general*) another term for an **action reply**

insurance (*general*) a tactical or strategic form of play that enables a team to build up an unbeatable or unmatchable **lead**

inswinger (*association football*) a **ball** kicked so as to swing in toward the **goal** or the center of the **pitch**; (*cricket*) a **ball** bowled so as to swerve from **off** to **leg**

intentional grounding (*American football*) the **offense** of deliberately throwing the **ball** to a place where it cannot be caught in order to avoid being **sacked**

Inter (*association football*) short name of the Italian **club** Inter Milan

Intercalated Games (*Olympics*) the special **Olympic Games** held in Athens in 1906 to commemorate the 10th anniversary of the birth of the modern Games [they were intercalated, or inserted in the calendar, between the quadrennial 1904 and 1908 Games]

interception (*American football*) a **pass** thrown by the **quarterback** that is caught by a member of the **defense**

interchange (*Australian Rules, rugby league*) another term for a **substitute**

intercollegiate football (*American football*) another term for **college football**

intermediates (*auto racing*) tires used in changeable weather, having more grooves and tread than dry-weather tires but fewer than **wets**

international (*general*) (1) (of) a contest between teams of different countries; (2) a participant in such a contest

International Cricket Council (*cricket*) the governing body of the world **game**, with headquarters at **Lord's**, founded in 1909 as the Imperial Cricket Conference and until 1993 administered by the MCC

International Olympic Committee (*Olympics*) the body that administers the modern **Olympic Games**, set up in 1894 and comprising representatives of national Olympic associations from all of the member countries

interstate (*baseball*) a **batting average** below 100 [all U.S. interstate highways have two-digit numbers]

interval running (*athletics*) another term for **interval training**

interval training (*athletics*) alternate fast and slow running at timed intervals in a single session, carried out as training for **marathons** and other **long-distance races**

intervarsity (*general*) (of) a **game** or **match** between universities, especially Oxford and Cambridge

inverted cross (*gymnastics*) a holding move on the **rings** in a **handstand** position, with the arms stretched out perpendicular to the body

invitational (*general*) a **match** or contest open only to those invited

inward (*swimming*) a **dive** in which the **diver** starts with his back to the water and continues with a rotation toward the **board**

inwick (*curling*) a **wick** in which the **stone** slides close to the **tee**

IOC (*Olympics*) abbreviation of **International Olympic Committee**

ippon (*judo, karate*) a winning score of one full **point**, awarded for a perfectly executed **throw** or **hold** [Japanese *ip* (from *ichi*), "one," and *pon*, a numerical counter for something long, as a staff or sword]

Irish (*rugby union*) short name of the English **club** London Irish

Irish Derby (*horse racing*) an annual **race** run at the **Curragh** since 1866 [named for the English **Derby**]

Irish Grand National (*horse racing*) an annual **race** run at **Fairyhouse** since 1870 [named for the English **Grand National**]

Irish whip (*wrestling*) a one-handed **throw** in which the arm is whipped back and forth forcing the opponent to execute an aerial **somersault**

iron (*golf*) a **club** with a thin metal head, used for shorter **shots** than a **wood**

Iron (*association football*) nickname of the English **club** Scunthorpe United [from the town's iron and steel industry]

iron man (*athletics*) a powerful **athlete**

Ironman (*general*) a test of endurance in the form of a **triathlon** at a **surf** carnival, held in Hawaii since 1978 and comprising a swim in the sea of 2.4 miles (3.9km), a **cycle race** of 112 miles (180km) around the island of Oahu, and a **marathon**

ironmongery (*mountaineering*) colloquial term for all the metal tools and equipment used for **climbing**, such as **ice axes**, **crampons**, and **pitons**

irons (*horse racing*) colloquial term for stirrups

Irons (*association football*) occasional nickname of the English **club** West Ham United [of the same origin as the better-known nickname **Hammers**]

Ironwoman (*general*) the semi-official title of a female winner of an **Ironman**

Iroquois Cup (*lacrosse*) the **cup** awarded since 1890 to the winners of the annual English **club** championship [named for the Iroquois people of Canada from whom the **game** was adopted]

Isis (*rowing*) the reserve **eight** of Oxford University, who race their Cambridge counterpart, **Goldie**, immediately before the **Boat Race** [name of the Thames River at Oxford]

Island Games (*general*) a biennial festival of sporting contests similar to the **regional games** of the Olympics held since 1985 for competitors from an island community, the **venue** varying but always on an island

Islanders (*ice hockey*) short name of the New York Islanders team

Isthmian Games (*general*) a festival of sporting contests similar to the **Olympic Games** held in ancient Greece on the Isthmus of Corinth

Italian Grand Prix (*auto racing*) the **Formula One** international **Grand Prix** held on the **circuit** at Monza, Italy

Ivy League (*American football*) a **conference** of colleges and universities in the northeastern United States whose teams largely founded and developed **college football** in the late 19th century [from the nickname of the colleges themselves]

jab (*boxing*) a short straight **punch**

jack (*bowls*) the small white (occasionally yellow) **object ball**, which in **crown green** bowls has a **bias**

Jack Adams Award (*ice hockey*) the **trophy** awarded annually to the **coach** of the year [named after Jack Adams, **manager** of the Detroit Red Wings in the late 1940s and early 1950s]

jack high (*bowls*) a **bowl** that is level with the **jack** [a term now officially obsolete]

jacket (*horse racing*) the loose-fitting silk or satin blouse (formerly jacket) worn by a **jockey** in the distinctive colors of the **owner** of the **racehorse**

jackknife (*swimming*) a **dive** in which the **swimmer** bends his body in two, grasps or touches his ankles, then straightens his body out again on entering the water

jackpot (*general*) a cash **prize** won on certain conditions, especially one that accumulates

jaffa (*cricket*) a well-bowled **ball** that is likely to **take a wicket** [said to be so called because "sweeter" than the other balls in a **bowler's spell**, as a Jaffa orange is sweeter than others]

Jags (*association football*) colloquial name of the Scottish **clubs** Inverness Caledonian Thistle and Partick Thistle [local term for the jagged leaves of a thistle, the Scottish national emblem]

Jaguars (*American football*) short name of the Jacksonville Jaguars team

jai alai (*sport*) a type of **pelota** resembling **handball**, played with a long curved basket strapped to the wrist [Spanish, from Basque *jai*, "festival," and *alai*, "merry"]

jam (*mountaineering*) the act of twisting a hand or foot in a crack to secure a **hold**

Jam Tarts (*association football*) nickname of the Scottish **club** Heart of Midlothian [rhyming slang for **Hearts**, with an additional reference to the maroon color of the team's shirts]

Jambos (*association football*) nickname for **supporters** of the Scottish **club** Heart of Midlothian [variant form of **Jam Tarts**]

James Norris Memorial Trophy (*ice hockey*) the **trophy** awarded to the outstanding **defenseman**

throughout a **season** [named for James Norris, owner of the Detroit Red Wings from 1932 to 1952]

jamming (*baseball*) a **pitch** aimed at the body of the **batter** so as to cramp his swing and rob him of power to hit the **ball**

Japanese Grand Prix (*auto racing*) the **Formula One** international **Grand Prix** held on the **circuit** at Suzuka, Japan

jar (*horse racing*) another term for **firm going**, especially as adversely affecting horses who perform better on softer ground

javelin (*athletics*) (1) a light spear for throwing; (2) the **field event** in which it is thrown

jaws (*snooker*) the corners of the **cushion** either side of a **pocket**

Jazz (*basketball*) short name of the Utah Jazz team

jenny (*billiards, snooker*) an **in-off** into one of the middle **pockets** made with the **object ball** close to a **cushion**

jerk (*weightlifting*) the second phase of the **clean and jerk** movement in which the **weightlifter** lifts the **barbell** from shoulder height to above his head with straightened arms and legs

Jesters Cup (*fives*) the **trophy** awarded annually to the winner of the **Rugby fives** national **championship** [named for the Jesters Club, founded in 1928 as a **cricket club** but now mostly associated with **court games**]

jet ski (*aquatics*) a jet-propelled craft, comparable to a motorcycle, used to skim across the surface of the water on a **keel** resembling a **ski**

jet skiing (*aquatics*) the riding of a **jet ski** in a competition or as a form of recreation

Jets (*American football*) short name of the New York Jets team

jeu de paume (*sport*) a former name for **real tennis** [French, *jeu de paume*, "game of the palm (of the hand)"]

jeu provençal (*sport*) a **game** similar to **boules** played in Provence, France [French *jeu provençal*, "Provençal game"]

jib (*sailing*) a triangular **sail** stretched in front of the **foremast**

jibe (*sailing*) another spelling of **gybe**

jigger (*golf*) a former type of **iron** used for **approach shots**

Jillaroos (*field hockey*) nickname of the Australian national under-21 women's team [from *jillaroos*, female novices on a sheep or cattle station, as an equivalent of the male *jackaroos*, from *Jack* and *kangaroo*, the national animal]

Jim Thorpe Trophy (*American football*) the **trophy** awarded annually since 1955 to the **Most Valuable Player** in the **National Football League** [named for the all-around **athlete** and talented football player Jim Thorpe (1888–1953)]

jink (*rugby union*) a quick deceptive turn, as made on getting the **ball** out from a **ruck**

jock (*general*) (1) colloquial term for a **jockstrap**; (2) colloquial term for a **sportsman**

Jock Scott (*angling*) a type of **artificial fly** [named for Jock Scott, the Scottish fisherman who designed it in the mid-19th century]

jockey (*association football*) to move backward, forward, or sideways in order to cover changes in direction by **opposition** players; (*horse racing*) a (usually professional) **rider** in a **horse race** [pet form of the male name *Jock*, applied to a young male, as jockeys were originally boys]

jockey cap (*horse racing*) a reinforced cap with a long peak, worn by **jockeys**

Jockey Club (*horse racing*) the organization founded at **Newmarket** in about 1750 to promote and regulate the sport and subsequently becoming the controlling authority for **flat racing** [in 2007 its regulatory powers passed to the **British Horseracing Authority**]

jockstrap (*general*) a genital support worn by **sportsmen** [from *jock*, slang term for the genitals, and *strap*]

jodhpur boots (*equestrianism*) ankle-high boots worn with **jodhpurs**

jodhpurs (*equestrianism*) riding breeches that are loose around the hip but tight-fitting from the knee to the ankle [originally worn in Jodhpur, northwestern India]

jods (*equestrianism*) colloquial shortening of **jodhpurs**

Joeys (*field hockey*) nickname of the Australian national junior men's team [from *joey*, a young kangaroo, the national animal]

jog (*athletics*) to run at a slow, steady pace, especially for exercise

jogging (*athletics*) running at a slow, steady pace, especially for exercise

John Player League (*cricket*) a former equivalent of the **Pro40 League** [name of sponsor]

join the dots (*cricket*) to bowl a **maiden over** [a **delivery** which scores no **run** is a **dot ball**, so that the six dots (in two columns of three) conventionally entered by the **scorer** for a maiden over can be joined up to form a capital "M" for "maiden"]

judge (*angling*) a type of **artificial fly**; (*boxing*) one of the three **ringside** officials who keep a record of the **scoring hits** in a **bout**; (*greyhound racing, horse racing*) the official who determines the finishing order in a **race**; (*weightlifting*) one of the three officials who decide whether a **lift** is valid or not; (*wrestling*) one of the three officials in charge of a **bout**, the others being the **chairman** and the **referee**

judo (*sport*) a Japanese **martial art** that evolved

from **jujitsu** as a physical discipline based on unarmed self-defense techniques involving principles of movement and balance [Japanese *ju*, "gentleness," and *do*, "way"]

judogi (*judo*) the costume of loose-fitting jacket and pants secured by a belt worn by a **judoka**

judoka (*judo*) a practitioner of or expert in **judo**

Jug, The (*horse racing*) colloquial name of the **Little Brown Jug** harness race

juggle (*baseball*) to fumble a hit **ball** without dropping it, thus failing to prevent a **runner** from reaching a **base**

jujitsu (*sport*) a Japanese **martial art** that evolved as system of unarmed combat, now often practiced in physical training, in which the aim is to turn an opponent's strength and weight to their disadvantage [Japanese *ju*, "gentle," and *jutsu*, "skill"]

juke (*American football*) to trick an opposing player by pretending to make one move but actually making another

jukskei (*sport*) a South African sport similar to **quoits**, in which bottle-shaped pegs (originally yoke pins) are thrown at stakes fixed in the ground [Afrikaans *yuk*, "yoke," and *skei*, "pin"]

Jules Rimet Trophy (*association football*) the **trophy** awarded from 1930 to 1970 that preceded the **World Cup** [donated by French **FIFA** president Jules Rimet (1871–1956)]

jumar (*mountaineering*) (1) a clamp which grips the rope when a weight is applied but which runs freely when it is removed; (2) a climb using such clamps [of Swiss origin]

jump (*athletics*) (1) a jump made as the main part of a movement or exercise, as a **high jump** or **long jump**; (2) a jump as a the third and final phase of the **triple jump**; (*general*) (1) a natural or man-made obstacle that has to be jumped over or across, as a **fence** in **horse racing**; (2) a leap in the air as part of a **routine**, as in **ice skating**; (3) a leap to catch, hit, or throw a **ball**, as in **basketball**; (4) a place from which a jump is made, as for a **ski jump**; (*parachuting*) a descent by **parachute**

jump ball (*basketball*) a **ball** thrown up by the **referee** between opposing players to restart the **game**

jump cue (*pool*) a **cue** used to make the **cue ball** jump

jump hook (*basketball*) a **hook shot** made while the player's feet are off the ground

jump jockey (*horse racing*) a **jockey** who rides in **steeplechases**

jump-off (*equestrianism*) in **showjumping**, an extra **round** to decide the winner if two or more **riders** tie for first place

jump racing (*horse racing*) **racing** over **jumps**, as distinct from **flat racing**

jump shot (*basketball, handball*) a **shot** made when the player's feet are off the ground; (*billiards, snooker*) a **shot** that makes the **cue ball** jump over another **ball**

jump the gun (*athletics*) to make a **false start** [by leaving before the **starting gun**]

jump turn (*skiing*) a turn made while jumping

jumper (*basketball*) colloquial term for a **jump shot**; (*general*) a person or animal, such as a horse, that jumps; (*rugby union*) a player who jumps to gain the **ball** in a **lineout**

jumping jack (*athletics*) a jumping exercise in which the legs are spread apart then brought together while the arms are swung above the head then back down to the sides

jumping pole (*athletics*) the pole used in the **pole vault**

jumpmaster (*parachuting*) a person in charge of parachutists

jungle (*golf*) colloquial term for tall **rough**, bushes, or trees

junior (*boxing*) lighter than the standard for a particular **weight**

junior bantamweight (*boxing*) the professional **weight** category of maximum 52kg (115lb)

junior circuit (*baseball*) colloquial term for the **American League** [so called as formed after the **National League**]

junior featherweight (*boxing*) the professional **weight** category of maximum 55kg (122lb)

junior flyweight (*boxing*) the professional **weight** category of maximum 49kg (108lb)

junior lightweight (*boxing*) the professional **weight** category of maximum 59kg (130lb)

junior middleweight (*boxing*) the professional **weight** category of maximum 70kg (154lb)

Junior TT (*motorcycle racing*) the lesser annual **TT race** [for smaller **bikes** than in the **Senior TT**]

junior welterweight (*boxing*) the professional **weight** category of maximum 63.5kg (140lb)

juvenile (*horse racing*) a two-year-old horse

K (*baseball*) colloquial abbreviation for a **strikeout**

k point (*skiing*) the point at which the hill flattens out in a **ski jump**, expressed as so many meters from the **takeoff** and for a **normal hill** rated as around 90 meters [part-translation of German *K-Punkt*, shortening of *kritischer Punkt*, "critical point"]

kabaddi (*sport*) a sport of Indian origin played between two teams of 7 players, in which players in turn make "raids" into the opposing teams' **court** in which they try to touch one of their opponents while chanting "kabbadi" to show that they are holding their breath as the rules require [said to derive from a word related to Kannada *kabalisu*, "to gulp"]

kaboom (*trampolining*) a type of **somersault** in which one part of the body lands on the **bed** immediately after another, such as the heels after the back [imitative of the action]

kahuna (*surfing*) a fictitious "god" of the sport [Hawaiian *kahuna*, "priest," "wise man"]

kamikaze (*surfing*) a deliberate **wipeout** [from the Japanese suicide pilots in World War II]

Kangaroos (*Australian Rules*) short name of the North Melbourne Kangaroos team; (*rugby league*) nickname of the Australian national team [from the Australian national animal]

karabiner (*mountaineering*) another spelling of **carabiner**

karate (*sport*) a Japanese **martial art** as a form of self-defense using blows of the hands and kicks of the feet, together with special breathing and shouts [Japanese *kara*, "empty," and *te*, "hand," denoting a weaponless sport]

karate chop (*karate*) a sharp, slanting blow of the hand

karateka (*karate*) a practitioner of or expert in **karate**

kart (*auto racing*) shortening of **go-kart**

karting (*auto racing*) the sport of racing in **go-karts**

kata (*karate*) a formal series of practice exercises and movements

kayak (*canoeing*) a type of small **canoe** based on an Inuit (Eskimo) original and propelled by a **paddle** with a blade on each end (or on one end only)

kayaker (*canoeing*) a person who paddles in a **kayak**

kayaking (*canoeing*) the sport or recreation of paddling in a **kayak**

kayo (*boxing*) a **knockout** [phonetic spelling of KO]

keel (*rowing*) the structure of the bottom of the boat that runs from **bow** to **stern**; (*sailing*) the fixed, fin-like structure on the bottom of the **hull** that stabilizes the boat

keelboat (*sailing*) a boat with a heavy **keel** that provides weight to offset the **sails**

keep goal (*association football*) to act as **goalkeeper**

keep one's end up (*cricket*) to be content to keep one's **wicket** standing without trying to score

keep wicket (*cricket*) to act as **wicketkeeper**

keeper (*American football*) an offensive **play** in which the **quarterback** keeps the **ball** and runs with it instead of attempting a **pass** to his receiver; (*association football*) shortening of **goalkeeper**; (*cricket*) shortening of **wicketkeeper**

keepnet (*angling*) a cone-shaped net in which fish that have been caught are kept in the water until they can be weighed

keepy-uppy (*association football*) the feat of keeping the **ball** from touching the ground by repeatedly flicking it up with the feet, knees, or chest

kegler (*general*) a person who plays **tenpin bowling**, **skittles**, or any related **game** [German *Kegel*, "skittle"]

keirin (*cycling*) a **track event** over 8 laps in which the **riders** follow a motorcyle **pacer** for the first 51/2 laps then sprint the remaining 21/2 laps after the motorcycle leaves the **track** [Japanese *keirin*, "bicycle race"]

Kelso (*horse racing*) a **National Hunt racecourse** at Kelso, southeastern Scotland

Kempton (*horse racing*) short name of **Kempton Park**

Kempton Park (*horse racing*) a **flat** and **National Hunt racecourse** at Sunbury, near London, England

kendo (*sport*) a Japanese **martial art** that uses cuts or thrusts from a bamboo sword to score blows on one's opponent [Japanese *ken*, "sword," and *do*, "way"]

kendoka (*kendo*) a practitioner of or expert in **kendo**

kennel (*greyhound racing*) a business that owns and races greyhounds

Kentucky Derby (*horse racing*) a **race** for three-year-old horses, run annually at Churchill Downs, Louisville, Kentucky, since 1875

Kentucky Futurity (*horse racing*) a **harness race** for three-year-old **trotters**, run annually at the Red Mile, Lexington, Kentucky, since 1893

Kentucky Three-Day Event (*equestrianism*) the nation's prime **three-day event**, held annually at the Kentucky Horse Park, Lexington, Kentucky, since 1978

kermesse (*cycling*) a **criterium** raced around a short town-center **circuit**, especially in Belgium [Flemish *kermesse*, "kermis" (an annual fair, literally "church mass")]

KERS (*auto racing*) acronym of kinetic energy recovery system, used by drivers to increase speed on a **lap**, as when overtaking [the system was abandoned in 2010]

key (*basketball*) the (usually painted) area on the **court** that includes the **foul lane** and the **foul circle** [so called because in shape it resembles a keyhole]

kick (*athletics*) a sudden increase in speed, as in the final **lap** of a **long-distance race**; (*shooting*) the recoil of a gun when fired; (*snooker*) a bad contact between the **cue ball** and the **object ball**, caused by dust or chalk on the **billiard table**

kick-and-rush (*association football*) (of) a type of **play** that is more energetic than skillful

kick from the hand (*rugby league, rugby union*) a kick of the **ball** as it is let fall from the hand of the kicker

kick-in (*association football*) a practice in **goal** shooting before the start of a **match**

kick-nose (*skateboarding*) the curved front end of the **skateboard**

kick out (*basketball*) to pass the **ball** from inside the **foul lane** to a player outside it

kick shot (*pool*) a **shot** in which the **cue ball** bounces off one or more **cushions** before hitting the **object ball**

kick-tail (*skateboarding*) the curved back end of the **skateboard**

kick turn (*skateboarding*) a 180-degree turn on the **skateboard** made by pressing down and pivoting on the back wheels; (*skiing*) a turn in which one **ski** is raised so that its tail touches the ground and then pivoted to point in the desired direction

kickabout (*association football*) an informal **game**

kickback (*horse racing*) loose material thrown up from the **track** by a galloping horse

kickball (*baseball*) a simple form of the **game** using a larger **ball** which is kicked, not batted

kickboxing (*sport*) a **martial art** of American origin similar to **karate** in which combatants kick with bare feet and punch with gloved fists

kicker (*cricket*) a **ball** that rebounds sharply from the **pitch**; (*general*) a player whose job is to take special kicks, as in **set pieces**; (*skiing, snowboarding*) a steep ramp used to propel performers into the air

kickflip (*skateboarding, snowboarding*) a **jump** into the air that makes the **board** rotate before the jumper lands on it

kicking coach (*rugby union*) a **coach** in kicking skills, and especially **place kicks**

kicking game (*rugby union*) play in which the **ball** is primarily advanced by being kicked, as against a **handling game**

kicking tee (*rugby union*) a plastic device used to hold the **ball** stationary for a **place kick**

kickoff (*American football*) a kick from the 35-yard line made at the start of each **half**; (*association football*) a kick to a teammate from the **center spot** made at the start or resumption of a **game**

kickout (*surfing*) a maneuver executed by pressing down on the rear of the **surfboard** and then turning it so as to ride up and over the crest of a wave

kickwax (*skiing*) another term for **gripwax**

Kilbeggan (*horse racing*) a **National Hunt racecourse** at Kilbeggan, Co. Westmeath, Ireland

kilian (*ice skating*) a fast **ice dance** performed by a pair of skaters side by side [origin uncertain]

kill (*association football, field hockey*) to stop a **ball** dead; (*badminton, tennis*) a **smash** that cannot be returned; (*boxing*) a **knockout**; (*trampolin-*

ing) the act of absorbing the recoil from the **bed** by flexing the body at the hips, knees, and ankles; (*volleyball*) another term for a **spike**

kill-devil (*angling*) an **artificial fly** that spins in the water like a wounded fish

Killarney (*horse racing*) a **flat** and **National Hunt racecourse** at Killarney, Co. Kerry, Ireland

Killies (*association football*) short name of the Scottish **club** Kilmarnock

kilo (*cycling*) colloquial term for a 1km **time trial**

King George (*horse racing*) short name of the **King George VI and Queen Elizabeth Diamond Stakes**

King George V Gold Cup (*equestrianism*) the **trophy** awarded for an international men's **showjumping** competition held at **Hickstead** since 1934 [named for George V (1865–1936)]

King George VI and Queen Elizabeth Diamond Stakes (*horse racing*) an annual **race at Ascot** founded in 1951 to mark the Festival of Britain [named for George VI (1895–1952) and his wife Queen Elizabeth (the Queen Mother) (1900–2002)]

King George VI Chase (*horse racing*) an annual **race** run traditionally on Boxing Day (December 26) at **Kempton Park** since 1947 [named for George VI (1895–1952)]

King of the Mountains (*cycling*) the title given to the **leader** in the competition for **points** gained on **climbs** in the **Tour de France** or **Giro d'Italia**

king pair (*cricket*) a **golden duck** in both **innings** of a **match**

King Willow (*sport*) a personification of **cricket** [from the **willow** from which the bat is traditionally made]

Kings (*basketball*) short name of the Sacramento Kings team; (*ice hockey*) short name of the Los Angeles Kings team

Kinnaird Cup (*fives*) the **cup** awarded since 1926 to the winner of an annual contest in **Eton fives** [donated by Lord Kinnaird (1880–1972)]

kip (*gymnastics*) a movement in which the body is rapidly straightened from an inverted **pike** position by pushing the hips forward and the legs back [origin uncertain, but perhaps related to Low German *Kippe*, "point"]

kiss (*billiards, snooker*) a light contact between two **balls** in motion

kiss the mistress (*bowls*) to lightly graze the **jack** [*mistress* in former sense "jack"]

kit (*general*) a set of sports clothes or equipment

kite (*general*) a type of specially designed **parachute** on which a person is suspended when being towed in a sport such as **kitesurfing** or **parakiting**

kiteboarding (*sport*) another term for **kitesurfing**

kitesurfing (*sport*) a sport similar to **windsurfing**

in which a person is towed on a **board** like a **wakeboard** behind a steerable **kite**

kitty (*bowls*) another term for the **jack**

Kiwis (*general*) a New Zealand sports team [from the country's national bird]

knee drop (*trampolining*) a landing position on the knees and shins with the rest of the body vertical

kneeboard (*water skiing*) a short **board** like a **surfboard** on which the **rider** kneels while sitting on his heels

Knickerbockers (*basketball*) short name of the New York Knickerbockers team

Knicks (*basketball*) short colloquial name for the **Knickerbockers**

Knights (*rugby league*) short name of the English **club** City Knights

knock (*cricket*) the **score** achieved by a **batsman** in a single **innings**; (*cycling*) another term for **bonk**

knock-back (*association football*) a downward **header** for a nearby teammate to take on

knock-down (*association football*) a downward **header** for a teammate to run to

knock in (*polo*) to put the **ball** back into play from one's own **backline**

knock-on (*rugby league, rugby union*) a contravention of the rules in which the **ball** is knocked forward with the hand or arm

knock out (*general*) to defeat in a **knockout competition**

knock the balls about (*billiards*) to play an informal **game**

knock up (*cricket*) to score **runs** rapidly

knock-up (*squash, tennis*) a practice **game** before a **match**

knockout (*boxing*) a blow that renders the opponent unconscious or incapable of recovering before the end of the **count**

knockout competition (*general*) a contest in which the losers in each **round** are eliminated

knots (*surfing*) the cuts and bruises sustained by a **surfer** that serve as a status symbol

knuckleball (*baseball*) a slow **pitch** with an unpredictable trajectory, effected by gripping the **ball** with the fingertips

knuckler (*baseball*) colloquial term for a **knuckleball**

knur and spell (*sport*) a **game** resembling **trapball** played chiefly in northern England in which a knur (**ball**) is thrown up by a spell (**trap**) to be hit with a **stick** or **bat**

KO (*boxing*) abbreviation of **knockout**

koka (*judo*) the lowest **score** awarded for a **throw** or **hold**, worth three **points** [Japanese *koka*, "result"]

kook (*surfing*) a novice or incompetent **surfer**

Kookaburras (*field hockey*) colloquial name of the Australian national men's team [from the bird associated with Australia]

kop (*association football*) a high bank of **terraces** for standing spectators at a **match**, especially that originally at **Anfield** [from the hill Spion Kop, near Ladysmith, South Africa, the site of a British defeat during the Boer War]

korfball (*sport*) a **game** of Dutch origin resembling **basketball** played between two teams of eight, the aim being to score **goals** in suspended baskets made of woven rattan or wicker [Dutch *korf*, "basket," and *bal*, "ball"]

Kovacs (*gymnastics*) a **flyaway** on the **horizontal bar** and **asymmetric bars** in which the **gymnast**, after swinging around the bar, releases the bar, performs a back **somersault** in the air, then regrasps the bar [introduced in 1979 by the Hungarian gymnast Peter Kovacs]

krav maga (*sport*) a form of self-defense using **martial art** techniques that was originally developed for Israeli defense forces as a system of unarmed combat [Hebrew *krav maga*, "contact fighting"]

kumite (*karate*) a form of **sparring** similar to that in **boxing** except that attacks are stopped short of contact with the **target** [Japanese *kumi*, "set," and *te*, "hand"]

Kumuls (*rugby league*) nickname of the Papua New Guinea national team [from the bird of paradise native to the islands]

kung fu (*sport*) a **martial art** of Chinese origin covering both armed and unarmed combat techniques and self-defense [Chinese *kung*, "merit," and *fu*, "master"]

kyu (*judo, karate*) one of the novice grades of proficiency [Japanese *kyu*, "class"]

kyudo (*archery*) a form of the sport designed to develop concentration and coordination [Japanese *kyu*, "bow," and *do*, "way"]

lacks (*sport*) colloquial term for **lacrosse**

lacrosse (*sport*) a **field game** of French-Canadian origin played by men and women (with different rules for each) in which a **crosse** is used to throw, catch, and **cradle** the **ball** and drive it into the opponents' **goal** [Canadian French (*le jeu de*) *la crosse*, "(the game of) the hooked stick"]

lad (*horse racing*) shortening of **stable lad**

ladder tournament (*general*) a **tournament** in which players are ranked according to performance and can move up only by defeating a higher-ranked player

Ladies' Day (*horse racing*) colloquial name of the day when the **Ascot Gold Cup** is run at **Royal Ascot** or the **Cheltenham Gold Cup** at **Cheltenham**, the emphasis being on fashion rather than **racing**

Ladies' Plate (*rowing*) the **trophy** awarded to the

winner of a **race** for men's **eights** at Henley Royal Regatta [first offered as a **prize** in 1845 by the local ladies of Henley]

Lady Byng Memorial Trophy (*ice hockey*) the **trophy** awarded annually to the player best combining clean play with a high standard of skill [presented in 1925 by Lady Byng, née Marie Evelyn Moreton (1870–1925), wife of Lord Byng (1862–1935), governor general of Canada (1921–26)]

lag (*billiards*) another term for **string**

lag a putt (*golf*) to play a **putt** with the aim of getting the **ball** near the **hole** but not necessarily in it

Lake Placid (*Olympics*) a noted **bobsled** course in New York State that was the **venue** of the **Winter Olympics** in 1932 and 1980 and remains so for **world championships**

Lakers (*basketball*) short name of the Los Angeles Lakers team

lamé (*fencing*) the metal mesh that covers the **target** area of a fencer, used with electronic recording equipment [French]

Lance Todd Trophy (*rugby league*) the **trophy** awarded to the **man of the match** in the **Challenge Cup final** [named in memory of the British player Lance Todd (1883–1942)]

land (*general*) to win a **race** or a **prize**

land yacht (*sailing*) a wheeled boat with **sails** for running on land, usually along beaches

landing mat (*gymnastics*) the mat on which a **gymnast** lands on completing a **routine** on **apparatus**

landing net (*angling*) a special net in which fish are landed after being caught.

lane (*athletics*) a marked division of the **track** within which an **athlete** must stay when running a **sprint race**; (*cycling*) a marked division of the **track** in a **velodrome**; (*swimming*) a marked channel of a swimming pool in which a **swimmer** must stay when competing in a **race**; (*tenpin bowling*) the smooth wooden runway along which the **balls** are bowled to the **pins**

langlauf (*skiing*) another term for **cross-country skiing** [German *lang*, "long," and *Lauf*, "run"]

lanterne rouge (*cycling*) the **rider** in last place in the **general classification** in a **stage race** [French *lanterne rouge*, "red light," from the red light on the rear of a train]

lap (*general*) a completed **circuit** of a **track** or **course**

lap of honor (*general*) a celebratory circuit of a **field** or **track** made by a team or individual competitor after a victory

lap shot (*cricket*) a **hit** by a **batsman** that goes straight into the lap of the **wicketkeeper**

lapped (*cycling*) more than one **lap** behind the **leader** in a **track race**

lappery (*sport*) colloquial term for **auto racing** [in which contestants complete **laps** of the **racetrack**]

large hill (*skiing*) the larger of the two **ski-jump** hills in the **Winter Olympics**, usually measuring 120m

Laser (*sailing*) a class of single-handed **dinghy** introduced in 1971 [apparently random name]

last man (*association football*) a sole **defender** between an **attacker** and the **goal**, who commits a **foul** if he prevents the attacker from taking a clear opportunity to score a goal; (*cricket*) the last **batsman** of his side to **go in**

late cut (*cricket*) a **cut** with a **stroke** played later than usual

late tackle (*association football*) a mistimed **tackle** made after the **ball** has been played and making contact with the player rather than with the ball, so resulting in a **foul**

lateral (*American football*) a sideways or backward **pass**

lateral water hazard (*golf*) a **water hazard** that runs parallel to the **hole**

lath (*equestrianism*) a thin white strip marking the boundary of a **water jump**, used to indicate if a horse fails to clear the jump.

Latics (*association football*) colloquial name of the English **clubs** Oldham Athletic and Wigan Athletic [apparently a form of *athletic*]

laugher (*baseball*) an easily won **match** [it was so easy to win it was laughable]

law 29 (*rugby union*) an imaginary law relating to conduct on the **field** that effectively equates to a law of common sense

lawn bowls (*bowls*) the outdoor **game**, as distinct from **indoor bowls**

lawn tennis (*sport*) the formal name of **tennis**, as distinct from **real tennis**

lay (*angling*) to lower a weight or **shot** into the water until it rests on the bottom with the **hook** and **bait**; (*horse racing*) to place a **bet** on a horse in a **race**

lay-in (*basketball*) a **shot** made at the top of a **jump**, usually by bouncing the **ball** off the **backboard** into the **basket**

lay off (*association football, field hockey*) to pass the **ball** to a teammate who is in a better position to make progress with it

lay on (*association football, field hockey*) to pass the **ball** acurately so that a teammate can make the next move

lay-up (*basketball*) a **shot** made at the top of a **jump** in which the **ball** enters the **basket** after being gently tipped onto the **backboard**; (*croquet*) a **shot** that leaves the **balls** in a position that favors the player but puts his opponent at a disadvantage; (*golf*) a **shot** played deliberately short of a **hazard** or **green**

layback (*mountaineering*) a method of climbing a crack by leaning back with the feet against the rock face; (*surfing*) an extreme maneuver in which the **surfer** lies back on a wave

layback spin (*ice skating*) an **upright spin** made with the back arched

layout (*gymnastics*) a position in which the body is fully extended, either straight or slightly arched; (*swimming*) a **dive** in which the body and legs are straight, with the feet together and the toes pointed

Laytown (*horse racing*) a **flat racecourse** at Laytown, Co. Meath, Ireland

lb (*cricket*) abbreviation of **leg before**

lbw (*cricket*) abbreviation of **leg before wicket**

lead ["first place"] (*bowls*) the first **bowler** in a team, who has the advantage of bowling the **jack**; (*boxing*) the first **punch** of two or more from the same fist; (*curling*) the member of the **rink** who plays first; (*equestrianism*) the leg that the horse puts first in a **canter**; (*general*) (1) the position of a competitor ahead of others in a **race**; (2) the distance by which a competitor is ahead of others; (*mountaineering*) the climber who goes first, attaching safety aids such as **belays**

lead ["metal"] (*angling*) the lead weight or piece of **shot** used at the end of a **fishing line**

lead change (*equestrianism*) a maneuver in **dressage** in which the horse's **lead** changes

lead dog (*sled dog racing*) the dog in the front place in the team formation

lead-off hitter (*baseball*) the player who bats first for the batting side

lead-out (*cycling*) the tactic whereby a **rider** allows a teammate to **slipstream** behind him as he rides at high speed in order to give him an advantage as he prepares to go into a **sprint**; (*greyhound racing*) the official who parades the dogs before a **race** and who retrieves them after it

lead pass (*association football*) a **pass** into the space in which a teammate has run forward, so creating a potential opportunity to score a **goal**

lead through (*mountaineering*) to act as an alternate **leader** over a particular stretch of rock

lead with one's chin (*boxing*) to adopt an awkward **stance** that makes one vulnerable to **punches** [a **boxer** normally leads with his fists]

leader (*angling*) a translucent connection between the end of a **fishing line** and the **hook** or **fly**; (*general*) (1) the player or animal (as a horse or dog) in the front place in a team; (2) the player or team ahead of others in a **race** or **match**

leaderboard (*golf*) the **scoreboard** that lists the names and **scores** of the current **leaders** in a competition

league (*general*) a group of **clubs** or teams who compete with one another for a **championship**

League Cup (*association football*) the former name of the **Carling Cup**

league football (*Australian Rules, rugby league*) the **game** as played in **leagues**

league match (*general*) a **match** between two **clubs** in the same **league**

league table (*general*) a table in which **clubs** in a **league** are listed according to their results

Leander (*rowing*) Britain's oldest and most prestigious rowing **club**, founded in London in 1818 but now based at Henley, the site of the **Henley Royal Regatta** [name of the rowboat from which it evolved]

leash (*surfing*) the rubber cord used to attach the **surfboard** to the **surfer**'s ankle

leather (*general*) colloquial term for the **ball** in sports such as **association football**, **baseball**, and **cricket** [from the leather covering (or formerly covering) the ball]

leather on willow (*sport*) a byname for **cricket** [from the **leather** struck by the **willow**]

leave (*billiards*) the position of the **balls** at the end of a player's **stroke** or **break**; (*tenpin bowling*) the **pins** that remain standing after the first **ball**

ledger (*angling*) short name for **ledger bait**, **ledger line**, or **ledger tackle**

ledger bait (*angling*) **bait** that is anchored to the bottom [from a word related to *lay* or *lie*]

ledger line (*angling*) a **fishing line** fixed in one place

ledger tackle (*angling*) the **tackle** used to keep the **ledger bait** on the bottom

lee-oh! (*sailing*) the warning called by the **helmsman** when the boat is about to **come about**

leech (*sailing*) the outside edge of a **sail**

leeward (*sailing*) toward the direction in which the wind is blowing, as distinct from **windward**

left (*boxing*) a **punch** with the left fist

left arm (*cricket*) a player who bowls with the left arm

left back (*field games*) a **back** who plays primarily on the left side of the **pitch**

left center (*field games*) a player who plays primarily to the left of the center of the **pitch**

left cross (*boxing*) a **punch** delivered from the left side

left defender (*field games*) a **left half** who plays deep

left field (*baseball*) the part of the **outfield** to the left of **second base** as viewed from **home plate**

left fielder (*baseball*) a **fielder** positioned in **left field**

left half (*field games*) a **halfback** who plays primarily on the left side of the **pitch**

left-hander (*boxing*) a **punch** delivered with the left hand; (*general*) a player whose left hand is dominant, as against the more common **right-hander**; (*surfing*) a wave breaking to the left, as seen by a **surfer** facing the beach

left midfield (*field games*) the **midfield** players who play primarily on the left side of the **pitch**

left wing (*field games*) the part of the **pitch** to the left of its center

left winger (*field games*) an attacking player on the **left wing**

leftie (*general*) colloquial term for a **left-hander**

leg (*athletics*) (1) a **stage** of a race; (2) a single runner's section of a **relay**; (*cricket*) shortening of **leg side**; (*general*) a distinct part of a contest or competition; (*sailing*) the distance covered on a single **tack**

leg bail (*cricket*) the **bail** nearest the **batsman**

leg before (*cricket*) shortening of **leg before wicket**

leg before wicket (*cricket*) an infringement in which the lower part of the leg of the **batsman** prevents the **ball** bowled by the **bowler** from hitting the **wicket**, as a result of which the batsman is **out**

leg break (*cricket*) a **ball** bowled by a slow **bowler** that deviates from the **leg side** to the **off side** on bouncing

leg bye (*cricket*) a **bye** scored after the **ball** bowled by the **bowler** has touched any part of the **batsman**'s person except his hands or the **bat**

leg circle (*gymnastics*) a move on the **pommel horse** in which the legs are kept together and swung in complete circles around the horse, the hands being lifted to allow the legs to pass

leg cutter (*cricket*) a a **ball** bowled by a fast **bowler** that deviates from the **leg side** to the **off side** on bouncing

leg drive (*cricket*) a **drive** to the **leg side**

leg glance (*cricket*) a **glance** to the **leg side**

leg rope (*surfing*) another name for a **leash**

leg side (*cricket*) the side of the **pitch** on which the **batsman** stands when waiting to receive a **ball** from the **bowler** [his legs are on that side]

leg slip (*cricket*) a **fielder** positioned slightly behind the **batsman** on the **leg side**

leg spin (*cricket*) the **spin** given to the **ball** by the **bowler** so that it causes a **leg break**

leg spinner (*cricket*) a **bowler** who bowls **leg spins**

leg stump (*cricket*) the **stump** nearest the **batsman**

leg theory (*cricket*) the theory that favors **body-line bowling**, with a large number of **fielders** on the **leg side** close to the **wicket**

leg trap (*cricket*) a group of **fielders** positioned for **catches** on the **leg side** close to the **wicket**

Leger (*horse racing*) short name of the **St. Leger**

leggie (*cricket*) another spelling of **leggy**

leggy (*cricket*) colloquial term for a **leg spinner**

Leicester (*horse racing*) a **flat** and **National Hunt**

racecourse at South Knighton, near Leicester, Leicesterhire, England

Le Mans (*auto racing*) short name of the **Le Mans 24-Hour race**

Le Mans 24-Hour race (*auto racing*) an annual 24-hour **race** for **sports cars** held since 1923 on an 8.3 miles (13.4km) **circuit** near Le Mans, northwestern France

length (*cricket*) a suitable distance for pitching a **ball**, a "good length" being one that the **batsman** finds hard to play; (*greyhound racing*) the length of a greyhound's body, used to indicate the distance between two dogs finishing a **race**; (*horse racing*) the length of a horse, used to indicate the distance between two horses at the **finishing post**; (*rowing*) the length of a boat, used to judge the distance between two boats in a **race**; (*swimming*) the length of a **swimming pool**, as a measure of distance covered by a **swimmer**; (*tennis*) the consistent ability of a player to make **shots** to the back of the **court**

Lents (*rowing*) the **boat races** held in the Lent (spring) term between colleges at Cambridge University

Leonard Trophy (*bowls*) the **trophy** awarded to the country with the best overall performances in the men's **world championship** [donated in 1966 by W.M. Leonard, managing director of the Australian company that originally sponsored it]

Leopardstown (*horse racing*) a **flat** and **National Hunt racecourse** near Dublin, Ireland

leotard (*gymnastics*) a close-fitting one-piece garment worn by **gymnasts** [first worn by the French trapeze artist Jules Léotard (1830–1870)]

les autres (*Olympics*) the term used for competitors in the **Paralympic Games** whose disability does not fit into any of the other defined groups [French *les autres*, "the others"]

Les Bleus (*rugby union*) nickname of the French national team [French *les bleus*, "the blues," for the color of their **strip**]

Lester B. Pearson Award (*ice hockey*) the **trophy** awarded to the outstanding player of the year [named in honor of the Canadian prime minister Lester B. Pearson (1897–1972)]

Lester Patrick Trophy (*ice hockey*) the **trophy** awarded since 1966 for outstanding service to the sport in the United States [named for Lester Patrick (1883–1960), **manager** and **coach** of the New York Rangers]

let (*squash*) a replayed **point** following unintentional obstruction; (*table tennis*) a replayed **point**; (*tennis*) (1) a **serve** that hits the **net cord** before landing, and is accordingly replayed; (2) a replayed **point** [not *let*, "permit," but *let*, "hinder"]

let-off (*cricket*) the reprieve of a **batsman** because a **fielder** has missed an opportunity of getting him **out**

letter (*general*) an award to a player for achievement in sport made by a school or college in the form of a monogram (letter) representing the name of the awarding establishment

letter jacket (*general*) a blouson-style jacket in school or college **colors** bearing an embroidered or sewn-on **letter** (originally as a sporting award but now more generally)

letterbox (*mountaineering*) a rectangular opening in a narrow rock ridge

levade (*equestrianism*) a movement in **dressage** in which the horse rears up to balance on its hindlegs with its forelegs drawn up [French *levade*, "a raising"]

leveller (*association football*) another term for an **equalizer**

libero (*association football*) another term for a **sweeper**; (*volleyball*) a player who can be brought on at any time to play in a defensive position [short for Italian *battitore libero*, literally "free beater" (i.e. "defender")]

lido (*swimming*) an open-air **swimming pool** [originally the name of a bathing beach near Venice, Italy]

lie (*golf*) the position from which the **ball** has to be played

Liège-Bastogne-Liège (*cycling*) an annual **road race** in Belgium from Liège to Bastogne and back (via a different route), first held in 1892

Liffey Descent (*canoeing*) an annual **long-distance race** in Ireland down the Liffey River, first held in 1959

lift (*ice skating*) in **pair skating**, a movement in which the man lifts the woman in the air, as in an **axel lift**; (*weightlifting*) the movement by which a **weightlifter** lifts the **barbell**; (*wrestling*) the movement by which a **wrestler** lifts an opponent

lifter (*cricket*) a **ball**, especially one bowled fast, that rises sharply after striking the **pitch**

liftoff (*general*) another term for a **takeoff**

ligger (*angling*) a fishing **line** with a **float** and **bait** which is left in the water, especially as a **nightline** for pike fishing [related to *lie*]

Light Blues (*association football*) a nickname of the Scottish **club** Rangers [the team's shirts are lighter in color than those of the **Dark Blues**]

light flyweight (*boxing*) another term for **junior flyweight**

light heavyweight (*boxing*) the professional **weight** category of maximum 79kg (175lb)

light middleweight (*boxing*) another term for **junior middleweight**

light welterweight (*boxing*) the professional **weight** category of maximum 63.5kg (140lb)

Lightning (*ice hockey*) short name of the Tampa Bay Lightning team

lightweight (*boxing*) the professional **weight** category of maximum 61kg (135lb)

lightweight rowing (*rowing*) a contest for **rowers** weighing less than 70kg (154lb)

Lilienthal Medal (*gliding*) the sport's highest award, instituted in 1928 [named in memory of the German aeronautical pioneer Otto Lilienthal (1848–1896)]

Lilywhites (*association football*) nickname of the English **club** Preston North End [so called from the color of the team's **strip**]

limb (*archery*) the upper or lower half of a **bow**

Limerick (*horse racing*) a flat and **National Hunt racecourse** in Co. Limerick, Ireland

limited-over (*cricket*) (of) a **match** in which the number of **overs** is restricted

Lincoln Handicap (*horse racing*) a flat race run annually at **Doncaster** [until 1965 run at Lincoln and known as the Lincolnshire Handicap]

line (*American football*) (1) the **odds** set by **bookmakers**; (2) the players who line up on or near the **line of scrimmage**; (*angling*) shortening of **fishing line**; (*cricket*) the direction of flight of a **ball** bowled by the **bowler**; (*general*) (1) a mark that limits an area of play or that must be crossed to **score** or to win a **race**; (2) a strategic formation of players in a row in a **team game** such as **American football** or **ice hockey**; (*golf*) the direction of the **hole** from the position of a player's **ball**

line call (*tennis*) a **call** on the status of a **shot**, made by an **umpire** or **line judge**

line drive (*baseball*) a hard-hit **ball** with a flat trajectory

line-fishing (*angling*) fishing with a **line** rather than a **net**

line judge (*American football*) the member of the officiating team who monitors the **line of scrimmage**; (*tennis*) an official who watches a **line** to judge whether a **shot** is in or out

line of scrimmage (*American football*) an imaginary **line** across the **field** behind which the **linemen** of a team position themselves at the start of play

line orienteering (*orienteering*) the following of a set route marked on a master map

line player (*handball*) another term for a **pivot**

linebacker (*American football*) a defensive player positioned just behind the **line of scrimmage**

lineman (*American football*) any player who lines up on the **line of scrimmage**

lineout (*rugby union*) the means of restarting play after the **ball** has gone into **touch**, in which the two sets of **forwards** form a line facing the **touchline** and a player from the opposing team throws the ball in, upon which the **jumpers** attempt to gain **possession**

liner (*baseball*) a **ball** which when struck flies through the air in a nearly straight line not far from the ground

linesman (*American football, tennis*) another term for a **line judge**; (*association football*) the former name of an **assistant referee**; (*ice hockey*) an official responsible for calling any infraction regarding the **blue line** or **red line**

lineup (*billiards*) the positioning of three **balls** in a direct line, with one's opponent's ball between the **cue ball** and the **red**; (*general*) a list of proposed or actual members of a team, entrants for a **race**, or the like; (*surfing*) the place where **surfers** wait for waves to break, lining themselves up with a particular point on the shore

Lingfield Park (*horse racing*) a **flat** and **National Hunt racecourse** near Lingfield, Surrey, England

linkman (*association football, field hockey*) a player who acts as a link between the **center forwards** and the **backs**

links (*golf*) shortening of **golf links**

lino (*association football*) colloquial name for a **linesman**

Lions (*American football*) short name of the Detroit Lions team; (*association football*) nickname of the English **club** Millwall [from their self-acclaimed prowess]; (*Australian Rules*) short name of the Brisbane Lions team; (*Canadian football*) short name of the British Columbia Lions team; (*rugby league*) short name of the English **club** Swinton Lions; (*rugby union*) popular name of the British and Irish Lions, a touring team made up of players from the British Isles [named from the lion on the team's official necktie]

lip (*golf*) the edge or rim of the **hole**

lip out (*golf*) to hit the **lip** of the **hole** but not fall in

liptrick (*snowboarding*) a trick performed on or near the lip of the wall of the **half-pipe**

listed race (*horse racing*) a **flat race** that is less important than a **pattern race** but still highly prized

Listowel (*horse racing*) a **flat** and **National Hunt racecourse** at Listowel, Co. Kerry, Ireland

Little Brown Jug (*horse racing*) an annual **harness race** for three-year-old **pacers**, run at Delaware, Ohio, since 1946 [named by newspaper vote after the popular song of 1869]

Little League (*baseball*) an international organization for children and young people, founded in Williamsport, Pennsylvania, in 1939

Little Three (*American football*) the **college football** teams of Amherst College, Wesleyan University, and Williams College; (*basketball*) the

teams of Canisius College, Niagara University, and St. Bonaventure College

live bait (*angling*) a living worm or small fish used as **bait**

Livi Lions (*association football*) nickname of the Scottish **club** Livingston

load (*horse racing*) to ride or lead a horse into the **starting stalls** before a **race**

load the bases (*baseball*) to place **baserunners** at **first base**, **second base**, and **third base**

loan (*association football*) the temporary **transfer** of a player from one **club** to another with no **transfer fee** involved

lob (*cricket*) a low underhand **ball** bowled by the **bowler**; (*general*) a **hit** or kick that sends the **ball** in a high arc, usually for strategic reasons, for example to score a **goal**

lob wedge (*golf*) a **wedge** with a high degree of **loft**, used to play **pitch shots** and **flop shots**

local derby (*association football*) a **match** between rival teams from the same area [after the **Derby**]

lock (*rugby league, rugby union*) one of the two players in the **second row** of the **scrum**, behind the **hooker**; (*wrestling*) a **hold** that prevents an opponent from moving the part held

lock forward (*rugby league, rugby union*) an alternate name for the **forward** who is a **lock**

locker room (*general*) (1) a room for changing clothes and storing belongings in a locker, as in a **pavilion**, **gymnasium**, or **sports center** or at a **swimming pool**; (2) the equivalent of a **changing room** as a place where individual participants and team members can discuss tactics or fellow players, be addressed by their **captain**, **manager**, or **coach**, and the like

loft (*general*) a **stroke** or **hit** that sends a **ball** up high; (*golf*) the degree of angle at which a **clubhead** is set

lofter (*golf*) a **golf club**, especially an 8-**iron**, used for a **loft**

log (*surfing*) a large, cumbersome **surfboard**

lollipop (*association football*) colloquial term for a **stepover**; (*auto racing*) colloquial term for the sign on a stick used to give instructions to a driver during a **pit stop**; (*bowls*) colloquial term for one of the small colored lollipop-shaped pieces of plastic held up by the **marker** to indicate the number of **shots** gained in an **end**

lolly (*cricket*) colloquial term for an easy **catch** [shortening of *lollipop*, with a suggestion of **dolly**]

London Marathon (*athletics*) an annual **marathon** run since 1981 over a course in London, England, to raise money for charity

London to Brighton Walk (*athletics*) an annual 53-mile (85km) **race walking** event between

London and Brighton, England, first held in 1919 but discontinued in 2003

long ball (*general*) a **ball** hit, kicked, or thrown a long way

long bomb (*American football*) a **play** in which a **quarterback** throws a **long ball** to a **receiver** positioned near the **end zone** to score a **touchdown**

long corner (*field hockey*) a **free hit** taken from the corner of the **goal line**

long-distance race (*general*) a **race** over a long distance, as in **long-distance running**

long-distance runner (*athletics*) a runner in a **long-distance race**

long-distance running (*athletics*) a blanket term for the **5,000 meters** and **10,000 meters foot races**

long field (*cricket*) a **fielding** position near the **boundary** on the **bowler**'s side, or more specifically **long off** or **long on**

long game (*golf*) the various kinds of **play** needed to reach the **green**

long hop (*cricket*) a **ball** bowled so that it makes a long **flight** after pitching or bouncing

long iron (*golf*) an **iron** used to play long **shots**

long jump (*athletics*) a **field event** in which an **athlete** sprints down a **runway** then leaps as far as possible off the **board** to land in the **pit**

long leg (*cricket*) a **fielding** position on the **boundary** behind the **batsman** on the **leg side**

long odds (*horse racing*) **odds** in a **bet** that are unfavorable in terms of risk but favorable in terms of potential gain

long off (*cricket*) a **fielding** position on the **boundary** behind the **bowler** on the **off side**

long on (*cricket*) a **fielding** position on the **boundary** behind the **bowler** on the **leg side**

long reliever (*baseball*) a **relief pitcher** used to pitch several **innings** if the **starting pitcher** has to be removed from the **game**

Long Room (*cricket*) a large room in the **pavilion** at **Lord's** which every player must pass through before going out to the field of play

long throw (*association football*) a **throw-in** that sends the **ball** into or near the **goal area** of the opposing team, thus giving an opportunity for a teammate to score

long-track racing (*motorcycle racing*) a form of **speedway** over 1,000-meter tracks

Long Western (*archery*) a **round** of 48 **arrows** for men and women respectively at 80 and 60yds (73m and 55m)

longboard (*surfing*) an extra long **surfboard**, such as a **Malibu**

Longchamp (*horse racing*) a noted **racecourse** near Paris, France

longeur (*equestrianism*) in **vaulting**, the person who leads round the horse while the **rider** performs gymnastic maneuvers [French *longeur*, "person who walks alongside"]

longstop (*cricket*) a now rarely used **fielding** position directly behind the **wicket** to stop **balls** missed by the **wicketkeeper**

Lonsdale Belt (*boxing*) the **trophy** in the form of a belt awarded for winning the same title three times in succession [presented in 1909 by Lord Lonsdale (1857–1944), president of the National Sporting Club]

look for runs (*cricket*) to take every opportunity, as a **batsman**, to score a **run**

look-in (*American football*) a quick **pass** made to a **receiver** running diagonally across the center of the **field**

loom (*rowing*) the long section of the **oar** between the handle and the **blade**

Loons (*association football*) nickname of the Scottish **club** Forfar Athletic [Scots *loon*, "boy," "lad"]

loop (*ice skating*) shortening of **loop jump**; (*table tennis*) a **shot** that places heavy **topspin** on the **ball**

loop jump (*ice skating*) a **jump** in which the skater takes off from the back **outside edge**, makes a full turn in the air, then lands on the same edge

loose (*rugby union*) (of) forward play that does not involve **scrums** or **lineouts**

loose ball (*association football*) a **ball** not in the **possession** of either team

loose box (*horse racing*) a part of a **stable** where horses are kept untied ["loose" because they can move about]

loose forward (*rugby league*) the **forward** who **binds** at the back of the **scrum** behind the two **second-row forwards**; (*rugby union*) (1) either of the two **wing forwards**; (2) the **forward** who **binds** at the back of the **scrum**

loose head (*rugby league, rugby union*) the **forward** in the **front row** of the **scrum** closest to the **scrum half** as he puts the **ball** in

loose-head prop (*rugby league, rugby union*) the **prop forward** on the left of the **front row** in the **scrum**

loose scrum (*rugby league, rugby union*) a **scrum** formed by the players around the **ball** during play, as distinct from one ordered by the **referee**

loosen up (*general*) to exercise gently in preparation for a full effort, as in **athletics**

loosener (*cricket*) an indifferent **ball** bowled by the **bowler** before he is fully warmed up

Lord's (*cricket*) the **home ground** of Middlesex **county cricket club**, London, that is the headquarters of the **Marylebone Cricket Club** and a regular **venue** for **test matches** [founded in Marylebone in 1787 by Thomas Lord (1755–1832) but in 1814 moved to St. John's Wood, to the northwest]

loser (*billiards, snooker*) colloquial term for a **losing hazard**

losing hazard (*billiards, snooker*) a **stroke** in which a player's own **ball** goes into a **pocket** after contact with another ball

lost ball (*cricket*) a situation in which the **ball** cannot be found or recovered, as a result of which it is declared **dead**

lot (*horse racing*) a batch of horses grouped for daily exercise, as in a **gallop**

love (*tennis*) a zero **score** [probably from *love* in the sense "nothing," as in "labor of love"]

love-all (*tennis*) a **score** of no **points** on either side

love-fifteen (*tennis*) a **score** of no **points** to the **server** and one point to the opponent

love-five (*tennis*) colloquial term for a **score** of **love-fifteen**

love-forty (*tennis*) a **score** of no **points** to the **server** and three points to the opponent

love game (*tennis*) a **game** in which a player fails to score a **point**

love set (*tennis*) a **set** in which a player fails to score a **point**

love-thirty (*tennis*) a **score** of no **points** to the **server** and two points to the opponent

low bar (*gymnastics*) the lower of the two **asymmetric bars**

low house (*shooting*) the lower **trap** in skeet

low post (*basketball*) the part of the **court** just outside the **foul lane** and under the **basket**

low side (*golf*) an underestimate of the **borrow** required when making a **putt**

lowball (*baseball*) a **ball** pitched in such a way that it passes over the **plate** below the level of the **batter**

Ludlow (*horse racing*) a **National Hunt racecourse** at Bromfield, near Ludlow, Shropshire, England

luff (*sailing*) to turn a boat toward the wind

lug (*sailing*) to carry too much **sail**

Lugano Trophy (*athletics*) the **trophy** awarded to the winner of the **world championship** in **race walking** [first won in 1961 in Lugano, Switzerland]

luge (*sport*) a **race** on the specially designed light toboggan so named [Swiss French *luge*]

lugworm (*angling*) a sluggish worm found in the sand on the seashore, used for **bait**

lunch (*cricket*) the first meal break of the day during a **match**, regarded as a time point for the number of **runs** scored

lunge (*fencing*) a sudden attack with the sword, made with the back leg straightened and the body and front leg thrust forward; (*gymnastics*) a sudden movement forward or sideways, made with one leg bent at the knee and the other stretched out behind

Lupi (*association football*) nickname of the Italian **club** AS Roma [Italian *lupi*, "wolves," from the legend that Rome was founded by Romulus and Remus, who were suckled by a she-wolf]

lure (*angling*) a type of brightly-colored **artificial fly**; (*greyhound racing*) the object resembling a hare that is chased by the dogs in a **race** as it is electrically driven around the inside of the **track**

lutz (*ice skating*) a **jump** from the back **outside edge** of one **skate** to the same edge of the other skate, with a complete rotation while in the air [said to have been invented by the Swiss skater Gustave Lussi (1898–1993)]

Luzhniki (*general*) a sports complex in Moscow, Russia, that was one of the main **arenas** for the 1980 **Olympic Games**

Lynx (*rugby league*) short name of the English **club** Chorley Lynx

m (*horse racing*) abbreviation of **mile** (or *miles*) in **racing** reports

M (*cricket*) abbreviation of **maiden over** in scoring

mace (*cricket*) the **trophy** in the form of an orb atop a **stump** awarded since 2001 to the top-ranked world team [official title **ICC Test Championship** Mace]

machine (*auto racing*) colloquial term for a **racecar**

MacRobertson International Shield (*croquet*) the **trophy** awarded to the winner of a **tournament** played between Britain, Australia, New Zealand, and the United States [donated in 1925 by the Australian philanthropist Sir MacPherson Robertson (1860–1945)]

made pony (*polo*) an experienced **pony**

madhouse (*darts*) the **score** of a double one [from the frustration felt by a player struggling to finish the **game** with this difficult **double**]

madison (*cycling*) a 50km **track race** with two teams of two **riders** competing for **points** during intermittent **sprints** [first ridden at **Madison Square Garden** in 1892]

Madison Square Garden (*general*) a major indoor sporting and entertainment center in New York City, successively rebuilt and renewed since its original opening in 1879

Magic (*basketball*) short name of the Orlando Magic team

magic ball (*cricket*) an unplayable **ball** which will invariably **dismiss** the **batsman**

magic minute (*general*) a time of one minute in a **race** or other contest, regarded as a challenge for a new **record** in a shorter time [as in the 1964 **Olympic Games** by the Australian **swimmer** Dawn Fraser in the women's 100 meters **freestyle** with a time of 59.5 seconds]

magic sponge (*association football*) colloquial term for the damp sponge at one time traditionally applied by the **trainer** to a sprain or muscular injury sustained by a player

magpie (*shooting*) the penultimate outermost division of a **target**, a **hit** on which is signaled by a black and white **flag**

Magpies (*association football*) nickname of the English **club** Newcastle United [from the players' black and white striped shirts]; (*Australian Rules*) short name of the Collingwood Magpies team

maiden (*cricket*) shortening of **maiden over**; (*greyhound racing*) a dog that has not run an official race; (*horse racing*) (1) a horse that has never won a race; (2) shortening of **maiden race**

maiden century (*cricket*) a **batsman**'s first **century**

maiden over (*cricket*) an **over** in which no **runs** are scored by the **batsmen**

maiden race (*horse racing*) a **race** for horses that have never won a race

maiden stakes (*horse racing*) the **prize** in a **maiden race**

maiden test (*cricket*) the first **test match** for which a **batsman** is selected

main course (*sailing*) the **mainsail** on a **square-rigged** boat

main wall (*real tennis*) the long wall of the **court** without a **penthouse**

mainmast (*sailing*) the principal **mast** on a boat

mainsail (*sailing*) the principal **sail** on a boat, usually attached to the **mainmast**

maître d'armes (*fencing*) an instructor in the sport [French *maître d'armes*, "master of arms"]

major (*angling*) a type of **artificial fly** used for salmon fishing; (*golf*) one of the four **majors**

major league (*baseball*) either of the two **majors**

majors (*baseball*) the two most prestigious **leagues**, as the **National League** and the **American League**; (*golf*) the four most important **championships**: the **British Open**, **U.S. Open**, **U.S. PGA**, and **U.S. Masters**

make all (*horse racing*) to lead all the way in a **race**

make the cut (*golf*) to equal or better a stated **score**, so avoiding elimination from the last two **rounds** of a four-round **tournament**

make-up game (*baseball*) a previously postponed **game** which is played to complete the number of scheduled **league matches**

makiwara (*karate*) an object designed to be struck during training to toughen the skin of the hands and feet [Japanese *maki*, "roll," and *wara*, "straw," referring to the original post or board covered with straw used for this purpose]

makunouchi (*sumo*) the highest division in the sport [Japanese]

Malaysian Grand Prix (*auto racing*) the **Formula One** international **Grand Prix** held on the **circuit** at Kuala Lumpur, Malaysia

malhini (*surfing*) a novice or beginner [Hawaiian *malhini*, "stranger"]

Malibu (*surfing*) a long narrow **surfboard** [originally used at Malibu, California]

mallet (*croquet, polo*) the long-handled hammer with which the **ball** is struck

Man City (*association football*) short name of the English **club** Manchester City

man coverage (*American football*) the strategy of assigning a **defender** to each **eligible receiver**

man in black (*association football*) colloquial term for a **referee** [who traditionally wears black to be differentiated from the **colors** of the two teams]

man in motion (*American football*) an offensive **back** allowed to move during a **scrimmage** before the **ball** is put into play

man in white (*Australian Rules*) colloquial term for an **umpire** [who wears white for distinction from the **colors** of the two teams]

man marking (*association football*) a defensive strategy in which a player is assigned an opposing player to **mark** throughout the **game**

Man of Steel (*rugby league*) the award made from 1977 by the **Super League** to the outstanding player of the **season**

man of the match (*general*) a semiofficial title granted to a player judged to have played best in a particular **match**, typically in **association football** or **cricket**

man-on-man (*general*) (of) a position in a **team game** in which one **defenseman** is assigned to one offensive player

Man U (*association football*) short name of the English **club** Manchester United

man who beat the man (*boxing*) a way of defining a **champion**, as the man who beat the previous champion

manager (*general*) the person who controls, counsels, and promotes a **sportsperson** or sports team

manege (*equestrianism*) the art of training horses [French *manège*, "training of a horse," from Italian *manegiarre*, "to manage," from Latin *manus*, "hand"]

manhattan (*cricket*) a bar chart showing the number of **runs** scored in each **over** of a **game** [the bars supposedly resemble the Manhattan skyline]

mankad (*cricket*) a way of causing a **batsman** to be **run out**, in which the **bowler** removes the **bails** instead of bowling if the batsman at the **non-striker**'s end **backs up** too far [popularized by the Indian player Mulvantrai Mankad]

Maple Leafs (*ice hockey*) short name of the Toronto Maple Leafs team

marathon (*athletics*) (1) a long-distance **foot race**, properly of 26 miles 385 yards (42.195km); (2) a city race run by **professionals** or **amateurs**, as the **Boston Marathon**, **London Marathon**, or

New York Marathon; (*equestrianism*) a **cross-country time trial** in **carriage driving**; (*general*) any demanding **race** or contest [originally so named from the tradition that a Greek messenger ran from Marathon to Athens with news of victory in a battle of 490 BC]

Marathon des Sables (*athletics*) an annual **ultramarathon** run over six days through the Sahara desert, North Africa [French *marathon des sables*, "**marathon** of the sands"]

Marcel Corbillon Cup (*table tennis*) the **cup** awarded to the winner of the women's world team **championship** [presented in 1934 by Marcel Corbillon (1890–1958), president of the French Table Tennis Association]

March Madness (*baseball*) the **postseason tournament** for colleges held in March

mare (*horse racing*) a female horse over the age of four

margin fishing (*angling*) a technique for catching carp at night, in which a **rod** is set up on the side of a lake with its **bait** floating on the water

Marilyn (*mountaineering*) any British hill with a reascent of 500 feet on all sides [named for U.S. movie actress Marilyn Monroe (1926–1962), punning on **Munro**]

marina (*sailing*) a specially-equipped berthing area for **yachts** and smaller craft

Mariners (*association football*) nickname of the English **club** Grimsby Town [from the town's seaside location]; (*baseball*) short name of the Seattle Mariners team

mark (*athletics*) (1) a measured achievement, as the distance of a **throw** or height of a **jump**, especially when a **record** or **personal best**; (2) the **starting line** in a race; (*Australian Rules*) a catch of the **ball** from a kick of at least 10 meters; (*bowls*) another term for the **jack**; (*boxing*) the pit of the stomach; (*general*) in **field games**, to stay close to an opposing player in order to prevent him from obtaining or passing the **ball**; (*horse racing*) shortening of **handicap mark**; (*rugby union*) a catch of the **ball** from a kick or **knock-on** or **throw-forward** by an opponent, formerly claimed by calling "mark!" and digging one's heel in the ground

mark someone's card (*horse racing*) to tip a possible winner at a **race meeting** [the card is the **racecard**]

marker (*billiards*) the person who records the **score**; (*bowls*) a person who generally assists the players; (*darts*) (1) a **dart** just outside the required **double** that helps the aiming of subsequent darts; (2) the person who records the **score**; (*general*) in **field games**, a player assigned to **mark** an opponent; (*real tennis*) another term for the **umpire**

market leader (*horse racing*) another term for the **favorite** [the market being the betting on a **race**]

Market Rasen (*horse racing*) a **National Hunt racecourse** at Market Rasen, Lincolnshire, England

marksman (*shooting*) a person who shoots well

marksmanship (*shooting*) the skill or art of a **marksman**

markswoman (*shooting*) a woman who shoots well

Marlins (*baseball*) short name of the Florida Marlins team

maroon jersey (*cycling*) the jersey worn by the **points** leader in the **Giro d'Italia** [Italian *maglia ciciamina*, "maroon jersey"]

marquee player (*general*) an outstanding player in a **professional** sports team [his name is as prominent as that of an entertainer billed on a marquee]

married man's side (*darts*) the lefthand side of the **dartboard** [where a player is less likely to make an expensive **mishit**, a married man being one who should aim to "play safe"]

marshal (*auto racing*) one of the officials posted around the **racetrack** to ensure the safety of drivers and spectators; (*general*) an official at a sporting **event** who supervises arrangements for competitors, controls spectators, and generally monitors proceedings

martial artist (*general*) a practitioner of the **martial arts**

martial arts (*sport*) a range of (mainly Japanese) combative sports and methods of self-defense such as **judo, karate,** and **kendo**

Marylebone Cricket Club (*cricket*) the **club** founded in 1787, with its headquarters at **Lord's**, that was formerly the governing body of the sport in England, is still responsible for making its laws, and is the official title of English teams when on **tour**

mascot (*association football*) a child **supporter** who with others accompanies the team on to the **pitch** at the start of a **match**, dressed in a scaled-down version of the team's **strip**; (*general*) a symbol of luck, often in the form of an animal or insect, representing a team or **club** and visibly present (as an outsize toy or a costumed person) at a **match** or **meeting**

mashie (*golf*) the former name of a 5-**iron** [perhaps from French *massue*, "club"]

mashie iron (*golf*) the former name of a 4-**iron**

mashie niblick (*golf*) the former name of a 7-**iron** [combining the features of a **mashie** and a **niblick**]

mass start (*general*) a **start** to a **race** in which all of the competitors set off together

massé (*billiards, snooker*) a **stroke** made with the **cue** held vertically or nearly so, causing the **cue**

ball to swerve sharply [French, from *masse*, "mace"]

mast (*sailing*) a long upright pole that carries the **sail** of a boat

mast foot (*windsurfing*) the part of the **sailboard** whose top fits into the lower end of the **mast**

Masters (*golf*) shortening of **U.S. Masters**; (*snooker*) an **invitational tournament** played at **Wembley** since 1979; (*tennis*) shortening of **Masters Cup**

Masters Club (*golf*) an annual dinner held since 1952 at the **Augusta National Golf Club** during the **U.S. Masters** for all previous winners of the **tournament**, hosted by the defending **champion**

Masters Cup (*tennis*) the **trophy** awarded to the winner of an annual men's **championship** featuring the top eight world players for the particular year

mat (*bowls*) the small piece of rubber on which players place their **back foot** when delivering a **bowl**; (*gymnastics*, *wrestling*) the area of padded material or canvas on which participants perform and which absorbs the shock when they land or fall

match (*general*) a formal contest or **game**

match angler (*angling*) an **angler** who takes part in **match fishing**

match ball (*cricket*) a **ball** that in its physical composition meets the standard of the sport; (*tennis*) a **ball** that could decide a **match**

match book (*cricket*) a book containing the **scores** of a **club** or particular team; (*horse racing*) a book containing the dates and **venues** of **races**

match card (*cricket*) a card that summarizes the **score** and lists the players in **batting order**

match fishing (*angling*) in central and northern England, a contest between teams at fixed locations to win the greatest weight of fish caught during a particular period of time

match-fixing (*general*) the fraudulent manipulation of a **match** result by a gambling syndicate

match point (*tennis*) the stage in a **match** at which only one **point** is needed to win

match race (*sailing*) a **one-design race** between two boats

match rifle (*shooting*) a **rifle** used in official competitions

match winner (*general*) a team player whose skill or performance helps win a **match**

matchday doctor (*general*) a physician who attends a **match** to give treatment if needed

matchmaker (*boxing*) a person who arranges **matches**

matchplay (*golf*) a **score** based on the number of **holes** won by each side rather than the overall total of **strokes** taken

matchup (*general*) a **game** or contest between two players

Matildas (*association football*) nickname of the Australian national women's team [from the colloquial phrase *waltz Matilda*, "carry one's swag"]

matman (*wrestling*) colloquial term for a **wrestler** [who performs on the **mat**]

maul (*rugby union*) a **loose scrum** formed by a teams' **forwards** around the player who holds the **ball** after a **lineout** and who has not been brought down by an attempted **tackle**

Mavericks (*basketball*) short name of the Dallas Mavericks team

maxi (*sailing*) a class of large **yacht** 15 to 20 meters in length

maximum (*darts*) a **score** of 180 with three **darts**, achieved through three **treble** 20s; (*snooker*) a **break** of 147 **points**, comprising 15 **reds** and 15 **blacks** followed by all six **colors**

May Week (*rowing*) the week in late May or early June when **boat races** are held between colleges at Cambridge University

mayfly (*angling*) (1) a **natural fly** of the genus *Ephemera*; (2) an **artificial fly** imitating it

Mays (*rowing*) the **boat races** held in **May Week**

MCC (*cricket*) abbreviation of **Marylebone Cricket Club**

McCarthy Cup (*hurling*) the **trophy** awarded to the winner of the **All-Ireland** senior **championship** [donated in 1921 by the player Liam McCarthy]

McHawk (*skateboarding*) a 720-degree rotational flip [introduced by the U.S. skateboarder Tony Hawk, with *Mc-* added from the **McTwist**]

McTwist (*skateboarding*) a 540-degree rotational flip [from the name of U.S. skateboarder Mike McGill, who introduced it, and the motion of the flip]

measure (*bowls*) the use of measuring instruments on completion of an **end** to determine which **bowl** is closer to the **jack** when this cannot be done with the naked eye

measuring line (*cycling*) another term for **pole line**

meat (*cricket*) the center of the **blade** of the **bat**

medal (*general*) an award, usually in the form of a coin with an inscription, for a sporting achievement

medal round (*golf*) a **round** of **medalplay**

medalist (*general*) a competitor who has been awarded a **medal**

medalplay (*golf*) another term for **strokeplay**

medicine ball (*general*) a heavy **ball** thrown and caught for exercise [it acts as a "medicine"]

Mediterranean draw (*archery*) a method of drawing and loosing an **arrow** in which the string is pulled back with three fingers, one above the arrow, the other two below

Mediterranean Games (*Olympics*) **regional games** held since 1951 for competitors from Mediterranean countries (in northern Africa or southern Europe)

medium bowler (*cricket*) a **bowler** who bowls at a medium **pace**, between a **fast bowler** and a **slow bowler**

medley (*athletics*) a **relay race** in which each participant runs a different distance; (*swimming*) a **relay race** in which the four main **strokes** (**backstroke**, **breaststroke**, **butterfly**, and **freestyle**) are used

meet (*general*) a gathering of **athletes** or **cyclists** for a competition or **race**

meeting (*general*) a gathering for a sports **event** or program, as typically in **athletics**; (*horse racing*) shortening of **race meeting**

Melbourne Cup (*horse racing*) a **race** for **three-year-olds** run at Flemington Park, Melbourne, Australia, since 1861

member's bounce (*golf*) a favorable **bounce** of the **ball** on to the **fairway** or **green** [so called because it is often a **club** member rather than a visitor who benefits]

Members' Enclosure (*horse racing*) an **enclosure** at a **racecourse** reserved for members of the racecourse **club**

Memorial Coliseum (*American football*) the **home ground** of the Los Angeles Rams team, Los Angeles, California

Mendoza line (*baseball*) a **batting average** of .200, regarded as the lower limit of respectability for a professional **hitter** [named for the weak-hitting player Mario Mendoza]

Merry Millers (*association football*) nickname of the English **club** Rotherham United [from their **home ground** at Millmoor Ground]

Messenger Stake (*horse racing*) an annual **harness race** held since 1957 for three-year-old **pacers** at Yonkers, New York [named for the English **thoroughbred** Messenger (foaled 1780), the great-grandfather of **Hambletonian**]

metric mile (*athletics*) colloquial name for the **1,500 meters race**

metronome (*cricket*) colloquial term for a consistently reliable **bowler**, especially a **seam bowler** [he will repeatedly "hit the spot" just as a metronome regularly ticks out the time]

Mets (*baseball*) short name of the New York Mets team

Mexican Grand Prix (*auto racing*) the **Formula One** international **Grand Prix** held on the **circuit** at Mexico City, Mexico

Mexican wave (*general*) the effect produced when adjacent groups of spectators stand up in turn with hands raised then sit down again to create an undulating movement around a **stadium** [popularized during the 1986 **association football World Cup** in Mexico]

Michelle (*cricket*) alternate term for a **five-fer**

mid-off (*cricket*) a **fielding** position behind the **bowler** on the **off side**

mid-on (*cricket*) a **fielding** position behind the **bowler** on the **on side**

midcourt (*tennis*) the area at the center of the **court**

middle (*cricket*) (1) shortening of **middle guard**; (2) to hit the **ball** with the middle of the **bat**

middle and leg (*cricket*) a **guard** taken by the **batsman** in front of his **middle stump** and **leg stump**

middle and off (*cricket*) a **guard** taken by the **batsman** in front of his **middle stump** and **off stump**

middle-distance race (*general*) a **race** over a medium distance, as in **middle-distance running**

middle-distance running (*athletics*) a blanket term for the **800 meters** and **1,500 meters foot races**

middle for diddle (*darts*) colloquial term for a method of starting a **game**, in which both players throw a single **dart** and the player who throws nearer the **bull** begins

middle guard (*American football*) a defensive **lineman** who plays between the defensive **tackles**; (*cricket*) a **guard** taken by the **batsman** in front of his **middle stump**

middle linebacker (*American football*) a defensive player positioned behind the middle of the **line of scrimmage**

middle order (*cricket*) the **batsmen** who come in the middle of the **batting order**

middle reliever (*baseball*) any **relief pitcher** other than the **closer**

middle stump (*cricket*) the middle **stump** of the **wicket**

middleman (*mountaineering*) the middle member of a climbing or descending team

Middleton Cup (*bowls*) the **cup** awarded since 1922 to the winner of an intercounty **championship** [presented by P.C. Middleton to replace an original award of 1911]

middleweight (*boxing*) the professional **weight** category of maximum 73kg (160lb)

midfield (*association football*) (1) the area in the center of the **pitch**; (2) the players who play between the **defense** and the **attack**

midfielder (*association football*) any of the players who play in **midfield**

midiron (*golf*) (1) a 5-, 6-, or 7-**iron**, used to play medium-range **shots**; (2) the former name of a 2-**iron**

Midsummer Classic (*baseball*) another name for the **All-Star game**

midwicket (*cricket*) a **fielding** position on the **leg**

side about midway between **mid-on** and **square leg**

Milan-San Remo (*cycling*) an annual **road race** from Milan to San Remo, northwestern Italy, first held in 1907

mile (*athletics*) the predecessor of the **1,500 meters**; (*horse racing*) a standard unit of distance [1 mile = 1.61km], together with the **furlong**

miler (*athletics*) an **athlete** running the **mile**; (*horse racing*) a horse running in a **race** of a **mile** or more

militaire (*equestrianism*) a continental European term for a **three-day event** [French *militaire*, "military," as originally a cavalry test for officers' horses]

military medium (*cricket*) straight, regular, medium-paced **bowling**

Milk Race (*cycling*) the former popular name of the **Tour of Britain** [sponsored by the Milk Marketing Board from 1958]

Mille Miglia (*auto racing*) an Italian **road race** from Brescia to Verona, Ferrara, Pesaro, Pescara, Rieti, Rome, Florence, Bologna, Cremona, and back to Brescia, a distance of around 1,600km, held from 1927 to 1957 [Italian *mille miglia*, "thousand miles"]

Millennium Dome (*general*) original name of the **O$_2$**

Millennium Stadium (*general*) a **stadium** built in Cardiff, Wales, in 1999 as the home of Welsh **rugby football**

miller (*trampolining*) a triple-twisting **double back** [named for its originator]

mini flyweight (*boxing*) the professional **weight** category of under 48kg (105lb)

miniature golf (*golf*) a simple, scaled-down version of the **game** in which a **club** is used to **putt** a small **ball** into a series of **holes** on a **green**

minibasketball (*basketball*) a simplified form of the **game** designed for young players

minibreak (*tennis*) a **point** against the **serve** in a **tie-break**

minigolf (*golf*) shortening of **miniature golf**

minilacrosse (*lacrosse*) a simplified form of the **game** designed for young players

minimal (*surfing*) a shorter version of a **Malibu**, popular with beginners

minirugby (*rugby union*) a simplified form of the **game** designed for young players

miniskis (*skiing*) short, slightly thick **skis** worn by beginners or in **skibobbing**

minitennis (*tennis*) a simplified form of the **game** designed for young players

minivolley (*volleyball*) a simplified form of the **game** designed for young players

minor county (*cricket*) a British county not having **first-class** status but with its own team.

minor league (*baseball*) any of the less prestigious professional **leagues**, often used to groom younger players for the **major leagues**

minors (*baseball*) short name for the **minor leagues**

Minstermen (*association football*) nickname of the English **club** York City [from York Minster, the city's medieval cathedral]

miscall (*general*) a bad or inaccurate call

miscue (*billiards, snooker*) a faulty **stroke** that results from a poor contact between the **cue tip** and the **cue ball**

misfield (*cricket*) a mistake made by a **fielder**, as when a **catch** is dropped

mishit (*general*) a faulty **hit**

miskick (*general*) a kick made with the wrong part of the foot, as in **association football**

misplay (*general*) an incorrect or faulty move or **play**

miss (*billiards, snooker*) a (sometimes deliberate) failure to hit the **object ball**, as a result of which the player is penalized; (*general*) a failure to hit the object aimed at, as in **shooting**

miss move (*rugby union*) a maneuver in which the attacking **three-quarters** miss out a **back** in order to move the **ball** more quickly to a player in a wider position

miss the break (*horse racing*) to start after the other horses in a **race**

miss the cut (*golf*) to fail to qualify for the final **round** of a **tournament**

miss the water (*rowing*) to start the **drive** before the **catch** has been completed

mittens (*boxing*) colloquial term for **boxing gloves**

mitts (*baseball*) the special padded leather gloves used to catch the **ball**

mix zone (*general*) an area at a sporting contest where reporters can interview players or performers immediately after their appearance

mixed doubles (*tennis*) a **match** with male and female players on the same side

mixed martial arts (*sport*) a **combat sport** that incorporates **boxing**, **wrestling**, **jujitsu**, and other disciplines

MK Dons (*association football*) short name of the English **club** Milton Keynes Dons

mod-pen (*Olympics*) colloquial abbreviation of **modern pentathlon**

modern pentathlon (*Olympics*) a contest in **swimming**, **riding**, **cross-country running**, **fencing**, and **pistol shooting**, introduced in 1912 as a variant of the original **pentathlon**

mogul (*skiing*) a mound of hard snow forming an obstacle on a **ski slope** [probably from a Norwegian dialect word meaning "heap," "mound"]

mohawk (*ice skating*) a turn from either edge of

the **skate** to the same edge on the other foot in the opposite direction [as distinct from a **choctaw**]

Monaco Grand Prix (*auto racing*) the **Formula One** international **Grand Prix** held on the **circuit** at Monte Carlo, Monaco

Monday morning quarterback (*American football*) a person (not just a **quarterback**) who expresses opinions about strategic decisions after the outcome of a **game** is known [the big games are played on Sunday afternoons]

Monkeyhangers (*association football*) nickname of the English **club** Hartlepool United [from a local legend about the hanging of a monkey for spying, represented by the team's **mascot**, H-Angus, depicted by a man in a monkey costme]

monocoque (*auto racing*) a one-piece structure housing the **cockpit** of a **race car**; (*cycling*) a one-piece construction method for bicycle frames and wheels [French *monocoque*, literally "single shell"]

monofil (*angling*) a **fishing line** made of a single strand of synthetic fiber

monohull (*sailing*) a boat with a single **hull**, as distinct from a **catamaran** or **trimaran**

monoski (*skiing*) a **ski** on which both feet are placed

moonball (*cricket*) colloquial term for a high, looping **ball** delivered by the **bowler**; (*tennis*) colloquial term for a very high **lob**

moonshot (*baseball*) another term for a **tape-measure shot**

morning glory (*horse racing*) a horse that runs faster in morning training than in the actual **race**

Mosconi Cup (*pool*) the **trophy** awarded since 1994 to the winner of an annual competition in **nine-ball pool** between the United States and Europe [named commemoratively for the U.S. **champion** player Willie Mosconi (1913–1993)]

Most Valuable Player (*baseball*) the annual award made to the player judged the most valuable to his team in each of the **major leagues**; (*basketball*) the annual award made to the outstanding player in the NBA; (*general*) a similar award in other sports

moto (*cycling*) colloquial name of **BMX** [from the full form of the name]; (*motorcycle racing*) (1) shortening of **motocross**; (2) a **heat** in this sport

motocross (*motorcycle racing*) a form of the sport on solo motorcycles, motorcycles with **sidecars**, or **quad bikes** on a **cross-country circuit** with natural obstacles such as **jumps**

MotoGP (*motorcycle racing*) an annual **race** for 500cc motorcycles, first held in 1949 [from *motorcycle* and *GP*]

motor racing (*sport*) another term for **auto racing**

motorcycle racing (*sport*) the racing of motorcycles, usually categorized by modification or engine size, around a specially-built **track** or over a **cross-country circuit**

motorcyclist (*motorcycle racing*) the **rider** of a motorcycle

motorsport (*sport*) any sport that involves motor-powered vehicles, as cars or motorcycles

mound (*baseball*) the raised area a short distance from **home plate** from which the **pitcher** throws the **ball** to the **batter**

mount (*equestrianism, horse racing*) the horse that a person is riding

mountain bike (*cycling*) a bicycle with strong heavy tires designed for **cross-country** use, whether in competition or for recreation

mountain biking (*cycling*) the sport or recreation of riding a **mountain bike**

mountainboard (*general*) a narrow board mounted on wheels and fitted with a steering mechanism, ridden down mountain tracks or other hilly terrain

mountaineer (*mountaineering*) a person who climbs mountains

mountaineering (*sport*) the climbing of rocks or mountains, either in competition or as a self-imposed physical challenge

mousetrap (*American football*) a **play** in which a defensive player crosses the **line of scrimmage** and is then blocked from the side while the **ball** carrier advances through the gap he has left

mouth guard (*rugby league, rugby union*) a guard worn to protect the mouth

mouthpiece (*boxing*) the piece of plastic placed in a boxer's mouth to protect his teeth and prevent him from biting his tongue

movement (*equestrianism*) a single maneuver in **dressage**

mow (*cricket*) another term for a **haymaker**

mud wrestling (*wrestling*) a form of the sport in an **arena** with a floor of wet mud

mudder (*horse racing*) colloquial term for a horse that performs well in muddy conditions

mudlark (*horse racing*) another term for a **mudder**

muff (*general*) (1) a bungling or inapt player or competitor; (2) a failure in a move or maneuver, as a dropped **catch** in **cricket** or a slip from a piece of **apparatus** in **gymnastics**

Muirfield (*golf*) a **championship golf course** east of Edinburgh, Scotland

mulligan (*golf*) a free extra **shot** allowed to a player who has made a bad shot [perhaps from the Canadian player David Mulligan, who played a "correction shot" after a bad shot]

multigym (*gymnastics*) (1) a piece of exercise equipment that can be used in several ways or by several people simultaneously; (2) a room with such equipment

multihull (*sailing*) a boat with two or more **hulls**, as a **catamaran** or **trimaran**

multiplier (*angling*) a geared **reel** on a **fishing rod**, used to draw the **line** in quickly [one turn of the handle makes the spool rotate several times]

Munro (*mountaineering*) a Scottish (now also English, Welsh, or Irish) mountain peak over 3,000 feet in height [named for the Scottish mountaineer Sir Hugh Thomas Munro (1856–1919), who published his original list in 1891]

Munro-bagger (*mountaineering*) a person who attempts to climb every (Scottish) **Munro**

Murrayfield (*rugby union*) the sport's Scottish **home ground**, in Edinburgh

musette (*cycling*) a small shoulder bag containing food handed to **riders** at **feeding stations** [French *musette*, "horse's nosebag"]

mush (*surfing*) the foam produced when a wave breaks

mush! (*sled dog racing*) the command to the dogs to start moving or to move faster [probably from French *marcher*, "to walk"]

musher (*sled dog racing*) the driver of a dog team [he calls **mush!**]

Musselburgh (*horse racing*) a **flat** and **National Hunt racecourse** at Musselburgh, central Scotland

muzzle (*greyhound racing*) the guard fitted over a greyhound's mouth to protect other dogs while racing and to serve as an aid in a **photo finish**

MVP (*general*) abbreviation of **Most Valuable Player**

Naas (*horse racing*) a **flat** and **National Hunt racecourse** at Naas, Co. Kildare, Ireland

nail (*baseball*) to put a **runner** out by throwing; (*general*) to defeat

naked bootleg (*American football*) a **bootleg** in which no players attempt to block in front of the **quarterback**

nap (*horse racing*) a horse that a **tipster** reckons has the best chance of winning [abbreviation of *napoleon*, a card game in which a player may try to win all five tricks]

NASCAR (*auto racing*) a form of **stock car racing** in specially modified cars [acronym of National Association for Stock Car Auto Racing]

nassau (*golf*) (1) a **match** in which a **point** is scored for winning the **front nine**, another for the **back nine**, and a third for the complete **round**; (2) a bet on these three results [from Nassau Country Club, New York, where it originated]

National (*horse racing*) shortening of **Grand National**

National Football Conference (*American football*) one of two **conferences** into which the **National Football League** was divided in 1969, the other being the **American Football Conference**

National Football League (*American football*) the major professional organization of the sport, founded in 1920 and merging (under its own name) with the **American Football League** in 1970

National Hockey League (*ice hockey*) the major professional organization of the sport, formed by five Canadian teams in 1917

National Hunt (*horse racing*) the term used in Britain for **racing** over **jumps**, as distinct from **flat racing** [short name of National Hunt Committee, the body that regulates the sport, founded in 1866 to fulfill a function similar to that of the **Jockey Club** in flat racing]

National League (*baseball*) one of the two most prestigious North American professional **leagues**, founded in 1876, the other being the **American League**

natural aid (*equestrianism*) a signal given to a horse by its **rider**, whether as a spoken command or by movement of the hands or legs

natural break (*cycling*) a euphemism for relieving oneself while continuing to ride, as in a long **road race**

natural fly (*angling*) a real insect such as a **mayfly** used as **bait**, as distinct from an **artificial fly**

natural footer (*surfing*) a **surfer** who rides with the left foot in front of the right

Navan (*horse racing*) a **flat** and **National Hunt racecourse** near Navan, Co. Meath, Ireland

navigator (*auto racing*) in **rally driving**, a term used for the **codriver** in a **road rally**, as the person who describes the route and directs the driver

nb (*cricket*) abbreviation of **no-ball** in scoring

near post (*association football*) the **post** nearest to where the **ball** is

neck (*horse racing*) the length of a horse's head and neck, used to measure its **lead** in a **race** [a scale exists whereby four **noses** equal one **head**, two heads equal one **neck**, and two necks equal half a **length**]

neck and neck (*general*) running level in a **race**

neck roll (*gymnastics*) a swing of the body backward to rest on the back of the neck

neck shot (*polo*) a **hit** of the **ball** made under the horse's neck

neck spring (*gymnastics*) a **vault** in which the weight of the body is initially borne by the neck and hands

needle match (*general*) a keenly competitive and critical **match**

negative split (*swimming*) a strategy whereby a **swimmer** completes the second half of a **race** faster than the first

nelson (*cricket*) a **score** of 111 **runs,** held to be unlucky because the figure resembles the three

stumps of the **wicket** with the **bails** missing [so called from the popular belief that Admiral Nelson had one eye, one arm, and one leg]; (*wrestling*) a **hold** in which a combatant passes his arms under both of his opponent's arms from behind and joins his hands so that he can exert pressure with his palms on the back of the other's neck [apparently from Nelson, Lancashire, England, a town noted for its wrestling matches]

Nemean Games (*Olympics*) the **games** held in Nemea, near Argos, Greece, in the second and fourth years of each **Olympiad**

Nerazzurri (*association football*) nickname of the Italian **club** Inter Milan [Italian *nero*, "black," and *azzurro*, "blue," the colors of the team's blue and black striped shirts]

net (*angling*) shortening of **fishing net**; (*association football*) (1) the wide mesh attached to the **goalposts** and **crossbar** that stops the **ball** when a **goal** is scored; (2) the entire structure forming the goal; (*badminton, real tennis, tennis, volleyball*) the length of netting that divides the **court**; (*field hockey, ice hockey*) the mesh across the **goal** that serves the same function as in **association football**; (*netball*) the net, hanging from a horizontal ring attached to a high pole, into which the **ball** is thrown; (*tennis*) another term for a **let**

net cord (*tennis*) the string or tape that runs across the top of the **net** and supports it

net fishing (*angling*) fishing with a **net** as distinct from a **rod** and **line**

net judge (*tennis*) an official who formerly sat with one hand resting on the **net cord** to feel if a **serve** was a **let**

net play (*badminton, tennis*) play near the **net**

net practice (*cricket*) a practice session in the **nets**

netball (*sport*) a **game** between two teams of seven in which **goals** are scored by throwing the **ball** into a **net**

netminder (*ice hockey*) another term for the **goaltender**

nets (*cricket*) (1) a practice **pitch** surrounded by nets to stop the **ball** from traveling too far; (2) a practice session in such nets

Nets (*basketball*) short name of the New Jersey Nets team

neutral corner (*boxing*) one of the two **corners** in the **ring** where neither **boxer** sits

neutral support (*cycling*) a mechanic who follows the **riders** in a **race** to give mechanical assistance where necessary

neutral zone (*American football*) the area between the two **lines of scrimmage**; (*cycling*) the section of a **road race** where the **riders** must ride behind a leading vehicle and cannot make an at-

tack; (*ice hockey*) the area between the attacking and defending **zones** in the middle of the **rink**

never up, never in (*golf*) a comment made to a **putter** who has hit the **ball** too gently

new ball (*cricket*) the new **ball** that a **captain** of either side (**batting** or **fielding**) may demand at the start of each **innings** or, in a **match** of more than a day's duration, that the captain of the fielding side may demand after a prescribed number of **overs**

New Den (*association football*) the **home ground** of Millwall **football club**, London

New Road (*cricket*) the **home ground** of Worcestershire **county cricket club**, Worcester

New York Marathon (*athletics*) a **marathon** run annually through all five boroughs of New York City since 1970

Newbury (*horse racing*) a **flat** and **National Hunt racecourse** at Newbury, Berkshire, England

Newcastle (*horse racing*) a **flat** and **National Hunt racecourse** at Newcastle upon Tyne, northeastern England

Newmarket (*horse racing*) the town in Suffolk, England, that is the historic center of English **racing**, with a **flat racecourse** where the **One Thousand Guineas** and **Two Thousand Guineas** are held as well as the **Cambridgeshire** and **Cesarewitch**

Newton Abbot (*horse racing*) a **National Hunt racecourse** at Newton Abbot, Devon, England

NFC (*American football*) abbreviation of **National Football Conference**

NFL (*American football*) abbreviation of **National Football League**

NHL (*ice hockey*) abbreviation of **National Hockey League**

nibble (*cricket*) to play indecisively at a **ball** bowled outside the **off stump**

niblick (*golf*) the former name of an 8- or 9-**iron**, used for playing out of a **bunker** [origin uncertain]

nick (*cricket*) a slight touch of the **ball** made by the **batsman** with the edge of the **bat**; (*real tennis, squash*) (1) the angle between two walls or between the wall and the floor in a **court**; (2) a **shot** that hits this angle

nickel defense (*American football*) a defensive formation involving five **defensive backs** rather than the usual four [so called because a nickel is worth five cents]

nickelback (*American football*) an additional **defensive back** brought into the **game** when the offensive team is likely to pass the **ball**

night crawler (*angling*) a large earthworm that comes to the surface at night, used as **bait**

night fishery (*angling*) a method or place of **fishing** at night

nightcap (*baseball*) the second of the two **games** in a **double header**; (*horse racing*) the last **race** of the day

nightline (*angling*) a **fishing line** set at night

nightwatchman (*cricket*) a relatively unskilled **batsman** sent in to bat after the **fall** of a **wicket** near the end of a day's play so that a better batsman does not have to go in and risk being **out** in unfavorable conditions [the player remains "in" overnight]

nil (*general*) a **score** of zero

nine (*baseball*) a team of nine players

nine-ball pool (*pool*) the **game** played with nine colored **object balls**, numbered 1 to 9

nine-dart finish (*darts*) a **game** of **501** won with nine **darts**, the fewest number with which the feat is possible

nine-hole (*golf*) a **course** with only nine **holes**, as against the standard 18

nine-meter line (*handball*) an arcing dotted line parallel to the **six-meter line**, extending 9m from the **goal**, marking the area where offensive players resume play after a **foul** by a **defender** inside it

nine, ten, jack (*cricket*) colloquial term for the last three **batsmen** in a team [numbers 9, 10, and 11, compared to playing cards]

ninepins (*sport*) a **game** in which nine **pins** are set up and bowled at to be knocked down

nineteenth hole (*golf*) a jocular name for the **clubhouse**, to which players usually repair after the 18th **green** [they can "sink" a drink in the bar there rather than **sink a putt**]

nineteenth man (*Australian Rules*) the first **substitute** player in a team (of 18)

ninjitsu (*sport*) a Japanese **martial art** originating in feudal times as a form of espionage and teaching stealth and camouflage [Japanese *nin*, "stealth," and *jutsu*, "art"]

niramiai (*sumo*) a method of intimidating an opponent before a fight by stamping, slapping one's thighs, and glaring [Japanese *niramu*, "to glare"]

no (*cricket*) abbreviation of **not out** in scoring

no-ball (*cricket*) a **ball** bowled in a way that is disallowed by the rules and so counts one **run** to the **batting** side, as when the **front foot** of the **bowler** is over the **popping crease**

no-cut contract (*American football*) a contract guaranteeing that a professional player will not be subject to a **cut** during either the **pre-season** practice or the subsequent **season**

no-hitter (*baseball*) a **game** in which a **pitcher** does not allow an opponent to score a **hit**

no-hoper (*horse racing*) a horse not good enough to stand a chance of winning

no-huddle offense (*American football*) an offensive strategy in which players line up for a **play** without a **huddle**

no-jump (*athletics*) a **foul** in the **long jump** or **triple jump**

no-lift (*weightlifting*) a **lift** deemed unsuccessful by the majority of the three **judges**

no man's land (*tennis*) the area of the **court** between the **baseline** and the **service line** [an area where effective action is difficult, as that between enemy trenches in World War I]

no-score draw (*association football*) a **match** in which neither side manages to score

no side (*rugby union*) the official end of a **match**

no-throw (*general*) a **throw** that is disallowed because it does not comply with the rules

noble art (*sport*) another term for **boxing** [short for "the noble art of self-defense"]

noble science (*sport*) another term for **boxing** [short for "the noble science of self-defense"]

nock (*archery*) the notch at the rear of an **arrow** that holds it in place on the **bowstring**

nod in (*association football*) to head the **ball** into the **goal**

nollie (*skateboarding*) an aerial maneuver in which the **front foot** pushes down on the **kick-nose** and then the feet stay close to the **board** in flight before the **back foot** guides the board back to the ground [the opposite of an **ollie**]

non-combativity (*judo*) the failure of a **judoka** to make an attack

non-contact (*general*) (of} a sport such as **handball** or **netball** in which no personal contact with the opponent is allowed

non-runner (*horse racing*) another term for a **non-starter**

non-starter (*horse racing*) a horse that was originally entered for a **race** but that was pulled out shortly before it

non-striker (*cricket*) the **batsman** who is not facing the **bowling**

Nordic skiing (*skiing*) the form of the sport that includes **cross-country skiing** and **ski jumps** [originating in Nordic countries such as Norway and Finland]

Nordic walking (*general*) **walking** as a form of exercise using poles like **ski sticks** to aid propulsion and strengthen the upper body

normal hill (*skiing*) the smaller of the two **ski-jump** hills in the **Winter Olympics**, usually measuring 90 or 95m

North End (*association football*) short name of the English **club** Preston North End

North Stars (*ice hockey*) short name of the Minnesota North Stars team

northpaw (*baseball*) a right-handed player [as distinct from a **southpaw**]

nose (*greyhound racing*) the smallest distance between two **greyhounds** finishing a **race** [as if by the length of a dog's nose]; (*horse racing*) the narrowest winning margin in a **race** [as if by the length of a horse's nose]; (*snowboarding*) the front edge of the **snowboard**; (*surfing*) the front of the **surfboard**

nose guard (*American football*) another term for a **nose tackle**

nose riding (*surfing*) a maneuver that involves standing on the very front of the **board**

nose tackle (*American football*) a defensive **lineman** lined up opposite the offensive **center**

not (*cricket*) abbreviation of **not out** in scoring

not out (*cricket*) of a **batsman** at the end of an **innings**, not having been **dismissed**

not out! (*cricket*) the response of an **umpire** to an **appeal** when giving his decision that the **batsman** has not been **dismissed** and so is not **out**

not up! (*squash*) the call made when the **ball** is not successfully retrieved

notch up (*general*) to score, as a **run** (or total of runs) in **cricket**

Notre Dame shift (*American football*) a former offensive maneuver in which the **backs** move just before the **snap** of the **ball** from their **T-formation** [popularized in the 1920s by Knute Rockne as **college football** coach at the University of Notre Dame, Indiana]

Nottingham (*horse racing*) a **flat racecourse** at Nottingham, Nottinghamshire, England

Nottingham Road (*cricket*) the **home ground** of Derbyshire **county cricket club**, Derby

novice (*horse racing*) a horse that has not won a **race** in a **season** before the current one

nudge (*association football*) a gentle **header**; (*cricket*) a slight tap of the **ball** with the **bat**

Nuggets (*basketball*) short name of the Denver Nuggets team

number eight (*rugby union*) the **loose forward**, who **binds** in the **back row** of the **scrum** [the position has no other name, although all other team players have alternate numerical designations, as follows: 1 **loose-head prop**, 2 **hooker**, 3 **tight-head prop**, 4, 5 **second-row forwards**, 6 **blind-side flanker**, 7 **openside-flanker**, 9 **scrum half**, 10 **standoff half**, 11, **left winger**, 12 **inside center**, 13 **outside center**, 14 **right winger**, 15 **fullback**]

nunchaku (*general*) a Japanese **martial arts** weapon consisting of two short sticks joined by a length of chain [Japanese *nunchaku*, from Okinawa dialect]

Nürburgring (*auto racing, motorcycle racing*) the **circuit** near Bonn, Germany, where the **German Grand Prix** is held

nurdle (*cricket*) to score **runs** by gently pushing the **ball** with the **bat** rather than hitting it [per-

haps blend of **nudge** or *nurse* and a word denoting a gentle movement, as *dandle*]

nurse (*billiards*) to keep the **balls** together for a series of **cannons**

nursery (*billiards*) shortening of **nursery cannon**; (*cricket*) a **club** devoted to the promotion and training of talented young players; (*horse racing*) shortening of **nursery stakes**

nursery cannon (*billiards*) a **cannon** with the three **balls** kept together and moved as little as possible

nursery slopes (*skiing*) **slopes** set apart for novices

nursery stakes (*horse racing*) a **race** for two-year-old horses [as young **colts**]

nutmeg (*association football*) a kick of the **ball** through the legs of an opposing player and its subsequent retrieval [perhaps from the path of the ball beneath the player's "nuts"]

nymph (*angling*) an **artificial fly** resembling the aquatic larva (nymph) of the **mayfly**

oakfly (*angling*) an **artificial fly** imitating the long-legged fly *Rhagio scolopacea*

Oaks (*horse racing*) an annual **race** for three-year-old **fillies** run at **Epsom** since 1779 [named for the estate of Lord **Derby** at Epsom]

oar (*rowing*) (1) the long pole, flattened at one end into a **blade**, used singly or in pairs for propulsion in water; (2) shortening of **oarsman**

oarsman (*rowing*) a **rower**

oarsmanship (*rowing*) the art of **rowing**

obi (*judo*) a belt worn by a **judoka** [Japanese *obi*, "belt"]

object ball (*snooker*) the **ball** that the player intends to strike with the **cue ball**

objection (*general*) a statement made in protest to a situation or action, especially as a transgression of the rules or laws of play or behavior

O'Brien shift (*athletics*) a special gliding or "step-back" technique in the **shot put** [introduced by the U.S. shot putter Parry O'Brien (1932–2007)]

obstacle (*equestrianism*) any **fence**, **gate**, or **water jump** that must be cleared in **showjumping** or a **three-day event**

obstructing the field (*cricket*) the offence by a **batsman** of deliberately hindering a **fielder** or interfering with the **ball** in order to avoid being given **out**

obstruction (*association football*) a **foul** committed by a player who, when not in **possession** the **ball**, uses his body to hinder his opponent; (*field hockey*) a **penalty** given when a player turns in front of the **opposition** or uses his **stick** to bar an opponent's passage; (*netball*) an infringement by which an opposing player blocks or hinders a **pass** or **shot**, as a result of which the obstructed team is awarded a **penalty pass** or **penalty shot**

ocean race (*sailing*) another term for an **offshore race**

oche (*darts*) the line behind which a player must stand when throwing **darts** [origin uncertain, but perhaps related to *notch*]

octave (*fencing*) the eighth of eight basic **parrying** positions, used to protect the lower outside of the body [French *octave*, "eighth"]

octopush (*sport*) a kind of underwater **field hockey** played in a **swimming pool**, in which a **squid** is used in place of a **ball** and **pushers** in place of **sticks** [devised in southern England in 1954 by **subaqua divers** and named as blend of *octopus*, both for the creature and punningly for the eight (now ten) team members, and *push*]

odd (*golf*) a **stroke** that makes a player's total for a **hole** one more than that of his opponent

odds (*horse racing*) the chances that a horse has of winning a **race**, as determined by the amount staked on it in a **bet**

odds-on (*horse racing*) **odds** in a **bet** that are better than those in **evens**, so that the winnings are less than double the amount staked

ODI (*cricket*) abbreviation of **one-day international**

off (*auto racing*) colloquial term for an accident in which the car leaves the **track**; (*cricket*) shortening of **off side**; (*horse racing*) the start of a **race**

off base (*baseball*) in between one **base** and the next, and so liable to be **tagged**

· **off break** (*cricket*) a **ball** bowled by a **slow bowler** that breaks from the **off side** toward the **leg side** on pitching

off course (*horse racing*) away from the **racecourse**

off cutter (*cricket*) a **cutter** from a **fast bowler** that moves from the **off side** to the **leg side** on pitching

off drive (*cricket*) a **drive** to the **off side**

off piste (*skiing*) away from a prepared **ski run**

off-roading (*auto racing*) the sport or recreation of driving over rough terrain in specially designed vehicles, often as a **race**

off side (*cricket*) the half of the **field** on the opposite side to that on which the **batsman** stands when waiting to receive the **ball** from the **bowler**

off spin (*cricket*) the **spin** imparted to a **ball** to turn it into an **off break**

off spinner (*cricket*) a **bowler** who bowls **off breaks**

off stump (*cricket*) the **stump** furthest from the **batsman**

off the ball (*association football*) (of) a dispute or fight between players away from the point where the **ball** is being played

off the bridle (*horse racing*) not running freely and having to be urged on by the **jockey**

off the pace (*horse racing*) lagging behind other runners in a **race**

off theory (*cricket*) a theory that favors concentrat-

ing the **fielders** on the **off side** and **bowling** the **ball** at the **off stump**

off track (*auto racing*) away from the **racetrack**

off-track betting (*horse racing*) a system for placing **bets** away from the **racecourse**

offense (*American football*) the team that has **possession** of the **ball** at the start of a **play**; (*general*) a breach of the rules

office manager (*auto racing*) colloquial term for the **codriver**

offload (*rugby league*) a very short **pass** made to a teammate running past; (*rugby union*) a very short **pass** made by a player taking a **tackle** to a teammate running past

offshore race (*sailing*) a **race** in which competing boats sail at some distance from the shore, often from one port to another

offside (*American football*) a situation in which a player is in front of the **line of scrimmage** at the time of the **snap**; (*association football*) a situation in which a player is nearer the **goal line** than one or both of the last two **defenders** when the **ball** is played toward him by a member of his own team; (*ice hockey*) a situation in which a player precedes the **puck** over the **blue line** of the **opposition**

offside trap (*association football*) a strategy in which defensive players move together toward the **halfway line** in order to catch attacking players **offside** when a forward **pass** is being made

Oilers (*ice hockey*) short name of the Edmonton Oilers team

Old Firm (*association football*) joint nickname for the Scottish **clubs** Celtic and Rangers, long traditional rivals

Old Trafford (*cricket*) the **home ground** of Lancashire **county cricket club**, Manchester

olive (*angling*) an **artificial fly** imitating a **mayfly** with an olive-colored body, especially *Ephemerella ignita*

ollie (*skateboarding*) an aerial maneuver in which the **rider** presses his **back foot** down on the **kick-tail** then keeps his feet close to the **board** in flight before guiding the **board** back to the ground with his **front foot** [said to be invented by U.S. skateboarder Alan "Ollie" Gelfand (1963–)]

Olympia (*Olympics*) the plain in southern Greece where the ancient **Olympic Games** were held [not to be confused with Mt. Olympus, the home of the gods in northeastern Greece]

Olympiad (*general*) alternate term for **Olympics** in its nonathletic application; (*Olympics*) (1) a period of four years between the ancient **Olympic Games**; (2) a celebration of either the ancient or the modern Olympic Games

Olympian (*Olympics*) a competitor in the **Olympic Games**

Olympian Games (*Olympics*) an alternate term for the ancient **Olympic Games**

Olympic city (*Olympics*) a city where the **Olympic Games** have been or will be held, among them Athens, Beijing, London, Los Angeles, Moscow, Munich, Paris, Rome, and Sydney

Olympic flame (*Olympics*) the flame lit by the **Olympic torch** that burns throughout the modern **Olympic Games**

Olympic Games (*Olympics*) (1) the festival in honor of Zeus held first held in ancient Greece in 776 B.C. and comprising athletic, literary, and musical competitions; (2) the modern international athletic contests inspired by this, first held in Athens, Greece, in 1896 and subsequently in different **Olympic cities**, sometimes more than once

Olympic motto (*Olympics*) the Latin slogan that has formed an integral part of the **Olympic Games** since 1920: "*Citius, altius, fortius*" ("Swifter, higher, stronger")

Olympic oath (*Olympics*) the pledge instituted in 1920 that is traditionally pronounced by a representative of the host country at the opening ceremony of the **Olympic Games**: "In the name of all competitors, I promise that we shall take part in these Olympic Games, respecting and abiding by the rules which govern them, in the true spirit of sportsmanship, for the glory of sport and the honor of our teams"

Olympic sport (*Olympics*) a sport officially recognized by the **International Olympics Committee**

Olympic torch (*Olympics*) the lighted torch brought from **Olympia** since 1936 to kindle the **Olympic flame**

Olympic village (*Olympics*) a specially designed residential and commercial center for participants and officials in the modern **Olympic Games**

Olympics (*general*) (1) a commonly used designation of the modern **Olympic Games**; (2) an international contest in a nonathletic sport or pastime, as chess or bridge

Olympism (*Olympics*) the spirit and ideals of the modern **Olympic Games**

Olyroos (*association football*) nickname of the Australian national under-23 men's team, who represent Australia at the **Olympics** [blend of *Olympic* and *kangaroos*, the national animal]

omnium (*cycling*) a series of contests in which competitors are awarded **points** on the basis of their performance in each [Latin *omnium*, "of all"]

on (*baseball*) shortening of **on base**; (*cricket*) another term for **leg**

on base (*baseball*) having safely reached a **base**

on board (*equestrianism, horse racing*) mounted on a horse

on deck (*baseball*) scheduled to bat after the next **batter**

on-deck circle (*baseball*) a circular area in **foul territory** where the next player to bat waits

on-drive (*cricket*) a **drive** to the **leg side**

on guard! (*fencing*) the equivalent of **en garde!**

on points (*boxing*) reckoned by the number of **points** scored rather than by a **knockout**

on side (*cricket*) another term for the **leg side**

on strike (*cricket*) facing the **bowling**

on the clock (*golf*) subject to time constraints as a result of playing too slowly

on the hill (*pool*) with one more **game** to win to gain victory

on the line (*horse racing*) at the **finishing post**

on the mark (*horse racing*) likely to win a **bet**

on the nose (*horse racing*) a **bet** to win only, not to come second or third

on the rails (*horse racing*) on the **track** of a racecourse nearest the **rails**

on the rivet (*cycling*) riding as fast as possible [from the rivet formerly at the front of a leather **saddle**]

on the rope (*mountaineering*) roped together

on the ropes (*boxing*) forced against the **ropes** by an opponent's attack, and thus in danger of defeat

on the up (*cricket*) (of) a **stroke** played as the **ball** rises from a **bounce**

on your marks! (*athletics*) the command given by the **starter** of a **foot race** to prepare the runners for the **starting signal** [the **mark** being the starting line]

one-base (*baseball*) (of) a **hit** that enables the **batter** to reach **first base**

one-day cricket (*cricket*) a **match** lasting only one day, with a limited number of **overs**

one-day international (*cricket*) an international **one-dayer**

one-dayer (*cricket*) colloquial term for **one-day cricket**

one-design (*sailing*) a class of boat with identical specifications

one down (*general*) one **point** behind in a **game**

one-horse race (*general*) a **race** with a single likely winner

100-meter hurdles (*athletics*) a **race** over **high hurdles** for women over the stated distance

100 meters (*athletics*) a **sprint** of the stated distance

110-meter hurdles (*athletics*) a **race** over **high hurdles** for men over the stated distance

one-old-cat (*baseball*) a form of the sport in which a **batter** runs to one **base** and **home** again, remaining as batter until **put out**

one short (*cricket*) a **run** in which the **batsman**, in turning to make another run, touches the ground with the **bat** short of the **popping crease**

One Thousand Guineas (*horse racing*) an annual **race** for three-year-old **fillies** run over the **Rowley Mile** at **Newmarket** since 1814 [original value of **prize**, a guinea being 21 shillings]

one-timer (*ice hockey*) a move in which the **puck** is hit toward the **goal** at the moment it is received in a **pass**

one-touch (*association football*) (of) a fast-moving play in which each player controls or passes the **ball** with a single touch of the foot

one-two (*association football*) a move in which a player makes a **pass** to a teammate, runs past an opponent, then receives the **ball** back; (*boxing*) a **jab** with the leading hand followed by a **cross** with the other hand; (*horse racing*) a double victory for a **trainer** whose horses finished first and second in a **race**

one-two-three (*horse racing*) a triple victory for a **trainer** whose horses were the first three to finish in a **race**

one up (*general*) ahead of an opponent by one **point**

onion bag (*association football*) colloquial term for the **net** behind the **goal**

onside (*association football*) not **offside**

onside kick (*American football*) a **kickoff** that travels only a short distance forward, enabling the kicking team to regain **possession** of the **ball**

Opals (*basketball*) nickname of the Australian national women's team [the opal is the national gemstone]

open (*general*) (1) a sporting contest or **tournament** that anyone can enter; (2) (of) a **game** or play that is spread out over the **field**; (3) (of) a player who is unmarked by a member of the opposing team

Open (*golf*) (1) shortening of **Open Championship**; (2) shortening of **U.S. Open**; (*tennis*) shortening of **U.S. Open**

open! (*wrestling*) the command of the **referee** to a **wrestler** to alter his position and use more open tactics

open championship (*general*) a **championship** that is open to both **professional** and **amateur** entrants

Open Championship (*golf*) (1) the world's leading **championship** in the sport, first held in Scotland in 1860 [formally the British Open]; (2) a similar championship elsewhere, as the **U.S. Open**, Open de España, Open de France, or European Open

open date (*general*) a future available date for which no **fixture** has yet been arranged

open goal (*association football*) (1) an undefended **goal**; (2) a goal scored into it

open one's account (*cricket*) (1) as a **batsman**, to begin scoring **runs**; (2) as a **bowler**, to take one's first **wicket**; (*horse racing*) as a horse or **jockey**, to achieve a first **win** in a **race**

open one's shoulders (*cricket*) to hit a **drive** [from the stance assumed by the **batsman**]

open side (*rugby league*) the side of the **pitch** with more space between the **scrum** or **play-the-ball** and the **touchline** than the **blind side**; (*rugby union*) the side of the **pitch** with more space between the **scrum**, **ruck**, or **maul** and the **touchline** than the **blind side**

open-side flanker (*rugby union*) the **flanker** binding on the **open side**

open table (*pool*) a situation in **eight-ball pool** in which a player can hit either the **solid ball** or the **stripe ball**

open-top bus (*general*) a double-decker bus with a roofless top deck on which a victorious team traditionally ride through their home town and parade their **trophy** as an equivalent of a **lap of honor**

open-water (*swimming*) (of) an **event** held in open water rather than in a **swimming pool**

opener (*cricket*) one of the two **batsmen** who start the side's **innings**; (*horse racing*) the first **race** of the day in a **meeting**

opening (*general*) (1) an initial move in a **game**; (2) an enterprising move during a game, that could lead to the advantage of one's team or oneself

opening batsman (*cricket*) one of the two **openers**

opening bowler (*cricket*) the **bowler** who bowls first

opposition (*general*) the team against which a given team is playing

Opposition (*basketball*) the team (who never wins) against which the Harlem Globetrotters play their **exhibition games**

option play (*American football*) a **play** in which an offensive player runs with the **ball** and, depending on the defensive formation, may either continue running or make a **pass**

Orange Bowl (*American football*) the intersectional **college football game** played annually since 1935 at the Orange Bowl **stadium**, Miami, Florida

order (*cricket*) shortening of **batting order**

order off (*association football*) alternate term for **send off**

Orient (*association football*) short name of the English **club** Leyton Orient

orienteering (*sport*) a form of **cross-country running** in which individuals or teams use a map and compass to reach their destination via a number of specified **control points** [Swedish *orientering*, literally "orientating"]

Orioles (*baseball*) short name of the Baltimore Orioles team

O's (*association football*) short name of the English **club** Leyton Orient

osaekomi waza (*judo*) the technique of holding down one's opponent [Japanese *osae*, "to press on," *komi*, "to be packed up," and *waza*, "technique"]

otter (*angling*) shortening of **otterboard**

otterboard (*angling*) a board manipulated to carry the end of a **fishing line**, or several hooked and baited lines, when fishing in a lake [from *otter*, the aquatic animal]

O₂ (*general*) an entertainment and exhibition center with a concert and sports **arena** in London, England, originally opened in 1999 as the Millennium Dome [name of sponsors]

out (*general*) (1) dismissed from a **game**, as a **batsman** who has been **bowled** in **cricket**; (2) the dismissal itself, as in **baseball**, in which an **inning** ends when three outs are recorded

out cricket (*cricket*) bowling and fielding, as distinct from **batting**

out for the count (*boxing*) failing to beat the **count** of the **referee** when down on the **canvas**

out lap (*auto racing*) (1) the **lap** covered by a driver after a **pit stop**; (2) in **qualifying**, the lap covered after leaving the **pits** and before doing the measured lap

out of (*horse racing*) born to a named **dam** [often coupled with **by** to name the **sire**]

out of bounds (*golf*) an area of the **course** designated as not to be played on, obliging a player whose **ball** enters it to play again and incur a **penalty**

out of the screws (*golf*) (of) a perfect **drive** [from the screws formerly surrounding the middle of the **clubface** of a wooden **driver**, an area now known as the **sweet spot**]

outbrake (*auto racing*) to brake later than another driver at a corner and so overtake him

outclassed (*boxing*) judged by the **referee** to be taking undue **punishment** from an opponent, in consequence of which the **bout** is stopped

outdoor bowls (*bowls*) the sport played on a **green**, as distinct from **indoor bowls**

outer (*archery, shooting*) the outermost ring of the **target**; (*darts*) the green circle around the **bull** on a **dartboard**

outfield (*baseball*) the part of the playing area beyond the **baselines**; (*cricket*) the outer part of the field, near the **boundary**

outfield player (*association football*) any player other than the **goalkeeper**

outfielder (*baseball, cricket*) a **fielder** in the **outfield**

outhalf (*rugby league*) another term for a **standoff half**

outing (*general*) an appearance in a **match** or **race**; (*horse racing*) another term for a **race**

outjump the hill (*skiing*) in **ski jumping**, to jump beyond the **k point**

outlet receiver (*American football*) a **receiver** near the **line of scrimmage** who can catch a **pass** if players further **downfield** are covered

outrigger (*canoeing*) a projecting device on a float, fixed to the side of a **canoe** to give extra stability; (*rowing*) a projecting **rowlock** that gives extra stability to the **oar**; (*sailing*) a projecting **spar** used to extend the **sails**

outrun (*skiing*) in a **ski jump**, the flat area at the bottom of the hill where skiers slow down and stop

outshot (*darts*) another term for a **checkout**

outside (*general*) a player nearer the edge of the **field** than a **center**; (*surfing*) the expanse of sea outside the breakers

outside center (*rugby union*) the **center** who plays between the **inside center** and the **winger**

outside edge (*cricket*) a deflection of the **ball** from the outer edge of the **bat**; (*ice skating*) the outer of the two edges of the **blade** of a **skate**

outside half (*rugby union*) another term for the **fly half**

outside lane (*athletics, cycling*) the outermost lane of the **track**, which is longest because of the curve

outside left (*association football, field hockey*) an attacking position on the left side away from the center of the **field**

outside right (*association football, field hockey*) an attacking position on the right side away from the center of the **field**

outsider (*horse racing*) a horse not regarded as a **favorite** to win a **race** and therefore at **long odds** as a **bet**

outswinger (*association football*) a **pass** that swerves away from the **goal** or from the center of the **pitch**; (*cricket*) a **ball** bowled so as to swing from **leg** to **off**

outwick (*curling*) to strike the outside of another **stone** and so send it within a **circle** [from **wick**]

oval (*Australian Rules*) a **ground** where the **game** is played; (*auto racing*) in **Indy car** and **NASCAR** racing, an oval-shaped **circuit** with gentle bends that can be taken at high speed

Oval (*cricket*) the **home ground** of Surrey **county cricket club**, London, where **test matches** are played [so named from the oval road built around the original area of land, which became a **sports ground** in 1845]

oval-ball game (*sport*) colloquial name for **rugby union**, as distinct from the **round-ball game**

over (*cricket*) a series of six **balls** bowled by the

bowler, after which a change is made from one end of the **wicket** to the other

over rate (*cricket*) the rate at which **overs** are bowled

over the sticks (*horse racing*) colloquial term for a **steeplechase**

over the top (*association football*) (of) a **tackle** in which a player goes over the **ball**

over the wicket (*cricket*) (of) a **ball** bowled with the arm of the **bowler** near the **wicket**, as against **round the wicket**

overarm (*cricket*) (of) a **delivery** by the **bowler** made with the hand raised above the shoulder; (*swimming*) (of) a **stroke** in which one or both arms are lifted out of the water and brought forward and down to their original position; (*tennis*) (of) a **serve** made with the hand raised above the shoulder

overbump (*rowing*) a **bump** in a **bumping race** in which the bumping boat goes up more than one place because the boat it bumps has also just bumped

overclub (*golf*) to use a **club** with too little **loft**, thus sending the **ball** too far

overhand (*swimming*) an **overarm stroke**

overhead (*tennis*) a **shot** played with the **racket** above the head

overhead kick (*association football*) another term for a **bicycle kick**

overhit (*golf*) a **putt** that sends the **ball** further than intended

overlap (*association football*) a situation in which a player moves up to overtake the player in **possession**, usually to take a **pass**; (*rugby league, rugby union*) a situation in which the team in **possession** has more players in an attack than can be marked by the **defenders**; (*sailing*) a situation in a **race** in which the **stern** of one boat is ahead of the **bow** of another, obliging the overtaking boat, if not yet clear, to give way

overpitch (*cricket*) to bowl a **ball** that pitches close enough to the **batsman** to be easily hit by him

overplay (*golf*) to hit the **ball** beyond the **green**

overrreach (*horse racing*) an injury caused when a horse's hindfoot strikes against the corresponding forefoot, typically on landing after jumping a **fence**

overrule (*tennis*) a **call** by the **umpire** to overturn the call of a **line judge**

overswing (*golf*) to swing the **club** too hard and so **follow through** more than is necessary

overthrow (*baseball*) a throw from a **fielder** that sends the **ball** beyond a **baseman**; (*cricket*) a return throw of the **ball** by a **fielder** to the **wicket** that not only misses it but is missed by the **bowler** or **wicketkeeper**, enabling the **batsmen** to run again and score another **run**

overtime (*American football*) an extra period of 15 minutes played at the end of a tied **game**

Owls (*association football*) nickname of the English club Sheffield Wednesday [from the district of Owlerton, Sheffield, South Yorkshire, where the club is based]

own goal (*association football*) a **goal** scored inadvertently against one's own team

owner (*horse racing*) the person who owns a particular **racehorse** and who, in consultation with the **trainer**, decides which **races** it should run

oxer (*equestrianism*) in **showjumping**, a **jump** consisting of a brush **fence** with a guardrail on one or both sides [short form of *ox fence*]

ozeki (*sumo*) a **champion wrestler** [Japanese]

p (*basketball*) abbreviation of **personal foul**

p point (*skiing*) the expected landing point in a **ski jump**

pa-kua (*sport*) a Chinese **martial art** in which fighters are arranged around a circle in positions they must defend [Chinese *pa*, "eight," and *kua*, "trigrams"]

Pac Ten (*American football*) colloquial shortening of **Pacific Ten**

pace (*cricket*) the speed of a bowled **ball**; (*equestrianism, horse racing*) (1) the **gait** of a horse, as **walk**, **trot**, **canter**, **gallop**; (2) a mode of stepping in horses in which the legs on the same side are lifted together

pace bowler (*cricket*) a fast **bowler**

pace car (*auto racing*) a car that sets the pace in the **formation lap** of a **race** but does not take part in the race

pace lap (*auto racing*) another term for **formation lap**

pace notes (*auto racing*) in **rally driving**, notes used by the **codriver** to alert the driver to bends and hazards ahead and to recommend a suitable speed for each section

paceline (*cycling*) a group of **riders** who each **slipstream** behind the one in front, taking turns to ride at the front to set the pace

pacemaker (*general*) a competitor who sets the pace in a **race**; (*horse racing*) a horse entered in a **race** to set the pace in such a way that it benefits a **stablemate**

paceman (*cricket*) another term for a **pace bowler**

pacer (*equestrianism, horse racing*) a horse whose usual **gait** is a **pace**, especially one bred to take part in **harness racing**

Pacers (*basketball*) short name of the Indiana Pacers team

Pacific Ten (*American football*) a **conference** of ten **college football** teams, comprising the universities of California at Berkeley, California at Los Angeles, Southern California, Oregon, Oregon

State, Stanford, Washington, Washington State, Arizona, and Arizona State

pacing (*cycling*) a technique of increasing speed by riding in the slipstream of a vehicle; (*horse racing*) **harness racing** for **pacers**

pack (*general*) the largest group of competitors in a **race**, especially when bunched together; (*parachuting*) the **parachute** when folded in its container; (*rugby league, rugby union*) the **forwards** in a team; (*snooker*) the **reds** when grouped together between the **black spot** and **pink spot**

pack down (*rugby league, rugby union*) to form a **scrum**

pack leader (*rugby union*) the **forward** assigned to organize the **pack**

Packers (*American football*) short name of the Green Bay Packers team

pad (*cricket*) the protective covering for the front of the legs worn by **batsmen** and **wicketkeepers**; (*general*) a guard shaped to protect a particular part of the body

pad up (*cricket*) to put on one's **pads** before a **game**

paddle (*canoeing*) the short, broad **oar** used to propel a **canoe**; (*paddleball, paddle tennis*) the wooden or plastic **bat** used to strike the **ball**; (*rowing*) to row at less than full speed; (*table tennis*) another term for a **bat**

paddle sweep (*cricket*) a gentle **sweep** played with a short **stroke**

paddle tennis (*sport*) a variant of **tennis** played on a small **court** with a deadened (deflated) **tennis ball** and a **paddle**

paddleball (*sport*) a variant of **handball** played between two or four players in a four-walled **court** with a light **ball** and a **paddle**

paddler (*canoeing*) a competitor in a **canoe** or **kayak**

paddock (*auto racing*) the enclosed area behind the **pits** where teams park their transporters and motorhomes; (*greyhound racing*) the area on a **track** where the dogs are kept before the start of the **race**; (*horse racing*) the area where the horses are displayed to spectators before the start of a **race**

Padres (*baseball*) short name of the San Diego Padres team

paint (*basketball*) another term for the **key**

pair (*cricket*) a **score** of no **runs** in each **innings** of a **match**; (*rowing*) a boat rowed by two people

pair of spectacles (*cricket*) another term for a **pair** [from the two zeros on the **scoreboard**]

pair skating (*ice skating*) a coordinated performance by a male and a female skater

pajama cricket (*cricket*) jocular term for **one-day cricket** [from the brightly-colored clothes often worn instead of **whites**]

Pak (*gymnastics*) a move on the **asymmetric bars** in which the **gymnast** releases the **high bar**, executes a backward **flip**, then catches the **low bar** [introduced by the North Korean gymnast Gyong Sil Pak]

Palace (*association football*) short name of the English **club** Crystal Palace

pallone (*sport*) an Italian **game** on the lines of **tennis**, in which a large **ball** is struck with an armguard [Italian *pallone*, "big ball"]

palm ball (*baseball*) a **pitch** with the **ball** gripped by the thumb and palm rather than with the fingers

palmer (*angling*) a type of bristly **artificial fly** imitating a hairy caterpillar

palooka (*boxing*) an inexperienced or incompetent **boxer** [from the comic strip *Joe Palooka* by the U.S. artist Ham Fisher, first published in 1930]

Pan-African Games (*Olympics*) **regional games** held since 1965 for contestants from African countries

Pan-American Games (*Olympics*) **regional games** held since 1951 for contestants from North, Central, and South America, Canada, and the Caribbean

Panthers (*ice hockey*) short name of the Florida Panthers team

par (*golf*) the number of **strokes** that a good average player should take for a particular **hole** or **course**, two **putts** being allowed on each **green** [Latin *par*, "equal"]

parachute (*parachuting*) the large, umbrella-like sheet of fabric with wires or ropes attached to a harness worn by a person jumping from an aircraft to slow his descent or, in modified form, to generate lift in a sport such as **paragliding**

parachuting (*sport*) the activity of descending from an aircraft by **parachute**, in competition involving the **disciplines** of style and **accuracy jumping**

parade (*fencing*) a general term for a **parry**; (*greyhound racing*) the display of the dogs to spectators before the start of a **race**; (*horse racing*) the display of the horses to spectators before the start of a **race**; (*motorcycle racing*) in **speedway**, the introduction of the **riders** to the public

parade lap (*auto racing*) another term for a **formation lap**

parade ring (*horse racing*) a **circuit** at a racecourse around which horses can be walked to warm up before a **race**

paraglider (*paragliding*) a type of modified **parachute** in the form of a flexible **wing**

paragliding (*sport*) the activity of drifting through the air to the ground on a **paraglider** after being towed up by an aircraft or jumping from it

parajetting (*sport*) another term for **paramotoring**

parajump (*parachuting*) a descent made by jumping from an aircraft with a **parachute**

parakiting (*sport*) the activity of **soaring** on a **kite** while being towed by a motorboat, car, or other fast-moving vehicle

parallel bars (*gymnastics*) a pair of horizontal bars arranged side by side and supported on posts used in men's competition for **routines** that include **giant** swings, releasing and regrasping movements, and **handstands**

parallel slalom (*skiing*, *snowboarding*) a **slalom event** in which two competitors race head-to-head down identical **courses**

parallel turn (*skiing*) a turn made by shifting the body while keeping the **skis** parallel

Paralympian (*Olympics*) a competitor in the **Paralympic Games**

Paralympic Games (*Olympics*) a series of sporting contests, run on the lines of the traditional **Olympic Games** since 1948, for competitors in six disability groups, each group subdivided into classes based on the type and extent of their disabilities [blend of *parallel* and *Olympic* but also suggesting *paraplegic*]

Paralympics (*Olympics*) popular name of the **Paralympic Games**

paramotor (*paramotoring*) a two-stroke engine that powers a propeller

paramotoring (*sport*) an **adventure sport** similar to **paragliding**, in which the participant flies suspended from a **wing** while propelled by a **paramotor** worn on the back, where there is also a packed **parachute**

parapenting (*sport*) an activity blending **hang-gliding** and **parachuting**, in which the participant jumps from a height wearing a modified type of **parachute**, which is then used as a **hang-glider** [blend of *parachute* and French *pente*, "slope"]

Paraplegic Games (*Olympics*) a former name for the **Paralympic Games**

parasailing (*sport*) the activity of **soaring** on a modified **parachute** while being towed by a motorboat, car, or other fast-moving vehicle

parascending (*sport*) an activity similar to **paragliding**, in which the participant is towed into the wind by a motor vehicle

paraskiing (*skiing*) an activity in which participants ski from a place to which they have been dropped by **parachute**

Parc des Princes (*rugby union*) the **stadium** in Paris where France have played most of their international **matches** since 1973

parc fermé (*auto racing*) (1) the cordoned-off area into which cars are driven after **qualifying** and the **race** itself and where teams can carry out servicing; (2) in **rally driving**, the cordoned-off area into which cars are driven after each day's rallying [French *parc fermé*, "closed park"]

pari-mutuel (*horse racing*) a form of **totalizator** in which those who backed the winner share the total **stakes** [French *pari mutuel*, "mutual stake"]

Paris-Dakar rally (*auto racing*) a periodical **race** for cars, motorcycles, and trucks from Paris, France, to Dakar, Senegal, first held in 1979

Paris-Roubaix race (*cycling*) an annual **road race** from Paris to Roubaix, France, first held in 1896

park (*association football*) colloquial term for the **pitch**; (*general*) another term for a **stadium**

parkour (*sport*) another term for **free running** [from French *parcours*, "route," "course"]

parry (*association football*) a **save** in which the **goalkeeper** pushes the **ball** away with his hands without actually catching it; (*fencing*) the blocking of an opponent's **thrust**

Pars (*association football*) nickname of the Scottish **club** Dunfermline Athletic [of disputed origin, but perhaps from a mocking alteration of "Athletic" to "Paralytic"]

partner (*general*) one of two people who play on the same side in a **game**

partnership (*cricket*) (1) the length of time for which two **batsmen** bat together; (2) the number of **runs** scored during such a time

pass (*fencing*) another term for a **thrust**; (*general*) a **hit**, kick, **throw**, or **header** of the ball (or its equivalent) to a teammate; (*real tennis*) a **service** which drops in the **pass court**; (*tennis*) a **shot** that goes beyond the reach of an opponent

pass court (*real tennis*) the area in front of the **grille** on the **hazard** side of the **court**, enclosed by the end wall, the **main wall**, the **service line**, and the **pass line**

pass interference (*American football*) illegal contact with an opponent made in order to stop a catch

pass line (*real tennis*) another term for the **fault line**

pass play (*American football*) a sequence of **passes** between members of the same team

pass roll (*croquet*) a **shot** that rolls a player's **ball** further than the one from which **croquet** is being taken

pass rush (*American football*) an attempt to tackle the **quarterback** before he can pass the **ball**

pass rusher (*American football*) a player who makes a **pass rush**

passage (*equestrianism*) a slow **trot** in which the horse raises its feet high before bringing them down

passback (*American football*) another term for a **snapback**; (*association football*) a **pass** back to a teammate, often the **goalkeeper**

passbook (*boxing*) the record of a **boxer's matches**, including injuries sustained, medical procedures applied, and the like

passed ball (*baseball*) a correctly thrown **pitch** that the **catcher** fails to gather in time to prevent a **baserunner** from advancing

passing game (*association football*) a style of play in which a player retains **possession** of the **ball** until an opportunity to score a **goal** arises

passing shot (*tennis*) a **shot** beyond the reach of one's opponent

passive play (*handball*) a team's undue delay with the **ball**, resulting in a **foul**

passivity (*judo*) another term for **non-combativity**; (*wrestling*) stalling tactics in which moves are avoided

passivity zone (*wrestling*) the outer circle of the **mat**

patball (*general*) any simple or gentle **ball game** in which the **ball** is hit back and forth between two players; (*sport*) derisory nickname for **tennis**, especially when played lazily or deliberately slowly for tactical reasons

paternoster (*angling*) a **fishing line** similar to a **ledger** [its many **hooks** are like the beads in a rosary that mark the saying of the paternoster (Lord's Prayer)]

Patriots (*American football*) short name of the New England Patriots team

pattern (*general*) a fixed sequence of tactical movements; (*shooting*) the arrangement of **shot** marks on a **target**

pattern race (*horse racing*) a **flat race** open to all comers in a particular category, as of age or weight, the aim being to find the best among the top-rank horses entered [so called for the organization of such races by **groups**]

pav (*cricket*) shortening of **pavilion**

pavé (*cycling*) the cobbled roads that form part of certain **road races** in France and Belgium [French *pavé*, "paved (way)"]

pavilion (*cricket*) a building for players and (certain) spectators at the side of a **pitch**

pay-as-you-play (*association football*) a contract that pays players for their appearances in a **match**, often with a bonus for **goals** scored or a team **win**

PB (*general*) abbreviation of **personal best**

pearling (*surfing*) the dipping of the nose of the **surfboard** under the waves

Pebble Beach (*golf*) a **championship golf course** near Monterey, California

pedigree (*horse racing*) (1) the ancestry of a **racehorse**, especially with regard to the identity of its progenitors and the purity of its stock; (2) the record of a horse's performance [apparently from French *pied de grue*, "crane's foot," from the arrowhead mark used to denote succession in a genealogical tree]

peel (*croquet*) to send another player's **ball** through the next **hoop** [from the British player Walter H. Peel (*fl.*1868)]; (*curling*) a **takeout** in which both the **stone** played and the stone hit leave the **house**

peel off (*general*) to leave a set formation or group, as a **scrum** in **rugby union** or a **peloton** in cycling

peg (*angling*) a stretch of a river or lake allocated to a single **angler** in **match fishing**; (*baseball*) a long, low throw at a **base**; (*cricket*) colloquial term for a **stump**; (*croquet*) the short wooden post in the center of the lawn; (*mountaineering*) another term for a **piton**

peg back (*general*) to reduce the **lead** of another contestant in a **race**

peg out (*croquet*) to finish a **game** by hitting the **ball** against the **peg**

pelota (*sport*) a **game** played in Spain, southern France, and Latin America in which two players hurl a **ball** against a marked wall using a basket-like wicker **racket** attached to a glove [Spanish *pelota*, "ball"]

peloton (*cycling*) the main group of **riders** in a **stage race** [French *peloton*, "small ball"]

pen (*association football*) abbreviation of **penalty** in sports reports

penalty (*association football*) shortening of **penalty kick**; (*general*) a punishment for a **foul**, usually involving the imposition of some sort of disadvantage or the award of an advantage to an opponent or opponents; (*horse racing*) an additional **weight** carried by a horse as a result of previous **wins** in a **handicap**; (*ice hockey*) suspension from play for a violation of the rules, especially for unruly behavior

penalty area (*association football*) the area in front of the **goal** in which a **foul** by the defending team may result in the award of a **direct free kick** to the attacking team as a **penalty kick**

penalty bench (*ice hockey*) the enclosed area at the side of the **rink** where players who have violated the rules must stay for the **penalty** period

penalty box (*association football*) another term for the **penalty area**; (*ice hockey*) another term for the **penalty bench**

penalty corner (*field hockey*) a **shot** taken on the **back line** for an **offense** committed within the **shooting circle** or **twenty-three-meter line**

penalty goal (*general*) a **goal** scored as the result of a **penalty**

penalty kick (*association football*) a **direct free kick** at **goal** taken from the **penalty spot**

penalty killer (*ice hockey*) a player responsible for preventing a member of the opposing side from scoring when his own team is reduced in number as a result of **penalties**

penalty line (*handball*) another term for the seven-meter line

penalty pass (*netball*) a **free pass** awarded when a team has committed a **foul**

penalty shoot-out (*association football*) a method of settling a tied **match** by having each team take a series of **penalty kicks**

penalty shot (*netball*) a **shot** awarded after an infringement in the **shooting circle**

penalty spot (*association football*) the spot in the **penalty area** from which a **penalty kick** is taken; (*field hockey*) the spot in front of the **goal** from which a **penalty stroke** is taken

penalty stroke (*field hockey*) a **shot** at **goal** awarded after an infringement

penalty try (*rugby league, rugby union*) a **try** awarded by the **referee** if a **foul** has prevented the opposing team from scoring a try

pendulum (*mountaineering*) a move in which a climber uses momentum to swing to a new position

Penguins (*ice hockey*) short name of the Pittsburgh Penguins team

penholder (*table tennis*) a grip in which the **bat** is held between thumb and forefinger, like a pen

pennant (*baseball*) a **flag** awarded to the winners of a **league championship**

Pensioners (*association football*) former nickname of the English **club** Chelsea [from the Chelsea pensioners, or veteran soldiers resident at the Royal Hospital, Chelsea]

pentathlete (*Olympics*) a competitor in the **modern pentathlon**

pentathlon (*Olympics*) (1) in ancient Greece, an athletic contest in leaping, **running, discus**-throwing, spear-throwing, and **wrestling**; (2) shortening of **modern pentathlon** [Greek *pente*, "five," and *athlon*, "contest"]

penthouse (*real tennis*) the roofed corridor that runs around three sides of the **court**

pepperbox (*fives*) in **Eton fives**, an irregular buttress that protrudes into the **court** and that serves as a **hazard**

percher (*cricket*) a **bouncer** that seems to hang in the air for a long time

perfect game (*baseball*) a **game** in which a **pitcher** does not allow any **batter** to reach **base**

perfect ten (*general*) a full **score**, achieved in ideal circumstances

perfecta (*horse racing*) a **bet** on which two horses will come first and second in a **race** [American Spanish *quiniela perfecta*, "perfect **quinella**"]

perfume ball (*cricket*) a **bouncer** on or just outside the **off stump** that narrowly misses the **batsman**'s face [it is so close that he can smell it]

perimeter (*basketball*) the area of the **court** beyond the **key**

period (*ice hockey*) one of the three time divisions that make up a **game**, each of 20 minutes

personal best (*athletics*) the best time or distance achieved by a particular **athlete**

personal foul (*basketball*) a **foul** by individual player in the form of physical contact that resulted in an unfair advantage

Perth (*horse racing*) a **National Hunt racecourse** at Perth, eastern Scotland

pesade (*equestrianism*) a former maneuver in **dressage** in which a horse rears up on its hind legs without moving forward [French *pesade*, from Italian *posata*, "pause"]

pesäpallo (*sport*) a Finnish form of **baseball** [Finnish *pesä*, "home," and *pallo*, "ball"]

pétanque (*sport*) a French **game** similar to **boules** in which steel **bowls** are rolled or hurled toward a wooden marker **ball** [French *pétanque*, from Provençal *pèd tanco*, "feet fixed," describing the throwing position]

petit final (*canoeing*) a **race** that determines the placing of **paddlers** who did not reach the **final** [French *petit final*, "little final"]

petticoat (*archery*) the part of a **target** outside the scoring area

phantom (*angling*) an **artificial bait** that closely resembles **live bait**

phantom goal (*association football*) another term for a **ghost goal**

Philadelphia Gold Cup (*Olympics*) the **cup** awarded to the winner of the men's **single scull championship** [presented in 1920 by Philadelphia rowing men in honor of John B. Kelly, Sr., that year's winner]

Phillies (*baseball*) short name of the Philadelphia Phillies team

photo finish (*general*) (1) a **finish** in a **race** that is so close that a special type of photography is needed to determine the winner; (2) any close finish

photograph (*general*) another term for a **photo finish**

physio (*general*) colloquial shortening of **physiotherapist** or **physiotherapay**

physiotherapist (*general*) a person who treats an injured player or sports participant by physical means such as massage, infrared heat treatment, exercise, and the like, rather than by drugs

physiotherapy (*general*) treatment administered by a **physiotherapist**

piaffe (*equestrianism*) in **dressage**, a type of slow **trot** in which the horse's neck is raised and arched [French *piaffer*, "to strut"]

pick (*basketball*) a (legitimate) maneuver in which an **attacker** who does not have the **ball** obstructs a **defender** from challenging the player who has the ball; (*general*) (1) a **game**, or a **team**, for which the **captains** select their players alternately from a single group or **squad**; (2) a player who is selected to play in such a team; (*horse racing*) a horse fancied as a likely winner

pick-and-roll (*basketball*) a maneuver in which an **attacker** frees a teammate holding the **ball** by using a **pick** on a **defender** then moves toward the **basket** for a **pass**

pick off (*baseball*) to **put out** a **runner** who has strayed off **base** by throwing the **ball** to a **fielder** who **tags** the runner before he is able to return to the base

pick up (*horse racing*) to take hold of the **bit** and run faster

pick-up (*angling*) the loop of metal that pays back the **line** onto the spool as it is reeled in; (*athletics*) the process of increasing speed at the beginning of a **race**; (*general*) a **game** or team for which **captains** select players alternately from a single group

pick up the bridle (*horse racing*) fuller term for **pick up**

picnic race (*horse racing*) in Australia and New Zealand, a rural **race** for **amateurs**

pie chucker (*cricket*) colloquial term for an inexpert **bowler**

pig board (*surfing*) a **surfboard** with a wide tail and a narrow nose

pigskin (*American football*) colloquial term for the **football** [originally made of leather from the skin of a pig]

pike (*gymnastics*) a position of the body in which the legs are kept straight but the torso bent at the hips; (*swimming*) a position for a **dive** in which the body is bent at the waist with the legs straight and toes pointed [not related to other senses of *pike*, as "fish" or "weapon"]

pile-up (*auto racing*) a large-scale collision of **cars** on the **track**; (*horse racing*) a tangled heap of fallen horses and **jockeys** on the **course**, usually the other side of a **jump**

piledriver (*general*) a strong blow or kick; (*wrestling*) the act of slamming down one's opponent's head so that it hits the **mat**

Pilgrims (*association football*) (1) nickname of the English **club** Boston United; (2) nickname of the English club Plymouth Argyle [for the Pilgrim Fathers who came to America from the English towns of Boston, Lincolnshire, and Plymouth, Devon]

pill (*general*) colloquial term for a **ball**, as a **basketball**, **football**, **golf ball**, or **tennis ball**

pills (*billiards*) colloquial term for the **balls** in a **game**

pilot (*croquet*) the **ball** off which a player will **run a hoop** in a **break** in which the **pioneer** and the **pivot** have already been set up

pin (*golf*) (1) the rod of a **flag**; (2) another term for the flag itself; (*ninepins, tenpin bowling*) one of the wooden pieces used as a target; (*wrestling*) another term for a **throw**

pin high (*golf*) (of) an **approach shot** or **chip** that finishes near the **pin**

pin hole (*archery*) the exact center of the **bullseye**

pin position (*golf*) the position of the **flag** on the **green**

pin splitter (*golf*) a **shot** that lands dead on the **pin**

pin spotter (*tenpin bowling*) the device that replaces the **pins** in position after each player's turn

pinch (*horse racing*) to overurge a horse

pinch hitter (*baseball*) a **batter** who bats in place of a teammate at a critical point in a **game**, as through injury or for tactical reasons; (*cricket*) a **batsman** in a **game** of limited **overs** who bats higher up the **batting order** than usual with the aim of scoring quick **runs**

pinch runner (*baseball*) a **substitute baserunner** who runs in place of a **batter** who has reached **base**, especially toward the end of a close **game**

Pine Valley (*golf*) a **golf course** at Clementon, New Jersey

ping (*horse racing*) (1) to jump a **fence** well; (2) to leave the **starting stalls** quickly

ping-pong (*sport*) another name for **table tennis** [properly a trademark, *Ping-Pong*, with *ping* as the sound of the **bat** striking the **ball**, *pong* as that of the ball hitting the table]

pink (*snooker*) the pink **ball**, worth six **points**

pink jersey (*cycling*) the jersey worn by the overall **leader** of the **Giro d'Italia** [Italian *maglia rosa*, "pink jersey"]

pink spot (*snooker*) the spot on the **billiard table** where the **pink** is positioned, in the center of the bottom half of the table, at the apex of the triangle of **reds**

pintail (*surfing*) a **surfboard** with a tapering tail

piolet (*mountaineering*) a two-headed **ice ax** [French *piolet*, from Piedmontese dialect]

pioneer (*croquet*) a **ball** sent to the **hoop** after the one next in turn, so as to be ready for when that hoop is attempted

pipe-opener (*general*) a practice **game** or **trial run**; (*horse racing*) a **gallop** or first **race** that gets a horse fit for subsequent races [it "opens the pipes" or clears the wind]

pipeline (*surfing*) the hollow formed by the breaking of a large wave

Pirates (*association football*) nickname of the English **club** Bristol Rovers [from the port city's connection with shipping]; (*baseball*) short name of the Pittsburgh Pirates team

pirouette (*equestrianism*) in **dressage**, a full turn made by pivoting on a hind leg; (*gymnastics*) a turn made by swiveling the foot through 180 degrees while standing erect or by moving the hand similarly when in a **handstand** position [French *pirouette*, "spinning top"]

piste (*fencing*) the dueling area; (*skiing*) a prepared downhill trail [French *piste*, "track"]

piste-basher (*skiing*) (1) a machine that compacts and levels the snow on a **piste**; (2) colloquial term for a person who enjoys skiing on pistes

pisteur (*skiing*) a person who prepares the snow on a **piste** [French *pisteur*, from *piste*]

pistol (*shooting*) the small, hand-held gun used in competitive **shooting**

Pistons (*basketball*) short name of the Detroit Pistons team

pit (*American football*) the center of the **line**, where opposing players battle to attack or defend the **quarterback** [from *pit* as an enclosure where animals fight]; (*athletics*) the sanded landing area in the **long jump** and **triple jump**; (*auto racing*) an area (in early days below ground level) close to the **circuit** where cars can be serviced or repaired during a **race**

pit area (*auto racing*) fuller term for the **pit**

pit babe (*auto racing*) colloquial term for an attractive young woman engaged by a team to grace its **pit area**

pit board (*auto racing*) a board held out from the **pit wall** to tell a driver his position, the time gap to the car ahead or behind, and the number of **laps** remaining

pit lane (*auto racing*) the lane that leads to the **pits** from the **circuit**

pit lizard (*auto racing*) colloquial term for a female fan or follower of the sport

pit road (*auto racing*) the road that leads to the **pits** from the **circuit**

pit stop (*auto racing*) a stop made by a driver in the **pits** to refuel or repair his car

pit wall (*auto racing*) the wall that separates the **pit** area from the **start straight** and **finish straight**

pitch (*angling*) the place in a river assigned to a particular **angler**; (*association football*) the area, bounded by the **goal lines** and **touchlines**, on which a **match** is played; (*baseball*) (1) to throw the **ball** to the **batter**; (2) the ball so thrown; (*cricket*) (1) the area of ground between the **wickets**; (2) the manner of bowling the **ball** so that it lands at a particular point or from a particular direction; (3) the point where the ball bounces; (*general*) the area of play in a **field game**; (*golf*) shortening of **pitch shot**; (*horse racing*) an area at a **racecourse** assigned to a **bookmaker**; (*mountaineering*) (1) a section of rock or ice between two **belay** points; (2) a steep descent; (*rowing*) the angle at which the **blade** of the **oar** enters the water

pitch-and-putt (*golf*) a type of **miniature golf**, in which the **green** can be reached in a single **stroke**

pitch-and-run (*golf*) a **pitch shot** played so that the **ball** runs some distance on landing

pitch invasion (*association football*) the incursion of spectators onto the **pitch** during or at the end of a **match**, either in celebration or in protest

pitch mark (*golf*) a dent or small depression left by a **ball** when it lands on the **green**

pitch-out (*baseball*) a tactic by which the **pitcher** deliberately throws the **ball** wide of the **plate** in order to make it easier for the **catcher** to **throw out** a baserunner regarded as likely to attempt to **steal a base**

pitch shot (*golf*) a **shot** that sends the **ball** in a high arc so that it runs only a short distance on hitting the ground

pitch the wickets (*cricket*) to fix the **stumps** in the ground and place the **bails** on them

pitcher (*baseball*) the player who throws the **ball** to the **batter**

pitching wedge (*golf*) a **club** giving good **loft** for playing **pitch shots**

piton (*mountaineering*) an iron peg that can be hammered into the rock and have a rope attached to it [French *piton*, "eyebolt"]

pits (*auto racing*) the area close to the **circuit** where each team is assigned its **pit**

pivot (*basketball*) a move in which the player with the **ball** takes a step while keeping the other foot on the floor; (*croquet*) a **ball** positioned between the **pioneer** and the **hoop** being attempted, in order to allow the **striker's ball** to change direction

place (*horse racing*) the positions of second and third (and sometimes fourth) in a **race**

place bet (*horse racing*) a **bet** on a horse to finish second or third (or sometimes fourth) in a **race**

place horse (*horse racing*) a horse that finishes second or third (or sometimes fourth) in a **race**

place kick (*rugby league, rugby union*) a kick taken with the **ball** placed on the ground, as for a **penalty** kick or **conversion**

placepot (*horse racing*) a **bet** staked on a **place horse** in the first six **races** on the **racecard**

plain ball (*billiards*) the all-white **cue ball**, as distinct from the **spot white**; (*snooker*) a **stroke** in the center of the **cue ball**, as distinct from a **topspin**

planche (*gymnastics*) a position in which the body is supported by the arms parallel to the ground, as on the **parallel bars** or the **rings** [French *planche*, "plank"]

plane (*surfing*) to ride a wave with the hands forming a spear shape to protect the face and cut through the water

plank (*auto racing*) a wooden board fitted to the underside of **Formula One** cars as a check that they are not too close to the ground

plant (*snooker*) a **stroke** in which the **cue ball** strikes the **object ball** which then (intentionally) strikes a another **ball** into a **pocket**

plasticine (*athletics*) the soft rubber section of the **board** in the **long jump** and **triple jump** that is imprinted by the jumper's **spikes** on **takeoff** and so determines whether the **jump** was a **foul** or not [from *Plasticine*, the proprietary name of a kind of soft modeling material]

plastron (*fencing*) a padded protective garment worn under the fencing jacket [French *plastron*, from Italian *plastrone*, from *plastra*, "breastplate"]

plate (*baseball*) the five-sided white slab over which the **pitcher** must throw the **ball**; (*general*) a **cup** or other **prize** awarded to the winner of a **race**; (*horse racing*) a light racing horseshoe

plater (*horse racing*) a moderate horse entered for a **selling race**

platform (*swimming*) a rigid **diving board**, as distinct from a **springboard**

platinum duck (*cricket*) a **duck** scored by a **batsman** who is **out** on the first **ball** of the **season** [it ranks as the rarest kind, above a **golden duck**]

platoon (*American football*) a group of players trained to act as a single unit of **attackers** or **defenders**, and sent into a **game** (or taken out of it) as a body; (*general*) a group of players who alternate in the same position in a team

play (*American football*) a single period of activity, beginning with the **snap**, in which players follow prearranged actions; (*angling*) to allow a fish to exhaust itself by its struggles to get away; (*general*) a particular move or maneuver

play! (*cricket*) the call of the **umpire** at the **bowler's** end at the start of a **match** and on resumption of play after any interval

play across the line (*cricket*) as a **batsman**, to play a strong but potentially risky **shot** of the **ball** that sends it far off its course on a line between the **wickets**

play action (*American football*) an attempt to disguise a passing **play** as a running play

play away (*general*) to play a **game** on an opponent's **ground**

play back (*cricket*) to step back to play a **stroke**

play-by-play (*general*) a running commentary on a sporting event

play forward (*cricket*) to step forward to play a **full toss**

play line (*real tennis*) the line running around the walls of the **court** above which the **ball** must not be hit

play off (*golf*) (1) to play the **ball** from the **tee**; (2) to have as a **handicap**

play-off (*general*) (1) an additional **game** or **match** played to decide a **draw** or **tie**; (2) a series of games or matches played to decide a **championship** or **promotion**

play on (*cricket*) to play the **ball** onto one's own **wicket**, thus putting oneself **out**; (*general*) to continue playing after a particular incident or temporary stoppage

play pepper (*baseball*) to warm up by catching and returning **balls**

play-the-ball (*rugby league*) a means of restarting play after a **tackle**, in which the tackled player rolls the **ball** behind him with his foot

play the percentages (*general*) to play safe **shots** or moves rather than risky ones on the basis that this is more likely to bring eventual success

play through (*golf*) to continue to play, overtaking other players who have temporarily ceased playing to allow this

player-manager (*general*) a person who both plays in a team and manages it

playfield (*Australian Rules*) the area of the **pitch** marked by the boundary lines within which the **game** is played

playing field (*general*) a **field** where a sport is regularly played

playmaker (*general*) a member of a team who is skilled at initiating **plays** that might lead to a **score**

pleasure angler (*angling*) an **angler** who fishes alone, as distinct from a competing **match angler**

plug (*angling*) a type of **lure** with one or more **hooks** attached; (*golf*) to become stuck in a **hazard**

plumb (*cricket*) indisputably **leg before wicket** [as a ruling on a **batsman**]

plummet (*angling*) a weight attached to a **fishing line**, used with a **float** to gauge the depth of the **swim** or to keep the float upright

Plumpton (*horse racing*) a **National Hunt** racecourse at Plumpton Green, East Sussex, England

plunge (*American football*) a quick thrust into the **line**, as often made by a **fullback**

plunging back (*American football*) another term for a **fullback**

plus fours (*golf*) a type of baggy knickerbockers formerly worn by **golfers** [so named from the four extra inches of cloth required to create the overhang at the knee]

plus twos (*golf*) a shorter and less baggy form of **plus fours** [from the two extra inches of cloth]

poach (*association football*) to lurk around the **penalty area** of the opposing team on the chance of scoring an opportunist **goal**; (*tennis*) to take a **ball** that should have been left to one's partner in **doubles**

pocket (*American football*) the area behind the offensive **linemen**, usually affording protection to the **quarterback** when attempting a **pass**; (*billiards, snooker*) one of the six open-mouthed bags or pouches at the corners and sides of the **billiard table** into which the **balls** are struck; (*general*) a position in a **race** in which a competitor is hemmed in by others and so has no chance of winning; (*lacrosse*) the strung part of the head of the **stick** which holds the **ball**

pocket billiards (*sport*) an alternate name for **pool**

podium (*general*) the raised platform on which the winners of a **race** or other contest stand

podium finish (*auto racing, motorcycle racing*) a finish in first, second, or third place, giving the winner a stand on the **podium**

point (*cricket*) a **fielding** position on the **off side** fairly near the **batsman** on a line with the **popping crease** [so called as originally close to the point of the **bat**]; (*general*) a unit of count in scoring or judging; (*lacrosse*) a defensive player positioned a short distance in front of the **goalkeeper** and behind the **cover point**, with the role of marking the opposing team's **first home**

point after (*American football*) another term for an **extra point**

point guard (*basketball*) a player positioned away from the **basket** who directs attacking play

• **point-to-point** (*horse racing*) an amateur **steeplechase** for **hunters** over a **cross-country course** [from one point to another]

point-to-pointer (*horse racing*) a horse entered in a **point-to-point**

pointbreak (*surfing*) the place where a wave breaks around an exposed pointed rock

pointer (*horse racing*) shortening of **point-to-pointer**

pointing (*horse racing*) competing in a **point-to-point**

points competition (*cycling*) a subsidiary competition in a **stage race**, won by the **rider** who has accumulated the most **points** from his finishing positions in **stages** and from **primes**

points race (*cycling*) a **track race** in which **riders** gain **points** for their position at the end of each **lap** and in individual **sprints** throughout the **race**

poke (*cricket*) a **stroke** made by jabbing at the **ball**

pole (*athletics*) the long rod used in the **pole vault**; (*auto racing*) shortening of **pole position**; (*horse racing*) the starting position closest to the inside fence surrounding a **racecourse**; (*skiing*) shortening of **ski pole**

pole line (*cycling*) the innermost line painted around the **track** in a **velodrome**

pole position (*auto racing*) the position on the **grid** in the front row and on the inside of the first bend; (*general*) the most advantageous position in any **race** or competition

pole-sitter (*auto racing*) a driver who stays in **pole position**

pole vault (*athletics*) a **field event** in which the competitor uses a **pole** to clear a high bar

poleman (*auto racing*) a driver in **pole position**

policeman (*ice hockey*) a hefty player whose main role is to protect his own **goalscorers**

polka-dot jersey (*cycling*) the red polka-dot jersey won by the **King of the Mountains** in the **Tour de France** [French *maillot à pois rouge*, "polka-dot jersey"]

polo (*sport*) a **game** of Eastern origin similar to **field hockey** played on horseback between teams of four, using **mallets** to propel a small hard **ball** into the opponent's **goal** [Tibetan *pulu*, "ball"]

polo ground (*polo*) the dedicated area where the game is played, as a grass field with marked white lines and **goalposts** at either end

polo pony (*polo*) fuller term for a **pony**

polo stick (*polo*) the **mallet** used in playing **polo**

polocrosse (*sport*) a **game** similar to **polo** played on horseback with **sticks** having a head resembling the **crosse** used in **lacrosse**

Polytrack (*horse racing*) proprietary name of a type of synthetic surface on a **racecourse**

pommel (*gymnastics*) one of the two handrails fitted to a **pommel horse**

pommel horse (*gymnastics*) a piece of **apparatus** similar to a **vaulting horse** having a stuffed leather body with **pommels** and used in men's competition for a variety of **routines**, including **swings**, **scissors**, **splits**, and **handstands**

Pompey (*association football*) nickname of the English **club** Portsmouth [of disputed but almost certainly naval origin]

Pontefract (*horse racing*) a **flat racecourse** at Pontefract, West Yorkshire, England

pony (*polo*) a horse used in the **game**

pony goal (*polo*) a **goal** that results from the **ball** making contact with a horse

pooch kick (*American football*) a short high kick made with the aim of making the receiving team restart behind its own 20-yard line

Pool (*association football*) short name of the English **clubs** Hartlepool United and Liverpool

pool (*sport*) a form of **billiards** played with a **cue** and **balls** on a table similar to (but smaller than) a **billiard table** and having the three main types **nine-ball pool**, **eight-ball pool**, and **straight pool** [from the collective **bet** formerly placed by players]; (*swimming*) shortening of **swimming pool**

pools (*association football*) popular name of the **football pools**

pools panel (*association football*) a specially convened group of advisers who decide the results of **football matches** that have been postponed through bad weather, enabling bets to be placed as usual on the **football pools**

pop (*baseball*) shortening of **pop-up**

pop lacrosse (*lacrosse*) a simplified form of the **game** designed for young players

pop-up (*baseball*) a **ball** hit high in the air by the **batter** and giving an easy **catch**

Pop Warner football (*American football*) a junior **league** program for young boys, founded in Philadelphia in 1929 [named for **college football coach** Glenn Scobey ("Pop") Warner (1871–1954)]

popinjay (*archery*) a **target** consisting of bunches of plumage arranged atop a pole

popout (*surfing*) a poorly made **surfboard**

popping crease (*cricket*) a horizontal line marked across the **pitch** in front of the **bowling crease**, behind which the **batsman** must have a foot or the **bat** in order not to be **run out** or **stumped** and which the **bowler** must not overstep when releasing the **ball** in order to avoid delivering a **no-ball** [the **crease** was originally a depression into which the batsman had to "pop" the bat on completing a **run**]

port (*bowls*) a passage remaining open between two **bowls**; (*curling*) a passage remaining open between two **stones**; (*sailing*) the left side of a boat when facing **forward**

Portuguese Grand Prix (*auto racing*) the **Formula One** international **Grand Prix** held on the **circuit** at Estoril, Portugal

Posh (*association football*) nickname of the English **club** Peterborough United [said to derive from a "posh" (smart) team that originally played on the **ground** before the club was founded in 1934]

position (*field games*) the desired location of a player or the **ball**

position player (*baseball*) any player other than a **pitcher**

possession (*general*) (1) the state of having control of the **ball** in a **game** such as **association football**; (2) the length of time that a team has such control during a **match**

post (*association football*) one of the two pillars that support the **crossbar** and **net** of the **goal**; (*general*) shortening of **starting post, finishing post** or **winning post**; (*greyhound racing*) a greyhound's box or position number at the **start** of a **race**

post and rail (*horse racing*) (of) a **fence** consisting of posts and one or more rails

post pattern (*American football*) a route taken by a **receiver** that involves running straight up the **field** then turning in toward the **goalposts**

post up (*basketball*) to establish **possession** outside the **key** with one's back to the **basket**

post weight (*greyhound racing*) a greyhound's weight as determined by officials before it has left its **post** to enter the **track**

postman's knock (*boxing*) colloquial term for two successive **punches**

postseason (*general*) taking place after the end of the regular **season**

pot (*billiards, snooker*) to send a **ball** into a **pocket**; (*general*) (1) colloquial term for a **cup**; (2) a group of teams or individuals awaiting a **draw**; (*horse racing*) (1) a large **bet**; (2) a horse on which such a bet has been placed; (*rugby league, rugby union*) to score a **drop goal**

pot bunker (*golf*) an artificially constructed small deep **bunker**

pot-lid (*curling*) a **stone** played in such a way that it rests exactly on the **tee**

potholing (*sport*) the exploration of potholes, as deep holes and caves in limestone country

pothunter (*general*) colloquial term for a person who competes purely to win **pots** or **prizes**

Potters (*association football*) nickname of the English **club** Stoke City [from the local pottery industry]

powder skiing (*skiing*) the art of skiing on powdered snow, like that found **off piste**

Power (*Australian Rules*) short name of the Port Adelaide Power team

power forward (*basketball*) the taller of a team's two **forwards**, who specializes in catching **rebounds**

power slide (*motorcycle racing*) a method used in **speedway** for rounding a corner in which the **rider** slides the back wheel out in a controlled skid while maintaining acceleration

powerboat racing (*sport*) the sport of navigating a motor-powered boat, either at sea or inland on a lake or river

powerlifting (*weightlifting*) a contest of strength involving a **bench press**, a **squat**, and a two-handed **dead lift**

powerplay (*cricket*) a period in a **limited-over match** during which there are special restrictions on the positions where **fielders** may be stationed; (*general*) a strong attacking play designed to put pressure on the **defense** by concentrating players in one small area; (*ice hockey*) a formation adopted when the opposing team has one or two players on the **penalty bench**; (*tennis*) tactics that involve hitting the **ball** with maximum speed and strength

practice swing (*golf*) a trial **swing** made without contacting the **ball** as a preliminary to the actual **stroke**

prayer (*American football*) colloquial term for a

desperate **pass**, especially when there is no obvious **receiver** to catch it

pre-season (*general*) (of) a period of **games** before the regular **season** begins

Preakness Stakes (*horse racing*) an annual **race** for three-year-old **thoroughbreds** held at Pimlico, Baltimore, Maryland, since 1873 [named for the **colt** Preakness]

Predators (*ice hockey*) short name of the Nashville Predators team

Premier League (*association football*) the **division** of 20 English **clubs** formed in 1992 from the old Division 1 of the **Football League**

premiership (*general*) a competition between the top **clubs** in a sport

Premiership (*association football*) another name for the **Premier League**

prep (*horse racing*) shortening of **prep race**

prep race (*horse racing*) a minor **race** that tests a horse's capabilities before the major one [shortening of *preparatory race*]

prep run (*horse racing*) another term for a **prep race**

present (*horse racing*) a sum of money paid by the **owner** of a horse to the winning **jockey**

President's Cup (*equestrianism*) the **trophy** awarded since 1965 to the winner, based on the results of earlier competitions, of a team **showjumping championship**

press (*basketball*) any kind of close guarding by the defending team; (*golf*) to send the **ball** in the wrong direction by trying to hit it too hard; (*gymnastics*) the raising of the body by continuous muscular effort; (*weightlifting*) the raising of a **weight** to shoulder level, then its gradual extension above the head

press-out (*weightlifting*) an illegal move in which the arms are not straight when a **lift** is attempted but are then straightened when it is completed

press-up (*gymnastics*) an exercise performed face down in which the body is raised and lowered on the arms while the trunk and legs are kept straight

pressure hold (*mountaineering*) a **hold** made by applying pressure downward or sideways

prevent defense (*American football*) a defensive strategy in which the **offense** is allowed to advance the **ball** by small degrees but denied the opportunity to advance and score quickly

priest (*angling*) a club or mallet for killing fish [by administering the "last rites"]

primary receiver (*American football*) the offensive **receiver** ear-marked to catch the **ball**

Primavera (*cycling*) an alternate name for the **Milan-San Remo** road race [Italian *primavera*, "spring," the season when it is held]

prime (*cycling*) the place in a **road race** or **stage** of a **stage race** at which **points** are assigned in the

points competition; (*fencing*) the first of eight basic **parry** positions, used to protect the upper inside of the body [French *prime*, "first"]

primitive bow (*archery*) a competitive **bow** made of wood

Princess Elizabeth Cup (*rowing*) the **trophy** awarded to the winner of a **race** for school **eights** at **Henley** [presented in 1946 by Princess Elizabeth, later Queen Elizabeth II (1926–)]

Prix de l'Arc de Triomphe (*horse racing*) a prestigious **race** for **colts** and **fillies** held annually at **Longchamp** since 1920 [named for the Arc de Triomphe, Paris, a noted commemorative monument]

prize (*general*) a reward or symbol of success, such as a sum of money or a **trophy**, won in a sporting contest

prize ring (*boxing*) a **ring** where **prizefights** are held

prizefight (*boxing*) a **boxing match** fought for a **prize** in the form of money

prizefighter (*boxing*) a contestant in a **prizefight**

prizewinner (*general*) the winner of a **prize**

pro (*general*) shortening of **professional**

pro-am (*golf*) a **tournament** for both **professionals** and **amateurs**

Pro Bowl (*American football*) a **game** played in Hawaii at the end of the **season** between teams selected from the best players in the **AFC** and **NFC**

pro-celebrity (*golf*) (of) a **tournament** involving **professionals** and celebrities

pro football (*American football*) shortening of **professional football**

Pro-Ride (*horse racing*) proprietary name of a type of synthetic surface on a **racecourse**

pro shop (*golf*) a shop run by a resident **professional** at a **golf club**

Probables v. Possibles (*general*) a **trial match** to select a team in a sport such as **association football** ["Probables" being more likely to be selected than "Possibles"]

procession (*cricket*) the rapid loss of a number of **wickets** [the outgoing and incoming **batsmen** form something of a procession across the **pitch**]; (*general*) a **race** in which the winner is so far ahead that the rest of the **field** trails in a long line behind him

proette (*golf*) a female **professional** [combination of **pro** and the feminine suffix *-ette*, designed to avoid the undesirable sense of *pro*]

professional (*general*) a person who regularly takes part in sport for payment, as distinct from an **amateur**

professional football (*American football*) the sport as played by **professionals**, introduced in 1895

professional foul (*association football*) an intentional **foul** made to prevent the opposing team from scoring

professional's side (*golf*) colloquial term for the **high side** [a player who misses a **putt** on this side has not underestimated the **borrow**, as an **amateur** might do]

profit foul (*basketball*) the equivalent of a **professional foul**

Pro40 League (*cricket*) a **league** of **county cricket** teams who play 40 **overs** a side

promoter (*general*) the organizer of a sporting event such as a **boxing match**

promotion (*association football*) the elevation of a **club** from a lower **division** to a higher following a **season** in which the club has finished in a high position in the **league**; (*general*) the staging for profit of a sporting event such as a **boxing match**

prone (*shooting*) a position lying face down in a **small-bore rifle** competition

prop (*boxing*) the extended arm of a **boxer**; (*horse racing*) to stop suddenly [the horse's rigid forelegs are like a prop]; (*rugby league, rugby union*) one of the two outside **front-row forwards** who support the **hooker** in a **scrum**

prop forward (*rugby league, rugby union*) fuller term for a **prop**

propeller (*angling*) a type of artificial **bait** with blades that rotate when drawn through the water

protection (*mountaineering*) the **running belays** necessary to safeguard a **pitch**

protection area (*wrestling*) the border of the **mat** beyond the **passivity zone**

proximity flying (*sport*) an extreme form of **base jumping** in which the participant, deploying a **parachute** and sometimes wearing a special "wingsuit," keeps deliberately close to the surface of the structure from which he jumps

prusik (*mountaineering*) a type of rope sling that enables a climber to ascend or descend a **climbing rope** [devised by the Austrian climber Karl Prusik (1895–1961)]

puck (*hurling*) a **stroke** of the **ball**; (*ice hockey*) the hard thick rubber disk used instead of a **ball** [origin unknown]

puck carrier (*ice hockey*) the player in **possession** of the **puck** during play

puck-chaser (*ice hockey*) colloquial term for a player of the **game**

puddle (*rowing*) the whirlpool effect when the **oar** comes out of the water at the end of a **stroke**

pugilism (*sport*) a formal alternate name for **boxing** [Latin *pugil*, "boxer"]

pugilist (*boxing*) an alternate term for a **boxer**

puissance (*equestrianism*) a **showjumping** competition that tests a horse's power to jump large **obstacles** [French *puissance*, "power"]

pull (*American football*) to withdraw from the **line**

of scrimmage and cross behind it in order to block opposing players and clear the way for a **runner**; (*cricket*) short for **pull the ball**; (*general*) to withdraw a player from a **game**; (*golf*) short for **pull a shot**; (*horse racing*) (1) to hold back a horse in order to prevent it from winning; (2) an advantage in **weight** over another horse; (*rowing*) short for **pull the oars**

pull! (*shooting*) the command given in **trapshooting** to release the **clay pigeon**

pull a punch (*boxing*) to hold back the full force of a **punch**

pull a shot (*golf*) to play a **shot** that sends the **ball** too much to the left (for a right-handed player) or to the right (for a left-handed player)

pull back (*association football*) to score a **goal** that brings a losing team level with the opposing side

pull drive (*cricket*) a **drive** that brings the **ball** from the **off side** to the **leg side**

pull hitter (*baseball*) a **hitter** who consistently **pulls the ball**

pull-out (*surfing*) the ending of a ride by steering the **surfboard** over or through the back of a wave

pull stroke (*cricket*) a **stroke** that brings the **ball** from the **off side** to the **leg side**

pull the ball (*baseball*) to hit the **ball** into **left field** from a right-handed stance (or into **right field** from a left-handed stance); (*cricket*) to hit the **ball** with a horizontal **bat** at waist height round to the **leg side**

pull the goalie (*ice hockey*) to replace the **goalkeeper** during a **game** with an additional attacking player

pull the oars (*rowing*) to row [by pulling the **oars** through the water]

pull the string (*baseball*) to throw a slow **ball**

pull up (*equestrianism, horse racing*) to come to a halt

pull-up (*gymnastics*) an exercise in which the **gymnast** hangs from a bar by his hands then pulls himself up so that his chin is level with the bar

Pumas (*rugby union*) nickname of the Argentine national team [so dubbed as a rival to the **Springboks** by a journalist who mistook the jaguar on the team's crest for a puma]

pump (*sailing*) to increase the speed of a boat by rapidly pulling the **sails** in and out

pump iron (*general*) to exercise with **weights** as a form of **bodybuilding**

punch (*boxing*) a blow with the fist; (*golf*) a **shot** that sends the **ball** in a low trajectory

Punch-and-Judy hitter (*baseball*) a **batter** who hits the **ball** softly [as if merely a puppet like Punch beating his wife Judy]

punch and retreat (*boxing*) a strategy of gradually wearing down an opponent by delivering a series of individual **punches** while otherwise avoiding any direct engagement or action

punch drunk (*boxing*) suffering from cerebral concussion inflicted by past blows in the sport [the sufferer moves as if drunk]

punch out (*baseball*) colloquial equivalent of **strike out**

punchbag (*boxing*) a large stuffed bag for **boxers** to practice punching

punchball (*boxing*) a suspended **ball** for **boxers** to practice punching; (*sport*) a **game** similar to **baseball** in which a rubber **ball** is punched with the fist or head

Punchestown (*horse racing*) a flat and **National Hunt racecourse** at Naas, Co. Kildare, Ireland

punching bag (*boxing*) another term for a **punchbag**

punishment (*general*) damaging treatment, as in the repeated **punches** of a **boxer** on his opponent or, in **cricket**, in the ready **runs** scored by a **batsman** from the **balls** of a **bowler**

punt (*American football*) the kick of a **ball** dropped from the hands before it touches the ground, and specifically such a kick **upfield** into the opposing team's territory, usually on the fourth **down**, so that the opposing team have to move the ball a greater distance when they gain **possession**; (*general*) a kick made by dropping the **ball** from the hands and kicking it before it touches the ground, as in **rugby league**

punter (*American football*) a player who specializes in **punts**; (*horse racing*) a person who bets on the results of **races**

Pura Cup (*cricket*) the **cup** awarded to the winner of an annual Australian interstate competition, first held in 1893 [name of sponsor]

pursuit (*cycling*) shortening of **pursuit race**

pursuit race (*cycling*) a **race** in which two **riders** start at opposite sides of a **track** and try to overtake each other

push (*cricket*) a **stroke** by the **batsman** that merely eases the **ball** away; (*snooker*) shortening of **push stroke**; (*table tennis*) a defensive **shot** played with **backspin**

push a shot (*golf*) to play a **shot** that sends the **ball** too much to the right (of a right-handed player) or to the left (of a left-handed player)

push and run (*association football*) a style of play in which players pass the **ball** quickly then run to receive a return **pass**

push hold (*mountaineering*) another term for a **pressure hold**

push-in (*field hockey*) the act of pushing the **ball** into play from the **sideline**

push-off (*swimming*) the act of pushing oneself off the end of the **pool** in turning

push pass (*athletics*) a method of **handover** in a relay race in which the incoming runner pushes the **baton** into the palm of the outgoing runner; (*general*) a **pass** made by pushing rather than hitting or kicking the **ball**

push shot (*general*) a **shot** in which the **ball** is pushed instead of being hit; (*snooker*) another term for a **push stroke**

push stroke (*snooker*) an illegal **stroke** in which the **cue** is still in contact (or comes into contact again) with the **cue ball** when the latter touches the **object ball**

push the ball (*field hockey*) to propel the **ball** in a continuous movement with the **stick** across the **pitch** in such a way that the ball does not leave the ground

push-up (*gymnastics*) (1) another term for a **press-up**; (2) an exercise on the **parallel bars** in which the body is supported on bent arms and raised when they are straightened

pushball (*sport*) a simple **game** for two teams in which one team tries to push a very large **ball** toward and into the opponent's **goal**

pusher (*octopush*) the **stick** used to propel the **squid**

pushout (*pool*) a **shot** allowed after the **break** in which a player can hit the **ball** anywhere on the **table** and the opponent can either take the next shot from where it finishes or ask the first player to begin again; (*wrestling*) the act of pushing an opponent out of the **ring**

pushover (*rugby union*) shortening of **pushover try**

pushover try (*rugby union*) a **try** scored after a **maul** or **scrum** close to the **try line** has been pushed over the line and enabled a **touchdown**

put down (*cricket*) to drop a **catch**

put-in (*rugby league, rugby union*) the throwing of the **ball** into the **scrum**

put on (*general*) to add a particular number of **points** or **runs** to a **score**

put out (*general*) to cause a player in a **game** or **match** to be **out**

put up (*cricket*) to score a particular number of **runs**

putt (*golf*) (1) to hit the **ball** gently so that it goes across the **green** and, ideally, into the **hole**; (2) a **stroke** that sends the ball thus [a Scottish form of *put*]

putt out (*golf*) to finish a **game** by **putting** into the **hole**

putter (*golf*) (1) a short-handled **club** with an upright striking face, used for hitting a **putt**; (2) a player hitting a **putt**; (*putting*) a player engaged in the sport

putting (*golf*) the act of hitting a **putt**; (*sport*) a **game** similar to **miniature golf**, played with **putters** and **golf balls** on a small **course** with several **holes**

putting cleek (*golf*) an old-fashioned **putter** similar to a **cleek**, with a long narrow blade running direct from the **shaft**

putting green (*golf*) (1) a formal term for the **green**; (2) a small **golf course** with several **holes** used for practice or for the sport of **putting**

putting the shot (*athletics*) another term for the **shot put**

pyramid (*snooker*) the triangle of 15 **reds** set up at the start of the **game** in the top half of the **billiard table**

pyramid rest (*billiards, snooker*) another term for a **spider**

pyramid spot (*billiards*) the **spot** on the table midway between the **center spot** and the top **cushion**, corresponding to the **pink spot** in **snooker**

pyramids (*snooker*) a variant of the **game** played with 15 **reds** arranged into a **pyramid** and one white **cue ball** (but no **colors**)

Q school (*golf*) abbreviation of **qualifying school**

QPR (*association football*) short name of the English **club** Queen's Park Rangers

quad (*rowing*) shortening of **quadruple scull**

quad bike (*motorcycle racing*) a four-wheeled motorcycle

quadrella (*horse racing*) a **bet** on the winners of a group of four **races** in a **meeting** [Latin *quadr-*, "four" with diminutive suffix *-ella*]

quadruple scull (*rowing*) a four-manned boat in which each **rower** has a pair of **sculls**

Quakers (*association football*) nickname of the English **club** Darlington [from the town's long association with the Quakers (Society of Friends)]

qualifier (*general*) shortening of **qualifying round**

qualifying round (*general*) a preliminary **round** of a competition, designed to limit the number of entrants

qualifying school (*golf*) a six-**round** competition held annually for players seeking one of 35 places on the **European Tour**

quarte (*fencing*) the fourth of eight basic **parry** positions, used to protect the upper inside of the left of the body [French *quarte*, "fourth"]

quarter (*American football*) (1) one of the periods of 15 minutes into which a **game** is divided; (2) shortening of **quarterback**; (*Australian Rules*) one of the periods of 20 minutes into which a **match** is divided

quarter court (*squash*) one half of the back part of the **court**

quarter-final (*general*) the **round** before the **semifinal** in a **knockout competition**

quarter-line (*rugby union*) another term for the **twenty-two**

quarter-miler (*athletics*) an expert in running the quarter-mile (now **400 meters**)

quarter-pipe (*skateboarding*) half of a **half-pipe**, as a curved ramp

quarter-race (*horse racing*) a **race** over a quarter of a mile

quarter stretch (*horse racing*) a part of a **racecourse** that is a quarter of a mile long

quarterback (*American football*) the player between the **linemen** and the **running backs**, who directs his team's attacking play

quarterback club (*American football*) an association of **supporters** who actively promote their team

quarterback sack (*American football*) an attack on a **quarterback** before he can make a **pass**

quarterback sneak (*American football*) a **play** in which a **quarterback** carries the **ball** instead of passing it to another **back**

quasimodo (*surfing*) a crouched position adopted when riding a **surfboard** [from the name of the "Hunchback of Notre Dame," the deformed bellringer in Victor Hugo's 1831 novel *Notre Dame de Paris*]

Queens (*association football*) short name of the Scottish **club** Queen of the South

Queen's Prize (*shooting*) the leading award for **rifle shooting** [founded in 1860 by Queen Victoria (reigned 1837–1901)]

Queensberry Rules (*boxing*) the standard rules of the modern form of the sport [introduced in 1867 under the patronage of the 8th Marquis of Queensberry (1844–1900)]

quickie (*cricket*) colloquial term for a **fast bowler**

quickstick (*lacrosse*) a **shot** made by a player without using a **cradle** between receiving the **ball** and sending it on

quinella (*horse racing*) a **bet** on the horses that will finish first and second in a **race** (but not on their order of finishing) [American Spanish *quiniela*]

Quins (*rugby union*) short name of the English **club** Harlequins

quinte (*fencing*) the fifth of eight basic **parry** positions, used to protect the lower inside of the body [French *quinte*, "fifth"]

quiver (*archery*) a long narrow case for holding **arrows**

quoit (*quoits*) a ring made of rubber, rope, or the like (originally iron), used for throwing in the **game** named for it

quoits (*sport*) a **game** in which a **quoit** is thrown to encircle or land as near as possible to a peg or small post [origin uncertain]

R&A (*golf*) abbreviation of the **Royal and Ancient Golf Club of St. Andrews**

rabbit (*athletics*) colloquial term for a **pacemaker**; (*cricket*) (1) colloquial term for a poor **batsman**; (2) colloquial term for a **batsman** often dismissed by the same **bowler**; (*golf*) colloquial term for a poor player [from the characteristic timidity of a rabbit]

rabbit ball (*baseball*) a **ball** that is lively in action [it springs like a rabbit]

rabbit punch (*boxing*) an illegal **punch** to the back of the neck [like that used by hunters and farmers to kill a rabbit]

Rabbitohs (*rugby league*) short name of the Australian team South Sydney Rabbitohs

rabbitry (*general*) (1) a poor player; (2) poor performance in a **game** [like that of a **rabbit**]

race (*general*) a competitive trial of speed, as in **auto racing, cycling, greyhound racing, horse racing, rowing, sailing,** and **swimming**

race-fixing (*general*) the fraudulent manipulation of the result of a **race**

race meeting (*horse racing*) a series of **races** on a particular day at a **racecourse**

race walking (*athletics*) a form of **racing** in which the competitors walk as fast as possible, with one or other of the feet always in contact with the ground

raceball (*horse racing*) a ball held in connection with a **race meeting**

racecar (*auto racing*) a specially constructed or modified automobile used for the sport

racecard (*horse racing*) the program of a day of **races** at a **race meeting**

racecourse (*horse racing*) a delimited area or **track**, with or without obstacles, that is specially prepared for **racing**

raceday (*horse racing*) the day when a particular **race** or **meeting** is held

racegoer (*horse racing*) a person who regularly visits **race meetings**, usually to place **bets**

racehorse (*horse racing*) a horse specially bred and trained to take part in **racing**

racemare (*horse racing*) a female **racehorse**

racer (*general*) a person or vehicle that takes part in a **race**

races (*horse racing*) another term for a **race meeting**

racetrack (*general*) an area marked out as the location of a **race**; (*horse racing*) another term for a **racecourse**

racewalk (*athletics*) a contest in **race walking**

raceway (*horse racing*) a **track** or **circuit** for running horses in **harness racing**

racing (*general*) the act of taking part in a **race**; (*sport*) shortening of (especially) **horse racing** or of any sport specified by the first word, as **auto racing, greyhound racing**

racing car (*auto racing*) another term for a **racecar**

racing colors (*horse racing*) the distinctive **colors** worn by a **jockey** to identify the **owner** of the horse

racing dive (*swimming*) a **dive** approached by a **run-up**

racing flag (*sailing*) a private flag flown on a boat or **yacht** when racing

racing form (*horse racing*) a record of a horse's performance in previous **races**

racing line (*auto racing*) the optimum line on a **track** on which to drive between one corner and the next

rack (*equestrianism*) a horse's **gait** in which the legs on the same side move almost simultaneously; (*pool*) (1) the arrangement of the **balls** at the beginning of the **game**; (2) a single **game**

racket (*general*) a **bat** with a round or oval frame strung with catgut or nylon, used in sports such as **tennis** and **squash**

racket abuse (*tennis*) an impetuous act in which a player hurls his **racket** to the ground or smashes it against something

racketball (*sport*) a British version of **racquetball**, played on a smaller **court** with a slower **ball**

rackets (*sport*) a **game** similar to **squash**, in which two or four people alternately strike a hard white **ball** with a **racket** against one of the walls of a four-walled **court**

racquet (*general*) another spelling of **racket**

racquetball (*sport*) a **game** of U.S. origin blending elements of **handball** and **squash**, played between two or four players with a short-handled **racket** and a small rubber **ball** in a four-walled **court**

racquets (*sport*) alternate spelling of **rackets**

rafting (*sport*) the sport of traveling down a river, especially over rapids, on a raft

ragworm (*angling*) the burrowing marine worm *Nereis diversicolor* used as **bait**

raider (*horse racing*) a horse brought over from abroad to run in a particular **race**

Raiders (*American football*) short name of the Oakland Raiders team; (*rugby league*) short name of the English **club** Barrow Raiders

rail (*equestrianism*) a wooden bar in an **obstacle**; (*pool, snooker*) another term for the **cushion**; (*squash*) a **shot** hit close to the side walls of the **court**; (*surfing*) the edge of the **surfboard**

rail turn (*surfing*) a trick turn in which the **rail** of the **surfboard** is submerged

rails (*horse racing*) the fence forming the inside boundary of a **racecourse**

Railwaymen (*association football*) nickname of the English **club** Crewe Alexandra [from the town's historic importance as a railroad center]

rainbow jersey (*cycling*) the multicolored jersey awarded to the winner of the **World Road Race Championships**

rainbow shot (*basketball*) a **shot** that curves from the player's hand down into the **basket**

raincheck (*general*) a ticket for future use given to a spectator if a **game** or sports meeting is **rained off**

rained off (*general*) cancelled or prematurely ended because of rain

raise (*curling*) a **draw** that knocks another **stone** into the **house** or into a better position within it

rally (*auto racing*) (1) formerly, a **race** as both a test of endurance and speed and a method of recording the performance of automobiles; (2) today, a competition to test skill in driving over long distances, sometimes over an unknown route, as either a **road rally** or a **stage rally**; (*badminton, squash, table tennis, tennis*) a vigorous or extended exchange of **shots**, especially to decide a **point**; (*boxing*) a sustained exchange of blows [French *rallier,* "re-ally," "bring together again"]

rally driver (*auto racing*) a driver in a **rally**

rally driving (*auto racing*) the sport of driving in a **rally**

rallycross (*auto racing*) a form of the sport that combines elements of **rally driving** and **autocross**, with a **circuit** that consists partly of paved road and partly of rough ground

rallye (*auto racing*) alternate spelling of **rally**

rallying (*auto racing*) shortening of **rally driving**

Rams (*American football*) short name of the St. Louis Rams team; (*association football*) nickname of the English **club** Derby County [from a local legend about the mythical Derby Ram]; (*rugby league*) short name of the English **club** Dewsbury Rams

randolph (*trampolining*) a forward **somersault** with two and a half **twists** [named from its similarity to a **rudolph**]

randy (*trampolining*) colloquial name for a **randolph**

Ranfurly Shield (*rugby union*) the **trophy** awarded to the winner of a New Zealand interprovincial competition [presented in 1902 by the 5th Earl of Ranfurly (1856–1933), governor of New Zealand]

range (*golf*) shortening of **driving range**; (*shooting*) shortening of **rifle range** or **shooting range**

ranger (*golf*) an official who monitors the rate of play on a **course**, encouraging slow players to speed up or to allow others to **play through**

Rangers (*association football*) short name of the English **club** Queen's Park Rangers [not to be confused with either of the Scottish clubs Queen's Park or Rangers]; (*baseball*) short name of the Texas Rangers team; (*ice hockey*) short name of the New York Rangers team

rappel (*mountaineering*) another term for **abseil** [French *rappel,* "recall"]

Raptors (*basketball*) short name of the Toronto Raptors team

rapture of the deep (*aquatics*) colloquial term for nitrogen narcosis, the intoxicating and anesthetic effect of too much nitrogen in the brain, experienced by **divers** at considerable depths

rate (*horse racing*) to ride at a moderate pace so as to save the horse's energy for the **finish**

rating (*rowing*) the total of **strokes** rowed per minute, used to advise a **crew** of its work rate

rattle (*association football*) a wooden instrument with a ratchet wheel which when whirled around makes a loud clacking noise, formerly sounded by a team's **supporters** at a **match**

Ravens (*American football*) short name of the Baltimore Ravens team

RBI (*baseball*) abbreviation of **run batted in**

reach (*boxing*) the distance between the fingertips of the outstretched arms of a **boxer**; (*cricket*) the extent to which a **batsman** can **play forward** without moving his **back foot**

reaction time (*athletics*) the fraction of time between the firing of the **starting pistol** and the departure of the **athlete** from the **starting block**

read the green (*golf*) to assess the physical features of the **green** on making an **approach shot**

ready golf (*golf*) a mode of playing in which players aim to keep up with those playing in front of them, as by selecting a **club** while walking to the **ball** rather than when stationary

Real (*association football*) short name of the Spanish **club** Real Madrid

real tennis (*sport*) the original form of **tennis**, played between two or four players, who hit a hard **ball** with a **racket** back and forth across a **net** in a **court** reminiscent of medieval cloisters with a **penthouse** along three of its sides [so named by contrast with **lawn tennis**]

rebound (*basketball*) an instance of catching the **ball** after a missed **shot** has bounced off the **backboard** or the edge of the **basket**

rec (*general*) colloquial abbreviation of **recreation ground**

recce (*auto racing*) in **rally driving**, inspection of the **course** by the driver and **codriver** in advance of the **rally** in order to draw up the **pace notes**

receiver (*American football*) an offensive player eligible to catch a **pass** from the **quarterback**; (*table tennis, tennis*) the player to whom the **server** serves the **ball**

record (*general*) an unsurpassed achievement or performance in a competitive sport

recordbreaker (*general*) a person who has set a new **record**

recordholder (*general*) a person whose **record** has not been beaten

recovery (*golf*) a **stroke** that brings the **ball** out of a **hazard**; (*rowing*) the phase in the **stroke** cycle in which the **rower** swings forward to take the next **catch**

recreation ground (*general*) a public open area for sports and **games**, often including **tennis courts** and a park

recumbent (*cycling*) a low-slung bicycle in an aerodynamic bodyshell in which the **rider** is in a recumbent position

recurve (*archery*) a **bow** with **limbs** curving away from the **archer**

recycle (*rugby union*) to keep **possession** of the **ball** after a **breakdown**

red (*billiards*) the red **ball**, worth three **points**; (*snooker*) the red **ball**, worth one **point**

red-ball game (*sport*) byname of **cricket** when played with a traditional red **ball**, as distinct from the modern **white-ball game**

red belt (*judo, karate*) a belt worn to indicate attainment of the **dan** rank

red card (*association football*) a red-colored card shown by the **referee** to a player who is being **sent off**, either because he has committed a serious **foul** or because he has already been shown two **yellow cards**

Red Devils (*association football*) nickname of the English **club** Manchester United [from the color of the team's shirts]

red dog (*American football*) a **play** in which one of the defensive team **rushes** the passer of the **ball**

red flag (*athletics*) a **flag** waved to an **athlete** who commits a **foul** in a **jump** or **throw**; (*auto racing*) a **flag** waved to show that a **race** has been stopped, as for bad weather conditions

Red Imps (*association football*) nickname of the English **club** Lincoln City [as for **Imps** with the color of the team's shirts]

Red Lichties (*association football*) nickname of the Scottish **club** Arbroath [from Scots *red licht*, "red light," from the red light cast by the Bell Rock lighthouse off the coast here]

red line (*cycling*) another term for the **sprinters' line**; (*ice hockey*) the line that divides the playing area into two

red rose (*general*) the emblem of a Yorkshire sports team, as opposed to the **white rose** [from the Wars of the Roses, the 15th-century dynastic struggle between the English houses of Lancaster and York, whose respective emblems were a white rose and a red rose]

Red Sox (*baseball*) short name of the Boston Red Sox team

red spinner (*angling*) an **artificial fly** imitating the olive dun **mayfly**

Red Stockings (*baseball*) short name of the Cincinnati Red Stockings team

Red Wings (*ice hockey*) short name of the Detroit Red Wings team

red zone (*American football*) the area between the **goal line** and the 20-yard line, within which the offensive team concentrate their attack strategy

Redbacks (*water polo*) nickname of the Australian national men's team [name of a type of poisonous spider]

Redcar (*horse racing*) a **flat racecourse** at Redcar, northeastern England

Reds (*association football*) nickname of the English **clubs** Barnsley, Liverpool, and Nottingham Forest [the color of the teams' shirts]; (*rugby league*) short name of the English **club** Salford City Reds

redshirt (*American football*) in **college football**, a player whose course is extended by one year, usually the sophomore year, during which he is not selected for a representative team in order to develop his skills and extend his period of eligibility [the color of his shirt, worn for distinction from members of the **varsity**]

Redskins (*American football*) short name of the Washington Redskins team

reefbreak (*surfing*) the point where a wave breaks over a shallow underwater reef

reel (*angling*) a cylindrical device attached to a **fishing rod**, used to wind the **line**

reel in (*angling*) to draw in a hooked fish by winding in the **line** onto the **reel**

re-entry (*surfing*) a trick that resembles "skating" on a **surfboard** along the top curl of a wave [the **board** leaves the wave, then comes back down to re-enter it]

ref (*general*) colloquial shortening of **referee**

referee (*American football*) the person in overall charge of the officiating team; (*association football*) the official in charge of a **game**, who upholds the rules with the aid of two **assistant referees** on the **touchlines** and a **fourth official** off the **pitch**; (*boxing*) the official stationed in the **ring** with the **boxers** who regulates the **bout**, intervening if necessary to stop a fight and administering the **count** to a boxer down on the **canvas**; (*cricket*) an official who deals with disciplinary matters in a **test match**; (*fencing*) the controller of a **bout**; (*wrestling*) one of the three officials in charge of a **bout**, adjudicating from the **mat**

referral (*cricket*) a referral to the **third umpire** of a disputed decision by the **umpire**

refusal (*equestrianism, horse racing*) the pulling up or running aside of a horse at a **fence**

regatta (*rowing, sailing*) an organized program of **races** [Venetian Italian *regata*, "contest"]

regional games (*Olympics*) a festival of **Olympic Games** held within a particular geographical region, as the **African Games** or **Pan-American Games**

registered player (*tennis*) an independent **professional** registered with the International Tennis Federation who is eligible to play for **prize money** in open **tournaments**

regular footer (*snowboarding*) a **boarder** who rides with the left foot in front of the right

reining (*equestrianism*) a **discipline** in which the **rider** uses the reins to perform a **routine** of figures, including turns and stops at different speeds

relative work (*parachuting*) a **free fall** in which competitors execute maneuvers relative to each other before opening the **parachute**

relay (*athletics*) shortening of **relay race**; (*baseball*) a **throw** to the **infield** by a **cut-off man** after he has intercepted a throw from the **outfield**

relay race (*athletics*) a **race** run by a team of four **athletes** over the same distance, each passing a **baton** to the next member of the team on completing a **stage**

release (*gymnastics*) the action of letting go one's hold of a piece of **apparatus** during or on completing a **routine**

relegation (*association football*) the demotion of a **club** from a higher **division** to a lower following a **season** in which they finished at or near the bottom of their division

relegation zone (*association football*) the positions at the bottom of a **league** which will result in **relegation** at the end of the **season**

reliability test (*auto racing*) former name for a **rally**

reliability trial (*auto racing*) alternate term for a **reliability test**

relief (*golf*) the option of moving one's **ball** if a normal **stroke** is obstructed

relief pitcher (*baseball*) a **pitcher** who enters the **game** as a **substitute**

reliever (*baseball*) another term for a **relief pitcher**

reload (*golf*) to take a second **tee shot** because the first **ball** is lost or **out of bounds**

rematch (*general*) (1) a second **match**, especially when the first had a questionable result; (2) a **return match**

remise (*fencing*) a second **thrust** made after the first one has missed [French *remise*, "put back"]

remove (*cricket*) to **dismiss** a **batsman**

rep (*general*) abbreviation of **replacement** in sports reports

repechage (*canoeing, cycling, fencing, rowing*) an extra contest in which competitors who lost in an earlier **heat** have a second chance to go on to the **final** [French *repêchage*, "fishing out again"]

repetition training (*athletics*) a training exercise in which an **athlete** alternately runs and rests over set distances

replacement (*general*) a player who replaces another, especially in a **field game**

replay (*general*) (1) a **game** or **match** that is played again, as when the original did not result in a winning **score** or was for some reason abandoned; (2) shortening of **action replay**

replay umpire (*cricket*) another term for a **third umpire**

reserve (*general*) a **substitute** kept in readiness

resistance (*equestrianism*) movements by a horse that indicate an imminent **refusal**

rest (*billiards, snooker*) a long wooden pole with a **bridge** at one end on which a player rests his **cue** when he cannot form a bridge with his hand; (*bowls*) a **shot** in which a **bowl** is delivered to push an opponent's bowl through and take its place [the opposing bowl is given a "rest"]; (*real tennis*) a series of **strokes** concluding with the **dead ball**

rest day (*general*) a day free of activity in an extended contest such as a **cycle race**

rest on one's oars (*rowing*) to stop rowing without removing the **oars** from the **rowlocks**

restart (*rugby union*) a **drop kick** from the **halfway line** to recommence play after the scoring of **points** by the opposing team

result (*general*) a satisfactory outcome against an opponent

retain (*association football*) to keep a player on in a **club** although his actual contract has expired

retire (*fencing*) to give ground before one's adversary

retired hurt (*cricket*) (of) a **batsman** who has left the **pitch** because of injury

retired shirt (*association football*) the symbolic removal of a former player's **squad number** in recognition of his value to the **club**

retrieve (*angling*) to **reel in** a **line**; (*association football*) to obtain **possession** of a **shot** or **pass** that is difficult to reach; (*tennis*) to make a **shot** that returns the **ball** successfully into the **court** when it seemed that it would land outside it

return (*general*) a **shot** that sends a **ball** back to an opponent, as in **tennis**

return crease (*cricket*) a line marked at right angles to the **bowling crease** and **popping crease** on either side of the **wicket**, inside which the **bowler** must bowl the **ball**

return match (*general*) a second **match** played at a different **venue** by the same teams

returner (*American football*) a player who collects the **ball** from a kick **downfield** and carries it back toward the opposing team

reversal (*wrestling*) a maneuver enabling a **wrestler** to escape from the **hold** of his opponent and move into a dominant position

reverse (*American football*) a **play** in which a player passes the **ball** to a teammate moving in the opposite direction, thus reversing the direction of attack; (*swimming*) a **dive** in which the **diver** starts facing forward then turns back to face the **board**

reverse cut (*lacrosse*) another term for a **backdoor play**

reverse pass (*association football*) a **pass** made when a player runs in one direction but passes in another direction

reverse sticks (*field hockey*) a move in which a player turns the **stick** so that the flat blade faces to the right, enabling a **shot** to be made in the opposite direction

reverse sweep (*cricket*) a **sweep** played on the **off side**, made by reversing the **grip** on the **bat**

reverse swing (*cricket*) the observed **swing** in a different direction to a **new ball** of a used ball that has been roughened on one side

revirginization (*ice skating*) the process by which professional skaters were declared "amateurs" so that they could compete in the 1994 **Olympics**

Rhinos (*rugby league*) short name of the English **club** Leeds Rhinos

rhubarb (*baseball*) an argument on the field of play between players or between the **umpire** and **managers** [from the use of the word to denote the indistinct sound of voices]

rhythmic gymnastics (*gymnastics*) a combination of traditional **floor exercises** and classical ballet in which female **gymnasts** perform with a **ball**, hoop, rope, ribbon, or the like

ride (*horse racing*) to urge a horse at an excessive speed

ride off (*polo*) to bump against an opponent's horse moving in the same direction

ride-off (*equestrianism*) an extra **round** to resolve a **tie** in a competition

ride out (*horse racing*) to exercise a horse by riding it

rider (*cycling*) a **cyclist** in a **race**; (*equestrianism*) a person riding a horse in a contest; (*general*) a person riding a **board** in a sport such as **skateboarding** or **surfing**; (*horse racing*) a person riding a horse in a **race**, as a **jockey**; (*motorcycle racing*) a person riding a motorcycle in a **race**

riding (*general*) the riding of horses for exercise or pleasure; (*Olympics*) another term for **showjumping** in the **modern pentathlon**

riding school (*equestrianism*) a school or establishment for teaching skills in the sport

rifle (*shooting*) (1) a firearm with a spirally grooved (rifled) barrel; (2) shortening of **air rifle**; (3) shortening of **small-bore rifle**

rifle range (*shooting*) a special enclosed area with **targets** for practice or competition in **rifle shooting**

rifle shooting (*shooting*) the **discipline** of shooting with a **rifle**

rig (*sailing*) the disposition of the **sails**, **masts**, and **spars** in a boat or **yacht** that define its type

rigger (*rowing*) shortening of **outrigger**

rigging (*sailing*) the wires and ropes that support a boat's **masts** and control or set the **sails**

right arm (*cricket*) a **bowler** who bowls with the right arm

right back (*field games*) a **back** who plays primarily on the right side of the **pitch**

right center (*field games*) a player who plays primarily to the right of the center of the **pitch**

right cross (*boxing*) a **punch** delivered from the right side

right defender (*field games*) a **right half** who plays **deep**

right field (*baseball*) the part of the **outfield** to the right of **second base** as viewed from **home plate**

right fielder (*baseball*) a **fielder** positioned in **right field**

right half (*field games*) a **halfback** who plays primarily on the right side of the **pitch**

right-hander (*boxing*) a **punch** delivered with the right hand; (*general*) a player whose right hand is dominant, as against the less common **left-hander**; (*surfing*) a wave breaking to the right, as seen by a **surfer** facing the beach

right midfield (*field games*) the **midfield** players who play primarily on the right side of the **pitch**

right wing (*field games*) the part of the **pitch** to the right of its center

right winger (*field games*) an attacking player on the **right wing**

rightie (*general*) colloquial term for a **right-hander**

rikishi (*sumo*) a **wrestler** [Japanese *riki*, "strength," and *shi*, "warrior"]

rim out (*basketball*) to hit the edge of the **basket** and bounce away

ring (*boxing, wrestling*) the roped rectangular area on a raised platform in which a **match** takes place [originally the space for a match surrounded by a circle of spectators]; (2) the sport itself as a profession; (*horse racing*) (1) an enclosure for **bookmakers** at a **racecourse**; (2) bookmaking itself as a profession; (3) shortening of **parade ring**; (*sumo*) the circular area within which a **match** takes place

ring rust (*boxing*) staleness of performance shown by a **boxer** who has been out of the **ring**

ring tennis (*sport*) a combination of **tennis** and **quoits** similar to **deck tennis** [played with rubber rings]

ring the bell (*American football*) to hit another player so hard on his helmeted head that he is disorientated and may even suffer slight concussion

ringer (*athletics*) an **athlete** competing under a false name; (*curling*) a **stone** inside the circle drawn around the **tee**; (*horse racing*) a horse raced under the name of another horse

ringette (*sport*) a sport similar to **ice hockey**, played mainly by women and girls, in which a rubber ring is used instead of a **puck**

ringman (*general*) colloquial term for a **bookmaker**

rings (*gymnastics*) two cylindrical handles suspended from wire cables on which, in men's competition, the **gymnast** executes **swings** and **handstands**

ringside (*boxing*) the area immediately surrounding the **ring**

ringside physician (*boxing*) the doctor who checks the physical condition of a **boxer** before the start of a **bout** and who determines whether a dazed boxer is fit enough to continue

ringside seat (*boxing*) a seat immediately next to the **ring**

ringsider (*boxing*) a spectator at a **prizefight**

rink (*bowls*) (1) one of the playing areas into which a **green** is divided; (2) a team of four players; (*curling*) (1) the playing area of prepared ice; (2) a team in this sport; (*ice hockey, ice skating*) shortening of **ice rink**; (*roller skating*) a smooth floor or area, usually of wood or asphalt, prepared for **skating** on **roller skates**

rip (*swimming*) a **dive** with an ideal **entry** [from the sound as the **diver** enters the water]

ripcord (*parachuting*) a cord pulled to inflate a **parachute** by opening the pack in which it is folded

Ripon (*horse racing*) a **flat racecourse** at Ripon, North Yorkshire, England

riposte (*fencing*) a quick **thrust** given after a **parry** [French *riposte*, from Italian *risposta*, "reply"]

rise (*angling*) the movement of a fish to the surface of the water to take food or a **bait**; (*cricket*) the upward course of a bowled **ball** after pitching

riverboarding (*sport*) the riding of a **bodyboard** down rapids

Riverside (*cricket*) the **home ground of** Durham **county cricket club**, Chester-le-Street, Co. Durham

ro (*cricket*) abbreviation of **run out** in scoring

road bike (*cycling*) a bicycle designed for **road races**, with dropped handlebars and several gears

road book (*auto racing*) in **rally driving**, a book of instructions, information, and maps issued to drivers by the organizers of a **rally**

road game (*general*) (1) a **game** played by a team on a **tour**; (2) another term for an **away game**

road race (*cycling*) a **race** ridden on roads, as distinct from a **track race**

road rash (*cycling, skateboarding*) colloquial term for skin abrasions caused by sliding across the road or other hard surface after a fall or crash

Road World Championships (*cycling*) an annual **road race** held in various countries since 1927

roadeo (*sport*) a contest and display of driving skills among truck drivers [blend of *road* and **rodeo**]

roadman (*cycling*) a competitor in a **road race**

roads and tracks (*equestrianism*) a phase of the **cross-country** section of the **three-day event**, involving riding on the **flat**

roadwork (*general*) **running** on roads as a method of training for **marathon** runners, **boxers**, and the like

roar (*curling*) to send a **stone** with great speed [in the **roaring game**]

roaring game (*sport*) another name for **curling** [from the sound made by the **stones** as they travel over the ice]

Robin Hood (*archery*) the feat of splitting the **shaft** of an **arrow** already in the **target** with another arrow [from the legendary English outlaw, who was skilled in archery]

Robins (*association football*) nickname of the English **clubs** Bristol City, Charlton Athletic, Cheltenham Town, and Swindon Town, and the Welsh club Wrexham [from the teams' red shirts]

rock climbing (*mountaineering*) the climbing of rock faces

rocker (*ice skating*) a figure in which the skater makes a 180-degree turn and continues to travel backward in the same direction; (*surfing*) the upward curve on a **surfboard**

Rockets (*basketball*) short name of the Houston Rockets team

Rockies (*baseball*) short name of the Colorado Rockies team

rod (*angling*) (1) shortening of **fishing rod**; (2) another term for an **angler**; (3) a permit to fish a particular stretch of river

rodeo (*sport*) a competitive display of riding and other skills among cowboys

rodman (*angling*) another term for an **angler**

Roehampton (*general*) a fashionable London sports club, founded in 1901, with **polo grounds, croquet lawns, tennis courts**, a **golf course**, and a **clubhouse**

Rokerites (*association football*) former nickname of the English **club** Sunderland [from Roker Park, their **home ground** until 1997, when they moved to the **Stadium of Light**]

role player (*basketball*) a player who performs a specific function and is brought on only when required

roll (*gymnastics, swimming*) a move in which the body, in a **tuck** position, rolls forward or backward

roll cast (*angling*) a **cast** in which the tip of the **rod** is rolled so that the **line** is picked off the water without being thrown behind the **angler**, as is more usual

roll-off (*tenpin bowling*) an extra **game** played to resolve a **tie**

roll-out (*American football*) a **play** in which a

quarterback moves out from the **blockers** before attempting a **pass**

roll with the punches (*boxing*) to move the body away to lessen the impact of an opponent's blows

roller (*baseball*) a **ball** that rolls along the ground after being hit; (*cricket*) a **ball** apparently bowled with a **spin** but actually running straight along the ground after pitching

roller arena (*roller skating*) another term for a **rink**

roller derby (*roller skating*) a **speed skating race** on **roller skates** [as a **derby**]

roller hockey (*sport*) a **game** resembling **ice hockey** played on a **rink** by teams on **roller skates** with a short **hockey stick** and a hard **ball** instead of a **puck**

roller seat drop (*trampolining*) a full **twist** to a **seat drop**

roller skates (*roller skating*) **skates** with four wheels instead of **blades**, the wheels set either at the corners of the shoe or in a single line to make **rollerblades**

roller skating (*sport*) the sport or competitive display of **skating** on **roller skates**, either on a **rink** or on a public street or other hard-surface area

roller sports (*general*) sports played on **roller skates**, as **roller hockey**

rollerblades (*roller skating*) **roller skates** in which the wheels are fixed in a single line akin to the **blades** of **ice skates**

rollerblading (*roller skating*) **skating** on **rollerblades**

rollerdrome (*roller skating*) another term for a **rink**

rolling maul (*rugby union*) a **maul** that is rolled or wheeled by its members with the aim of preventing the **opposition** from obtaining the **ball**

romp (*general*) an easily won **game** or **race**

romp home (*general*) to win by a substantial margin, as in a **race**

rookie (*general*) a person new to a sport or inexperienced in it

rooster tail (*surfing*) the curved plume of water thrown up by a **surfboard**

rope (*baseball*) shortening of **frozen rope**; (*horse racing*) to hold back a horse in order to lose a **race** intentionally; (*mountaineering*) (1) shortening of **climbing rope**; (2) a climbing party roped together; (*rodeo*) to lasso, as in **calf-roping** and **team roping**

rope-a-dope (*boxing*) a tactic in which a **boxer** pretends to be trapped on the **ropes** in order to incite his opponent to tire himself out with **punches** [an expression popularized in the 1970s by **heavyweight champion** Muhammad Ali, a noted employer of the tactic, the "dope" being the baited opponent]

rope down (*mountaineering*) another term for **abseil**

roper (*horse racing*) a **jockey** who pulls on the reins to slow his horse down and so lose a **race**, usually for financial reasons

ropes (*boxing*) the cords around the **ring**; (*cricket*) the cords marking the **boundary** of the **field**

roque (*croquet*) a version of the **game** with nine **hoops** played on a walled, hard-surface **court** [from *croquet*]

roquet (*croquet*) a **stroke** in which the **striker's ball** is played against another **ball**, whereupon the **striker** can play a **croquet shot** [probably from *croquet*]

Roscommon (*horse racing*) a **flat** and **National Hunt racecourse** at Roscommon, Co. Roscommon, Ireland

Rose Bowl (*American football*) (1) a **postseason college football** contest held annually (from 1916) in Pasadena, California, where it was first organized in 1902 as part of the festival inaugurated in 1890 as the Battle of the Flowers; (2) the **stadium** opened in 1922 for this **game**; (*cricket*) the **home ground** of Hampshire **county cricket club**, Southampton

rosette (*general*) (1) a rose-shaped badge of colored ribbons worn by a sports participant or animal (such as a horse) as a symbol of a **prize**; (2) a similar badge worn by a **supporter**

Rossoneri (*association football*) nickname of the Italian **club** AC Milan [Italian *rosso*, "red," and *nero*, "black," the colors of the team's red and black striped shirts]

rot (*cricket*) a rapid loss of **wickets** in an **innings**

rotation (*baseball*) the order of play assigned to **pitchers** for the **matches** of a particular series; (*gymnastics*) the period during which a team of **gymnasts** work on a particular piece of **apparatus**; (*volleyball*) the clockwise movement of players when the **service** changes

rouge (*Canadian football*) a single **point** awarded when the **ball** is played into the opponents' **goal area** and becomes **dead**; (*Eton field game*) a **score** awarded when a **attacker** touches a **ball** that has been sent over the **goal line** by a **defender** [origin obscure, apparently not French *rouge*, "red"]

rough (*golf*) an area of rough ground, especially uncut grass, around a **fairway** or **green**; (*tennis*) the side of a **racket** from which the loops of twisted string project, used as a call (opposed to **smooth**) when the racket is spun to decide on the **server** or choose an **end**

Rough Riders (*Canadian football*) short name of the Ottawa Rough Riders team

Roughriders (*Canadian football*) short name of the Saskatchewan Roughriders team

Roughyeds (*rugby league*) short name of the English **club** Oldham Roughyeds

rouleur (*cycling*) a **cyclist** who specializes in riding long flat **stages** or **races** [French *rouleur*, "roller"]

round (*archery*) a specified number of **arrows** shot over different distances; (*boxing*) a subdivision of a **bout** in the form of a period of action over a given number of minutes, separated from the next period by a rest; (*general*) a specified stage in a competition; (*golf*) a complete series of played **holes**; (*shooting*) a single **shot** fired from a **rifle**

round-arm (*cricket*) (of) a **ball** bowled with an almost horizontal swing of the arm

round-ball game (*sport*) colloquial name for **association football** [played with a round **ball**, as against the **oval-ball game**]

round heels (*boxing*) colloquial term for a poor **boxer** [who might easily fall]

round-off (*gymnastics*) a move in which the **gymnast** begins a **cartwheel** but lands on both feet instead of one, facing the opposite direction

round robin (*general*) a **tournament** in which each competitor competes once with each of the others; (*horse racing*) a form of multiple **bet** on three horses that adds up to ten bets

round-the-cans (*sailing*) colloquial term for a **harbor race** [the cans being the buoys]

round-the-clock shooting (*shooting*) colloquial term for **skeet**

round-the-houses (*auto racing*) colloquial term for a **street race**

Round-the-Island Race (*sailing*) an annual 50-mile **race** around the Isle of Wight, southern England, starting from and returning to Cowes, the location of **Cowes Week**

round the wicket (*cricket*) bowled from the hand of the **bowler** that is further away from the **wicket**

round trip (*baseball*) to score a **home run** and so make a complete circuit of all four **bases**

rounder (*rounders*) a complete circuit of the **bases** run by the **batter**

rounders (*sport*) a **game** similar to **baseball** in which players hit the **ball** with a **bat** and run to a **base** or if possible around all four bases (scoring a **rounder**) before the ball is thrown back to the **bowler**

roundhouse (*baseball*) a **pitch** made with a sweeping swing of the arm; (*boxing*) a wild swinging **punch**

route (*horse racing*) a long **race** of more than a mile

Route du Rhum (*sailing*) a solo transatlantic **race** held every four years from St. Malo, France, to Pointe-à-Pitre, Guadeloupe [French *route du rhum*, "rum route"]

route one (*association football*) (of) a style of play in which long high **passes** are made **upfield**

route orienteering (*orienteering*) a form of the sport in which the route is marked on the ground but not on the map

routegoer (*baseball*) a **pitcher** who **goes the route**

routine (*general*) a series of movements in a display, as in **gymnastics** or **ice skating**

rover (*American football*) a defensive **linebacker** assigned to anticipate the moves of the opposing team; (*archery*) a competitor in **field archery**; (*Australian Rules*) a (usually small and fast) player who forms part of the **ruck** and is skillful at receiving the **ball**; (*croquet*) a **ball** that has passed through all the **hoops** and is now ready to **peg out**

rover hoop (*croquet*) the last **hoop** through which a **ball** must pass before it can **peg out**

Rovers (*association football*) short name of the English **clubs** Blackburn Rovers, Bristol Rovers, Doncaster Rovers, and Tranmere Rovers, and the Scottish club Raith Rovers; (*rugby league*) short name of the English **clubs** Featherstone Rovers and Hull Kingston Rovers

row (*rowing*) to propel a boat through water by making **strokes** with one or more **oars**

row over (*rowing*) to win a **heat** in a **race** by rowing the **course** unopposed

rower (*rowing*) a person who **rows** or is a member of a **rowing club**

rowing (*sport*) the sport or recreation of using **oars** to propel a boat through water

rowing club (*rowing*) a **club** for people who **row**, especially competitively in a **race**

Rowley Mile (*horse racing*) a racecourse at **Newmarket**, on which the **One Thousand Guineas** and **Two Thousand Guineas** are run [from "Old Rowley," nickname (from a favorite horse) of Charles II, who proclaimed Newmarket as the headquarters of **racing**]

rowlocks (*rowing*) U-shaped swivels that hold the **oars** in place [originally *oarlock*]

Royal and Ancient (*golf*) short name of the **Royal and Ancient Golf Club of St. Andrews**

Royal and Ancient Golf Club of St. Andrews (*golf*) a **golf club** in St. Andrews, eastern Scotland, dating back to 1754 and today the accepted international authority on the **game** ["Royal" from 1834, when William IV agreed to be its patron]

Royal Ascot (*horse racing*) an annual **race** and society occasion at **Ascot** attended by the monarch [founded in 1711 by Queen Anne]

Royal Birkdale (*golf*) a **golf course** near Southport, Lancashire, northwestern England

royal duck (*cricket*) a **duck** scored by a **opening batsman** on the first **ball** of the **innings**

Royal Lytham (*golf*) a **golf course** at Lytham St. Annes, Lancashire, northwestern England

Royal Melbourne (*golf*) a **golf course** at Black Rock, near Melbourne, Australia

Royal Portrush (*golf*) a **golf course** at Portrush, northeastern Northern Ireland

Royal St. George's (*golf*) a **golf course** at Sandwich, Kent, England

royal tennis (*sport*) another spelling of **real tennis** [despite the historically attested association of royalty with the sport, the derivation of the name is in *real*, not *royal*]

Royal Troon (*golf*) a **golf course** at Troon, southwestern Scotland

Royals (*association football*) nickname of the English **club** Reading [from the royal blue of the team's **strip**]; (*baseball*) short name of the Kansas City Royals team

Rozelle rule (*general*) the provision in a contract between a **free agent** and a professional team which requires the team to give the free agent's former team an agreed compensation [established by Alvin Ray Rozelle (1927–1996) commissioner of the **National Football League** from 1960]

Rs (*association football*) colloquial abbreviation for the English **club** Queens Park Rangers

rub (*bowls*) an interference to the course of a rolling **bowl** caused by a snag on the **green**

rub of the green (*golf*) an accidental interference with the course of the **ball**

rubber (*baseball*) colloquial term for the **mound**, and formerly for the **home plate**; (*general*) a series of **games**, as in **cricket** or **tennis**

ruck (*Australian Rules*) the three players (a **rover** and two **ruckmen**) who follow the **ball** closely but do not have fixed positions; (*rugby union*) a **loose scrum** formed by the players around the **ball** on the ground with the aim of pushing back their opponents

ruckman (*Australian Rules*) one of the three players in a **ruck** whose function is to knock the **ball** to the **rover**

ruckrover (*Australian Rules*) fuller term for a **rover**

rudolph (*trampolining*) a forward **somersault** with one and a half **twists** [performed in the music hall of the 1920s by Dave Rudolph]

rudy (*gymnastics*) a **vault** consisting of a **handspring** off the **springboard** followed by a forward **salto** with one and a half **twists** off the **horse**; (*trampolining*) shortening of **rudolph**

rugby (*sport*) short name of either **rugby league** or **rugby union** [the basic sport evolved from **football** in the early 19th century at Rugby School, Warwickshire, England]

rugby academy (*rugby union*) a national or regional organization set up with the support of England's Rugby Football Union to recruit good players

Rugby fives (*fives*) the most common variant of the **game**, played between **singles** or **doubles** and

distinguished from **Eton fives** in that the **court** is four-walled and the **hazards** different [originally played at Rugby School]

rugby football (*sport*) another term for **rugby union**

rugby league (*sport*) a **field game** based on **rugby union**, played with an oval **ball** between teams of 13 players, each side having six attempts or **tackles** to move the ball **upfield** and score a **try** by grounding the ball in the **in-goal** area [mostly played in northern England, where an association of **clubs** was formed in 1922 as the Rugby League (originally Northern Union)]

rugby tackle (*rugby league, rugby union*) fuller term for a **tackle**

rugby union (*sport*) a **field game** played with an oval **ball** between teams of 15 players, with handling of the ball permitted and each side aiming to amass more **points** than the other [named for the Rugby Union, an association of **clubs** formed in 1871 to regularize the original form of **rugby**]

rugger (*sport*) colloquial term for **rugby football**

rugger bugger (*rugby football*) colloquial term for a player or fan, especially if burly or boisterous

Rules (*horse racing*) (1) shortening of the **National Hunt** Rules of Racing; (*sport*) shortening of **Australian Rules**

run (*baseball*) a **point** scored by the **batter** after completing a circuit of the **bases** and returned to **home plate**; (*cricket*) (1) the basic unit of scoring; (2) a **point** scored by a **batsman** after running from one **popping crease** to the other; (*general*) a spell of forward movement, as by an **athlete** in a **foot race** or a player with the **ball** in **American football**; (*horse racing*) another term for a **race**; (*skiing*) (1) a snow slope prepared for skiers; (2) a descent on such a slope

run a cracker (*horse racing*) to perform excellently in a **race**

run a hoop (*croquet*) to hit the **ball** through a **hoop**

run-and-gun (*basketball*) (of) a style of fast freeflowing play with few **set plays**

run-and-shoot (*American football*) (of) a style of play in which a fast-paced **quarterback** makes quick short **passes** while evading **tacklers**

run batted in (*baseball*) a credit awarded to a **batter** for every **run** scored as a result of his action, as a **hit**, **sacrifice**, or **walk**

Run for the Daisies (*horse racing*) colloquial name of the **Preakness Stakes** [from the chain of daisies hung around the winner's neck]

Run for the Roses (*horse racing*) colloquial name of the **Kentucky Derby** [from the chain of roses hung around the winner's neck]

run green (*horse racing*) to be distracted during a **race** through lack of experience

run-in (*horse racing*) another term for the **home straight**; (*rugby league, rugby union*) the act of running over the **touchline** of the opposite side with the **ball**

run interference (*general*) in **team games**, the **offense** of hindering opposing players while a teammate is in **possession** of the **ball** or **puck**

run-off (*auto racing*) an area of gravel or other material near a corner, designed to slow down cars if they run off the **track**; (*general*) an additional contest such as a **race** to decide a winner in the event of a **dead heat** or **tie**

run out (*cricket*) to **dismiss** a **batsman** by dislodging the **bails** of the **wicket** while he is still running and so out of his **ground**

run-out (*mountaineering*) the length of rope required to climb a particular **pitch**

run rate (*cricket*) a statistic in which a team's total number of **runs** scored is divided by the number of **overs** faced

run the line (*association football*) to act as **assistant referee** [on the **touchline**]

run up (*golf*) to send the **ball** rolling or low in the air toward the **hole**

run-up (*general*) a running approach to a key physical action such as a **jump** or **throw** in **athletics** or a **bowl** in **cricket**

runback (*American football*) a forward run made after catching a kick or intercepting a **pass**; (*tennis*) the area behind the **baseline** at either end of the **court** [in which the **receiver** can run back to make a **return**]

rundown (*baseball*) a **play** in which defending players attempt to **tag out** a **runner** caught between two **bases**; (*horse racing*) a list of entries and **odds** for the horses in a **race**

runner (*American football*) a player who runs with the **ball** in an attacking **play**; (*baseball*) shortening of **baserunner**; (*cricket*) a player who runs on behalf of an injured **batsman**; (*general*) a person who runs in a **foot race** such as a **marathon**; (*horse racing*) a horse entered in a **race**

runner-up (*general*) a competitor taking second place in a **race**

runner's high (*athletics*) the sense of euphoria that can be experienced by a **runner** at a particular stage in a **long-distance race** such as a **marathon**

running (*general*) fast forward motion on foot, either for exercise or as a **race**; (*Olympics*) another term for **cross-country running** in the **modern pentathlon**

running back (*American football*) a **back** whose main function is to run with the **ball** from the **line of scrimmage**

running belay (*mountaineering*) a device attached to the rock face through which the rope runs freely, acting as a pulley if the climber falls

running mate (*horse racing*) a horse entered in a **race** to set the pace for another horse from the same **stable** which is intended to win

running rugby (*rugby union*) play in which the **ball** is primarily advanced by being carried, as against a **kicking game**

running shot (*handball*) a **shot** made while running

running side (*snooker*) a **side** that causes the **cue ball** to rebound off the **cushion** at a greater angle than in a normally struck **shot**

running target (*shooting*) a **target** that moves across a track to simulate a moving animal or another target

runway (*athletics*) the section of **track** along which an **athlete** approaches a **jump** or **throw**; (*gymnastics*) the approach on which a **gymnast** makes his **run-up** to the **vaulting horse**

rush (*American football*) (1) to run with the **ball** or gain ground by doing so; (2) a move to push through a line of **defenders** while in **possession** of the **ball**; (*croquet*) a form of **roquet** in which the **ball** is struck with a strong swing of the **mallet**; (*rugby league, rugby union*) an attempt by one or more players to force the **ball** through a line of **defenders**

rush line (*American football*) a line of **defenders**, prepared for a **rush**

rusher (*American football*) a player, such as a **forward**, who specializes in **rushing**

rushing (*American football*) attempting to advance the **ball** by means of a **rush**

Ryder Cup (*golf*) the **trophy** awarded to the winners of a biennial **tournament** for male **professionals**, held since 1927 between teams from the United States and Europe (until 1979 USA and Britain) [donated by British seed merchant Samuel A. Ryder (1859–1936)]

saber (*fencing*) a light sword with a flattened triangular blade and a blunt point

sabermetrics (*baseball*) the measurement and analysis of statistics for the sport [from *SABR*, abbreviation of Society for American Baseball Research, and *-metrics*, as in *biometrics*]

sabre (*fencing*) another spelling of **saber**

Sabres (*ice hockey*) short name of the Buffalo Sabres team

sack (*American football*) to tackle a **quarterback** behind the **line of scrimmage** before he can pass the **ball**; (*baseball*) another term for a **base**; (*general*) another term for a **footbag**

sacker (*baseball*) a **fielder** who guards a **base**

sacrifice (*baseball*) a **play** in which a **batter** deliberately makes an **out** in order to enable a **baserunner** to score or advance to another **base**

saddle (*general*) a seat for a **rider**, as on a horse, **bicycle**, or **motorcycle**; (*horse racing*) (1) to put a saddle on a horse; (2) to be responsible, as a **trainer**, for preparing and entering a horse in a **race**

Saddlers (*association football*) nickname of the English **club** Walsall [from the town's saddle-making industry]

safe (*baseball*) having reached **base** before being **thrown out** by the **fielding** side

safety (*American football*) (1) one of two defensive players positioned behind the other **defenders**; (2) a **play** in which the **offense** carries the **ball** over their own **goal line** rather than back into the field of play, an act that scores two **points** for the **defense**; (*snooker*) a period of play in which each player tries to prevent his opponent from scoring **points** by keeping the **cue ball** in positions where he will find it hard to **pot** it

safety bindings (*skiing*) devices that hold the feet to the **skis** and that release automatically to prevent injury if the wearer falls

safety car (*auto racing*) a saloon car that comes out on to the **track** after an accident and that sets the speed of the **race cars** that follow it, especially if there are **marshals** on the track

safety lane (*cycling*) a **lane** in a **velodrome** between the **pole line** and the center of the **track**

safety play (*snooker*) fuller term for a **safety**

safety shot (*snooker*) a defensive **shot** designed to make it hard for one's opponent to **pot** the **cue ball**, as in a **safety**

safety squeeze (*baseball*) a tactical maneuver in which a **baserunner** at **third base** begins to run toward **home plate** as soon as the **batter** makes contact with the **ball**

safetyman (*American football*) fuller term for a **safety**

sag wagon (*cycling*) colloquial term for a vehicle that follows the **cyclists** in a **road race** to give mechanical assistance or pick up exhausted **riders**

sail (*sailing*) a sheet of material spread to catch the wind and so propel a boat through the water

sail-off (*sailing*) an additional contest held in case of a **tie**

sailboard (*windsurfing*) a craft consisting of a **board** like a **surfboard** with a **mast** that has a single **sail**

sailboarding (*sport*) another term for **windsurfing**

sailer (*baseball*) a pitched **fastball** that takes off [it "sails"]

sailing (*sport*) the sport or recreation of traveling across water in a boat or **yacht** propelled by one or more **sails**, as a competitive sport alternately known as **yachting** until 2000

sailplane (*gliding*) a **glider** that can rise with an upward current and remain long in the air

St. Andrews (*golf*) the **golf course** of the **Royal and Ancient Golf Club of St. Andrews**

St. George's (*archery*) a **round** of 36 **arrows** each for men at 100, 80, and 60yds (91m, 73m, and 55m)

St. Leger (*horse racing*) an annual **race** for three-year-old **colts** and **fillies** run at **Doncaster** since 1778 [founded by Colonel Barry St. Leger (1737–1789)]

St. Moritz (*bobsledding*) a town in eastern Switzerland with a **run** constructed in 1902

Saints (*American football*) short name of the New Orleans Saints team; (*association football*) (1) nickname of the English **club** Southampton [from the club's original name, Southampton St. Mary's]; (2) short name of the Scottish club St. Johnstone; (*Australian Rules*) short name of the St. Kilda Saints team; (*rugby league*) short name of the English **club** St. Helens; (*rugby union*) short name of the English **club** Northampton Saints

Salchow (*ice skating*) a **jump** in which the skater takes off from the back **inside edge** of one **skate**, spins in the air, then lands on the back **outside edge** of the other skate [first performed by the Swedish **figure skater** Ulrich Salchow (1877–1949)]

sales race (*horse racing*) a **race** of horses purchased at a sale in which they were grouped by age or sex (as **yearlings**, **colts**, or **fillies**)

Salisbury (*horse racing*) a **flat racecourse** at Netherhampton, near Salisbury, Wiltshire, England

Sally Gunnell (*golf*) colloquial name for a **shot** that travels a long distance along the **fairway** [after the English **champion athlete** Sally Gunnell (1966–)]

salto (*gymnastics*) an **aerial somersault** in which the **gymnast**'s feet come up over his head and his body rotates around his waist [Italian *salto*, "leap"]

Saltoun (*angling*) a type of **artificial fly** [probably after the 18th Lord Saltoun (died 1886)]

salute (*fencing*) the formal performance of certain movements before engaging

sambo (*wrestling*) a variant of the sport resembling judo [Russian acronym of *samozashchita bez oruzhiya*, "self-defense without weapons"]

San Marino Grand Prix (*auto racing*) the **Formula One** international **Grand Prix** held on the **circuit** at Imola, northern Italy, there being no circuit in San Marino itself

San Siro (*association football*) a **stadium** in Milan, Italy, that shared as a **home ground** by the **clubs** AC Milan and Inter Milan

sand iron (*golf*) another term for a **sand wedge**

sand save (*golf*) a **shot** with a **wedge** from a **bunker** followed by a single **putt** that sends the **ball** into the **hole**

sand trap (*golf*) another term for a **bunker**

sand wedge (*golf*) a **club** giving a good **loft** that is specially adapted to lift the **ball** out of a **bunker**

sandbag (*motorcycle racing*) to let the rest of the field go on ahead in the confidence that one can regain the **lead** and win the **race**

Sandown Park (*horse racing*) a **flat** and **National Hunt racecourse** at Esher, Surrey, England, the location of the **Eclipse Stakes**

sandwich boat (*rowing*) the **crew** that finishes top of a **division** in a **bumping race**, when they have the option of starting again at the bottom of the next higher division on the chance of making another **bump** and remaining in that higher division

Sanzar (*rugby union*) an acronymic name for the competitive union of South Africa, New Zealand, and Australia, who individually contest the **Tri-Nations Championship**

Sarries (*rugby union*) short name of the English **club** Saracens

sausage board (*surfing*) a **surfboard** rounded at both ends

savate (*boxing*) a form of the sport in which both feet and fists are used [French *savate*, originally a type of shoe]

save (*association football*) a **goalkeeper**'s successful attempt at stopping the **ball** from entering the **net**; (*baseball*) the credit given a **relief pitcher** for successfully preserving a team's narrow **lead** to the end of a **game**

SBX (*snowboarding*) abbreviation of **snowboard cross**

Scarlets (*rugby union*) short name of the Welsh **club** Llanelli Scarlets

scatback (*American football*) colloquial term for a fast-running **backfield** player

scatter (*baseball*) to keep the **score** down as a **pitcher** with a play that yields few **hits**

school (*equestrianism, horse racing*) to train a horse

schuss (*skiing*) a straight slope on which a fast downhill **run** can be made [German *Schuss*, "shot"]

schussboom (*skiing*) to ski at high speed [combination of **schuss** and **boom**, "to sail fast"]

scissor kick (*association football*) a kick in which the player jumps in the air with one leg outstretched then brings forward the other leg to kick the **ball**

scissors (*association football*) shortening of **scissor kick**; (*athletics*) a **high jump** in which the **athlete** crosses the **bar** in a seated position, bringing his trailing leg up as his leading leg goes down on the other side of the bar; (*gymnastics*) any movement involving the opening and closing of the legs; (*rugby league, rugby union*) shortening of **scissors pass**; (*swimming*) shortening

of **scissors kick**; (*wrestling*) a **hold** in which a contestant uses his legs to grip his opponent's head and then locks them at the instep or ankles to apply pressure

scissors hold (*wrestling*) fuller term for **scissors**

scissors kick (*swimming*) a kick used in the **sidestroke** in which the legs are parted slowly then brought suddenly together

scissors pass (*rugby league, rugby union*) a move in which the **ball** is passed by a player running diagonally across the **pitch** to a teammate running behind him at a different angle

sclaff (*golf*) a **stroke** in which the **sole** of the **club** scrapes the ground before striking the **ball** [probably alteration of *scruff*]

scoop (*general*) a sweeping **shot** that sends the **ball** up into the air, as with the **bat** in **cricket** or the **stick** in **field hockey**; (*surfing*) the upturned nose of the **surfboard**

scope (*horse racing*) the potential of a horse to improve with age

scorcher (*general*) a fast or powerful **shot** or **stroke**

score (*general*) a total or record of **points** won in a **game**, either by an individual or a team

score draw (*association football*) a **drawn game** in which both teams have scored at least once

score orienteering (*orienteering*) a form of the sport in which the competitors must visit as many **control points** as they can, each point having a different **score** value

scoreboard (*general*) a large board for publicly displaying the current **score** in a **game**, as in **cricket** or **tennis**

scorebook (*cricket*) a book specially prepared for entering the **score**

scorebox (*cricket*) a hut or other structure in which the **scorers** work

scorecard (*general*) a card specially prepared for entering the **score**, as in **baseball**, **cricket**, or **golf**

scoreline (*general*) a line in a newspaper or other publication giving the **score** in a contest

scorer (*association football*) a player who scores **goals**; (*general*) an official who keeps a record of the **score** in a **game** or contest

scoresheet (*general*) a sheet specially prepared for entering the **score**, as in **association football**, **baseball**, or **cricket**

scoring hit (*boxing*) a fair **hit** which, if the **judges** agree, earns the **boxer** one **point**

scoring space (*association football*) the part of the **pitch** in which most of the **goals** are scored

scorpion kick (*association football*) an unconventional **save** by a **goalkeeper** in which he places his hands on the ground and then, in a near **handstand**, raises his legs to kick the **ball** away with his heels [his body assumes the shape of a scorpion with raised tail]

Scottish FA Cup (*association football*) the **trophy** awarded to the winners of the **final** in a competition held by the Scottish Football Association since 1874

Scottish Football League (*association football*) a **league** of 3 **divisions** founded in 1890

Scottish League (*association football*) shortening of **Scottish Football League**

Scottish Premier League (*association football*) a **league** formed in 1998 by the top teams in the **Scottish Football League**

scout (*general*) a person who searches for new talent among the players of a team or **club** other than his own

scramble (*American football*) a series of movements made by a **quarterback** to evade **tacklers**; (*auto racing, motorcycle racing*) a **race** with a **course** over rough or hilly terrain; (*golf*) to play erratically but with the odd good **stroke** and even a chance of winning a **match**

scramble leg (*skiing*) the first **leg** of a **relay race** in **cross-country skiing** [so called from its bunched **mass start**]

scrambler (*golf*) a player who **scrambles**; (*motorcycle racing*) a modified motorcycle of the type used in a **scramble**

scrambling (*auto racing, motorcycle racing*) dedicated participation in **scrambles**

scratch (*golf*) having a **handicap** of zero; (*horse racing*) to remove a horse from a **race** after entering it; (*snooker*) to hit the **cue ball** into a **pocket**, thereby incurring a **penalty**

scratch hit (*baseball*) a poor **hit** that even so allows the **batter** to reach **first base**

scratch race (*cycling*) a straightforward **track race** over a distance of 15km (10km for women)

scratch sheet (*horse racing*) a publication listing horses **scratched** from **races** and giving their **odds**

screamer (*general*) a powerful **shot** or kick, as in **tennis** or **association football**

screen (*American football, basketball*) a maneuver in which an attacking player is protected by a group of teammates; (*cricket*) shortening of **sight screen**

screw (*billiards, snooker*) a **stroke** that imparts **backspin** or **sidespin** to the **cue ball** by striking it below its center so that it recoils backward or sideways after striking the **object ball**

screw shot (*billiards, snooker*) fuller term for a **screw**

screwball (*baseball*) a **pitch** that breaks in the opposite direction to a conventional **curveball** or **slider**

scrimmage (*American football*) (1) a sequence of play beginning with the **snap** and ending when the **ball** is **dead**; (2) a practice session of this sequence

scrub (*general*) (1) an inferior player; (2) a team made up of such players; (*horse racing*) a back-and-forth movement of the arms and legs made by a **jockey** on the neck and flanks of a horse to urge it forward, especially near the end of a **race**

scrubber (*general*) an inferior player

scruff (*golf*) alternate form of **sclaff**

scrum (*rugby league, rugby union*) a formation to restart play in which the **forwards** of both teams close in, in three rows, then with arms interlocked and heads down push against each other, whereupon the **ball** is thrown in between them and they attempt to kick it out to their own team [shortening of **scrummage**]

scrum down (*rugby league, rugby union*) to form a **scrum**

scrum half (*rugby league, rugby union*) the **halfback** who puts the **ball** into the **scrum** and attempts to secure it as soon as it emerges and send it to the **backs**

scrummage (*rugby league, rugby union*) formal term for a **scrum** [variant of **scrimmage**]

scrutineering (*auto racing*) the inspection of cars by the officials before a **race** to ensure compliance with technical regulations; (*motorcycle racing*) the inspection of **bikes** before a **race** by the officials to ensure compliance with technical regulations

scuba (*aquatics*) an apparatus used by **skindivers**, consisting in a breathing tube attached to a cylinder of compressed air [acronym of self-contained underwater breathing apparatus]

Scuderia (*auto racing*) a name used to refer to the Ferrari **Formula One** team [Italian *scuderia*, "stable"]

Scudetto (*association football*) informal name of the Italian **Serie A championship** [Italian *scudetto*, "shield," from the shield that the winners wear on their shirts for the following season]

scull (*rowing*) (1) a short, spoon-bladed **oar** used in pairs by a single **rower**; (2) a light boat propelled by such oars; (*swimming*) a movement of the hands against the water in **synchronized swimming**

sculling race (*rowing*) a **race** between **rowers** who are each in a **scull**

sculls (*rowing*) another term for a **sculling race**

scurry (*equestrianism*) a short **race** in **show-jumping** and **carriage-driving**, a contest in which a **fault** is counted as a time **penalty**

Seagulls (*association football*) nickname of the English **club** Brighton and Hove Albion [for the birds that frequent the coastal city]

Seahawks (*American football*) short name of the Seattle Seahawks team

seam (*cricket*) the raised stitching on a **cricket ball**

seam bowler (*cricket*) a **bowler** who uses the **seam** of the **ball** to make it deviate on pitching

seam bowling (*cricket*) the fast or medium-paced **bowling** of a **seam bowler**

seamer (*cricket*) (1) shortening of **seam bowler**; (2) a **ball** bowled by a seam bowler

Seasiders (*association football*) nickname of the English **club** Blackpool [from the town's fame as a seaside resort]

season (*general*) (1) the natural period of the year appropriate for a particular sport, as traditionally (in Britain) the summer for **cricket** and the winter for **association football**; (2) the calendar period of the year usually devoted to a particular sport; (3) the period during which an individual or team has played a particular sport

season's best (*athletics*) the best time or distance achieved by an **athlete** in a **season**

seat drop (*trampolining*) a basic landing in a seated position with the legs fully extended

second (*boxing*) an assistant who helps a **boxer** before a **bout** and during the rests between **rounds**; (*mountaineering*) the second **climber** of a team, who follows the **leader**

second base (*baseball*) the second of the **bases** to which a player must run, located on the far side of the **mound** from **home plate**

second baseman (*baseball*) the **fielder** stationed near **second base**, on the side nearer **first base**

second eleven (*cricket*) the second-best **eleven** to represent a school, college, or the like

second five-eighth (*rugby league*) a player positioned on the outside of a **five eighth** [a term used in Australia and New Zealand]

second half (*general*) the half of a **game** or **match** after **half time**

second home (*lacrosse*) the attacking player who is the second of the three **homes**

second row (*rugby league, rugby union*) the two **forwards** who make up the second row of the **scrum**

second service (*tennis*) the second of a player's two permitted **serves**

second slip (*cricket*) the second of the three **fielders** positioned in the **slips**

secondary (*American football*) the defensive **backfield**, behind the **linebackers**

seconde (*fencing*) the second of eight basic **parry** positions, used to protect the lower outside of the right of the body [French *seconde*, "second"]

sedge (*angling*) an **artificial fly** resembling a sedge fly

Sedgefield (*horse racing*) a **National Hunt racecourse** at Sedgefield, Co. Durham, England

see off the new ball (*cricket*) to bat until the shine has been removed from the **new ball** at the start of an **innings**

seed (*tennis*) a good player who as the result of a **draw** has been assigned a place in the order of playing that will avoid an encounter with another good player early in a **tournament** [the player is listed numerically in programs, for example No. 6 seed]

selection (*horse racing*) a horse selected by a bettor as likely to win a **race**

selector (*cricket*) an official who selects a team **captain**

self-defense (*general*) the principle of physically protecting oneself that applies in most of the **martial arts** and that originally applied to **boxing**, regarded as the **art of self-defense**

sell a dummy (*association football, rugby league, rugby union*) to deceive an opponent by means of a **dummy**

seller (*horse racing*) shortening of **selling race**

selling race (*horse racing*) a **race** whose winner must be put up for auction at a previously fixed price

selling plate (*horse racing*) another term for a **selling race**

semi (*general*) colloquial shortening of **semifinal**

semiamateur (*general*) not playing for payment, like a **professional**, but partly supported by a sponsor

semifinal (*general*) a **match** or **round** held immediately before the **final**

semipro (*general*) shortening of **semiprofessional**

semiprofessional (*general*) a part-time **professional** player, receiving payment for his participation but not relying on it for a living

Senators (*ice hockey*) short name of the Ottawa Senators team

send back (*cricket*) to **dismiss** a **batsman** [he is sent back to the **pavilion**]

send down (*cricket*) to bowl a **ball** [the **bowler** sends it down the **pitch**]

send in (*cricket*) (1) to send a **batsman** into the field to bat; (2) to nominate the opposing side to bat first after winning the **toss**

send off (*association football*) to order a player to leave the **pitch** following an **offense** that merited a **red card** or two offenses that merited two **yellow cards**

senior circuit (*baseball*) colloquial term for the **National League** [so called as formed before the **American League**]

Senior TT (*motorcycle racing*) the principal annual TT race [for larger **bikes** than in the **Junior TT**]

sensei (*karate*) an instructor in the sport [Japanese *sen*, "previous," and *sei*, "birth"]

seoi nage (*judo*) a shoulder throw [Japanese *seoi*, "to bear on the back," and *nage*, "throw"]

sepak takraw (*sport*) a **game** of Asian origin resembling a cross between **badminton** and **vol-**

leyball played with a rattan **ball** on a badminton **court** [Malay *sepak*, "kick," and Thai *takran*, "rattan ball"]

septime (*fencing*) the seventh of eight basic **parry** positions, used to protect the lower inside of the body [French *septime*, "seventh"]

Serie A (*association football*) the premier **division** in the Italian national **league**

serve (*tennis*) the opening **shot** of a **point**, in which the player throws the **ball** up into the air then hits it diagonally across the **net** to his opponent; (*general*) the opening **shot** in a **game** such as **badminton** or **squash**

serve and volley (*tennis*) a style of play in which a player runs up to the **net** after a **serve** in order to take up a position for a **volley**

server (*general*) the player making a **serve**

service (*tennis*) another term for a **serve**

service box (*squash*) the square area in each **quarter court** within which the **server** serves

service court (*badminton*) one of the two boxes into which the rear part of the **court** is divided and from which the **server** serves; (*tennis*) the box on the other side of the **net** into which the **server** must place the **ball** when serving

service game (*tennis*) a **game** in which it is a particular player's turn to serve

service line (*badminton, tennis*) the boundary of the **service court**

service park (*auto racing*) in **rally driving**, the area where a **crew** carries out any running repairs to a car

service side (*real tennis*) the half of the **court** from which the **ball** is served

service winner (*tennis*) a **shot** by the **receiver** that sends the **ball** out of **court** [it is a winner because the **serve** was an **ace**]

session (*cricket*) one of the three periods of play in a full day's play, the first being from the start of play to **lunch**, the second from lunch to **tea**, and the third from tea to the close of play

set (*badminton, squash*) to extend a **game** by a specified number of **points**; (*general*) a group of **games** counting as a unit, as in **volleyball**; (*snooker*) another term for a **plant**; (*tennis*) a series of **games** in which the winner is the first to win at least six games and at least two games more than his opponent

set! (*general*) the command given by the **starter** of a **race** to prepare competitors for the **starting signal** [short for "get set!"]

set blow (*shinty*) the equivalent of a **free hit**

set one (*squash*) a winning **score** of nine **points**

set piece (*association football*) a carefully planned and executed **play** from a **corner kick** or **free kick** near the **penalty area**; (*rugby union*) a **scrum** or a **lineout**

set play (*general*) a prearranged maneuver carried out after a restart by the team then in the **lead**

set point (*tennis*) a **point** that wins a **set**

set scrum (*rugby league, rugby union*) an organized **scrum**, as ordered by the **referee**

set shot (*basketball*) a **shot** at the **basket** made by a stationary player

set-to (*boxing*) a renewed attack

set two (*squash*) a winning **score** of ten **points**

set up (*general*) (1) to prepare the way for a move or maneuver, as a **shot** at **goal** in **association football**; (2 to contrive to place a player or team in a vulnerable position

set-up (*billiards, snooker*) a position of the **balls** from which it is easy to score; (*boxing*) a **boxer** who can be easily defeated by a particular opponent and who is selected for this very reason

set-up man (*baseball*) a **relief pitcher** who usually enters the game in the seventh or eight **inning** with the aim of preserving a **lead** for the **closer**

setter (*volleyball*) a player who plays the **ball** in a **volley** for a teammate to **spike**

seven-a-side (*rugby union*) a form of the **game** played by seven players on each side instead of 15, the emphasis being on speed and **ball skills**

seven-meter line (*handball*) the line, seven meters from the **goal**, from where a **seven-meter throw** is taken

seven-meter throw (*handball*) a **penalty** throw taken as a direct **shot** on **goal** from the **seven-meter line**, which the player must not cross before the **ball** leaves his hand

sevens (*rugby union*) shortening of **seven-a-side**

seventh-inning stretch (*baseball*) a break after the **top** half of the seventh **inning**, during which spectators can stand up and walk about before settling again to watch the climax

76ers (*basketball*) short name of the Philadelphia 76ers team

sex test (*general*) popular name for a gender verification test, a medical procedure that determines the sex of a female competitor suspected of being wholly or partly male

shadow boxing (*boxing*) **sparring** practice with an imaginary opponent

shadow skating (*ice skating*) a **routine** in **pair skating** in which the skaters perform with coordinated movements but not in physical contact with each other

shaft (*darts*) the part of the **dart** that screws into the **barrel** and holds the **flight**; (*golf*) the long handle of the **club**, on which the **clubhead** is set

shag (*baseball*) to chase after **fly balls** as part of **fielding** practice

shake 'n' bake (*basketball*) colloquial term for

showy play, with rapid changes of direction and neat handling of the **ball**

shakedown (*auto racing*) in **rally driving**, the testing of cars by their drivers on roads similar to those used in a **rally**, usually carried out the day before the rally itself

shakehands (*table tennis*) a grip of the **bat** that resembles "shaking hands" with it

Shakers (*association football*) nickname of the English **club** Bury [from the religious sect of "Shaking Quakers" (not the American Shakers), historically connected with the town]

shamateur (*general*) rather dated term for a **sportsperson** who retains **amateur** status while receiving payment (like a **professional**) for playing or competing [a "sham amateur"]

shanghai (*darts*) colloquial term for the feat of scoring a **single**, **double**, and **treble** of the same number with a set of three **darts** [from a form of the **game** in which players failing to score were eliminated or "shanghaied"]

shank (*golf*) a **mishit** close to the **heel** of the **club** in which the **ball** makes contact with the **hosel**, causing it to fly to the right (for a right-handed player)

Sharks (*ice hockey*) short name of the San Jose Sharks team; (*rugby union*) short name of the English **club** Sale Sharks

sharpshooter (*general*) a player having very good aim

Shaymen (*association football*) nickname of the English **club** Halifax Town [from the Shay, the team's **home ground**]

sheet (*curling*) the strip of ice on which the **game** is played; (*sailing*) a rope attached to the lower corner of a **sail**

Sheffield Shield (*cricket*) name until 1999 of the **Pura Cup** [from the 3d Lord Sheffield, who took an English team to Australia in 1891 and donated £150 for a **trophy**]

shell (*rowing*) a light narrow racing boat

shell out (*baseball*) to score heavily against an opposing team

shepherding (*Australian Rules*) the (legitimate) blocking of an opponent from tackling a teammate in **possession** of the **ball**

shield (*general*) a **trophy** in the form or shape of a shield, awarded to the winner of a contest

shift (*American football*) the movement of two or more offensive players into different starting positions before the **snap**

shime-waza (*judo*) a stranglehold [Japanese *shimeru*, "to tighten," and *waza*, "technique"]

shinty (*sport*) a **game** of Scottish origin similar to **field hockey**, played between teams of 12 with a **caman** and a leather-covered cork **ball** [said to derive from *shin ye!*, a cry used in the game]

Shire (*association football*) short name of the Scottish **club** East Stirlingshire

shirt swapping (*association football*) a traditional exchange of shirts between a player and his **marker** at the end of a **match**

shirtfront (*cricket*) (of) a smooth and even **pitch**

shodan (*judo, karate*) a degree of proficiency equivalent to first **dan** or first degree **black belt** [Japanese *sho*, "primary," and *dan*, "grade"]

shoo-in (*horse racing*) a horse allowed to win a **race** fraudulently [the **jockeys** decide which horse is to win and everyone else "shoos it in" past the **post**]

shoot (*association football*) to take a **shot** at **goal**; (*shooting*) a **match** or contest

shoot-off (*shooting*) an additional contest to resolve a **tie**

shoot-out (*American football*) a method of resolving a **tie** in which five players from both teams are given five seconds each to score against the **goalkeeper**, the team with the most **goals** receiving one point to break the tie; (*association football*) shortening of **penalty shoot-out**; (*general*) a keen and decisive contest

shoot set (*volleyball*) a **volley** in the form of a **pass** that travels fast and low over the **net**

shooter (*cricket*) colloquial term for a bowled **ball** that stays low after pitching

shooting (*sport*) the competitive sport of firing at a **target** with a **pistol** or **rifle**

shooting circle (*field hockey, netball*) the D-shaped area in front of the **goal** from which a **shot** at goal must be taken

shooting glove (*archery*) a glove worn to protect the hand when drawing a **bow**

shooting guard (*basketball*) a **guard** who specializes in taking long-range **shots**

shooting range (*shooting*) a specially prepared area with **targets** for practice or competition in the sport

shop (*billiards*) to **pot** one's opponent's **ball** [as when one "shops" (betrays) an accomplice to the police]

short (*cricket*) (1) a **fielding** position closer than normal to the **batsman**; (2) (of) a bowled **ball** that bounces at some distance from the batsman; (*horse racing*) not on top form

short ball (*cricket*) a **ball** that pitches with a short **length**

short corner (*field hockey*) another term for a **penalty corner**

short field (*baseball*) the part of the **field** in which the **shortstop** plays

short fielder (*baseball*) another term for a **shortstop**

short game (*golf*) play on and around the **green**

short-handed (*ice hockey*) having one or more players on the **penalty bench**

short head (*greyhound racing, horse racing*) a narrow **win** that is shorter than a **head** but longer than a **nose**

short iron (*golf*) an **iron** (usually an 8- or 9-iron or a **wedge**) used to play **shots** from close to the **green**

short leg (*cricket*) a **fielding** position very near (and in line with) the **batsman** on the **leg side**

short line (*squash*) a line extending the full width of the **court** 18ft (5.44m) from the front wall

short odds (*horse racing*) **odds** in a **bet** that are favorable in terms of risk but unfavorable in terms of potential gain

short program (*ice skating*) a **routine** in which the skaters have to perform preset movements, unlike a **free program**

short run (*cricket*) a **run** not properly completed by the **batsman**

short slip (*cricket*) another term for **first slip**

short square leg (*cricket*) a **fielder** at a **square leg** position close to the **wicket**

short stuff (*golf*) colloquial term for the **fairway** [where the grass is short by contrast with the **rough**]

short tennis (*tennis*) a form of the **game** for children, played on a small **court** with a small **racket** and a soft **ball**

short-track (*speed skating*) a form of the sport in which contestants race in packs around an oval **track** over distances varying from 500m to 5,000m

shortarm (*boxing*) (of) a **punch** delivered with a bent arm rather than an extended one

shortboard (*surfing*) a **board** shorter than the norm, ridden mainly by experienced **surfers**

shorten up (*rowing*) to row too fast at too high a **rating**, with the **oar** not pulled its full length through the water

shortstop (*baseball*) the **fielder** positioned between **second base** and **third base**

shot (*angling*) a **cast** of the net; (*archery*) (1) a discharged **arrow**; (2) the point where it strikes the **target**; (*association football*) a kick of the **ball** at **goal**; (*athletics*) the heavy metal ball resembling a cannonball thrown in the **shot put**; (*bowls*) (1) the **point** gained for placing one's **bowl** nearer the **jack** than the nearest bowl of one's opponent; (2) the position closest to the jack; (*general*) a **stroke**, **throw**, or **hit**; (*rowing*) an attempt to overtake and touch the boat in front in a **bumping race**; (*shooting*) (1) a discharged bullet; (2) the point where it strikes the **target**

shot bowl (*bowls*) the **bowl** nearest the **jack**

shot clock (*basketball*) the clock that records the length of time a team retains **possession** of the **ball** before attempting a **shot**, an excess of the prescribed time being an **offense**

shot put (*athletics*) a **field event** in which an athlete throws a **shot** as far as possible

shot to nothing (*snooker*) an attempt to **pot** a **ball** in such a way that if the **shot** is missed the player's opponent will not be left with an easy opportunity

shotgun (*American football*) an offensive formation to facilitate passing in which the **quarterback** stands some way behind the **center** and the other **backs** are stationed to act as **pass receivers** or **blockers**

shotmaker (*basketball, golf, tennis*) a player noted for making skillful **shots**

shotokan (*karate*) one of the five main forms of the sport [Japanese *sho*, "true," *to*, "way," and *kan*, "mansion"]

shoulder (*cricket*) the curved upper edge of the **blade**, near to where it joins the handle; (*surfing*) the calm portion of a wave breaking on the beach

shoulder arms (*cricket*) to hold the **bat** over one's shoulder in order to allow the **ball** to pass without attempting a **stroke**

shoulder stand (*gymnastics*) a movement in which the **gymnast** holds his body and legs up in the air, supporting them on his shoulders

shovel pass (*American football*) a **pass** in which a player flicks the **ball** out of his hand without extending his arm

show (*horse racing*) the third place in a **race**

show eyes (*bowls*) to roll with a wobble so that the side disk of the **bowl** continually "winks"

show the bowler the maker's name (*cricket*) to bat defensively with a straight **bat** [so that the **bowler** can read the name of the bat's manufacturer]

showjumper (*equestrianism*) a horse or **rider** who takes part in **showjumping**

showjumping (*equestrianism*) a **discipline** in which horse and **rider** clear a number of **obstacles** on a fixed **course**, usually within a time limit, earning **penalty** points for **faults**

shredding (*snowboarding*) to travel fast downhill while moving one's body from one side of the **board** to the other

Shrews (*association football*) short name of the English **club** Shrewsbury Town

Shrimpers (*association football*) nickname of the English **club** Southend United [from the shrimps gathered in the sands of this seaside resort]

shunt (*auto racing*) an accident in which one car crashes into another

shuriken (*martial arts*) a missile in the form of a star with projecting blades or points [Japanese *shu*, "hand," *ri*, "inside," and *ken*, "blade"]

shut the door (*auto racing*) to steer across the **track** in order to prevent a rival from passing

shuto (*judo, karate*) a movement of the hand in the

manner of a sword [Japanese *shu*, "hand," and *to*, "sword"]

shutout (*general*) a **game** in which the **opposition** fails to score

shuttle (*badminton*) shortening of **shuttlecock**

shuttlecock (*badminton*) the object hit back and forth in the **game**, as a lightweight cone in the form of a rounded cork stuck with **flights**

side (*billiards, snooker*) a **spin** given to a **ball** by striking it to left or right of its center, causing it to swerve and alter its angle of rebound

side charge (*Gaelic football*) a shoulder charge on an opponent who is in **possession** of the **ball** or about to play it

side judge (*American football*) a member of the officiating team whose duties are similar to those of the **back judge**

sideboards (*polo*) the short boards along the side of the **field** which help to keep the **ball** in play

sidecar (*motorcycle racing*) a small passenger car attached to a motorcycle

sidefoot (*American football, association football*) to kick with the inside of the foot

sideline (*general*) to remove a player from a team because of injury; (*table tennis*) a white line along each side of the table

sideline kick (*Gaelic football*) a kick taken from the side of the **pitch** after the **ball** has gone out of play

sidelines (*general*) in **field games**, the lines marking either side of the playing area

sideslip (*skiing*) a sideways downward slide

sidespin (*table tennis*) **spin** imparted to the **ball** by striking it sideways with the **bat**

sidestep (*rugby league, rugby union*) a sudden change of direction made in order to avoid a **tackle** from an opponent

sidestroke (*swimming*) a **stroke** performed by a swimmer lying on one side

sidewinder (*boxing*) a blow struck from the side

sight (*archery*) a guide to the eye on a **bow**; (*shooting*) a guide to the eye on a **rifle**

sight screen (*cricket*) a white board on wheels placed outside the **boundary** behind the **bowler**, used to help the **batsman** pick out the approaching **ball**

sighter (*archery, shooting*) a practice **shot** fired at the beginning of a **match** to check the adjustments of the **sights**

signal (*general*) a sound or gesture made by an official to convey a particular point of information during play, as of a **referee** in **association football** or an **umpire** in **cricket**

signal caller (*American football*) a player who signals the next move or formation to his teammates

Silkmen (*association football*) nickname of the En-

glish **club** Macclesfield Town [from the local silk-manufacturing industry]

silks (*horse racing*) the shirt and cap worn by a **jockey**, made in the **racing colors** of the horse's owner

silly (*cricket*) (of) a **fielding** position very close to the **batsman** [where one risks being struck by the **ball**]

silly mid-off (*cricket*) a **fielder** positioned in front of the **bowler** on the **off** side, close to the **batsman**

silly mid-on (*cricket*) a **fielder** positioned in front of the **bowler** on the **on** side, close to the **batsman**

silly point (*cricket*) a **fielder** positioned on the **off** side very close to the **batsman** on a line with the **popping crease**

silver (*Olympics*) shortening of **sliver medal**

silver duck (*cricket*) a **duck** scored by a **batsman** on his second **ball** [from **silver** as a second award]

Silver Ferns (*netball*) nickname of the New Zealand national team [from the tall tree fern native to New Zealand]

silver goal (*association football*) the first **goal** scored in a period of 15 minutes **extra time**, as a method of settling a **draw**, with a further 15 minutes if still a draw, at the end of which, if still a draw, a **penalty shoot-out** was held [a system in force from 2002 to 2004, when it was withdrawn, like the **golden goal**]

Silver Goblets and Nickalls Challenge Cup (*rowing*) the **trophy** awarded to the winner of a **race** for **coxless pairs** at Henley Royal Regatta [inaugurated in 1845 with the Goblets introduced as presentation **prizes** in 1850 and the Nickalls Challenge Cup donated in 1895 by Tom Nickalls in commemoration of his sons, Guy Nickalls (1866–1935) and Vivian Nickalls (1870–1947), who between them won 11 Goblets]

silver medal (*Olympics*) the medal awarded as second **prize** [silver is a less valuable metal than gold but more valuable than bronze]

silver ring (*horse racing*) an enclosure at a **racecourse** where smaller **bets** are laid [the bets were originally laid in silver coins rather than banknotes]

silver slugger (*baseball*) an annual award made to the outstanding **batter** in the **league** at each position

Silverstone (*auto racing*) a **circuit** at the village of Silverstone, Northamptonshire, England, the regular location of the **British Grand Prix**

silverware (*general*) sporting **trophies** made from (or coated with) silver

simple grip (*weightlifting*) a grip for holding the **barbell** that has four fingers on one side balanced by the thumb on the other side

sin bin (*general*) colloquial term for the enclosure to which a player is sent for a given period of time when suspended from a **game** for unruly behavior; (*ice hockey*) colloquial term for the **penalty bench**

Singapore Grand Prix (*auto racing*) the **Formula One** international **Grand Prix** held on the Marina Bay **street circuit** in Singapore

single (*baseball*) a **hit** that allows the **batter** to reach **first base**; (*cricket*) a **hit** for one **run**; (*tennis*) a **game** played with one player on each side

single-foot (*equestrianism*) in **dressage**, a brisk walking **pace** with one foot on the ground at a time

single leg tackle (*wrestling*) a move in which a **wrestler** brings his opponent down by using an armhold on one of his legs

single scull (*rowing*) a one-manned boat in which the **rower** has a pair of **sculls**

single-wicket (*cricket*) a form of the **game** in which individual players take it in turns to bat for a limited number of **overs**

sink (*billiards, snooker*) colloquial term for **pot**

sink a putt (*golf*) to send a **putt** into the **hole**

sink-and-draw (*angling*) a method of taking fish by weighting a **deadbait** with **lead**, arming it with **hooks**, and allowing it to sink to the bottom, after which it is drawn up in a motion that causes it to dive and swoop

sinker (*angling*) a weight used to sink a **fishing line**; (*baseball*) a **fastball** with a downward movement; (*windsurfing*) a short **board** used by experienced **surfers** for sailing in high winds

sire (*greyhound racing*) the father of a greyhound; (*horse racing*) the father of a **foal**

sit down (*golf*) to land on the **green** and not roll any further

sit in (*cycling*) to ride close to the **rider** in front in order to **slipstream**

sit on the splice (*cricket*) to bat defensively [as if sitting on the **splice** of the **bat**]

sit out (*sailing*) to keep the boat flat in the water by **hiking**

sit spin (*ice skating*) a **spin** performed in a seated position close to the ice, with one leg bent and the other fully extended [originated by the U.S. skater Jackson Haines (1840–1879)]

sit-ups (*general*) a series of exercise movements, typically carried out in a **gymnasium**, in which the head and torso are raised from a lying position while the legs remain still

sitter (*general*) (1) an easy **catch**, as in **baseball** or **cricket**; (2) an easy **shot**

sitting sports (*general*) sports in which the participant is seated, as **cycling, equestrianism, rowing** or **sailing**

sitzmark (*skiing*) an impression in the snow made by a skier falling backward [German *sitzen*, "to sit," and English *mark*]

six (*cricket*) a **score** of six **runs** gained by hitting the **ball** over the **boundary** without its touching the ground

six-day race (*cycling*) a **track race** held on six successive evenings

six-meter line (*handball*) the curving line six meters from the **goal** that marks the **goal area**

Six Nations (*rugby union*) an annual **championship** in which teams from England, Ireland, Scotland, Wales, France, and Italy compete against one another [until 2000, when Italy joined, known as the **Five Nations**]

six-yard area (*association football*) another term for the **six-yard box**

six-yard box (*association football*) the rectangular area in front of the **goal** from which a **goal kick** can be taken

six-yard line (*association football*) the line marking the limit of the **six-yard box**

six-zero defense (*handball*) a defensive formation in which all of the players (except the **goalkeeper**) line up along the **six-meter line** to block the attackers

sixte (*fencing*) the sixth of eight basic **parry** positions, used to protect the upper right-hand side of the body [French *sixte*, "sixth"]

sixth man (*basketball*) the best **substitute** player in a team

sixth tackle (*rugby league*) the last of the six allowable **tackles** in the set, leading to a **handover**

skateboard (*skateboarding*) a narrow **board**, similar to a small **surfboard**, that is mounted on **trucks** that bear small wheels

skateboarding (*sport*) the sport of riding on a **skateboard**, on which the **rider** stands and coasts along, turning it by shifting his weight and occasionally pushing one foot against the ground, in the manner of a scooter, in order to maintain forward progress

skatepark (*skateboarding*) a park or area for riding a **skateboard**

skates (*ice hockey, ice skating*) shortening of **ice skates**; (*roller skating*) shortening of **roller skates**

skating (*sport*) (1) shortening of **ice skating**; (2) shortening of **roller skating**

skating rink (*ice hockey, ice skating*) alternate term for an **ice rink**; (*roller skating*) fuller term for a **rink**

skeet (*shooting*) a form of **clay-pigeon shooting** in which the **targets** are thrown from **traps** and the shooter moves in a semicircle to different stations [apparently alteration of *shoot*]

skeg (*rowing*) a stabilizing fin attached to the **stern** section of the **hull**; (*sailboarding*) a stabilizing fin on the underside of a **sailboard**; (*surfing*) a stabilizing fin on the underside of a **surfboard** [Dutch *scheg*, "cutwater"]

skeleton (*bobsledding*) shortening of **skeleton bob**

skeleton bob (*bobsledding*) a form of **bobsled** with no brakes or steering mechanism on which a person races head-first down an ice-covered **course** ["skeleton" because basic]

ski archery (*sport*) a combination of **archery** and **cross-country skiing**

ski blades (*skiing*) a type of very short **skis**, although often wider than regular skis, resembling a cross between a ski and a **snowboard**

ski boat (*water skiing*) a type of small powerboat, used to tow **water skiers**

ski bum (*skiing*) a devotee of the sport, especially one who travels widely in search of snowy conditions

ski-flying (*skiing*) jumping from a high **takeoff** point, so that a greater time is spent in the air

ski jump (*skiing*) (1) a steeply-sloping, snow-covered **track** ending in an elevated platform from which a skier jumps; (2) the jump itself

ski-kiting (*water skiing*) a form of the sport in which the skier holds on to a bar attached to a kitelike device

ski lift (*skiing*) a mechanism for carrying skiers uphill, consisting of seats suspended from an overhead cable

ski mountaineering (*sport*) a combination of **skiing** and **mountaineering**, using light **skis**

ski-o (*orienteering*) a form of **orienteering** on **skis**

ski pole (*skiing*) another term for a **ski stick**

ski run (*skiing*) a snow slope prepared for skiing on

ski slope (*skiing*) a snowy slope prepared for skiers to descend

ski stick (*skiing*) one of a pair of pointed sticks, with a disk near the tip, used by skiers for balance, propulsion, or braking

ski touring (*skiing*) the sport or recreation of traveling across country on **skis**

ski tow (*skiing*) a type of **ski lift** in the form of an endless moving chain of bars or seats, suspended from an overhead cable; (*water skiing*) a tow rope for **water skiers**

skibob (*skiing*) a vehicle resembling a bicycle with **skis,** used for descending a snow slope

skibobbing (*skiing*) the sport of riding on a **skibob**

skid lid (*cycling*) colloquial term for a helmet

skier (*cricket*) a **ball** hit high in the air by the **batsman**

skiff (*rowing*) a type of small light boat

skiing (*sport*) the recreation or competitive sport of descending a snowy slope on **skis**

skijoring (*skiing*) a form of the sport in which the skier is towed by a horse or motor vehicle [Nor-

wegian *skikjøring*, from *ski*, "ski," and *kjøring*, "driving"]

skimboard (*surfing*) a type of thin **surfboard** without a **skeg** used for riding shallow water

skimmer (*cricket*) a **ball** from the **bowler** that travels with a low trajectory

skin the cat (*gymnastics*) to execute a move in which the **gymnast** passes his feet and legs between his arms while hanging by his hands from the **horizontal bar**, so drawing his body up and over the bar

skindiver (*aquatics*) a person who engages in **skindiving**

skindiving (*aquatics*) the recreation of **diving** and **swimming** underwater, with breathing equipment (usually a **scuba** or **aqualung**) carried on the back

skins (*golf*) a type of **matchplay** in which each **hole** is worth a particular number of **points**; (*skiing*) strips of fabric (originally sealskin) attached to the underside of **skis** to prevent a skier from slipping backward when climbing

skinsuit (*cycling*) an aerodynamic garment like a swimsuit worn by racing **cyclists**

skip (*athletics*) another term for **step**; (*bowls, cycling*) colloquial abbreviation of **skipper**

skipper (*bowls, cycling*) the captain of a team

skipping (*golf*) the technique of hitting a **ball** over water so that it skips the surface

skis (*skiing*) long narrow runners (originally of wood), usually pointed and turned up at the front, fastened under the feet to enable travel over snow downhill or on the level; (*water skiing*) shortening of **water skis** [a Norwegian word]

skish (*angling*) a contest in which **fishing tackle** is used to **cast** on dry land [origin uncertain but perhaps a blend of *skill* and *fish*]

skitter (*angling*) to fish by drawing the **bait** over the surface of the water

skittle (*skittles*) one of the **pins** used in the **game**

skittle alley (*skittles*) fuller term for an **alley**

skittle out (*cricket*) to **dismiss** a team for a low **score** [their **wickets** fall like **skittles**]

skittles (*sport*) (1) a **game** in which nine **skittles** are set up at the end of an **alley** to be bowled at and knocked down in as few attempts as possible

Skolars (*rugby league*) short name of the English **club** London Skolars

skull (*golf*) another term for **thin**

skurfing (*skateboarding*) colloquial term for the sport [blend of **skating** and **surfing**]

Sky Blues (*association football*) (1) nickname of the English **club** Coventry City; (2) nickname of the Scottish club Forfar Athletic [from the color of the teams' shirts]

skyboard (*parachuting*) a **board** similar to a **skateboard**, used by **skysurfers**

skybox (*general*) a luxurious high seated area in a **stadium**

skydiver (*parachuting*) a participant in **skydiving**

skydiving (*parachuting*) the carrying out of acrobatic maneuvers while in **free fall**

skyer (*cricket*) another spelling of **skier**

skyhook (*basketball*) a variant of the **jump hook** in which the **ball** is released from a point high above the shooter's head; (*mountaineering*) a type of grappling-iron in the form of a small flattened hook with an eye for attaching a rope, fixed temporarily into a rock face

skyscraper (*baseball, cricket*) a **ball** hit high in the air

skysurfer (*parachuting*) a participant in **skysurfing**

skysurfing (*parachuting*) a form of **skydiving** in which participants are attached to **skyboards**

slab (*mountaineering*) a smooth body of rock lying at an angle to the horizontal

slalom (*canoeing*) a type of **race** in **whitewater** in which **paddlers** have to pass through **gates**; (*skiing*) a **downhill race** on a zigzag **course** between artificial obstacles such as flags [Norwegian *slalåm*, from *sla*, "sloping," and *låm*, "track"]

slam (*general*) to score a **goal** with a forceful **hit** or kick

slam dunk (*basketball*) a forceful (and usually dramatic) **dunk**

slam-dunk smash (*tennis*) a **smash** suggestive of a **slam dunk** in which a player jumps above the **ball** to strike it down as forcefully as possible [popularized in the 1990s by the U.S. player Pete Sampras (1971–)]

slamball (*sport*) a **game** resembling **basketball** with eight **trampolines**

slant (*American football*) a **play** in which the player in **possession** of the **ball** enters or leaves the **line of scrimmage** diagonally

slant pattern (*American football*) the route of a **receiver** running diagonally from the outside of the **field** toward the middle

slap skates (*speed skating*) another term for **clap skates**

slapshot (*ice hockey*) a fast powerful **shot** made with the **stick** taken above the player's head

sled (*sled dog racing*) a low conveyance on runners drawn over snow by horses or dogs

sled dog racing (*sport*) **races** between teams of dogs harnessed to **sleds**, especially as organized in Alaska

sledge (*sled dog racing*) alternate form of **sled**

sledging (*cricket*) the barracking of a **batsman** by **fielders** in order to upset his concentration [from *sledge* in the sense "sledgehammer"]

sleeper (*tenpin bowling*) a **pin** that is not easily seen because it is hidden behind another pin; (*horse racing*) an apparently indifferent **runner** that suddenly livens up and wins a **race**

sleigh (*sled dog racing*) another term for a **sled**

slice (*association football*) a **miskick** that sends the **ball** in an unintended direction; (*golf*) a **mishit** that sends the **ball** from left to right in the air (for a right-handed player) or from right to left (for a left-handed player); (*tennis*) a **shot** played with a slicing action that imparts **backspin** to the **ball**

slicks (*auto racing*) untreaded tires, used in dry-weather conditions [following a **Formula One** ruling, slicks had grooves from 1998 through 2009]

slide (*baseball*) a sliding approach along the ground to a **base**; (*rowing*) shortening of **sliding seat**; (*surfing*) a ride across the face of a wave

slider (*baseball*) a fast **pitch** that deviates from its original path; (*bobsledding*) colloquial term for a participant in the sport; (*cricket*) a **ball** to which the **bowler** has imparted **backspin**, so that it bounces less than the **batsman** expects

sliding seat (*rowing*) a seat that slides back and forth with the movement of the **rower**

sliding tackle (*rugby league, rugby union*) a **tackle** made by a player in a sliding approach

Sligo (*horse racing*) a flat and **National Hunt** racecourse in Co. Sligo, Ireland

sling (*mountaineering*) a short length of rope that provides extra support for the body in **abseiling**

sliotar (*hurling*) the leather-covered **ball** [Irish *sliotar*]

slip (*cricket*) one of the three **fielders** (**first slip**, **second slip**, **third slip**) positioned next to the **wicketkeeper** on the **off side**

slips (*cricket*) the positions of the three **slips**

slipstream (*auto racing*) to drive close behind another car in order to benefit from the vacuum created and so attempt to pass; (*cycling*) to ride close behind another **rider** or riders in order to benefit from the decreased wind resistance and so save energy

slob (*angling*) a large soft worm, used as **bait**

slog (*cricket*) a forceful and often unrefined **hit** of the **ball**

slog overs (*cricket*) in **limited-over games**, the **overs** at the end of an **innings**, when **batsmen** attempt to score a large number of **runs**

slog sweep (*cricket*) a **sweep** in which the **ball** is hit hard and in the air

slope soaring (*gliding*) increasing altitude in a **sailplane** by using the moving air forced up by a ridge

slopes (*skiing*) the snowy areas on a hill or mountain down which skiers make their descent

slot (*American football*) a gap in the **defense** line, usually between the **end** and the **tackle**; (*auto racing*) in **rally driving**, a turning or opening marked for the driver to take; (*ice hockey*) an (unmarked) area in front of the **goal** where an attacking player would be well placed to take a successful **shot** at goal

slot receiver (*American football*) a **receiver** who lines up further **infield** than a **wide receiver**

slotback (*American football*) a **back** positioned behind the **slot**

sloucher (*horse racing*) a **jockey** who deliberately rides slowly in the early stages of a **race**

slow back! (*golf*) a direction to a new player when the **club** is swung back from the **ball** in making a **stroke**

slow bowler (*cricket*) a **bowler** who bowls the **ball** at a slow speed

slow bowling (*cricket*) **bowling** by a **slow bowler**

slow side (*association football*) the longest distance, as the **goalkeeper** sees it, for the **ball** to travel from a player toward or into the **net**

slug nutty (*boxing*) colloquial term for **punch drunk**

slugfest (*baseball, boxing*) colloquial term for a hard-hitting contest

slugger (*baseball*) a **batter** who specializes in hitting **home runs**

smack (*cricket*) a hard **hit** with the **bat**

small-bore rifle (*shooting*) a **rifle** with a narrow bore, usually of .22in caliber

small forward (*basketball*) the smaller of a team's two **forwards**, the other being the **power forward**

smash (*badminton, tennis*) a powerful overhead **stroke** hit downward; (*table tennis*) a hard flat attacking **stroke**

smashball (*sport*) a **game** similar to **tennis** but without a **net** in which two or more players smash a **ball** back and forth with **rackets**

smooth (*tennis*) the side of a **racket** opposite to the **rough** side, used as a call when the racket is spun to decide on the **server** or choose an **end**

smother (*rugby league, rugby union*) a high **tackle** in which a player overwhelms an opponent

Snakeboard (*skateboarding*) proprietary name of a form of **skateboard** consisting of two footplates joined by a bar, allowing greater maneuverability than a standard **board**

snap (*American football*) the action of starting a **play**, as a **pass** of the **ball** from the **line of scrimmage** back to the **quarterback**; (*surfing*) a sharp turn back into the face of a wave

snapback (*American football*) fuller term for a **snap**

snatch (*weightlifting*) a type of **lift** in which the **barbell** is raised in one continuous movement from the floor to above the head with the arms straight

sneak (*American football*) an attempt to advance the **ball** a short distance by diving forward straight after receiving the **snap**; (*cricket*) another term for a **daisycutter**

snick (*cricket*) a slight deflection of the **ball** off the edge of the **bat**

sniggle (*angling*) to catch a fish by hooking it with a slight turn of the wrist

snooker (*sport*) (1) a **game** played on a standard **billiard table** by two players with 21 colored **balls** (15 of them **red**) and one white **cue ball**, the aim being to **pot** the colored balls in a certain order and gain more **points** than one's opponent in doing so; (2) a situation in which the path between the cue ball and the **object ball** is blocked, obliging the player to take an indirect **shot** [said to derive from army slang for a raw recruit, a term adopted for the game among British troops in India, where it originated in 1875]

snorkel (*aquatics*) a short breathing tube used by submerged **swimmers** [German *Schnorchel*]

snorter (*cricket*) a dangerously fast **ball** delivered by the **bowler**

snow bunny (*skiing*) an inexperienced skier, especially if female

snow sports (*general*) sports that take place on snow, such as **skiing** and **snowboarding**

snowblading (*skiing*) a form of the sport using short **skis** and no **poles**

snowboard (*snowboarding*) a **board** similar to a **skateboard** but without wheels, guided by the user with movements of the feet and body

snowboard cross (*snowboarding*) an **event** in which groups of competitors race down a **course** featuring **jumps**, turns, and **moguls**

snowboarding (*sport*) a sport similar to **skiing** or **skateboarding** in which participants travel down snow-covered slopes with their feet strapped to a **snowboard** rather than **skis**

snowcross (*motorcycle racing*) **races** between **snowmobiles** over a **motocross circuit**

snowdome (*general*) an indoor **arena** where **winter sports** can take place around the year

snowmobile (*motorcycle racing*) a motorized **sled** or tractorlike vehicle for traveling over snow

snowplow (*skiing*) the act of turning the front points of the **skis** inward to slow down

snowsurfing (*skiing*) the sport of traveling downhill on a large single **ski** like a **surfboard**

snurfing (*skiing*) colloquial name for **snowsurfing** [blend of *snow* and **surfing**]

soaring (*general*) the act of flying high in a **glider** or while being towed when suspended from a **kite**

soccer (*sport*) colloquial term for **association football**, originally used to distinguish it from **rugby football** [from *assoc.*, abbreviation of *association*]

soccer fan (*association football*) a keen **supporter** of the sport

soccer field (*association football*) a **field** where the sport is played

soccer match (*association football*) another term for a **football match**

soccer mom (*association football*) colloquial term for a mother who spends many hours driving her children to organized sports activities, such as **soccer**, and to supporting them in their participation

Socceroos (*association football*) nickname of the Australian national team [blend of **soccer** and *kangaroo*, the Australian national animal]

socket (*golf*) the part of the **clubhead** that houses the **shaft** of the **club**

soft (*horse racing*) a category of **going**

soft wicket (*cricket*) a **wicket** with damp, yielding turf

softball (*sport*) a **game** similar to **baseball** played between teams of nine with a large soft **ball** pitched underarm, the aim being to gain **runs** by hitting the ball with the **bat** and running past all three **bases** before returning to **home plate**

soigneur (*cycling*) an official who is responsible for a team's food, drink, and **kit** and who provides massage for **riders** after a **race** or **stage** [French *soigneur*, "carer"]

soldier palmer (*angling*) a type of **artificial fly**

sole (*golf*) the undersurface of a **clubhead**

Solheim Cup (*golf*) the **cup** awarded to the winner of a biennial **tournament** played between **professional** women's teams from the United States and Europe [founded in 1990 by Karsten Solheim, owner of Karsten Manufacturing Corporation]

solid ball (*pool*) a colored **ball** bearing a number in a small white circle

soling (*bowls*) the action of delivering a **bowl** to run evenly

Soling (*sailing*) a class of **keelboat** with a **crew** of three [named from the initials of the boat's sponsor, Sverre Olsen, and the surname of its 1950s designer, Jan Herman Linge]

solo (*Gaelic football*) to drop the **ball** from hand to foot and then kick it back into the hands; (*motorcycle racing*) a single-seater motorcycle (as opposed to one with a **sidecar**)

somersault (*general*) a complete turn of the body head over heels on the ground or in the air; (*gymnastics*) another term for a **salto** [Old French *sombresaut*, from Provençal *sobre*, "over," and *saut*, "leap"]

Sons (*association football*) nickname of the Scottish **club** Dumbarton [from "Sons of the Rock," nickname of the inhabitants of Dumbarton, a town dominated by a hill of basalt]

soop (*curling*) to assist the passage of a **stone** by sweeping the ice in front of it as it travels over the ice [Scots *soop*, "sweep"]

sophomore (*horse racing*) another term for a **three-year-old**

soup (*surfing*) another term for **mush**

souple (*wrestling*) a **hold** in which a **wrestler** holds his opponent from behind and throws him in a sweeping movement

southpaw (*baseball*) a left-handed **pitcher**; (*boxing*) a left-handed **boxer**, who leads with his right hand [when right-handed **batters** faced east to avoid the afternoon sun in their eyes, pitchers faced west, but if left-handed would throw with their south-side hand]

Southwell (*horse racing*) a **flat** and **National Hunt racecourse** at Rolleston, Nottinghamshire, England.

SP (*horse racing*) abbreviation of **starting price**

Spa (*auto racing*) a town in eastern Belgium, whose Spa-Francorchamps **circuit** is the **venue** for the **Belgian Grand Prix**

spaceball (*sport*) a **game** of American origin played by two or four players on a **trampoline** divided into two **courts** by a gantry holding a funneled basket, each court having a **backstop** below a rebound **net**, the aim being to throw the **ball** through the basket so that it scores by hitting the court or the backstop

spade mashie (*golf*) the former name of a 6-**iron**

spaghetti-legs routine (*association football*) a stagy wobbling of the legs performed by a supposedly fearful **goalkeeper** as a ruse to distract the taker of a **penalty kick**

Spanish Grand Prix (*auto racing*) the **Formula One** international **Grand Prix** held on the **circuit** at Barcelona, Spain

Spanish walk (*equestrianism*) another term for the **piaffe**

spanker (*sailing*) a **fore-and-aft sail** on the **mast** nearest the **stern** of a boat

spar (*boxing*) to exchange light blows by way of practice or demonstration; (*sailing*) a general term for a **boom**, **gaff**, **mast**, or **yard**

spare (*skittles, tenpin bowling*) knocking down all the **pins** with one's first two **balls** [so that one has a ball to spare]

spare ride (*horse racing*) a ride by a **jockey** on a horse for which he has not been booked

sparring partner (*boxing*) a **boxer** chosen to **spar** with another

spartakiad (*general*) a sporting competition with a great number of participants in a wide range of **events** [Russian *spartakiada*, after Spartacus, 1st-century B.C. leader of a slave revolt against Rome]

spear (*American football*) to butt an opponent with one's helmet; (*athletics*) colloquial term for a **javelin**; (*ice hockey*) to use one's **stick** as a spear to attack opponents

spear chucker (*athletics*) colloquial term for a **javelin** thrower

spear tackle (*rugby league, rugby union*) an illegal

tackle in which a player is lifted up and thrown down head first [like a spear]

Special Olympics (*Olympics*) a series of motivational games for the physically and mentally disabled, first held in the United States in 1968

special stage (*auto racing*) in **rally driving**, a timed competitive section of the **rally**

special team (*American football*) a group of players used for **kickoffs**, **punts**, and other special **plays**, as distinct from the regular **offense** and **defense**

spectator sport (*general*) a sport that is exciting and entertaining to watch as well as to play, such as **American football** or **hurling**

speed and endurance (*equestrianism*) the second day of a **three-day event**, consisting of a **steeplechase**, a **cross-country obstacle course**, and **roads and tracks**

speed bag (*boxing*) a small **punchbag** used for practicing quick **punches**

speed riding (*skiing*) an **extreme sport** in which the skier skis downhill until the wind inflates a **wing** on his back, allowing him to fly over obstacles

speed skating (*ice skating*) a form of the sport in which two or more skaters race on an oval **track**

speed walking (*athletics*) another term for **race walking**

speedball (*boxing*) a type of small fast **punchball**; (*sport*) a **field game**, played between teams of 11 players, that grew out of **association football** and that resembles **Gaelic football** in that the **ball** can be handled

speedway (*motorcycle racing*) a form of the sport in which **riders** on **bikes** with fixed gears and no brakes race several **laps** around an oval shale **track** in a **stadium**

speleology (*sport*) a formal term for **caving**

spell (*cricket*) a number of **overs** bowled successively by a particular **bowler**

spelunker (*caving*) colloquial term for a **caver** [whose sport or pastime is **speleology**]

sphairistike (*sport*) the name under which **lawn tennis** was patented in 1874 and by which it was quite widely known for a time [Greek *sphairistike tekhne*, "the art of playing ball"]

spider (*billiards, snooker*) a **rest** with wide arches that can be placed over a **ball** without touching it; (*darts*) the wire grid fixed to the front of a **dartboard** that shows the **score** numbers

Spiders (*association football*) nickname of the Scottish **club** Queen's Park [from the black and white hoops on the team's shirts, which suggest a spider's web]

spike (*American football*) to throw the **ball** forcefully to the ground, as when celebrating a **touchdown**; (*volleyball*) a forceful downward hit of the **ball** into the opposing team's **court**

spikes (*athletics*) running shoes with spiked soles

spin (*general*) (1) a twisting motion imparted to a **ball**, as by a **spin bowler** in **cricket**; (2) a rapid rotation of the body, as in **ice skating**; (*horse racing*) another term for a **race**

spin bowler (*cricket*) a **slow bowler** who imparts **spin** to a **ball** by means of his wrist or fingers, so that it deviates after pitching

spinach (*golf*) alternate term for **cabbage**

spinnaker (*sailing*) a three-cornered lightweight **sail**, set **forward** of or opposite the **mainmast** to increase sail area when running before the wind

spinner (*angling*) an **artificial fly** that revolves when pulled through the water; (*cricket*) (1) another term for a **spin bowler** (2) a **ball** that has had **spin** imparted to it

spinning (*angling*) fishing with a **spinner**

spinout (*auto racing*) a spinning skid that throws a car off the road or **track**

spiral (*American football*) a kick or **pass** that causes a **ball** to spin around its long axis

Spireites (*association football*) nickname of the English **club** Chesterfield [from the unusual twisted spire of the town's parish church]

spitball (*baseball*) the swerving **pitch** of a **ball** moistened with saliva or spit

SPL (*association football*) abbreviation of **Scottish Premier League**

splice (*cricket*) the wedge-shaped part of the handle of a **bat** that fits into the **blade**

split (*croquet*) shortening of **split shot**; (*general*) the time taken to complete a particular part of a **race**; (*horse racing*) the widening gap between two horses running side by side in a **race** that is entered by a following **rider**; (*tenpin bowling*) a **leave** situation in which the remaining **pins** are widely spaced; (*weightlifting*) the action of thrusting forward with one foot and back with the other during a **lift**

split decision (*boxing*) a decision made by a majority of the **judges** but not by all of them

split end (*American football*) an offensive player lined up a few yards from the end of the **line of scrimmage** so that he can immediately run **downfield** to catch **passes**

split-finger pitch (*baseball*) another term for a **splitter**

split jump (*ice skating*) a **jump** in which the legs are briefly kicked out into the **splits** position

split roll (*croquet*) another term for a **split shot**

split shot (*croquet*) a **stroke** that drives two touching **balls** in different directions

splits (*gymnastics*) the action of lowering the body to the **floor** or a piece of **apparatus** with the legs extended to either side or one forward and one back

splitter (*baseball*) a **fastball** thrown with fingers apart, giving it a late downward movement

spoon (*angling*) an artificial **bait** in the form of the bowl of a spoon, used in **spinning** or **trolling**; (*cricket*) a weak **hit** which sends the **ball** high in the air; (*golf*) an old-fashioned **club** with a slightly hollowed face, corresponding to a 3-**wood**; (*surfing*) the slight upward slope of a **surfboard**

spoonbait (*angling*) formal term for a **spoon**

sport fishing (*angling*) a name for the sport that distinguishes it from commercial fishing

sport of kings (*sport*) a byname for **horse racing** [a sport long patronized by royalty]

sportfish (*angling*) a fish caught for sport rather than as food

sports car (*auto racing*) a specially designed high-performance car built for highway driving

sports day (*general*) a meeting at a school or college for contests in various sports

sports ground (*general*) an area with equipment and facilities for sports

sports injury (*general*) an injury suffered as a result of participation in a sport

sports medicine (*general*) the branch of medicine concerned with the treatment of **sports injuries** and the assessment and improvement of the health of those involved in sport

sports writer (*general*) a person such as a reporter or columnist who writes regularly on sport

sportscast (*general*) a broadcast about sport

sportscaster (*general*) (1) a presenter of sports programs on radio or television; (2) a sports commentator

sportsman (*general*) a person who practices or is skilled in sport

sportsmanship (*general*) the performance or practice of a **sportsman**, especially one showing fairness and good humor

sportsperson (*general*) a person of either sex who practices or is skilled in sport

sportswoman (*general*) a woman who practices or is skilled in sport

spot (*billiards*) (1) one of the three marked points on the **billiard table** (**billiard spot, center spot, pyramid spot**) on which the **balls** are placed at certain stages in the **game**; (2) shortening of **spot white**; (*greyhound racing*) one hundredth of a second as a timing unit; (*snooker*) one of the six marked points on the **billiard table** on which the **colors** are placed at the start of a **frame** and to which they are returned (so long as there are still **reds** on the table) after being sent into a **pocket**

spot ball (*billiards*) another term for the **spot white**

spot-barred (*billiards*) bound to the rule that the **spot stroke** may not be played more than twice consecutively

spot kick (*association football*) a kick made from the **penalty spot**

spot stroke (*billiards*) a **stroke** by which a player **pots** the **red** from the **spot**, leaving his own **ball** in place to repeat the stroke

spot white (*billiards*) the white **cue ball** that has two small black spots on it to differentiate it from the **plain ball**

spotter (*archery*) a person appointed to identify the **score** of an **archer**; (*gymnastics, trampolining*) a person stationed to prevent a possible accident

spray deck (*canoeing*) a waterproof **cockpit** cover worn around the waist by a **kayaker** and attached to the **coaming** to prevent water entering the **kayak**

spray skirt (*canoeing*) another term for a **spray deck**

spread (*general*) a term used in betting for the number of **points** or **goals** by which a stronger team may be expected to beat a weaker team in a **match**

spread a plate (*horse racing*) to lose a shoe or **plate** during (or before) a **race**

spreadeagle (*ice skating*) a maneuver performed on the **outside edges** or **inside edges** of both **skates** in which the skates point in opposite directions; (*skiing*) an aerial maneuver in which the skier extends his arms and legs to the side while keeping the **skis** parallel and perpendicular to his body

spring double (*horse racing*) a bet on the **Lincoln Handicap** and **Grand National**, both **races** run in the spring

springboard (*gymnastics*) a flexible board used by a **gymnast** to take off when executing a **vault**; (*swimming*) a flexible **diving board**

Springboks (*rugby union*) nickname of the South African national team [from the agile antelope native to South Africa that is the team's emblem]

springer (*horse racing*) a horse on which the betting **odds** suddenly shorten

sprint (*athletics*) a **100 meters, 200 meters,** or **400 meters** race; (*cycling*) a **track race** ridden over 1km by individuals against one or two opponents; (*general*) (1) a short spell or burst of forward motion, as in **running, rowing,** or **cycling**; (2) a short **race**; (*horse racing*) a short **race** of five or six **furlongs** on the **flat**

sprint car (*auto racing*) a fast **racecar** used for racing over short distances

sprint hurdles (*athletics*) the **100-meter hurdles** or **110-meter hurdles**

sprinter (*cycling*) a **cyclist** whose specialty is the **sprint**

sprinters' lane (*cycling*) the inner **lane** of a **track** in a **velodrome**, between the **pole line** and the **sprinters' line**

sprinters' line (*cycling*) the red line on a **track** in a **velodrome**, between the **stayers' line** and the **pole line**, used by **riders** to overtake the **lead** rider

sprit (*sailing*) a **spar** set diagonally to extend a **fore-and-aft sail**

Spurs (*association football*) short name of the English **club** Tottenham Hotspur; (*basketball*) short name of the San Antonio Spurs team

spurt (*general*) a sudden increase of speed or energy, as in a **sprint**

squad (*general*) (1) a group of players trained in readiness to form a team; (2) the team itself

squad number (*association football*) the number on a player's shirt that identifies him and that originally indicated his playing position

square (*association football*) in a line across the **pitch** at right angles to the direction of play; (*cricket*) (1) the close-cut, rectangular area in the center of the **ground** on which the **wickets** are prepared; (2) at right angles to the wicket

square cut (*cricket*) a **cut** hit **square** on the **off side**

square drive (*cricket*) a **drive** hit **square** on the **off side**

square hit (*cricket*) a **hit** to **square leg**

square leg (*cricket*) a **fielding** position on the leg side in a line with the **popping crease**

square leg umpire (*cricket*) the **umpire** at **square leg**, who answers **appeals** for **run out** and **stumped**, as against the umpire who stands behind the **wicket** of the **bowler**

square-rigged (*sailing*) with square **sails** placed at right angles to the length of the boat

square-rigger (*sailing*) a **square-rigged** boat

squash (*sport*) a **game** played by two or four players with a small rubber **ball** that is struck with a **racket** against the walls of an enclosed **court** [the ball squashes on impact]

squash rackets (*sport*) the formal name of **squash**

squash tennis (*sport*) a **game** for two players similar to **squash** but played with an inflated ball and larger **rackets**

squat (*gymnastics*) shortening of **squat thrust**; (*weightlifting*) a **lift** in which the competitor squats with a **barbell** across his shoulders then rises again

squat rack (*weightlifting*) a pair of posts with a support that holds a **barbell** at a convenient height for a **squat**

squat thrust (*gymnastics*) a move in which the **gymnast** thrusts his legs back to their full extent from a squatting position while supporting his weight on his hands

squatter (*cricket*) another term for a **shooter**

squeaker (*general*) colloquial term for a **game** won by a very narrow margin

squeeze (*baseball*) shortening of **squeeze play**

squeeze play (*baseball*) a tactic in which a **batter** uses a **bunt** so that a **runner** at **third base** can attempt to reach **home plate** safely

squib (*American football*) a **kickoff** with a short kick

squid (*octopush*) the circular lead disk used as a **puck** in the **game**

st (*cricket*) abbreviation of **stumped** in scoring

stab (*billiards, snooker*) a short sharp **stroke** that makes the **ball** stop dead or travel slowly after making contact with the **object ball**

stab stroke (*billiards, snooker*) fuller term for a **stab**

stabilizer (*archery*) a device attached to the **bow** to increase stability during a **shot**

stable (*horse racing*) (1) an establishment where **racehorses** are kept and trained; (2) the horses belonging to a single **trainer**; (*sumo*) an establishment in which a group of **wrestlers** live and receive training

stable lad (*horse racing*) a man or boy employed to look after horses at a **stable**, one of his jobs at the **racecourse** being to lead a horse around the **parade ring**

stable lass (*horse racing*) a woman or girl employed to look after horses at a **stable**

Stableford (*golf*) a competition in which **points** are awarded for **scores** achieved on each **hole**, the player's **handicap** and the **stroke index** being used to help calculate the points [named for its inventor in 1931, English physician Frank Stableford (1870–1959)]

stablemate (*horse racing*) a horse from the same **stable** as another

Stade (*rugby union*) short name of the French **club** Stade Français [French *stade*, "stadium"]

stadium (*general*) a **sports ground** or **arena** with rows of seats or stands for spectators [Latin *stadium*, "racecourse," from Greek *stadion*, "running track for foot races," originally a unit of length in ancient Greece equivalent to 606 3/4 ft (184m), the most noted track or course at Olympia being of this length]

Stadium of Light (*association football*) (1) the **stadium** of the English **club** Sunderland, built in 1997 [named from the lamps formerly worn by local miners]; (2) English name of the Estádio da Luz, the stadium of the Portuguese club Benfica, Lisbon, built in 1954 [translated as if "stadium of light" but really named for its location in the suburb of Luz]

stag leap (*ice skating*) a leaping **jump** performed with the leading leg tucked under the body and the trailing leg kicked out straight behind

stage (*general*) one of the timed sections into which a **long-distance race** or **rally** is divided

stage race (*cycling*) a **race** in **stages**, usually as a series of **road races** ridden on successive days

stage rally (*auto racing*) in **rally driving,** a **rally in stages,** usually ridden over several days

staggered start (*athletics*) the **start** to a **race** in which the **athletes** are spaced at intervals along the **track** to compensate for the curve of the **bend**; (*general*) a **race** in which competitors leave the **start** at timed intervals

Stags (*association football*) nickname of the English **club** Mansfield Town [apparently from the animal on the town's former coat of arms, denoting its proximity to Sherwood Forest]

stake (*horse racing*) the money wagered on a **bet**

stake and rider fence (*horse racing*) a **fence** made of stakes with a top bar

stake boat (*rowing, sailing*) a boat anchored to mark the **start** or **course** of a **race**

stakes (*greyhound racing, horse racing*) (1) money staked or contributed as a **prize** in a **race**; (2) the race itself

Stalder (*gymnastics*) in the **horizontal bar** and **asymmetric bars,** a 360-degree **swing** around the bar in a **straddle pike** position [first performed by the Swiss **gymnast** Josef Stalder]

stallion (*horse racing*) a male horse kept for breeding

Stallions (*Canadian football*) short name of the Baltimore Stallions team

stalls (*horse racing*) shortening of **starting stalls**

Stamford Bridge (*association football*) the **home ground** of Chelsea **football club,** London

Stampeders (*Canadian football*) short name of the Calgary Stampeders team

stance (*boxing*) the position adopted by a **boxer** in readiness to land or receive **punches**; (*cricket*) the position adopted by a **batsman** in front of the **wicket** as he holds his **bat** in readiness for a **ball** from the **bowler**; (*golf*) the position of a player's feet when making a **stroke**

stand (*cricket*) another term for a **partnership**; (*general*) a raised structure with sitting or standing accommodation for spectators at a **match** or on a **racecourse**

stand down (*general*) to withdraw from a **game, match,** or **race**

stand still (*cycling*) to stop altogether in a **sprint** as a tactical maneuver to avoid taking the **lead** before the climax of the **race**

stand-up (*boxing*) a fight in which the contestants stand up fairly to each other without any special moves or maneuvers

standard (*horse racing*) a category of **going**

standardbred (*horse racing*) a breed of horse developed as **trotters** and **pacers** in **harness racing** [they are bred to attain a minimum standard speed]

standing (*general*) a current ranking in a grade scale

standing count (*boxing*) a **count** of eight taken by a **boxer** who although not knocked down appears unable to continue fighting

standing shot (*handball*) a **shot** taken from a stationary position

standoff (*rugby league, rugby union*) shortening of **standoff half**; (*rugby union*) another term for a **fly half**

standoff half (*rugby league, rugby union*) a **back** who stands next to the **scrum half** and links play with the **three-quarters**

stands (*general*) another term for a **stand,** especially where extensive or arranged in sections

Stanley Cup (*ice hockey*) the **cup** awarded annually since 1893 to the winner of the world **professional championships** [donated by Frederick Arthur Stanley, Lord Stanley of Preston (1841–1908), governor general of Canada]

stanza (*general*) a **half** or other period of a **game**

Star (*sailing*) a class of double-handed **keelboat**

star drag (*angling*) an adjustable tension device in a **reel** [so called for its star-shaped nut]

star jump (*gymnastics*) a **jump** in which the arms and legs are thrust out to give a star shape

starboard (*sailing*) the right side of a boat when facing **forward**

Stars (*ice hockey*) short name of the Dallas Stars team

start (*general*) (1) the beginning of a sporting contest; (2) the point where a **race** begins

start hut (*skiing*) the small building from which skiers start in a **downhill race** or **slalom**

start straight (*auto racing*) the straight section of track where the **grid** is and where **races** start

starter (*baseball*) shortening of **starting pitcher**; (*general*) (1) the official who gives the signal for the **start** of a **race** or other contest; (2) one of the competitors assembled for the start of a race; (*golf*) a member of the **pro shop** staff who marshals the players starting the first **hole**; (*horse racing*) one of the horses assembled for the **start** of a **race**

starting block (*athletics*) a device for helping a **sprinter** make a quick **start** to a **race,** in the form of a framework with wood or metal blocks attached, on which the sprinter braces his feet; (*cycling*) a device that holds the rear wheel of a bicycle at the **start** of **track race,** releasing the wheel when the **start** is signaled

starting box (*greyhound racing*) the boxlike stall from which a greyhound is released at the beginning of a **race**

starting gate (*horse racing*) the mechanical barrier behind which the horses are held in their stalls before the **start** of a **race** and which opens to release them simultaneously; (*motorcycle racing*) in **motocross,** the board across the starting area that drops down to start the **race**; (*skiing*) the point from which skiers start their **run** in **downhill** racing

starting grid (*auto racing*) fuller term for a **grid**

starting gun (*general*) another term for a **starting pistol**

starting line (*general*) a line marking the **start** of a **race**

starting pistol (*general*) a small pistol used to give the signal for the **start** of a **race**

starting pitcher (*baseball*) the **pitcher** who initiates play in a **game**

starting post (*general*) a post marking the starting point of a **race**

starting price (*horse racing*) the **odds** on a horse at the **start** of a **race**

starting signal (*general*) the signal given to competitors to begin a **race**

starting stalls (*horse racing*) the stalls with **starting gates** in which the horses are held before the **start** of a **race**

startline (*general*) another term for a **starting line**

State of Origin series (*rugby league*) a series of annual **matches** played since 1980 between the Australian states of Queensland and New South Wales

station (*rowing*) the position on one or other side of a river occupied by the crew of an **eight** at the **start** of a **boat race** [the crews in the **Boat Race** start from the Middlesex station and Surrey station, named for their historic counties on the respective north and south banks of the Thames River]

Statue of Liberty (*American football*) a **play** in which the **quarterback** holds the **ball** up as if to throw it while a **back** circles behind to take it from him and then attempt to advance it by **rushing**

stay all day (*horse racing*) to consistently maintain speed and stamina in a **race**

stay on (*horse racing*) of a racehorse, to give of its best toward the end of a **race**

stayer (*horse racing*) a horse that does not tire as quickly as others in a **race**

stayers' line (*cycling*) the blue outermost line on a **track** in a **velodrome** used by **riders** in a **madison** to ease up and ride slowly between efforts

steady (*cricket*) (of) a **batsman** who is reliable and does not take risks

steal (*baseball*) to gain a **base** without the help of a **hit** or **error** by running to it without being **tagged out**; (*basketball*) to take **possession** of the **ball** from an opponent; (*golf*) to play a long **putt** with a delicate **stroke** that sends the ball into the **hole**

steamer (*horse racing*) a horse whose **odds** shorten

rapidly because a large sum of money has been unexpectedly staked on it

steamy (*golf*) a short **shot** or **putt** that passes over or through the **green**

Steelers (*American football*) short name of the Pittsburgh Steelers team

Steelmen (*association football*) nickname of the Scottish **club** Motherwell [from the town's former noted steel industry]

steeplechase (*athletics*) (1) another term for **cross-country running**; (2) a 3,000-meter **track race** with obstacles in the form of **hurdles** and **water jumps**; (*equestrianism*) a phase of the **speed and endurance** section of the **three-day event** in which **riders** clear low **fences** along a turf **track**; (*horse racing*) a **race** with obstacles to be jumped [originally a race on horseback across country with a visible church steeple as the goal]

steeplechaser (*horse racing*) a horse trained for **steeplechases**

steepler (*cricket*) a lofty **hit** by the **batsman**, often providing an easy **catch**

steer-wrestling (*rodeo*) an **event** in which a competitor drops from horseback onto the horns of a galloping steer and throws it to the ground

stem (*darts*) another term for the **shaft**; (*sailing*) the curved timber at the **bow** of a boat

stem turn (*skiing*) a turn performed by **stemming** with one ski and then placing the other parallel with it

stemming (*skiing*) the act of moving the tail of one or both **skis** outward in order to turn

step (*athletics*) the second phase of the **triple jump**; (*fives*) in **Eton fives**, the shallow step that divides the **court** into an inner and outer part

step up (*horse racing*) a "promotion" to a **race** with a greater **distance**

stepover (*association football*) a move in which a player aims to throw an opponent off balance by stepping over the **ball** without actually kicking it

stepover turn (*water skiing*) a maneuver executed on one or two **skis** in which the skier lifts a ski over the **tow rope** while executing a 180-degree turn

stern (*rowing, sailing*) the rear part of a boat

steward (*auto racing*) a senior official who makes decisions about the running of a **race**, including the awarding of **penalties**; (*horse racing*) an official who supervises arrangements on a **racecourse** and sees that the rules of the sport are upheld

Stewards' Challenge Cup (*rowing*) the **cup** awarded to the winner of a **race** for **coxless fours** at **Henley Royal Regatta**, inaugurated in 1841

Stewards' Cup (*horse racing*) a famous annual **sprint** at **Goodwood**

stewards' inquiry (*horse racing*) an investigation by **stewards** into the conduct of a **race** in cases where a contravention of the rules is suspected, the result being signaled by the hoisting of **flags** on the **racecourse**

stick (*athletics*) colloquial term for the **baton** in a **relay race**; (*general*) (1) the implement with which the **ball** is struck in **field hockey**, **ice hockey**, and **rounders**; (2) the implement with which the **ball** is struck in some regional or improvised **games** such as **trapball** and **knur and spell**; (*gymnastics*) to make a perfect landing, without any movement of the feet; (*polo*) another term for a **mallet**; (*skiing*) shortening of **ski stick**; (*surfing*) colloquial term for a **surfboard**

stick up (*cricket*) to put a **batsman** on the defensive

stickball (*sport*) a form of **baseball** or **lacrosse** adapted to playing in a small area, often with a makeshift **stick** and nonstandard **ball**

sticker (*cricket*) a batsman who plays slowly and carefully and who is hard to **dismiss**

stickhandling (*general*) the controlling of a **ball** or **puck** in a **game** played with a **stick**

stickout (*general*) colloquial term for an excellent sports player or performer

sticks (*association football*) colloquial term for the **goalposts**; (*cricket*) colloquial term for the **wicket** (with its three **stumps**); (*field hockey*) a **foul** committed by raising the **stick** above the shoulder when swinging it back to play the **ball**; (*horse racing*) the **hurdles** in a **steeplechase**

stickwork (*general*) another term for **stickhandling**

sticky dog (*cricket*) another term for a **sticky wicket**

sticky wicket (*cricket*) a **wicket** made soft and sticky by rain [a condition less common than formerly thanks to the use of **covers**]

stiff (*general*) a competitor who is sure to fail; (*golf*) another term for **stone dead**; (*horse racing*) a horse that is certain not to win

stiff-arm (*American football, rugby league, rugby union*) to fend off an opponent with the arm straight

stiff track (*horse racing*) a physically demanding **course**, as one with a long **home straight** or an uphill **finish**, as at **Cheltenham**

still-ball game (*general*) a **game** such as **golf** or **snooker** in which the **ball** is always still when being played

stimpmeter (*golf*) a device that measures the speed of a **green** by rolling a **golf ball** down a ramp at a standard initial velocity and measuring how far it travels [named for its U.S. inventor, Edward Stimpson (died 1985)]

stock bowler (*cricket*) a dependable but unenterprising **bowler**

stockcar (*auto racing*) a car with a basically standard chassis that has been specially modified and strengthened for use in **stockcar racing**

stockcar racing (*auto racing*) a **race** between **stockcars** in which the cars are often damaged and even destroyed in collisions

stocker (*auto racing*) colloquial term for a **stockcar** or its driver

stomach roll (*athletics*) a form of **high jump** in which the **athlete** clears the **bar** stomach down

stone (*curling*) the heavy smooth stone with a handle at the top that players send over the ice

stone dead (*golf*) (of) a **ball** that is so near the **hole** that a **putt** seems a mere formality

stonewall (*cricket*) to bat extremely defensively

stonewaller (*cricket*) a **batsman** who **stonewalls**

stoolball (*sport*) a **game** resembling **cricket**, now played mainly by children, in which a hard **ball** is bowled **underarm** at a **wicket** defended by a player with a **bat**

Stoop (*rugby union*) the **home ground** of the **game** at **Twickenham** [in full Stoop Memorial Ground, named commemoratively for Adrian Stoop, an England **back**]

stoopball (*sport*) a **game** resembling **baseball**, in which the **ball** is thrown against a stoop (a set of steps leading to the front door of a house) instead of to a **batter**

stop (*boxing*) (1) a **guard** or attack that prevents a **punch** from landing on its mark; (2) to defeat an opponent with a **knockout**; (*cricket*) shortening of **longstop**; (*horse racing*) to slow down (but not actually stop) in a **race**

stop-go penalty (*auto racing*) a **penalty** imposed for exceeding the speed limit in the **pit lane**, obliging the driver to return to the lane and remain stationary for a stated period of time (10 seconds in **Formula One**) before rejoining the **race**

stop hit (*fencing*) a **thrust** made at the precise moment the opponent prepares for his own thrust

stop shot (*croquet*) a **croquet shot** that sends the croqueted **ball** as far as possible in relation to the **striker's ball**

stop thrust (*fencing*) another term for a **stop hit**

stop volley (*tennis*) a blocked **volley**, played close to the **net**, causing the **ball** to drop dead on the other side

stoppage time (*association football*) time added on to the regulation time (90 minutes) for a **game** to make up for time lost through injury or other interruptions

stopper (*association football*) a **defender** noted for his ability to block attacks on **goal**; (*baseball*) (1) a pitching **ace** relied on to win a **game** or reverse a losing streak; (2) a **relief pitcher** who prevents the opposing team from scoring highly

Stow (*association football*) short name of the English **club** Walthamstow

straddle (*archery, shooting*) a combination of one **shot** beyond the mark and one short of it; (*athletics*) a style of **high jump** in which the **athlete** clears the **bar** horizontally and face down, with his legs straddled either side; (*gymnastics*) a position with the legs spread far apart to the side, as assumed in a **vault** or when dismounting from **apparatus**

straight (*general*) a straight section of a **track** or **course**

straight-arm (*rugby league, rugby union*) (of) a **tackle** with the arms extended straight

straight bat (*cricket*) a **bat** held so as not to deviate to either side

straight bet (*horse racing*) a **bet** that backs a horse to win

straight drive (*cricket*) a **drive** in which the **batsman** hits the **ball** back down the **pitch** toward (or past) the **bowler**

straight games (*tennis*) a series of **games** won in succession

straight pool (*pool*) a variant of **eight-ball pool** in which any **object ball** can be pocketed in any order

straight red (*association football*) a **red card** shown to a player for a serious **offense**, entitling the **referee** to **send off** the offender immediately

straight sets (*tennis*) a run of **sets** won in succession

straight tip (*horse racing*) a tip for a **bet** that comes straight from an **owner** or **trainer**

straightaway (*auto racing, horse racing*) another term for a **straight**

strangle (*horse racing*) to hold back a horse from winning by pulling hard on the reins

stranglehold (*judo, wrestling*) another term for a **choke hold**

Stratford-on-Avon (*horse racing*) a **National Hunt racecourse** at Stratford-on-Avon, Warwickshire, England

strawweight (*boxing*) the professional **weight** category of under 48kg (105lb)

streaker (*general*) a spectator who runs naked across the **pitch** during a **match**

streamer (*angling*) an **artificial fly** with feathers attached, resembling a small fish

street circuit (*auto racing*) a **circuit** laid out with temporary walls for a **street race**

street hockey (*roller skating*) a type of **field hockey** played on **roller skates**, originally in the street

street race (*auto racing*) a **race** with a **circuit** over the streets of a city, rather than on a special **track**, as for the **European Grand Prix** in Valen-

cia, Spain, or the **Singapore Grand Prix** in Singapore

stretch (*baseball*) a pitching stance that is more upright than a **wind-up**, used when a **baserunner** is likely to **steal a base**; (*general*) another term for a **straight** [the words *straight* and *stretch* are related in origin]

stretcher (*rowing*) an adjustable support for the feet of the **rowers**; (*wrestling*) a **bout** with no **rounds**, **timeouts**, or breaks for injury [it ends when one of the contestants leaves the **ring** on a stretcher]

stride (*horse racing*) (1) an act of forward movement by a horse, completed when its feet have returned to their original position; (2) a horse's regular movement in a **race**

strike (*American football*) a forward **pass** straight to a **receiver**; (*angling*) a sudden jerk of the **line** to impale the **hook** in the mouth of a fish; (*association football*) another term for a **shot**; (*baseball*) (1) a **ball** thrown by the **pitcher** into the **strike zone**; (2) a ball at which the **batter** swings and misses; (*cricket*) the position of a **batsman** ready to receive the next **ball** from the **bowler**; (*rugby league, rugby union*) an attempt to **hook** the **ball** from the **scrum**; (*tenpin bowling*) the knocking down of all of the **pins** with the first **ball** bowled

strike out (*baseball*) to dismiss or be dismissed from a **game** by means of three **strikes**

strike zone (*baseball*) the area above **home plate** extending from the knees of the **batter** to the middle of his torso, as a target for the **pitcher** to aim at

striker (*association football*) an attacking player whose main role is to score **goals**; (*cricket*) the **batsman** facing the **bowling**; (*general*) a player who hits the **ball**

striker's ball (*croquet*) the **ball** played at the start of a turn

striking circle (*field hockey*) another term for the **shooting circle**

string (*archery*) the cord of a **bow**; (*billiards*) (1) the beads hung on a wire that serve to keep the **score**; (2) to decide the order of play by striking the **cue ball** from **balk** to rebound off the top **cushion**, the first **stroke** going to the player whose ball comes to rest nearer the bottom cushion; (*horse racing*) (1) the horses belonging to a particular **yard** or **stable**; (2) a single file of horses led out for morning exercise

strip (*cricket*) colloquial term for the **pitch**; (*general*) (1) to take off one's normal clothing in preparation for a contest; (2) the distinctive clothing worn by members of a sports team, typically in the **colors** of their **club**

strip fitter (*horse racing*) to be revealed as a horse

in good physical shape when its blankets are taken off just before a **race**

stripe ball (*pool*) a **ball** with a broad colored stripe and a number on it

stroke (*general*) to hit or kick the **ball** smoothly and carefully; (*golf*) a **hit** of the **ball** that serves as a unit of scoring; (*rowing*) (1) the complete single movement of the **oars** in and out of the water; (2) the **rower** who sits nearest the **stern** of the boat and whose stroke sets the time for the rest of the rowers; (*squash*) a **point** awarded to a player who has been deliberately obstructed; (*swimming*) a particular set of movements of the arms and legs, appropriate for the position of the body, that propel a **swimmer** through the water

stroke index (*golf*) a measure of the relative difficulty of the **holes** on a **course**

stroke oar (*rowing*) fuller term for the **stroke**

strokeless (*cricket*) unable to play **strokes** freely because of the style of **bowling**

strokemaker (*cricket*) a **batsman** who plays well-executed, attacking **strokes**

strokeplay (*cricket, tennis*) the playing of a range of well-executed **strokes**; (*golf*) a method of scoring by counting the number of **strokes** played rather than the number of **holes** won

strokeside (*rowing*) the right side of the boat as viewed by the **rowers**

stroll (*baseball*) another term for a **base on balls**; (*general*) another term for a **walkover**

strong safety (*American football*) a defensive **back** positioned opposite the **strong side** that usually covers the **tight end**

strong side (*American football*) the side of a standard offensive formation on which the **tight end** lines up

stud (*horse racing*) (1) a male horse used for breeding; (2) a horse-breeding establishment

studbook (*horse racing*) a record of horses' **pedigrees**

stuff (*basketball*) to throw or **slam** the **ball** down through the **basket**

stump (*cricket*) (1) one of the three small posts which, together with the **bails**, form the **wicket**; (2) as a **wicketkeeper**, to **dismiss** a batsman who is out of his **ground** by dislodging a **bail** or by knocking down a stump while holding the **ball**

stumped (*cricket*) **dismissed** from a **game** because **stumped** by the **wicketkeeper**

stumps (*cricket*) (1) another term for the **wicket**; (2) the end of a **game**, when it is time to **draw stumps**

stun (*snooker*) to check the forward momentum of the **cue ball** by imparting a small amount of **backspin** to it

stun and be gone (*boxing*) another term for **punch and retreat**

style jumping (*parachuting*) a **jump** in which a series of predetermined maneuvers are carried out while in **free fall**

stymie (*golf*) a situation on the **green** in which an opponent's **ball** blocks the way to the **hole** (an impasse overcome by a rule of 1951 which allowed the obstructed ball to be lifted and its position marked) [origin obscure]

sub (*general*) colloquial shortening of **substitute**

subaqua (*aquatics*) the sport or recreation of underwater **swimming** or **diving** using an **aqualung** or similar apparatus

submission (*wrestling*) the surrender of a competitor to a **hold**

subsidiary goal (*polo*) a **goal** scored by sending the **ball** into a space to the side of each **goalpost**

substitute (*general*) a player who replaces a teammate during a **match**, either as a tactical move or as the result of injury or sickness

subway alumni (*American football*) city-dwelling **supporters** of a **college football** team who are not graduates (alumni) of the college in question

sucker (*golf*) a **ball** embedded in mud which can be lifted without **penalty**

sucker punch (*boxing*) a **punch** that takes advantage of an opponent's momentary lack of concentration

sudden death (*general*) (1) an extra period of play to settle a **tie**, ending when one of the competitors scores; (2) a **game** or **match** shortened from its usual duration by a time limit

Sugar Bowl (*American football*) a **postseason college football** contest held annually (from 1935) at New Orleans, Louisiana, where it was conceived in 1927

sugarbag (*wrestling*) to toss an opponent onto the **canvas** [as if he were a bag of sugar]

suicide squad (*American football*) the team who defend the player who took the **kickoff** [so called as subjecting themselves to a continuing onslaught from their opponents]

suicide squeeze (*baseball*) a tactical maneuver in which a **baserunner** at **third base** begins to run toward **home plate** as soon as the **pitcher** begins to throw the **ball**

sulky (*horse racing*) a light two-wheeled vehicle used in **harness racing**

sumi-gaeshi (*judo*) a move in which one of the contestants falls to the **mat** and throws his opponent over his left shoulder [Japanese *sumi*, "corner," and *kaeshi*, "overturning"]

Summer Eights (*rowing*) another name for **Eights Week**

Summer Olympics (*Olympics*) a name sometimes used for the main **Olympic Games** to distinguish them from the **Winter Olympics**

sumo (*sport*) a Japanese form of **wrestling** in which the aim is to force an opponent out of the **ring** or force him to touch the ground within it with any part of the body other than the soles of the feet [Japanese *sumo*]

sumo wrestling (*sport*) fuller name of **sumo**

sumotori (*sumo*) another term for a **rikishi** [combination of **sumo** and **tori**]

Sunday League (*cricket*) the name of the **Pro40 League** until 2007

Suns (*basketball*) short name of the Phoenix Suns team

super bantamweight (*boxing*) the professional **weight** category of maximum 55kg (122lb)

Super Bowl (*American football*) the annual **championship** of the **National Football League**, played since 1976 between the respective **champions** of the **National Football Conference** and **American Football Conference**

super featherweight (*boxing*) the professional **weight** category of maximum 69kg (130lb)

super flyweight (*boxing*) the professional **weight** category of maximum 52kg (115lb)

Super 14 (*rugby union*) a competition established in 1996 for the 14 (originally 12) leading state and provincial teams in Australia, New Zealand, and South Africa

super G (*skiing*) an **event** combining **downhill** and **giant slalom** [G for giant (slalom)]

super heavyweight (*boxing*) the amateur **weight** category of above 91kg (201lb)

Super League (*rugby league*) an annual competition held since 1996 between the top six teams in the **league**

super lightweight (*boxing*) the professional **weight** category of maximum 63.5kg (140lb)

super middleweight (*boxing*) the professional **weight** category of maximum 76kg (168lb)

super over (*cricket*) an extra **over** added to settle the **score** after a **match** ends in a **tie**

Super Saturday (*general*) nickname for a key contest held on a Saturday, as the men's **semifinals** in the **U.S. Open** on Saturday, September 12, 2009, the day before the **finals**

super special stage (*auto racing*) in **rally driving**, a short **special stage** with two parallel **tracks**

Super Sunday (*general*) nickname for a key contest held on a Sunday, as on Sunday, November 29, 2009, when in **association football** there was a **double header** in two **Premier League derbies**: Arsenal v. Chelsea and Everton v. Liverpool

super welterweight (*boxing*) the professional **weight** category of maximum 70kg (154lb)

superbike (*motorcycle racing*) a 750cc four-cylinder or 1,000cc twin-cylinder motorcycle

supercross (*motorcycle racing*) the racing of motocross bikes in a **stadium** on a temporary dirt or sand **track** with obstacles such as **jumps**

superfecta (*horse racing*) a **bet** in which the bettor must select the first four horses to finish in the correct order [blend of *super-* and **perfecta**]

supermoto (*motorcycle racing*) the racing of **solo** motorcycles or **quad bikes** on a part surfaced, part natural **circuit** with obstacles such as **jumps**

superpipe (*snowboarding*) a large **half-pipe**

Supersonics (*basketball*) short name of the Seattle Supersonics team

superspeedway (*auto racing*) in **NASCAR** and **Indy** racing, a **track** over a mile long

supersub (*association football*) a player who often scores as a **substitute** [shortening of *supersubstitute*]

suplex (*wrestling*) a **hold** in which the opponent is grasped around the waist from behind and thrown [apparently Latin *supplex*, "supplicant"]

supplement (*horse racing*) to pay a **supplementary fee**

supplementary fee (*horse racing*) a (high) fee paid on top of an **entry fee** to enter a horse late in a **race**

supporter (*general*) a person who maintains a loyal interest in the fortunes of a **club** and who regularly attends their **matches**, in many cases wearing their **colors**

surf (*surfing*) shortening of **surf riding**

surf bum (*surfing*) an enthusiast who frequents beaches suitable for the sport

surf canoe (*surfing*) a **canoe** or **kayak** used for the sport

surf riding (*sport*) an older term for **surfing**

surface fishing (*angling*) a method of fishing that involves a **cast** of **bait** (rather than an **artificial fly**) that floats on the surface of the water

surfboard (*surfing*) the long narrow board used in the sport

surfer (*surfing*) (1) a person who participates in the sport; (2) shortening of **windsurfer**

surfie (*surfing*) a young unemployed person who spends a lot of time engaged in the sport

surfing (*sport*) the sport or recreation of riding breaking waves on a **surfboard**

Surlyn (*golf*) proprietary name of a tough thermoplastic resin used to cover **golf balls**

suspension (*general*) the temporary barring of a player from a **game**

sutemi-waza (*judo*) the technique of throwing from a lying position [Japanese *sute-mi*, "self-abandonment," and *waza*, "art," referring to the thrower's sacrifice of an upright posture]

swallow dive (*swimming*) a **dive** made with the arms outstretched to the sides [like the wings of a swallow]

swan dive (*swimming*) another term for a **swallow dive** [with arms like the wings of a swan]

Swans (*association football*) short name of the Welsh **club** Swansea City; (*Australian Rules*) short name of the Sydney Swans team

Swaythling Cup (*table tennis*) the **cup** awarded since 1926 to the winner of the world men's team **championship** [presented by Lady Swaythling, later president of the English Table Tennis Association]

sweat (*horse racing*) a training run given to a horse before a **race**

sweat serve (*table tennis*) an illegal **serve** in which the **ball** has been deliberately coated in sweat by the **server**, making it difficult to return

sweatband (*tennis*) an absorbent wristlet worn to prevent sweat running down to a player's hands

Swedish fall (*gymnastics*) a move in **floor exercises** in which the **gymnast** drops straight to the ground, his hands shooting out for support at the last moment

sweep (*cricket*) a **stroke** in which the **batsman** goes down on one knee to play the **ball** to the **leg side** with a horizontal **bat**; (*general*) victory in all of the **games** in a contest by a team or competitor

sweep rowing (*rowing*) rowing with only one **oar**, worked with both hands

sweeper (*association football*) a player who plays behind the **defenders** but who does not **mark** any opponent [he "sweeps up" any problems if the line of defenders is breached]; (*cricket*) a **fielder** positioned on the **boundary** in front of **square** to stop **balls** hit through the **infield**; (*cycling, motorcycle racing*) the negotiation of a bend or turn with a controlled sideways skid of the rear wheel

sweepstake (*horse racing*) a **race** in which the competitors' **stakes** are taken by the winner or winners

sweet science (*sport*) a byname for **boxing**

sweet spot (*cricket*) the area on the face of the **bat** where the **ball** bowled by the **bowler** should ideally make contact for a good **stroke**; (*golf*) the spot on the **clubface** where the **ball** should ideally make contact for best effect and control; (*tennis*) the point on the face of a **racket** where the **ball** should ideally make contact for a good **return**

swerve (*baseball*) a **ball** that deviates in flight from the **spin** imparted to it by the **pitcher**; (*cricket*) a **ball** that deviates in flight from the **spin** imparted to it by the **bowler**

swim (*angling*) a stretch of river fished by a particular **angler**

swim the stream (*angling*) to send **bait** along the course of a **swim** by means of **float tackle**

swimathon (*swimming*) a long-distance swimming **race**

swimmer (*swimming*) a person who takes part in **swimming** or **diving**

swimming (*sport*) the competitive sport or leisure activity of propelling one's body through the water, which may be entered by a **dive**

swimming pool (*swimming*) an indoor or outdoor pool designed for swimming

swimpool (*swimming*) another term for a **swimming pool**

swing (*boxing*) a **punch** made with a sweep of the arm; (*cricket*) a curving deviation of the **ball** in its path through the air after its **delivery** by the **bowler**; (*golf*) the curving path of a **golf club** as a player makes a **stroke**, first moving up and back from the **ball** then down and through to strike it; (*gymnastics*) a rotation of the body on a piece of **apparatus** such as the **asymmetric bars**, **horizontal bar**, **parallel bars**, **pommel horse**, or **rings**

swing bowler (*cricket*) a **bowler** who imparts a **swing** to the **ball**

swing pass (*American football*) a short **pass** to a **back** running to the outside

swinger (*cricket*) a **ball** from the **bowler** that travels with a **swing**

swingman (*general*) a versatile player, who can play in different positions

swingtime (*trampolining*) a movement performed immediately after another, with no **free bounce** in between

swish (*basketball*) a **shot** that drops the **ball** cleanly into the **basket**; (*cricket*) colloquial term for a careless attacking **stroke**

Swiss ball (*general*) a large inflatable plastic ball used in fitness exercises

switch (*horse racing*) to race a horse under the name of another horse

switch hitter (*baseball, cricket*) a player who can bat equally well right-handed or left-handed

switchfoot (*surfing*) a **surfer** who can ride the **board** with either foot forward

swivel (*angling*) a device that prevents rotary action of the **bait** in the water from twisting or kinking of the **line**

swivel hips (*trampolining*) a **seat drop** followed by a **half twist** into another seat drop

SW19 (*tennis*) a byname of the **courts** at **Wimbledon** [the local London postcode]

swordplay (*sport*) another term for **fencing**

synchro (*swimming*) shortening of **synchronized swimming**

synchronized diving (*swimming*) an **event** in which **divers** perform side by side

synchronized skating (*ice skating*) a **discipline** in which teams of skaters perform **routines** in formation

synchronized swimming (*swimming*) a form of

the sport in which groups of **swimmers** carry out gymnastic and balletic **routines** to music

syndicate (*horse racing*) a group of people who own a **racehorse**

T (*basketball*) abbreviation of **technical foul**; (*squash*) the T-shaped configuration formed by the juncture of the **half-court line** and the **short line**

T-car (*auto racing*) a team's reserve car [originally known as the training car]

T-formation (*American football*) a T-shaped formation of offensive players, with the left **halfback**, **fullback**, and right halfback lined up parallel to the **line of scrimmage** and the **quarterback** in front of them directly behind the **center**

table (*billiards, snooker*) shortening of **billiard table**; (*general*) shortening of **league table**

table tennis (*sport*) a **game** like **tennis** played on a table, with players using a small rubber-coated **bat** to propel a hollow celluloid **ball** over a **net** strung across the table

tabletop (*skiing*) (1) a large **jump** constructed with a flat surface before it and a big drop after it; (2) a **freestyle event** using this jump

tac-au-tac (*fencing*) a combination of a **parry** and a **riposte** [French *tac-au-tac*, "clash for clash"]

tack (*horse racing*) a general term (from *tackle*) for riding harness, **saddles**, **bridles**, and the like; (*sailing*) (1) the course of a boat with respect to the side of the **sail** against which the wind is blowing; (2) one of the **port** or **starboard** sections of a zigzag **course** made when sailing to **windward**

tack room (*horse racing*) a room in or near a **stable** where **tack** is kept

tackle (*American football*) (1) an offensive player positioned outside a **guard** on the **line of scrimmage**; (2) a defensive player positioned on the inside of the line of scrimmage; (3) the act of forcing the player with the **ball** to the ground; (*angling*) shortening of **fishing tackle**; (*association football*) an attempt to win the **ball** from an opponent by using the leg or foot; (*Australian Rules*) an attempt to stop an opponent; (*field hockey*) an attempt to take the **ball** from an opponent by using the **stick**; (*rugby league*) one of six attempts to move the **ball** up the **field** by running, passing, and kicking; (*rugby union*) the stopping of an opponent by using one's arms to bring him down

tackler (*general*) a player who executes a **tackle**

tackling bag (*American football, rugby league, rugby union*) a suspended stuffed bag used for practicing **tackles**

tackling dummy (*American football*) another term for a **tackling bag**

tae kwon do (*sport*) a Korean **martial art** similar to karate but differing from it in its wide range of kicking techniques and the importance it attaches to different methods of breaking objects [Korean *tae*, "kick," *kwon*, "fist," and *do*, "way"]

tag (*angling*) a piece of brightly-colored wire or fabric tied to the tail of an **artificial fly**; (*baseball*) to **put out** a **baserunner** by touching him with the **ball** or with the hand holding the ball

tag team (*wrestling*) a team of **wrestlers** engaged in **tag wrestling**

tag wrestling (*wrestling*) a contest between two teams of two **wrestlers** in which only one wrestler from each team is in the **ring** at any one time and may be replaced by the wrestler outside the ring after touching ("tagging") the latter's hand

tagout (*baseball*) fuller term for a **tag**

t'ai chi (*sport*) a Chinese **martial art** centering on sequences of very slow controlled movements [Chinese *tài*, "greatest," and *jí*, "limit"]

t'ai chi ch'uan (*sport*) fuller form of **t'ai chi** [Chinese *quán*, "fist"]

tai-otoshi (*judo*) another term for a **body drop** [Japanese *tai*, "body," and *otoshi*, "drop"]

tail (*cricket*) the weaker **batsmen** at the end of a team's **batting order**

tail fly (*angling*) the fly at the end of the **leader**

tail shot (*polo*) the hitting of the **ball** behind and under the **pony's** rump

tailback (*American football*) a **running back** who lines up behind a **fullback**

tailer (*angling*) a device with a metal loop for landing large fish such as salmon by the tail

tailgate (*general*) to picnic around the trunk of one's car outside a **stadium** before a **match**

take (*cricket*) (1) to catch the **ball** after it has been struck by the **batsman** (before it touches the ground); (2) to **dismiss** a batsman by catching the ball thus; (3) to dismiss a batsman by bowling a **ball** that hits his **wicket**; (*rugby league, rugby union*) an act of catching the **ball**

take a dive (*boxing*) to feign a **knockout** [by a **dive** to the **canvas**]

take a toss (*equestrianism, horse racing*) to fall from a horse

take a wicket (*cricket*) to **dismiss** a **batsman** with a bowled **ball**

take off (*cricket*) to replace a **bowler** after a **spell**

take strike (*cricket*) to prepare, as a **batsman**, to face the **bowling**

takeaway (*golf*) the initial movement of the **club** at the beginning of a **backswing**

takedown (*wrestling*) a move in which a standing **wrestler** throws his opponent to the ground

takeoff (*croquet*) a **stroke** in a **croquet** in which the **striker's ball** goes further than the croqueted one; (*general*) (1) the moment when a person, animal, or vehicle leaves the ground, water, or other surface in a **jump, dive,** or flight; (2) the point where this happens, as the end of the **inrun** in a **ski jump**

takeoff area (*cricket*) the area by the **wicket** where the **bowler** ends his **run-up** and releases the **ball**

takeout (*bowls*) a **shot** that knocks an opponent's **bowl** away from the **jack;** (*curling*) a **shot** that hits an opponent's **stone** and removes it from play

takeover zone (*athletics*) the section of **track** in which the **baton** must be passed in a **relay race**

Talbot Handicap (*bowls*) an annual competition in **crown green bowls** [first held in 1873 at the Talbot Hotel, Blackpool, Lancashire]

Tall Blacks (*basketball*) nickname of the New Zealand national men's team [referring to the players' height and **strip** color and punning on the name of the **All Blacks**]

Tall Ships Race (*sailing*) an international biennial race for high-masted **square-riggers** and **fore-and-afters** crewed partly by trainees and held over different courses since 1956

tally (*baseball*) a single **run**

tambour (*real tennis*) a projecting part of the **main wall** of the **court** on the **hazard side** [French *tambour,* "drum"]

tandem (*cycling*) a bicycle for two **riders,** one behind the other [punning use of Latin *tandem,* "at length"]

Tangerines (*association football*) nickname of the Scottish **club** Dundee United [from the orange color of the players' **strip**]

tank (*tennis*) to lose or fail to finish a **match** deliberately

tap (*bowls*) a **shot** in which a **bowl** makes light contact with another bowl that is touching the **jack**

tap-in (*association football*) a simple **shot** from a short distance into an undefended **goal;** (*basketball*) an act of striking the **ball** in the air with the hand so that it goes into the **basket,** typically following an unsuccessful **shot**

tap kick (*rugby union*) a light kick of the **ball** to restart play from a **penalty,** the same team retaining **possession** of the ball

tap penalty (*rugby union*) a **penalty** taken with a **tap kick**

tap tackle (*rugby union*) a **tackle** made by diving and touching the ankle of the player with the **ball,** so that he falls over

tap up (*association football*) to approach a player under contract to a **club** with the aim of persuading him to leave that club and move to another

tape (*athletics*) a strip of material stretched across the **track** at the **finishing line** of a **foot race**

tape-measure shot (*baseball*) a **home run** that travels far beyond the field of play

Targa Florio (*auto racing*) the **trophy** awarded to the winner of an annual **time trial** held in Sicily, Italy [Italian *Targa Florio,* "Florio Shield"]

target (*archery, shooting*) a mark to shoot at for practice or competition; (*boxing, fencing*) the part of an opponent's body to which an attack is directed

target archery (*archery*) a form of the sport in which competitors shoot at circular **targets**

target man (*association football*) a tall **forward** in a central position to whom a high **pass** can be made

target pin (*archery*) a mark on a **bow** used as a **sight**

tariff (*gymnastics*) the degree of difficulty of a **vault**

tartan (*angling*) an **artificial fly** used in salmon fishing

Tartan (*athletics*) proprietary name of a synthetic resin material used to lay all-weather running **tracks**

Tartan Army (*association football*) nickname of the **supporters** of Scotland's national team, especially when playing abroad

Tartans (*association football*) nickname of a Protestant youth gang in Northern Ireland, the traditional **supporters** of the Scottish **club** Glasgow Rangers

tatami (*judo*) the rectangular vinyl-coated foam **mat** on which contests take place [Japanese *tatami*]

Tattersalls (*horse racing*) (1) a leading auction house for **thoroughbreds,** based in **Newmarket** [founded in 1766 by Richard Tattersall (1724–1795)]; (2) an **enclosure** at a **racecourse,** with cheaper admission than the **Members' Enclosure**

tattoo (*greyhound racing*) an identification number on the inside of a registered greyhound's ear

Tatts (*horse racing*) colloquial abbreviation of **Tattersalls**

Taunton (*horse racing*) a **National Hunt** racecourse at Taunton, Somerset, England

taxi squad (*American football*) players who train with a team but are not selected for **matches** [originally a nickname for a group of extra players which Arthur McBride, owner of the Cleveland Browns in the 1940s, kept on in the team by employing them in a taxi company which he owned]

tchoukball (*sport*) a **game** in which one team throws the **ball** against a highly sprung **net** and the other team tries to prevent it from landing when it rebounds, physical contact with other players being against the rules [from the sound of the ball hitting the net]

tea (*cricket*) the second meal break of the day during a **match**, regarded as a time point for the number of **runs** scored

team foul (*basketball*) a **personal foul** that counts toward a team's permitted number of **fouls** in a period of play

team game (*general*) a (usually outdoor) **game** played by two teams in opposition

team handball (*sport*) the formal name for **handball**

team orders (*auto racing*) an agreement that applies when teams have more than one driver in a **race**, whereby drivers can allow another member of their team to win if they are leading themselves and their teammate is in second place

team pursuit (*cycling*) a **track race** ridden on the same principle as a **pursuit race**, but by teams of four instead of two individual **riders**

team race (*sailing*) a **race** in which two or more teams of evenly matched boats compete against one another

team roping (*rodeo*) a form of **calf-roping** involving two mounted competitors, one of whom heads off the calf, then throws and ties it after the other has lassoed it

team sport (*general*) another term for a **team game**

team sprint (*cycling*) a **track race** ridden in teams of three over three **laps**, with competing teams starting on opposite sides of the **track**

team tactics (*horse racing*) a prearranged agreement on a maneuver to favor a particular **rider**, as when one rider moves off the **rails** to let another through

team time trial (*cycling*) a **time trial** ridden by a team of **riders**

Team 2012 (*Olympics*) a collective name for all competitors in the 2012 **Olympic Games** and **Paralympic Games**

teamsheet (*cricket*) a final list of the members of a team, exchanged with that of the opposing side before a **match**

teapot (*cricket*) colloquial term for a **fielder** who stands with hands on hips and fails to stop the **ball** [from the pose, suggesting the handle and spout of a teapot]

teaser (*cricket*) a **ball** that is difficult for the **batsman** to play

technical area (*association football*) an area marked by white lines at the side of the **pitch** to which **managers**, **trainers**, and **substitutes** are restricted during play

technical crew (*auto racing*) the team of mechanics and engineers who service and repair cars in the **pit area** during a **race**

technical foul (*basketball*) a **foul** awarded for a non-contact **offense** such as unsporting conduct

technical knockout (*boxing*) a decision by the ref-

eree that one of the combatants, although not losing to a physical **knockout**, is too badly beaten to continue the fight, so that his opponent is the winner

technical points (*wrestling*) **points** scored from moves other than **falls**

technical superiority (*wrestling*) a **lead** of ten **points** by one **wrestler** over the other, resulting in a **win**

Teddy Bears (*association football*) nickname of the Scottish **club** Rangers [rhyming slang for **Gers** in a local pronunciation]

tee (*curling*) the spot aimed at in the center of the **house**; (*golf*) (1) a small support for the **ball**, with a concave top, used when it is first played at each **hole**; (2) the place where this is done; (*rugby union*) shortening of **kicking tee**

tee box (*golf*) a box containing sand for filling **divots** made on the **tee**

tee marker (*golf*) a colored marker on the ground showing the forward limit of the **tee**

tee off (*golf*) to start play with a **shot** from the **tee**

tee-off (*golf*) the strip of ground where **tees** are placed and where play begins at each **hole**

tee shot (*golf*) the first **shot** at a **hole**

tee time (*golf*) the moment when a **golfer** moves to **tee off**

tee up (*golf*) to place a **ball** on a **tee** ready for a **shot**

teeing ground (*golf*) a fuller term for the **tee**

teeline (*curling*) the line that passes through the **tee** across the width of the **sheet**

teesra (*cricket*) a **ball** similar to a **doosra** but with an extra **bounce** from the **topspin** imparted by the **bowler** [Hindi *tisra*, "third"]

telegraph (*general*) a large board displaying **scores**, **results**, or other information at a **cricket match**, **race meeting**, or the like

telemark (*canoeing*) a sudden turn made with the **paddle**; (*skiing*) a sudden turn on the outer of the two **skis** [first practiced by skiers in the Telemark region of southern Norway]

telemark position (*skiing*) the position adopted by a skier on landing in a **ski jump**, with one of the **skis** in front of the other

telemetry (*auto racing*) the system used to relay information on a car's performance back to the **technical crew** in the **pit area**

telltale (*squash*) another term for the **tin**

1080 (*wakeboarding*) a triple **spin** [in which the body turns through 1080 degrees]

ten-foot rule (*ice hockey*) a rule that prohibits a player from standing within 10 feet of the two players engaged in a **face-off**

ten-man rugby (*rugby union*) a style of play in which the eight **forwards** and **scrum half** or **fly half** are dominant

ten strike (*tenpin bowling*) a **throw** that knocks down all ten **pins**

10,000 meters (*athletics*) a **long-distance race** of the stated distance run over 25 **laps**

tenikoit (*tennis*) another name for **deck tennis** [blend of respelled **tennis** and **quoits**]

tennis (*sport*) a **game** for two or four players played with **racket** and **ball** on a **court**, the aim being to gain **points** by hitting the ball over a **net** dividing the court in such a way that the opposing player or players cannot return it [probably from French *tenez!*, "take (it)!," "here you are!," as the call of the **server** to his opponent]

tenpin (*tenpin bowling*) one of the **pins** aimed at in the **game**

tenpin bowling (*sport*) an indoor **game** for individuals and teams similar to **skittles**, in which the aim is to knock down as many **pins** as possible by rolling a heavy **ball** down a **lane** at them

tenpins (*sport*) shortening of **tenpin bowling**

terminal speed (*auto racing*) in **drag racing**, the speed that is recorded as the racer crosses the **finishing line**

terraces (*association football*) the open areas rising in tiers around a **stadium**, where spectators stand

Terriers (*association football*) nickname of the English **club** Huddersfield Town

Terrors (*association football*) nickname of the Scottish **club** Dundee United

test (*cricket*) shortening of **test match**; (*croquet, rugby league*) an international **match**

test match (*cricket*) a five-day **match** played as one of a series between international teams, the first taking place between England and Australia in 1877 [so called as a test of which is the better team]

tester (*cycling*) a **time trial** specialist

testimonial (*general*) shortening of **testimonial match**

testimonial match (*general*) a **match** played to raise money for a player nearing retirement

tetrathlon (*general*) a scaled-down version of the **modern pentathlon** for younger competitors, comprising **swimming**, **riding**, **running**, and **shooting** [Greek *tetra*, "four," and *athlon*, "contest"]

Texans (*American football*) short name of the Houston Texans team

Texas leaguer (*baseball*) a **blooper** that drops between an **infielder** and an **outfielder**, resulting in a **base hit**

Texas scramble (*golf*) an informal version of the **game** in which all of the players hit each **shot** from the same place, the best **ball** fixing the location of the next shot

Texas wedge (*golf*) a **putter** when used to putt from off the **green** [from the **shots** made on the dry, hard **fairways** of some Texas **golf courses**]

Thai boxing (*boxing*) a form of the sport practiced in Thailand, using not only gloved fists but feet, knees, and elbows

Thames Cup (*rowing*) the **cup** awarded since 1868 to the winner of a **race** for **eights** at **Henley Royal Regatta** [from the river on which Henley stands]

thermal (*gliding*) an ascending current of warm air, used by **gliders** to gain height

thermaling (*gliding*) the exploitation of **thermals** to gain altitude

thin (*golf*) to hit the **ball** too near the top so that it travels parallel to the ground but only just above it

third (*curling*) the member of the **rink** who plays third; (*netball*) one of the three equal areas (attacking third, center third, and defending third) into which the **court** is divided

third-ball attack (*table tennis*) a strategy intended to win the **point** on the third **shot** of the **rally,** with the **server** attempting a **loop** or **smash** as the **return**

third base (*baseball*) the third of the **bases** to which a player must run, located on the left-hand side of the **infield** as viewed from **home plate**

third baseman (*baseball*) the **fielder** stationed near **third base**

third half (*rugby union*) colloquial term for the invariable drinking session after a **game** [following the **first half** and **second half**]

third home (*lacrosse*) the attacking player who is the third of the three **homes**

third man (*boxing*) colloquial term for the **referee**; (*cricket*) a **fielder** positioned near the **boundary** on the **off side** behind the **slips**; (*lacrosse*) a defensive player whose role is to mark the **third home** of the opposing team; (*polo*) an official who sits on the sidelines and makes a final decision when the two mounted **umpires** are in disagreement

third slip (*cricket*) the third of the three **fielders** positioned in the **slips**

third umpire (*cricket*) an official who does not appear on the field of play but who adjudicates on disputed decisions by the **umpire** by means of TV **replays** or the record of special cameras such as **Hawk-Eye** [he is third after the umpire behind the **bowler** and the **square leg umpire**]

Thirsk (*horse racing*) a **flat racecourse** at Thirsk, North Yorkshire, England

thirty-all (*tennis*) a level **score** of two **points** each

thirty-fifteen (*tennis*) a **score** of two **points** to one to the **server**

thirty-five (*tennis*) colloquial shortening of **thirty-fifteen**

thirty-forty (*tennis*) a **score** of two **points** to three against the **server**

thirty-love (*tennis*) a **score** of two **points** to nil to the server

Thomas Cup (*badminton*) the **cup** awarded to the winner of an international **championship** for men, first held in 1949 [donated in 1939 by Sir George Thomas (1881–1972), winner of many national and international championship **titles**]

thoroughbred (*horse racing*) a **racehorse** bred from a **dam** and a **sire** of the best blood [all thoroughbreds descend from three Arab **stallions** that were mated with English **mares**]

thrash (*auto racing*) colloquial term for a fast and exciting **race**

Thrashers (*ice hockey*) short name of the Atlanta Thrashers team

thread the needle (*American football*) to pass the **ball** into a small gap between **defenders**

three (*bowls*) the third **bowler** in a **rink**, who assists the **skipper** and measures disputed **shots**

three-ball (*golf*) a **match** between three players, each with their own **ball**

three-cushion (*billiards*) (of) a form of the **game** in which the **cue ball** must contact a **cushion** at least three times, as well as both **object balls**, in order to score

three-day event (*equestrianism*) a contest in **dressage**, **showjumping**, and **cross-country**, held over three days

three-letter man (*general*) a competitor awarded a mark of distinction in three different sports

Three Peaks Challenge (*mountaineering*) the challenge to climb the three mountains Ben Nevis (Scotland), Scafell Pike (England), and Snowdon (Wales) within 24 hours.

Three Peaks Race (*cyclo-cross*) an annual **race** with a **course** over the summits of Pen-y-ghent, Whernside, and Ingleborough, all in Yorkshire, England

three-point goal (*basketball*) a **field goal** worth three **points**, scored from beyond the **three-point line**

three-point line (*basketball*) an arc painted on the **court** at a specified distance from the **basket**, a line beyond which a **field goal** scores three **points** rather than two

three-pointer (*basketball*) shortening of **three-point goal**

three positions (*shooting*) the standing, kneeling, and **prone** positions taken by competitors in a **small-bore rifle** contest

three-quarter (*rugby league, rugby union*) one of the four **backs**, between the **halfbacks** and the **full backs**, who aim to run with the **ball** and prevent their opposites from doing so

three-quarter back (*rugby league, rugby union*) fuller term for a **three-quarter**

three-year-old (*horse racing*) the prime age category for **racehorses**, as the **colts** and **fillies** entered in the **English classics**

threepeat (*general*) the winning of a **trophy** or other award on three consecutive occasions [blend of *three* and *repeat*]

threesome (*golf*) a **match** in which one person, playing his own **ball**, plays against two opponents, who play one ball alternately

Throstles (*association football*) nickname of the English **club** West Bromwich Albion [from local *throstle*, "song thrush," a bird formerly seen and heard in large numbers in the hawthorn bushes that gave the name of The Hawthorns, the team's **home ground**]

through ball (*association football*) a **ball** passed forward between **defenders**

through pass (*association football*) another term for a **through ball**

through the green (*golf*) a term for the whole area of the **golf course** except the **teeing ground**, the **putting green** of the **hole** being played, and all **hazards**

throw (*boxing*) to deliver a **punch**; (*cricket*) to bowl the **ball** illegally by bending and then suddenly straightening the elbow; (*general*) to cast an object such as a **ball, bowl, discus,** or **javelin** through the air or along the ground; (*judo, wrestling*) to cast one's opponent to the ground

throw-down (*cricket*) a **throw** of a **ball** from a short distance to a **batsman** as practice

throw down (*cricket*) to knock down a **wicket** with a **throw-in** and so **run out** the batsman

throw forward (*rugby league, rugby union*) another term for a **forward pass**

throw-in (*association football*) the act of throwing the **ball** back into play from behind the **touchline** when it has been put out by an opposing player; (*cricket*) the act of throwing in the **ball** from the **outfield**, either to the **bowler** or in order to **throw out** the **batsman**; (*polo*) the start or resumption of a **match** in which an **umpire** rolls the **ball** down the center of a line-up of players

throw-off (*handball*) a **throw** of the **ball** from the center line of the **court** at the beginning of a **game** or after a **goal**

throw out (*baseball*) to **put out** the **batter** by throwing the **ball** to a **fielder** to prevent the batter from reaching a **base**; (*cricket*) to **dismiss** a **batsman** who is out of his **ground** by throwing the **ball** at (and hitting) his **wicket**

throwaway (*athletics*) the pushing away of the **pole** by a competitor as he clears the **bar** in the **pole vault**

thrown in (*horse racing*) given a lenient **weight** in a **handicap**

thrust (*fencing*) a sudden attack with the sword, but without the body moves of a **lunge**

thruster (*surfing, windurfing*) a **sailboard** or **surfboard** with one or more additional **fins** and a more streamlined shape than usual, giving increased speed and maneuverability

thumb ring (*archery*) a ring for the thumb to help **draw** the **bow**

Thunder (*rugby league*) short name of the English **club** Gateshead Thunder

Thurles (*horse racing*) a **flat** and **National Hunt racecourse** at Thurles, Co. Tipperary, Ireland

tic-tac (*horse racing*) another spelling of **tick-tack**

tice (*croquet*) a **ball** played as a decoy to tempt one's opponent (in the hope that they will miss it) [shortening of *entice*]

tick-tack (*horse racing*) a system of communication by hand signals used by **bookmakers** on a **racecourse** to exchange information on current **odds** [imitation of semaphore arms]

tick-tack man (*horse racing*) a man who uses **tick-tack** to communicate the current **odds**

ticket tout (*general*) a person who buys up numbers of tickets for a sporting event and sells them at a profit, often in the vicinity of the event itself

tickle (*cricket*) another term for **feather**

tie (*general*) an equal **score** in a **game** or **match**

tie break (*tennis*) a further **game** played when the **score** in a **set** is six games all, a situation in which a player must go on to be two games ahead of his opponent to win the set

tie game (*general*) a **game** that ends in a **tie**

tie-off (*equestrianism*) another term for a **jump-off**

tierce (*fencing*) the third of eight basic **parry** positions, used to protect the upper sword-arm portion of the body [Old French *tierce*, "third"]

tiercé (*horse racing*) (1) the French equivalent of a **tricast** or **trifecta**, as a **bet** in which the first three horses to finish a **race** must be named in the correct order; (2) a **race** at which this method prevails [as **tierce**]

tifosi (*auto racing*) followers of the **Scuderia** [Italian *tifosi*, "fans"]

tiger (*general*) an outstanding **sportsman**; (*mountaineering*) a skillful and confident climber

Tiger Cats (*Canadian football*) short name of the Hamilton Tiger Cats team

tiger country (*golf*) colloquial alternate term for **jungle**

tiger line (*golf*) the most direct line for a **drive** or **approach shot** [so called from its risk]

Tigers (*association football*) nickname of the English **club** Hull City; (*Australian Rules*) short name of the Richmond Tigers team; (*baseball*) short name of the Detroit Tigers team; (*rugby league*) short name of the English **club** Castleford Tigers; (*rugby union*) short name of the English **club** Leicester Tigers

tight (*rugby union*) (of) forward play in **set pieces**, and especially **scrums**; (*squash*) (of) a **shot** played so that the second **bounce** lands so close to a side wall that it is unreturnable

tight end (*American football*) an **eligible receiver** lined up next to a **tackle** at the end of the **line of scrimmage**

tight five (*rugby union*) the **front row** and **second row** of the **scrum**

tight head (*rugby union*) shortening of **tight-head prop**

tight-head prop (*rugby union*) the **prop forward** on the right of the **front row** of the **scrum** [with his head right inside the scrum]

timbers (*cricket*) colloquial term for the **stumps**

Timberwolves (*basketball*) short name of the Minnesota Timberwolves team

time (*general*) the end of a contest or **match**, as of a **round** in boxing

time control (*auto racing*) in **rally driving**, the location where cars must stop to have their time recorded by officials

time fault (*equestrianism*) a **penalty** for exceeding the time limit in a round of **jumps**

time hit (*fencing*) a **hit** made on a **time thrust**

time on (*Australian Rules*) time added on for injuries or for when the **ball** was out of play

time thrust (*fencing*) a former term for a **stop hit**

time trial (*cycling*) an **event** in which competitors set off individually or in small teams and attempt to achieve the fastest time over a set distance (or the furthest distance in a set time)

time-trial bike (*cycling*) a **road bike** specially designed for a **time trial**, usually with closer ratio gears, **aero bars**, and more aerodynamic wheels and frame

time wasting (*association football*) a tactic of prolonging the time taken for **throw-ins, corner kicks, goal kicks**, and the like by a team in a winning position, a ruse punishable by the **referee** in the form of **stoppage time** added at the end of the **match**

timed out (*cricket*) failing to take **guard** at the **wicket** within three minutes of the **fall** of the previous wicket, as a result of which the incoming **batsman** is **out**

Timeform (*horse racing*) proprietary name of a rating in pounds based on the past performance of **racehorses** as recorded by the periodical *Timeform*, with horses in **flat races** given different ratings to those in **steeplechases**

timekeeper (*general*) a person who records the time (as of a **start** or **finish**) or the time taken (as in a **race**) in a sporting contest

timeless test (*cricket*) a former type of **test match**, the last being that of 1938 between South Africa and England, in which there was no restriction on the length of the **game**

timeout (*general*) a brief break in a **game** or **match** in order to rest, discuss tactics, substitute a player, or the like

tin (*cricket*) a metal rectangle with a number painted on it, set on a **scoreboard** to show the **score** during a **match**; (*squash*) a strip of tin along the lower boundary of the playable area of the front wall of the **court**, serving to rule out of play any **ball** heard to strike it

tip (*angling*) the topmost joint of a **fishing rod**; (*archery*) the pointed end of an **arrow**; (*basketball*) to send the **ball** into the **net** with a light touch; (*cricket*) to hit the **ball** lightly with the edge of the **bat**; (*horse racing*) a horse selected as a likely winner of a **race**; (*ice hockey*) to send the **puck** into the **net** with a light touch; (*snooker*) the small circular area made of leather at the narrow end of the **cue**, as the part that strikes the **cue ball**

tip-and-run (*sport*) an informal type of **cricket** in which the **batsman** must run if he hits the **ball**

tip-in (*basketball*) a **score** made by **tipping** the **ball** into the **basket**

tip-off (*basketball*) the opening **jump ball** in a **game**

tipster (*horse racing*) a person who offers tips to **punters**, often making a living by doing so

Titans (*American football*) short name of the Tennessee Titans team

title (*general*) another term for a **championship**

title fight (*boxing*) a **match** held to decide a **championship**

Tkatchev (*gymnastics*) a form of **release** on the **horizontal bar** or **asymmetric bars** in which the **gymnast** swings up in an arched position as in a **back giant**, sails over the bar with his back to it, then sits up and catches the bar again [introduced in 1977 by the Soviet gymnast Aleksandr Vasilyevich Tkachyov (1957–)]

TKO (*boxing*) abbreviation of **technical knockout**

toe (*field hockey*) the tip of the curved end of a **hockey stick**; (*golf*) the part of the **clubhead** furthest from the player

toe jump (*ice skating*) a **jump** in which the skater pushes off with his free foot

toe loop (*ice skating*) a **jump** in which the skater takes off and lands on the same back **outside edge**

toe pick (*ice skating*) the serrated teeth at the front of the **blade** of a **skate**, used in certain **jumps** and **spins**

toe poke (*association football*) a powerful **shot** struck with the end of the foot

toe rake (*ice skating*) another term for a **toe pick**

toe spin (*ice skating*) a **spin** made on the toe or toes of the **skates**

toe-tap (*Gaelic football*) another term for **solo**

toe the line (*athletics*) to line up before a **race** with one's toes touching the **starting line**

toeboard (*athletics*) the board marking the limit of the thrower's run in the **shot put**

toeclips (*cycling*) devices on the pedals that hold the foot firm, now generally superseded by **clipless pedals**

toehold (*mountaineering*) a small **foothold** used in climbing; (*wrestling*) a **hold** in which the **wrestler** grasps his opponent's toes and twists his foot or bends it back

Toffeemen (*association football*) nickname of the English **club** Everton [from the local manufacture of toffee]

Toffees (*association football*) colloquial shortening of **Toffeemen**

tombstoning (*swimming*) a hazardous form of **diving** in which the participant jumps into the sea from a height [his descent is vertical and upright, like a tombstone]

ton (*cricket*) colloquial term for a **century** [originally a measure of 100 cubic feet]

Ton (*association football*) short name of the Scottish **club** Greenock Morton

tonguestrap (*horse racing*) a band that prevents the horse's tongue from going over the **bit**, making it easier for the **rider** to control him

tonk (*cricket*) a powerful **stroke** with the **bat**

tonker (*cricket*) a **batsman** with a hard-hitting style [of **tonks**]

tools of ignorance (*baseball*) colloquial term for the protective equipment worn by the **catcher**

Toon Army (*association football*) nickname for the **supporters** of the English **club** Newcastle United [from local dialect *toon*, "town"]

top (*baseball*) the first part of an **inning**, during which the visiting team bats; (*golf*) to hit the **ball** (usually inadvertently) on its upper part, so that it travels only a short distance along the ground

top and tail (*rugby league, rugby union*) an illegal **tackle** in which one player grasps an opponent by the knees and another by the chest, so wrenching him to the ground

top edge (*cricket*) (1) the upper edge of a **bat** as held by the **batsman**; (2) a (usually inadvertent) **stroke** off this part

top order (*cricket*) the **batsmen** who come first in the **batting order**

top out (*mountaineering*) to reach the top of the route

top pocket (*billiards, snooker*) one of the two **pockets** at the far end of the **billiard table**

top-score (*cricket*) to score the greatest number of **runs** in an **innings**

top shelf (*ice hockey*) the roof of the **net**, into which the **puck** is sometimes hit

top weight (*horse racing*) the heaviest **weight** carried by a horse in a **handicap**

topo (*mountaineering*) a diagram showing the route of a rock climb [short for *topographical map*]

toprope (*mountaineering*) a rope fixed at the top of a route

topspin (*general*) a forward-spinning motion imparted to a **ball** as it is struck or thrown, making it travel higher, further, or faster

topspinner (*cricket*) (1) a **bowler** who imparts a **topspin** to the **ball**; (2) a ball given such a spin

tori (*judo*) the active partner in carrying out a **hold** or **throw** [Japanese *tori*, "taking"]

Tornado (*sailing*) a class of double-handed **multihull**

Torpids (*rowing*) an annual **bumping race** between college **eights** at Oxford University [originally held for second eights, regarded as unenthusiastic or lethargic]

toss (*general*) the tossing of a coin before a **match** to give one of the sides the choice of play, such as whether to bat or field in **cricket** or which **end** to take in **association football**

toss the oars (*rowing*) to raise the **oars** vertically in a victory salute

tossing the caber (*sport*) in **Highland games**, an event in which the contestant holds a **caber** upright in both hands against one side of his neck, moves slowly forward while balancing it, then brings his hands up to up-end it, so that it describes a loop in the air before falling

total football (*association football*) a style of the **game** in which all of the players, including **defenders**, can be involved in attack

totalizator (*horse racing*) (1) a ticketed betting system in which the total amount staked is divided among the winners in proportion to the size of their stake; (2) a machine that shows the number and amount of **bets** placed on each horse under this system

tote (*horse racing*) abbreviation of **totalizator**

Tote (*horse racing*) proprietary name of the Horserace Totalisator Board, established in 1963 to operate **totalizators** on British **racecourses** (and subsequently offering **bets** on any sporting event)

touch (*association football, rugby league, rugby union*) the area outside the field of play; (*general*) shortening of **touch football** or **touch rugby**

touch-finder (*rugby union*) (1) a player who kicks the **ball** into **touch**; (2) the kick itself

touch football (*American football*) a form of the **game** in which touching takes the place of tackling

touch in (*swimming*) to touch the end of the **swimming pool** on winning a **race**, as the equivalent of **breasting the tape** in a **foot race**

touch-in-goal (*rugby league, rugby union*) the areas at each end of the **pitch** behind the **try lines** and outside the **touchlines**

touch judge (*rugby league, rugby union*) an official who marks with a **flag** when and where the **ball** goes into **touch**, corresponding to the **assistant referee** (formerly **linesman**) in **association football**

touch kick (*rugby union*) a kick of the **ball** into **touch**

touch rugby (*rugby union*) a form of the **game** in which touching takes the place of tackling

touch rugger (*rugby union*) another name for **touch rugby**

touch shot (*tennis*) a gentle **stroke** of the **ball** with the **racket**

touchback (*American football*) a **play** in which the **ball** is made dead by a player on or behind his own **goal line** after it has been sent over the line by the opposing team

touchball (*rugby union*) another name for **touch rugby**

touchdown (*American football*) **possession** of the **ball** by a player behind the **goal line** of the opposing team; (*rugby league, rugby union*) the touching of the **ball** to the ground by a player behind the **try line**

touché! (*fencing*) an acknowledgment of a **hit** [French *touché!*, "touched!"]

toucher (*bowls*) a **bowl** that touches the **jack** before coming to rest when first bowled on the **green**

touching ball (*snooker*) a situation in which the **cue ball** is touching another **ball** and must be played away from it without moving it

touchline (*association football*) the line around the **pitch** within which play takes place; (*rugby union*) the line marking the edge of the **pitch**, from which **lineouts** are taken

touchline ban (*association football*) a ban on a seat in the **dugout** imposed for a stated period on a player or official as a **penalty** for improper conduct or other **offense**

tour (*auto racing*) (1) a **circuit** or **lap** of the **track**; (2) to travel very slowly; (*general*) a visit abroad by a sports team to play a series of **matches**

Tour de France (*cycling*) an annual **stage race** over the roads of France and adjoining countries to finish in Paris, first held in 1903 [French *Tour de France*, "Tour of France"]

Tour de l'Avenir (*cycling*) an annual **stage race** similar to the **Tour de France** for riders under the age of 23, first held in 1963 [French *Tour de l'Avenir*, "Tour of the Future"]

Tour of Britain (*cycling*) an annual **stage race** over the roads of England and Wales (but rarely Scotland) on the pattern of the **Tour de France**, first held in 1952

Tour of Spain (*cycling*) a frequently used English name for the **Vuelta a España**

touring car (*auto racing*) a large automobile with room for passengers, entered in **races** on the same **circuits** as purpose-built **racecars** [properly a car designed for touring]

tourist (*general*) a member of a sports team making a **tour**

Tourist Trophy (*motorcycle racing*) the **trophy** awarded to the winner of an annual **race** held on the roads of the Isle of Man since 1907 but discontinued as a world **championship** in 1976 because of the high incidence of injuries [originally open to motorcycles known as "touring machines"]

tournament (*general*) a series of **games** to determine a winner (or winning team) by process of elimination

Tournament of the Roses (*American football*) alternate name for the **Rose Bowl**

tourney (*general*) alternate form of **tournament**

tout (*general*) shortening of **ticket tout**; (*horse racing*) a person who lurks around **stables** to report on the movements and condition of **racehorses**

tow (*athletics*) to spur on competitors by setting a fast pace on the **track**

Towcester (*horse racing*) a **National Hunt racecourse** at Towcester, Northamptonshire, England

Town (*association football*) short name of the English **clubs** Ipswich Town and Shrewsbury Town

towplane (*gliding*) an aircraft that tows **gliders**

toxophily (*sport*) a formal term for **archery**

trace (*angling*) a short piece of wire or nylon that connects the **hook** to the **fishing line**

track (*cricket*) another term for the **pitch** between the **wickets**; (*general*) the prepared **course**, often oval-shaped, on which **races** are held between people (as in **athletics**), animals (as in **greyhound racing**), or machines (as in **auto racing**); (*horse racing*) shortening of **racetrack**

track and field (*athletics*) a collective term for **track events** and **field events**

track athlete (*athletics*) an **athlete** specializing in **track events**

track bike (*cycling*) a bicycle with a fixed rear wheel and no brakes, designed for **track races**

track event (*athletics*) any form of **foot race**, as the **middle-distance race**, **long-distance race**, **sprint**, **hurdles**, **relay**, and **steeplechase** [all run on a **track**, unlike **field events**]

track race (*cycling*) a **race** that takes place in a **velodrome**

track record (*general*) a record of past performance, especially of an **athlete**

track shoes (*athletics*) lightweight spiked running shoes worn by participants in **track events**

trackman (*athletics*) another term for a **track athlete**

trackwork (*athletics*) practice or performance on a **track**

Tractor Boys (*association football*) nickname of the English **club** Ipswich Town [from the local agricultural industry]

traffic (*auto racing*) cars that are further back in the **field** and going more slowly than the **leaders**; (*general*) the bunching together of players in a team of runners or **riders** in a **race**

traffic problems (*general*) problems experienced by participants in a **race** when caught up in **traffic**

trail (*general*) to be losing in a **game** or contest

trail the jack (*bowls*) to send down a **bowl** that strikes the **jack** flush and moves it along in the same direction as that of the bowl itself [which thus trails the jack or follows behind it]

Trailblazers (*basketball*) short name of the Portland Trailblazers team

trailing (*bowls*) a form of the **game** in which the object is to send down a **bowl** that will **trail the jack** into a semicircle marked beyond two bowls three feet apart

trails (*cycling*) a variant of **dirt jumping** in **BMX** in which **riders** ride over a series of dirt jumps

train (*general*) (1) to instruct and rehearse a person or team (or animal) in a sport; (2) to prepare oneself by practice and discipline for participation in a sport

train down (*general*) to reduce one's weight by diet and exercise in order to be fit for a particular sport or sporting event

trainer (*general*) a person whose profession is to **train** others in a sport; (*horse racing*) a person who schools **racehorses** and prepares them for **races**

training camp (*general*) a training center or **venue** for sports participants

Tralee (*horse racing*) a **flat** and **National Hunt racecourse** at Tralee, Co. Kerry, Ireland

tramlines (*tennis*) a pair of parallel lines either side of the **court**, the inner line in each case marking the boundary of the court for **singles** and the outer marking the boundary for **doubles** [the lines suggest those along which trams (streetcars) run]

Tramore (*horse racing*) a **flat** and **National Hunt racecourse** at Tramore, Co. Waterford, Ireland

trampet (*gymnastics*) a small **trampoline** used in place of a **springboard** in **vaulting**

trampoline (*trampolining*) an **apparatus** in the form of a strong fabric sheet connected by springs to a horizontal frame, on which various bouncing **routines** can be performed

trampolining (*sport*) the performance in competition or for recreation of **routines** on a **trampoline**

transfer (*association football*) the move of a **professional** player from one **club** to another, usually for a **transfer fee**

transfer fee (*association football*) the sum of money paid by one **club** to another in exchange for the acquisition of a **professional** player

transfer list (*association football*) a list of players available for **transfer** to another **club**

transfer window (*association football*) the time limit within which a **transfer** must be made

transition (*basketball*) the period of play immediately following a change of **possession**

transition phase (*Olympics*) the phase in the **triathlon** between the **disciplines** of **swimming** and **cycling** or cycling and **running**, during which competitors exchange one form of dress for another

transverse lines (*netball*) the lines dividing the **court** into **thirds**

trap (*American football*) a tactic in which an attacking team allows a **defender** to cross the **line of scrimmage** and blocks him from the side, enabling the player in **possession** of the **ball** to pass unopposed through the gap created; (*association football*) to control the **ball** with the feet and stop it dead; (*basketball*) to guard the player in **possession** of the **ball** with two **defenders** so that he has little or no opportunity to make a **pass**; (*golf*) shortening of **sand trap** (as an alternate term for a **bunker**); (*greyhound racing*) another name for the **starting box**; (*shooting*) a mechanical device that releases the **clay pigeons** at a particular speed and trajectory; (*trapball*) a shoe-shaped wooden device with a pivoted bar used to send the **ball** into the air

trap play (*American football*) fuller term for a **trap**

trapball (*sport*) a **game** in which a **ball** placed on one end of a **trap** is sent up into the air and struck with a **stick**

trapshooting (*shooting*) the sport of shooting at **clay pigeons** catapulted into the air by a **trap**

trash sports (*general*) competitive sports featuring celebrities and shown on television as popular entertainment

travel (*horse racing*) to run (in a specified manner) along a **racetrack**

traveling (*basketball*) the **offense** of carrying the **ball** for too many steps without **dribbling**; (*netball*) the **offense** of carrying the **ball**

traverse (*mountaineering*) a sideways progression across a rock face or slope from one conventional line of ascent (or descent) to another; (*skiing*) (1) a zigzag course down a slope; (2) one of the diagonal **runs** made in such a descent

treadmill (*general*) a machine in a **gymnasium** used for exercising, having a continuously moving surface of adjustable speed on which the user can run or walk

treble (*association football*) the winning of three **trophies** in a single **season**; (*darts*) a **score** of three times the normal amount, gained by hitting the inner **bed** of the **dartboard**; (*horse racing*) (1) a **bet** on three **races**, in which the winnings and stake from the first race are transferred to the second, and those from the second, if successful, to the third; (2) a total of three races won by the same horse; (3) a total of three races won by the same **jockey** in a **meeting**

treble chance (*association football*) a form of betting in **football pools**, in which three **points** are awarded for a **score draw**, two points for a **no-score draw**, and one point for a **home win** or **away win**

treble hook (*angling*) a **hook** with three points

trebles for show, doubles for dough (*darts*) big scorers do not always win **matches**, as although **trebles** give a high **score**, it is the **doubles** that often bring in the money (dough)

trench (*shooting*) a concrete structure in front of a **firing line** from which **clay pigeons** are thrown up by **traps**

trenches (*American football*) the offensive and defensive lines, as a scene of strenuous effort

Trent Bridge (*cricket*) the **home ground** of Nottinghamshire **county cricket club**, Nottingham

trey (*basketball*) a three-**point field goal**

tri (*sailing*) colloquial abbreviation of **trimaran**

Tri-Nations Championship (*rugby union*) an annual **championship** contested by the national teams of Australia, New Zealand, and South Africa since 1996

Tri-Nations Series (*rugby league*) former name of the **Four Nations Championship**

trial (*general*) a **match** or competition to select members of a major team

trial of strength (*general*) a contest such as **wrestling** in which two or more opponents strive to determine who has the greater strength

trialist (*general*) a competitor or player under consideration for a place in a major team

trials (*motorcycle racing*) an **event** held over a cross-country **circuit** with a series of sections in which competitors have to negotiate obstacles

triangle (*angling*) a set of three **hooks** fastened together so that the **barbs** form a triangle; (*snooker*) a triangular wooden frame in which the **red balls** are positioned before the start of a **game**

triathlete (*Olympics*) a competitor in a **triathlon**

triathlon (*Olympics*) a **race** in which **athletes** compete in **swimming**, **cycling**, and **long-distance**

running [Greek *tri-*, "three," and *athlon*, "contest"]

tricast (*horse racing*) a **bet** on the first three horses in a **race** in the correct order [blend of *tri-*, "three," and *forecast*]

trick skiing (*water skiing*) the execution of different maneuvers, such as **somersaults**

trickle (*golf*) to strike a **ball** so that it travels slowly over the ground

Tricolores (*rugby union*) nickname of the French national team [French *tricolores*, "tricolors," the blue, white, and red colors of the team's **strip**, those of the national flag]

trifecta (*horse racing*) a **bet** on the first three horses to finish in a **race** in the correct order [blend of *tri-*, "three," and **perfecta**]

triffis (*trampolining*) a triple **somersault** with a **twist**

trimaran (*sailing*) a boat with three **hulls** [blend of *tri-*, "three," and **catamaran**]

trimmer (*angling*) a **float** with a **reel** attached to a **line** with a baited **hook**, used in fishing for pike

trip (*horse racing*) the **distance** of a **race**

triple (*baseball*) a **hit** that allows the **batter** to reach **third base**; (*horse racing*) another term for a **trifecta**; (*trampolining*) a triple **somersault**

triple bogey (*golf*) a **score** of three **strokes** over **par** for a **hole**, three times that of a **bogey**

triple century (*cricket*) a **score** of 300 **runs** by a **batsman**, the equivalent of three **centuries**

triple crown (*auto racing*) the (unofficial) feat of winning the **Indianapolis 500, Le Mans 24-Hour race**, and **Monaco Grand Prix**; (*baseball*) the feat of leading the **league** in **home runs**, **batting average**, and **runs batted in** in a single season; (*cycling*) a collective name for the **Giro d'Italia, Tour de France**, and **World Road Race Championship**; (*horse racing*) (1) a collective name for the **Two Thousand Guineas, Derby**, and **St. Leger** or (in modern times) **Prix de l'Arc de Triomphe**; (2) a collective name for the **Kentucky Derby, Preakness Stakes**, and **Belmont Stakes**; (3) a collective name for the **Hambletonian, Yonkers Futurity**, and **Kentucky Futurity**; (4) a collective name for the **William H. Cane Futurity, Messenger Stake**, and **Little Brown Jug**; (*rugby union*) the victory by England, Scotland, Wales, or Ireland in all three **matches** against the other British Isles teams in the **Six Nations championship**

triple double (*basketball*) the feat of recording double figures in **points, rebounds**, and **assists** in a single **game**

triple event (*horse racing*) another name for the **triple crown**, as three of the five **English Classics**

triple header (*general*) an **event** at which three consecutive **matches** are held

triple jump (*athletics*) an **event** in which an **athlete** sprints down a **runway** then performs a **hop, step**, and **jump** into a **pit**; (*ice skating*) a **jump** incorporating three aerial turns

triple play (*baseball*) a defensive **play** that **puts out** three **runners** in a row

triples (*bowls*) a **game** in which three play against three, each playing three **bowls**

troll (*angling*) to fish by drawing a revolving or otherwise moving **bait** through the water

trophy (*general*) a **cup** or other decorative object awarded to the winner of a sporting contest

trot (*angling*) shortening of **trotline**; (*equestrianism*) a slowish **gait** in which the horse's legs move in diagonal pairs; (*horse racing*) colloquial term for a **trotting race**

trotline (*angling*) a long **line** across a stream or river to which shorter lines with baited **hooks** are attached

trotter (*horse racing*) a horse bred or trained for **trotting** in a **harness race**

Trotters (*association football*) nickname of the English **club** Bolton Wanderers [so named from the team's early **home ground** next to a piggery]

trotting (*horse racing*) the action of moving or racing at a **trot**

trotting race (*horse racing*) a **harness race** in which **trotters** compete

trout rod (*angling*) a **fishing rod** for trout

trout spoon (*angling*) a small revolving spoon used as a **lure** for trout

truck (*skateboarding*) the steerable axle on a **skateboard**

truck and trailer (*rugby union*) an illegal move in which the player carrying the **ball** (the "trailer") moves forward in **loose** play behind a teammate (the "truck") who shields him

trudgen (*swimming*) a **stroke** similar to the **crawl** in which each hand in turn is raised above the surface, thrust forward, and pulled back through the water [first demonstrated in 1873 by the English swimmer John Trudgen (1852–1902)]

trudgeon (*swimming*) an alternate (but incorrect) spelling of **trudgen**

try (*American football*) an attempt to score an extra **point** after a **touchdown**; (*rugby league, rugby union*) the act of placing the **ball** down in the **in-goal** area, scoring **points** and entitling the scoring side to a kick at **goal**

try a fall (*wrestling*) to take a **bout**

try line (*rugby league, rugby union*) the line on which the **goalposts** stand and over which a **touchdown** is made

Tsukahara (*gymnastics*) a **vault** consisting of a quarter-turn or half-turn onto the **horse** followed by one and half **somersaults** off it [introduced by the Japanese **gymnast** Mitsuo Tsukahara (1947–)]

tsurikomi (*judo*) the technique of lifting and pulling one's opponent off balance during a **throw** [Japanese *tsuri*, "lifting," and *komi*, "pushing in"]

TT (*motorcycle racing*) abbreviation of **Tourist Trophy**

tube (*surfing*) another term for a **barrel**

tubing (*sport*) the activity of floating down a stream or sliding downhill on snow on the inflated inner tube of an automobile tire

tuck (*gymnastics*) a position in which the **gymnast** folds his body at the waist with his knees and hips bent and pulled up into his chest; (*skiing*) a squatting position adopted by some **downhill** skiers, with the **poles** tucked under their arms; (*swimming*) a position in **diving** in which the **diver** pulls his thighs up to his chest, bends his knees, and clasps his hands around his shins

tuck position (*gymnastics, skiing, swimming*) fuller term for a **tuck**

tucked up (*cricket*) forced as a **batsman** to **play back** and so make a cramped **stroke**

tug (*gliding*) the aircraft that tows the **glider** into the air

tug of war (*sport*) a contest, formerly included in the **Olympics**, in which opposing teams tug at either end of a rope and endeavor to pull one another over a central line

tumble run (*gymnastics*) a **run** incorporating a **roll** in **floor exercises**

tumble turn (*swimming*) an underwater **roll** at the end of a **length** in which the swimmer pushes off from the end of the **pool** with his feet

tunnel (*general*) a covered way by which players enter or leave the field of play in a sport such as **association football**

turbo tennis (*tennis*) a **sudden death match** with a 30-minute time limit imposed [from *turbo-* in its implied sense of "boosted"]

turf (*horse racing*) (1) the grass surface of a **racecourse**, as distinct from an **all-weather** one; (2) a synonym for the sport itself and its world [in this sense often spelled with a capital letter, as "the Turf"]

turf accountant (*horse racing*) another term for a **bookmaker**

turf season (*horse racing*) the traditional **flat-racing season**, from March to November

turfite (*horse racing*) colloquial term for a person devoted to the sport

turfman (*horse racing*) alternate term for a **turfite**

TurfTrax (*horse racing*) proprietary name of a solar-powered weather system used at **racecourses** to give readings for atmospheric conditions and ground and soil temperatures

turkey (*tenpin bowling*) colloquial term for three successive **strikes**

turkey brown (*angling*) the **mayfly** *Paraleptophlebia submarginata* as an **artificial fly**

Turkish grand prix (*auto racing*) the **Formula One** international **Grand Prix** held on the **circuit** at Istanbul, Turkey

turn (*cricket*) the deviation of a **ball** on a **turner**; (*golf*) the halfway point on a **golf course**, at which the players turn to begin the return nine **holes**

turn of foot (*horse racing*) a horse's speed

turn one's arm over (*cricket*) to bowl, especially when not a regular **bowler**

turnaround (*general*) the point in a **team game** at which the two teams change **ends**

turnaround jump shot (*basketball*) a **jump shot** in which the player turns his back to the **basket** and twists in midair

Turnberry (*golf*) a **golf course** at the village of the same name on the east coast of Scotland

turner (*cricket*) a **pitch** on which the **ball** spins a long way after landing

turnover (*general*) the loss of **possession** of the **ball** to the opposing team, due to error or breach of a rule

turntable (*trampolining*) a **front** drop with a lateral rotation of 360 degrees as a side **somersault** performed in the horizontal plane

turnverein (*gymnastics*) a **club** on the lines of those founded for German immigrants to the United States by Friedrich Ludwig Jahn (1778–1852) [German *turnen*, "to do gymnastic exercises," and *Verein*, "club"]

TV umpire (*cricket*) an official who has access to TV **replays** and who may be consulted by a **fielder** in cases of a questionable decision by the **umpire** in response to an **appeal**

tweaker (*cricket*) colloquial term for a **spin bowler**

Tweddle (*gymnastics*) a **release** on the **horizontal bar** or **asymmetric bars** in the form of a **Tkatchev** with a late **half twist** [pioneered by the British **gymnast** Beth Tweddle (1985–)]

twelfth man (*association football*) colloquial term for the **supporters** of a team or **club** (*cricket*) a player selected beyond the regular **eleven** as a **reserve**

twelve men (*association football*) colloquial phrase implying that a regular team of **eleven** had been unfairly advantaged in a **match** by an erroneous decision of the **referee**

twenty-five (*field hockey, rugby league, rugby union*) shortening of **twenty-five-yard line**

twenty-five-yard line (*field hockey*) former name

of the **twenty-three-meter line**; (*rugby league*) a line formerly marked 25 yards from the **try line**, replaced by the **twenty-meter line**; (*rugby union*) a line formerly marked 25 yards from the **try line**, replaced by the **twenty-two-meter line**

24 Hours of Le Mans (*auto racing*) another name for the **Le Mans 24-Hour race** [translation of French name *les vingt-quatre heures du Mans*]

twenty-meter line (*rugby league*) a line marked 20 meters from the **try line**

twenty-three-meter line (*field hockey*) a line marked 23 meters from the **backline**

twenty20 (*cricket*) a fast-paced form of the **game** introduced in 2002 in which each side can bat for a maximum of 20 **overs**

Twenty20 Cup (*cricket*) the **cup** awarded to the winner of the annual competition in the **twenty20** form of the **game** between **first-class** counties, first held in 2003 and superseding the **Benson & Hedges Cup**

Twenty20 World Championship (*cricket*) an annual international **championship** in the **twenty20** form of the **game**, first held in 2007

twenty-two (*rugby union*) shortening of **twenty-two-meter line**

twenty-two-meter line (*rugby union*) a line marked 22 meters from the **try line**, showing the limit of the area within which **marks** can be made and from which kicks direct to **touch** can gain ground

twi-night (*baseball*) a set of two **games** played on the same day, the first by daylight in the afternoon, the second by artificial light in the evening [blend of *twilight* and *night*]

Twickenham (*rugby union*) the **home ground** of the England national team, in the London district of this name

Twickers (*rugby union*) colloquial name of **Twickenham**

twiddler (*table tennis*) colloquial term for a player using a **combination bat**, who turns it between **shots** to confuse his opponent

twin double (*horse racing*) a **bet** on the winners of four successive **races**

twin killing (*baseball*) colloquial term for a **double play**

twinbill (*baseball*) another term for a **double header**

Twins (*baseball*) short name of the Minnesota Twins team

twirler (*cricket*) colloquial term for a **spin bowler**

twist (*cricket*) a lateral **spin** imparted to the **ball** by a **bowler** or the **batsman**; (*gymnastics*) a rotation of the body around the spine in the longitudinal axis; (*swimming*) a lateral rotation of the body by a **diver**, often in addition to a **somersault**; (*table tennis*) a lateral **spin** imparted to

the **ball** by the **bat**; (*tennis*) a lateral **spin** imparted to the ball by the **racket**

twizzle (*ice skating*) a rapid rotation of the body

two (*bowls*) the second **bowler** in a **rink**, who usually updates the **scorecard**; (*cricket*) (1) a **hit** for two **runs**; (2) a **guard** of **middle and leg** [shortening of *two leg*]

two and six (*darts*) a **score** of 26, gained by hitting 20, 5, and 1 when aiming for a **treble** 20

two-bagger (*baseball*) another term for a **double**

two-eyed stance (*cricket*) the **stance** of a **batsman** in which he turns his head to face the oncoming **ball** as far as possible, keeping his left shoulder on the line of the ball

two-fisted (*tennis*) holding the **racket** with both hands

two-footed (*association football*) able to kick the **ball** equally well with either foot

200 meters (*athletics*) a **sprint** of the stated distance

two-minute suspension (*handball*) a **suspension** of two minutes awarded by the **referee** to a player who has received a second **warning** or shown faulty or unsportsmanlike conduct

two-minute warning (*American football*) a mandatory **timeout** occurring when two minutes remain in the second and fourth **quarters** of a **game**

two-platoon system (*American football*) the system of training and playing two separate **platoons**

Two Thousand Guineas (*horse racing*) an annual **race** for three-year-old **colts** and **fillies** run over the **Rowley Mile** at **Newmarket** since 1809 [original value of **prize**, a guinea being 21 shillings]

two-wheeler (*cycling*) colloquial term for a **cyclist**

twosome (*golf*) a **game** between two players

Tykes (*association football*) nickname of the English **club** Barnsley [from *tyke*, local term for a Yorkshireman]

Uber Cup (*badminton*) the **cup** awarded to the winner of a biennial international team competition for women first held in 1957 [named for the English player Betty Uber (*c.*1905–1983)]

uchimata (*judo*) an inner thigh **throw** made with the thrower's leg braced between the legs of his opponent [Japanese *uchi*, "inside," and *mata*, "thigh"]

ude-garami (*judo*) an armlock applied to the arm of an opponent when bent at the elbow [Japanese *ude*, "arm," and *karami*, "lock"]

ude-gatame (*judo*) an armlock applied to the arm of an opponent when straight [Japanese *ude*, "arm," and *katame*, "hold"]

UEFA (*association football*) abbreviation of **Union of European Football Associations**

UEFA Champions League (*association football*) formal name of the **European Champions' Cup**

UEFA Cup (*association football*) the **cup** awarded from 1958 to 2009 (when renamed the **Europa League**) to the winners of a contest between **clubs** finishing near the top of their domestic **league**

uglies (*rugby union*) colloquial term applied to a team's **forwards** by the **backs**

uke (*judo*) general term for the combatant who is in a **hold** or the object of a **throw** [Japanese *ukeru*, "to receive"]

ukemi (*judo*) the art of falling safely [**uke** and Japanese *mi*, "body"]

uki-gatame (*judo*) a ground **hold** applied after an opponent has been thrown [Japanese *uki*, "floating," and *katame*, "to lock"]

uki-otoshi (*judo*) a **throw** made with the hand alone [Japanese *uki*, "floating," and *otoshi*, "dropping"]

ultimate fighting (*sport*) a **combat sport** in which two opponents fight each other without protective gear and with only minimal rules as to the type of blow permitted

ultimate Frisbee (*sport*) another name for **airborne soccer**

ultra (*athletics*) colloquial shortening of **ultramarathon**

ultramarathon (*athletics*) a **long-distance race** greater than a **marathon**, especially a **foot race** of 36 miles or more

ump (*general*) colloquial abbreviation of **umpire**

umpire (*general*) an official in sports such as **baseball**, **cricket**, and **tennis**, in many ways corresponding to a **referee**, who supervises a **game** or **match**, enforces the rules, and decides disputes

uncapped (*cricket*) not having been awarded the **cap** given to regular members of a **county cricket** team; (*general*) not having been selected to play for a national team

Uncle Charlie (*baseball*) colloquial term for a **curveball**

under (*golf*) under **par** [in this adverbial usage, *under* is invariably preceded by the number of **strokes** involved, as "three under"]

under orders (*horse racing*) shortening of **under starter's orders**

under starter's orders (*horse racing*) ready to begin a **race** and awaiting the **starting signal**

under way (*sailing*) having begun to move in the water

under wraps (*horse racing*) (of) a horse restrained from running at its best in order to disguise its true **form** before an important **race**

underarm (*cricket*) (of) a **delivery** made with the hand lower than the level of the shoulders, now not generally permitted; (*swimming*) (of) a **stroke** made with the arm below the level of the body; (*tennis*) (of) a **serve** made with the hand lower than the level of the shoulders

undercard (*boxing*) a contest placed second on the billing

underclub (*golf*) to use a **club** with too much **loft**, so that the **ball** is not sent far enough

undercut (*golf*) to strike a **ball** below the center, causing it to rise high; (*mountaineering*) to cut a **handhold** from below in order to maintain the climber's balance; (*tennis*) to **slice** down on a **ball** below the center so that **backspin** is imparted

underedge (*cricket*) the inside or bottom edge of a **bat**

undergrip (*gymnastics*) a **hold** on the **horizontal bar** made by passing the hands beneath it, rather than over it, so that the palms face the **gymnast**

underhold (*mountaineering*) a **hold** in which the climber grasps a downturned edge or point from beneath with his palm turned upward in order to maintain his balance

underpitched (*cricket*) not pitched far enough by the **bowler**, so that the **ball** falls short

underspin (*general*) a backward **spin** imparted to a **ball** so that it stops quickly or bounces backward on making contact with the ground or some other surface

undertie (*angling*) to tie the wings of a **fly** so that they cover the point of the **hook**

underwater sports (*aquatics*) sports played below the surface of the water, some being submerged versions of **field games** such as **field hockey** or **rugby union**

underwater swimming (*aquatics*) a former term for sports such as **skin diving** or **subaqua**

underwear cricket (*cricket*) mocking term for **twenty20 cricket** [as punningly compared to **pajama cricket**, both being shortened forms of the **game**]

unearned run (*baseball*) a **run** conceded because of an **error** by the **fielding** side

uneven bars (*gymnastics*) another term for the **asymmetric bars**

unexposed (*horse racing*) having an unknown or uncertain **racing form**, like a **dark horse**

Union of European Football Associations (*association football*) the sport's international association for Europe, founded in 1954 and affiliated to **FIFA**

United (*association football*) short name of a British **club** with "United" in its name, as Leeds United or Manchester United

United States Grand Prix (*auto racing*) the **Formula One** international **Grand Prix** held on various **circuits**, such as those at Detroit (Michigan), Long Beach (California), the Indianapolis Motor Speedway (site of the **Indianapolis 500**), Caesars Palace, Las Vegas (California), Riverside

(California), Phoenix (Arizona), and Watkins Glen (New York)

University Boat Race (*rowing*) formal name of the **Boat Race**

unload (*boxing*) to deliver a forceful **punch**

unpaced (*general*) without the assistance of a **pacemaker**

unplaced (*horse racing*) not among the first thee horses to win a **race**

unplayable (*golf*) in a position where the **ball** cannot be struck

unseated (*equestrianism, horse racing*) thrown from a horse

unseeded (*tennis*) not placed in the **draw** of top players

unshipped (*equestrianism, horse racing*) another term for **unseated**

unsuited (*horse racing*) disadvantaged in a **race** by factors adversely affecting a horse's best performance, as by the state of **going**

up (*baseball*) another term for **at bat**; (*equestrianism, horse racing*) mounted on a horse; (*general*) ahead in scoring

up-and-down (*golf*) an act of completing a **hole** from a point close to the **green** with a single **pitch shot** or **chip shot** ("up") and a single **putt** ("down")

up-and-under (*rugby league, rugby union*) a very high kick ("up") that gives the kicker and his teammates time to rush forward to the point ("under") where the **ball** will come down

up the jumper (*rugby union*) a style of play in which a team advances the **ball** down the **pitch** through the **forwards**, with little passing and much use of the **drive** [the ball in such a move is difficult to locate, as if one of the players had put it "up his jumper"]

upfield (*general*) in or toward the farther end of a **playing field**

uppercut (*boxing*) an upward **punch** that comes from underneath the opponent's **guard**

upright (*association football*) another term for a **goalpost**

upright spin (*ice skating*) a **spin** in which the skater stands and rotates on one foot

upset (*general*) an unexpected defeat of the favorite

upshot (*archery*) the final **shot** of a contest

upstart (*gymnastics*) a series of movements on the **parallel bars** or **asymmetric bars**, especially at the start of a **routine**, by which a **gymnast** swings to a position in which he supports his body by his arms above the bars

upstream gate (*canoeing*) on a **slalom** course, a **gate** to be negotiated against the direction of the current

urn (*cricket*) the **trophy** awarded to the winner of the **Ashes**

U's (*association football*) short name of a **club** with "United" in its name, as Cambridge United, Colchester United, Oxford United

US Masters (*golf*) an annual **invitational** contest held at the **Augusta** National Club since 1934

US Open (*golf*) an annual **tournament** first held in 1895; (*tennis*) an annual **tournament** first held in 1881 and since 1978 played at **Flushing Meadows** [so named as open to both **amateur** and **professional** players]

US PGA (*golf*) a U.S. **championship** first held in 1916 and a **matchplay** event until 1958 [abbreviation of Professional Golfers' Association]

useful (*general*) playing or performing competently, if not outstandingly well

utility club (*golf*) a **club**, often used for long **shots** from difficult **rough**, that combines the favorable characteristics of an **iron** with those of a **wood**

utility player (*association football*) a player capable of playing in different positions

Uttoxeter (*horse racing*) a **National Hunt** racecourse at Uttoxeter, Staffordshire, England

v (*general*) abbreviation of *versus* ("against"), used to name the two teams or individuals in a **game** or **match**, as "France v New Zealand," "Rangers v Celtic"

V (*cricket*) the area on the **field** between **mid-off** and **mid-on**, used to describe the path of a **ball** hit by the **batsman**

V-position (*skiing*) the position of the **skis** adopted by most skiers during a **ski jump**, touching at the tail and spread apart at the tips to form a "V"

Valderrama (*golf*) a **golf course** at San Roque, southwestern Spain

Vale (*association football*) short name of the English **club** Port Vale

Valentine's Brook (*horse racing*) a difficult **jump** on the **Grand National** course at **Aintree** [named for a horse that spectacularly cleared it]

valet (*horse racing*) the person responsible for looking after a **jockey**'s equipment

Valiants (*association football*) nickname of the English **clubs** Charlton Athletic and Port Vale

van (*tennis*) abbreviation of **advantage**

Vardon grip (*golf*) a common grip of the **club**, in which the pinkie of the right hand overlaps the forefinger of the left [popularized by the English **champion** Harry Vardon (1870–1937)]

varsity (*general*) a team representing a university or college

varsity match (*general*) an annual **match** between the teams of Oxford and Cambridge universities, notably in **association football** and **rugby union**

vault (*athletics*) shortening of **pole vault**; (*gymnastics*) a leap from a **springboard** onto and over a **vaulting horse**, on which the hands are briefly rested to gain height during the flight; (*equestrianism*) a gymnastic leap or **routine** made by a **rider** on horseback

vaulting (*gymnastics, equestrianism*) the execution of a **vault** as a distinctive **event** or **discipline**

vaulting horse (*gymnastics*) a piece of **apparatus** in the form of a wooden block used for **vaulting** [it represents a horse to be mounted by a **vault**]

veer (*American football*) an offensive **play** in which a modified **T-formation** with a split **backfield** gives the **quarterback** the option of either passing to the **fullback**, pitching to a **running back**, or running with the **ball** himself; (*sailing*) to change course away from the wind

velodrome (*cycling*) an indoor or outdoor **stadium** with a banked **track** for **races** [borrowing of French *vélodrome*, from *vélo*, "bicycle," and -*drome* as in *hippodrome*]

Vendée Globe (*sailing*) a solo, non-stop round-the-world **race** held every four years, sailing westward from and back to Les Sables d'Olonne on the west coast of France [from *Vendée*, the French department where the race begins and ends]

vent (*parachuting*) the opening in a **canopy** through which air escapes at a controlled rate

venue (*general*) the chosen location for a **match** or other sporting contest

verbal abuse (*general*) the **offense** by a player of berating a **referee** or other official for an apparent misjudgment, such as an alleged **miscall** by a **line judge** in **tennis** (where it may be accompanied by **racket abuse**)

vert (*skateboarding, snowboarding*) a vertical extension to a ramp, from which stunts are performed [abbreviation of *vertical*]

vertical (*equestrianism*) a high **obstacle**

vertical gate (*skiing*) a **gate** on a **slalom** course with poles placed vertically rather than horizontally

Vezina Trophy (*ice hockey*) the **trophy** awarded annually since 1927 to the **goalkeeper** voted the best at his position [named in commemoration of the Canadian player Georges Vézina (1887–1926)]

victor ludorum (*general*) a title awarded in some schools and colleges to the overall **champion** in a sports competition [Latin *victor ludorum*, "winner of the games"]

Victorian Football League (*Australian Rules*) former name of the **Australian Football League**

victory lane (*auto racing*) in **NASCAR**, the place on the **infield** of the **racetrack** where the winner parks for the prize-giving

victory lap (*athletics*) a celebratory **lap** run by an **athlete** after winning a **race**

video referee (*rugby league, rugby union*) an official in the **stands** who has access to TV **replays** and

who may be consulted by the **referee** in cases of a doubtful **try**

video review (*general*) the video **replay** of an incident during a **match** in order to determine whether an **offense** had been committed

vigoro (*sport*) a **team game** played mainly by women that combines elements of **cricket** and **baseball** [abbreviation of *vigorous*]

VIII (*rowing*) conventional designation of an **eight** in sports reports [Roman numerals]

Vikings (*American football*) short name of the Minnesota Vikings team; (*rugby league*) short name of the English **club** Widnes Vikings

Villa (*association football*) short name of the English **club** Aston Villa

village cricket (*cricket*) an informal **game** or **match**, as played between local village teams

Villans (*association football*) short name of the English **club** Aston Villa [pun on *villains*]

Vince Lombardi Trophy (*American football*) the **trophy** awarded since 1967 to the winners of the **Super Bowl** [named for Vince Lombardi (1913–1970), **coach** and **manager** of the Green Bay Packers team]

violation (*basketball*) a breach of the rules not considered to be a **foul**, such as **traveling**

visitors (*general*) a team that comes to play a **match** on the **home ground** of their rivals

visor (*horse racing*) a headpiece worn by a horse to concentrate its attention on the **course** ahead in the manner of **blinkers** but unlike them having slits that allow some side vision

voiture balai (*cycling*) alternate French term for the **broom wagon**

volley (*association football*) a **shot** or **pass** in which the **ball** is struck before it hits the ground; (*squash, tennis*) a **shot** played before the **ball** bounces; (*volleyball*) a **shot** of the **ball** over the **net** with the fingers, fist, or forearm

volleyball (*sport*) a **game** for two teams of six players played with a large **ball** on a **court**, the aim being to gain **points** by hitting the ball by a **volley** over a high **net** dividing the court in such a way that the opposing team cannot return it

volte (*equestrianism*) the **gait** of a horse moving sideways around the center of a circle [French *volte*, from Italian *volta*, "turn"]

Volvo Ocean Race (*sailing*) a round-the-world **race** for **one-design** boats, first held in 1973 [name of sponsors]

vorlage (*skiing*) a position in which the skier leans forward without lifting his heels from the **skis** [German *Vorlage*, "presentation"]

vorlaufer (*skiing*) a skier who travels a **course** before a **race** to check that it is within the capacity of the competitors [German, *Vorläufer*, "runner ahead"]

vs (*general*) another form of **v** as an abbreviation of *versus* ("against"), as in "Barbarians vs All Blacks"

Vuelta a España (*cycling*) an annual **stage race** over the roads of Spain, first held in 1935 [Spanish *Vuelta a España*, "Tour of Spain"]

w (*cricket*) abbreviation of **wide** in scoring

waders (*angling*) high waterproof boots, used by **anglers** for standing in streams or rivers

wager (*horse racing*) another term for a **bet**

waggle (*golf*) an act of waggling the **clubhead** over the **ball** before playing a **shot**

waggler (*angling*) a type of long **float** that indicates the slightest movement of the **bait**

wagonwheel (*cricket*) a graphic representation or "map" of the paths of the **balls** hit by a particular **batsman** [the lines resemble the spokes of a wagonwheel]

WAGS (*association football*) acronym of "wives and girlfriends," referring to the glamorous, free-spending partners of celebrity **footballers**, as depicted in the British TV drama series *Footballers' Wives* (2002–06)

wahine (*surfing*) colloquial term for a young female **surfer** [Maori *wahine*, "woman"]

wait out (*baseball*) to force a **pitcher** to throw a maximum number of **pitches** by deliberately not striking at them

waiting blocks (*karate*) an area where nonplaying members of a team wait as **reserves** or where players go when **out**

waiting race (*horse racing*) a **race** in which a horse is kept a little way behind the **leaders** until the final stages

waive (*association football*) to refrain from using the right to buy or sign a player from a **club** in the same **league** before he is offered to a club in another league

wake (*water skiing*) the V-shaped track of water behind a boat as it moves forward

wakeboard (*water skiing*) the short wide **board** similar to a **snowboard** used in **wakeboarding**

wakeboarding (*water skiing*) the sport of riding and performing acrobatic maneuvers on a **wakeboard** while it is towed behind a motorboat

walk (*baseball*) another term for **base on balls**; (*cricket*) to leave the **pitch** when **dismissed** without waiting for the **umpire** to adjudicate on an **appeal**; (*equestrianism*) a horse's slowest **gait**, in which the legs move individually in a diagonal pattern

walk-on (*general*) a member of a team who has no regular status

walk-up (*general*) (of) spectators who attend a sporting contest without buying tickets in advance; (*horse racing*) the walking of a horse up to the **starting line**

walkathon (*athletics*) a long-distance competitive walk, undertaken to raise funds for charity [blend of *walk* and **marathon**]

walkaway (*general*) a **race** in which the winner leaves the other competitors far behind

Walker Cup (*golf*) the **cup** awarded to the winner of a biennial competition between **amateur** men's teams from the United States and the British Isles, first held in 1922 [named for George H. Walker, president of the United States Golf Association in the 1920s]

walking (*athletics*) shortening of **race walking**

walkover (*general*) (1) a **race** in which there is only one competitor, who has merely to walk over the **finishing line** to win; (2) an easy victory

wall (*association football*) a formation of defensive players lined up to defend their **goal** against a **free kick**; (*athletics*) the onset of extreme fatigue encountered by runners in a **long-distance race** or **marathon** as a physical and psychological barrier to be overcome; (*baseball*) the barrier marking the outer limit of the **outfield**; (*equestrianism*) a high **jump** built to look like a wall; (*Eton wall game*) each of the players who form the **bully** against the wall; (*mountaineering*) a steep smooth rock face; (*surfing*) the steep face of a wave before it breaks

wall bars (*gymnastics*) a set of horizontal bars extending up the wall of a **gymnasium**

wall game (*sport*) short name of the **Eton wall game**

wall pass (*association football*) another term for a **one-two**

Wallabies (*rugby union*) nickname of the Australian national team [from the animal, a member of the kangaroo family, that is native to Australia]

walley (*ice skating*) a **jump** that starts from a back **inside edge** and lands on the back **outside edge** of the same **blade** [origin disputed]

wallyball (*volleyball*) a form of the **game** played in a walled **court** [bland of *wall* and **volleyball**]

Walthamstow (*greyhound racing*) the **stadium** in the district of this name in London, England, that until its closure in 2008 was the country's leading **venue** for the sport

waltz (*ice skating*) a **jump** in the form of a **takeoff** from a front **outside edge** of one **blade**, a half-revolution, and a landing on the back **outside edge** of the other blade

ward (*fencing*) a defensive posture or movement

warm-down (*general*) a period of gentle exercise after keen physical exertion

warm-up (*general*) a practice exercise before a contest

warm-up lap (*auto racing*) another term for a **formation lap**

warn off (*horse racing*) to ban a person from all **race meetings** or from a particular **course**

warning (*boxing*) an official admonition from the **referee**, three of which lead to a **disqualification** from the **bout**

warning track (*baseball*) a grass-free strip around the outside of the **outfield**, warning approaching **fielders** that they are near a wall

Warriors (*association football*) nickname of the Scottish **club** Stenhousemuir; (*basketball*) short name of the Golden State Warriors team; (*rugby league*) short name of the English **clubs** Whitehaven Warriors and Wigan Warriors; (*rugby union*) short name of the English **club** Worcester Warriors

Warwick (*horse racing*) a **flat** and **National Hunt racecourse** at Warwick, Warwickshire, England

wash (*rowing*) (1) the rough water behind a moving boat that can affect the progress of competing boats in a **race**; (2) the water disturbed by an **oar**

washboard (*motorcycle racing*) in **motocross**, a series of hillocks [suggesting the corrugations on a washboard]

Wasps (*association football*) nickname of the Scottish **club** Alloa Athletic [from the yellow and black colors of the team **strip**]; (*rugby union*) short name of the English **club** London Wasps

watchet (*angling*) an **artificial fly** imitating a pale blue **mayfly** [name of color]

water ballet (*swimming*) another term for **synchronized swimming**

water hazard (*golf*) a **hazard** in the form of a lake, river, stream, ditch, or other body of water, defined by stakes or lines painted on the ground

water jump (*athletics*) an obstacle in the **steeplechase**, in which **athletes** land in a shallow pool of water; (*equestrianism, horse racing*) an **obstacle** in the form of a **fence** or hedge followed by a stretch of water

water polo (*sport*) a **game** played in a **pool** between two teams of seven **swimmers**, the aim being to throw a large **ball** into the netted **goal** of the opposing side [the game has no connection with or resemblance to **polo** but merely borrowed its name]

water skiing (*sport*) the sport of being towed at speed on one or two **skis** behind a motorboat

water skis (*water skiing*) lightweight runners made of fiberglass, in some versions fitted with **fins**, that enable the skier to skim the surface of the water

water sports (*sport*) another term for **aquatics**

Waterloo Cup (*bowls*) the **cup** awarded to the winner of a contest in **crown green** bowls first held at the Waterloo Hotel, Liverpool, in 1907

watery grave (*golf*) colloquial term for a stretch of water into which a **ball** has been hit

wave sailing (*windsurfing*) a form of the sport in which participants attempt to become airborne and perform stunts on the edges of waves

wave soaring (*gliding*) the gaining of altitude by riding vertical waves of wind, as on the lee side of a mountain

Waysiders (*association football*) nickname of the Scottish **club** Airdrie United

waza-ari (*judo*) a **score** of half a **point**, or half an **ippon**, awarded to a contestant for an incompletely executed **throw** or **hold** [Japanese *waza*, "act," and *ari*, from *aru*, "to be"]

weak side (*American football*) the side of a standard offensive formation on which there is no **tight end**

weasel (*cricket*) a very poor **batsman** [as one "sent in after a **rabbit**"]

weave (*boxing*) to dodge **punches** by making twisting and turning movements

wedeln (*skiing*) a style of traveling downhill in which the **skis**, kept parallel and close together, are swiveled rapidly from side to side [German *wedeln*, "to wag the tail"]

wedge (*golf*) a **club**, especially a 10-**iron**, with a broad low-angled face and a high degree of **loft**

Wednesday (*association football*) short name of the English **club** Sheffield Wednesday

Wee Rangers (*association football*) nickname of the Scottish **club** Berwick Rangers [they are "wee" (small) as less successful and prosperous than Rangers]

Wee Rovers (*association football*) nickname of the Scottish **club** Albion Rovers [they are "wee" (small) as less successful and prosperous than Raith Rovers]

weigh in (*boxing*) to be weighed as a **boxer** before a **match**; (*horse racing*) to be weighed as a **jockey** after a **race**

weigh-in (*angling*) the weighing of a **catch** after a competition; (*boxing*) the weighing of a **boxer** before a **match**; (*horse racing*) the weighing of a **jockey** after a **race**

weigh out (*horse racing*) to be weighed as a **jockey** before a **race**

weigh-out (*horse racing*) the weighing of a **jockey** before a **race**

weigh sling (*angling*) a bag attached to a sling, used for weighing a **catch**

weighing room (*horse racing*) the room in which the **jockeys** and their **saddles** are weighed before and after a **race**

weight (*athletics*) another term for the **shot**; (*bowls*) the force given a **delivery** of a bowl; (*boxing*) the standard amount that a **boxer** should weigh [categorized by a defining prefix, as **flyweight**, **heavyweight**]; (*horse racing*) the weight that a **handicapper** assigns to a horse to carry, based on its **form**; (*weightlifting*) shortening of **disk weight**

weight cloth (*horse racing*) a cloth under a horse's **saddle** that contains lead weights to bring the horse's **weight** up to the required amount

weight training (*weightlifting*) the sport as a form of physical exercise or training

weightlifter (*weightlifting*) a person who takes part in the sport

weightlifting (*sport*) a sport in which competitors strive to lift and hold above their heads a **barbell** which becomes increasingly heavy (by the addition of **disk weights**) as the competition progresses

weights (*weightlifting*) (1) shortening of **weightlifting** or **weight training**; (2) the **barbell** or other heavy object of a particular weight used in these

Well (*association football*) short name of the Scottish **club** Motherwell

Wellydrome (*cycling*) nickname of the roofless Meadowbank **velodrome**, Edinburgh, Scotland [pun on *welly*, short form of *wellington boot*, worn in wet conditions]

welsh (*horse racing*) to run off from a **racecourse** without settling one's **bets** [of uncertain origin, not related to *Welsh*]

welter (*horse racing*) an unusually heavy weight, carried mostly in **steeplechases** and **hurdle races** [origin uncertain]

welter race (*horse racing*) a **race** in which a **welter** is carried

welterweight (*boxing*) the professional **weight** category of maximum 67kg (147lb)

Wembley (*general*) shortening of **Wembley Stadium**

Wembley Arena (*general*) a former sports **venue** near **Wembley Stadium**, London, that is now used for rock concerts, comedy acts, and musical shows

Wembley Stadium (*general*) a **stadium** in Wembley, London, England, that opened in the 1920s as a general sports center but was rebuilt in 2007 primarily as a covered **association football** stadium with facilities for staging concerts and **athletics events**

Wentworth (*golf*) a **golf course** and **tennis club** at Virginia Water, Surrey, England

West Brom (*association football*) short name of the English **club** West Bromwich Albion

Westchester Cup (*polo*) the **cup** awarded to the winner of a contest inaugurated in 1886 between England and the United States [named for the Westchester Polo Club, Westchester County, New York]

Western (*archery*) a **round** of 48 **arrows** for men and women respectively at 60yds and 50yds (55m and 46m)

western grip (*table tennis*) anther term for the **shakehands**

western roll (*athletics*) a style of **high jump** in which the **athlete** takes off from the inside foot, swings up the other leg, and rolls over the **bar** face downward

wet bob (*rowing*) a boy at Eton College who rows during the summer term, as distinct from a **dry bob**

wet fly (*angling*) an **artificial fly** that sinks below the surface of the water

Wetherby (*horse racing*) a **National Hunt racecourse** at Wetherby, West Yorkshire, England [the name has no connection with Weatherbys, the firm founded in 1773 that now performs major administrative duties in British racing]

wets (*auto racing*) tires with a full tread designed to disperse surface water in wet conditions [colloquial shortening of *wet-weather tires*]

wetsuit (*general*) a close-fitting waterproof garment worn mainly by **skin divers** and **surfers** for protection against the cold

Wexford (*horse racing*) a **flat** and **National Hunt racecourse** at Wexford, Co. Wexford, Ireland

wheel (*rugby union*) to push the **scrum** unevenly, so that it rotates

Wheelchair Games (*Olympics*) an early name for the **Paralympic Games**

Wheelchair Olympics (*Olympics*) alternate name for the **Wheelchair Games**

wheelchair sports (*general*) sports played by people with physical disabilities (not just wheelchair users), with *wheelchair* prefixed to the name of the sport, as *wheelchair tennis*

wheeler (*cycling*) colloquial term for a **cyclist** [some **clubs** use the word in their name, as the Manchester Wheelers]

wheelhouse (*baseball*) the area immediately surrounding a **batter**, especially when favoring a good swing at a **pitch**

wheelie (*general*) a stunt in which a **cyclist** or **motorcyclist** travels a short distance with the front wheel of the machine off the ground, or in which a **boarder** travels on a **skateboard** with one pair of wheels off the ground

wheelsucking (*cycling*) colloquial term for the technique of riding close to the **rider** in front in order to **slipstream**

whereabouts rule (*general*) a requirement whereby **athletes** must give advance notice of the location where they can be reached by **dope** control officers at any time

whiff (*baseball*) to cause a **batter** to **strike out**; (*general*) to aim at a **ball** but miss it; (*golf*) another term for an **air shot**

whiffleball (*baseball*) a light, hollow, plastic **ball** used in a form of the **game** as played by young children [from *whiffle*, "puff of air"]

whip (*cricket*) a springy action of the wrist in hitting or bowling a **ball**; (*equestrianism*) the driver in **carriage driving**; (*horse racing*) the flexible switch with which a **jockey** urges on his horse; (*wrestling*) a technique by which an opponent is forced into a **somersault** by a sudden wrench of his forearm

whipback (*gymnastics*) a back **handspring** in which the hands do not touch the floor

whipper-in (*horse racing*) colloquial term for the last horse in a **race** at any given moment [a term borrowed from hunting, in which the whipper-in keeps the hounds from straying by driving them back into the main body of the pack with a whip]

whippet (*greyhound racing*) a racing dog developed from a cross between a greyhound and a spaniel or terrier

whistle (*general*) a blast on a whistle by a **referee**, typically in **association football**, to signal a halt in play, either because a **foul** has occurred or because it is **half time** or **full time**

Whitbread Round the World Race (*sailing*) name of the **Volvo Ocean Race** to 2001 [name of sponsor]

white (*snooker*) the white **cue ball**

white-ball game (*sport*) byname of **cricket** when played with a white **ball**, as against the traditional **red-ball game**

White City (*general*) a former **stadium** and center of **greyhound racing** in west London [originally an exhibition center of white-stuccoed buildings laid out in 1908]

white flag (*athletics*) a **flag** waved to an **athlete** to indicate a fair **jump** or **throw**; (*auto racing*) a **flag** waved to show that a slow-moving vehicle such as the **safety car** is on the **track**

White Hart Lane (*association football*) the **home ground** of Tottenham Hotspur **football club**, London

white jersey (*cycling*) the jersey awarded to the best-placed **rider** aged 25 or under [French *maillot blanc*, "white jersey"]

white rose (*general*) the emblem of a Lancashire sports team, as opposed to the **red rose** [from the Wars of the Roses, the 15th-century dynastic struggle between the English houses of Lancaster and York, whose respective emblems were a white rose and a red rose]

White Sox (*baseball*) short name of the Chicago White Sox team

Whitechapel (*billiards*) a **shot** that unintentionally sends an opponent's **ball** into a **pocket** [from Whitechapel, a formerly poor district of London, where the **game** was popular]

whites (*cricket, tennis*) the white clothes traditionally worn by players

Whites (*association football*) nickname of the English **club** Leeds United [the color of the team **strip**]

whitewash (*general*) a total defeat in a **game** or series of games

whitewater (*canoeing*) the type of foaming water created by rapids, as found in **slalom**

whoop (*general*) a bump on a **track** or **course** in **off-roading** or **rally driving**

wick (*curling*) to strike another **stone** and move it

wicket (*cricket*) (1) the upright arrangement of three **stumps** with two **bails** atop which the **batsman** defends against the **bowling**; (2) a batsman's turn at this; (3) a batsman's **innings**; (4) another term for the **pitch**, especially with regard to its condition (as a **soft wicket**)

wicket-taker (*cricket*) a **bowler** regularly able to **take a wicket**

wicketkeeper (*cricket*) the **fielder** who stands immediately behind the **wicket** defended by the **batsman** and whose main aim is stop any **balls** that the latter misses

wide (*cricket*) a **delivery** of the **ball** by the **bowler** judged by the **umpire** to be beyond the reach of the **batsman** and so counting one **run** to the batsman's side; (*horse racing*) running on a course that deviates from the most direct, as a horse may be obliged to do when starting from an unfavorable **draw**

wide receiver (*American football*) a **receiver** who stands to the side of the rest of the team, his prime task being to catch **passes** and run quickly **downfield** with the **ball**

wideout (*American football*) another term for a **wide receiver**

wiffleball (*baseball*) another spelling of **whiffleball**

Wightman Cup (*tennis*) the **cup** awarded to the winner of an annual **championship** played between British and American women's teams from 1923 to 1989 [donated in 1923 by the U.S. player Hazel Hotchkiss Wightman (1886–1974)]

Wild (*ice hockey*) short name of the Minnesota Wild team

wild card (*general*) a player or team allowed to enter a sporting contest although lacking the usual qualifications or not meeting the official requirements [from the term for a playing card having any value its player chooses to give it]

wild pitch (*baseball*) a **pitch** thrown so inaccurately that it is not hit by the **batter** or stopped by the **catcher**, thus enabling a **baserunner** to advance

Wildcats (*rugby league*) short name of the English **club** Wakefield Wildcats

William H. Cane Futurity (*horse racing*) an annual **harness race** for three-year-old **pacers** run at Yonkers, New York, since 1955 [named for **breeder** William H. Cane (1874–1956), who in 1950 converted the former Empire City **racetrack** to the Yonkers Raceway]

willow (*cricket*) byname for a **cricket bat** [traditionally made of willow]

Wimbledon (*tennis*) short name of the All England Lawn Tennis and Croquet Club at Wimbledon, London, England, founded in 1869 and since 1877 the site of the annual men's and women's **singles** and **doubles championships**

win (*general*) a victory in a contest

Wincanton (*horse racing*) a **National Hunt racecourse** at Wincanton, Somerset, England

Winchester fives (*fives*) a variant of **Rugby fives** played between **doubles** in a four-walled **court**, in which a buttress on a side wall makes one end of the court slightly narrower than the other [originally played at Winchester College, Hampshire]

Winchester football (*sport*) a form of **rugby union** played exclusively at Winchester College, Hampshire, with a round **ball** as in **association football**

wind (*boxing*) a point on the body covering the stomach, a blow on which causes winding

wind-assisted (*athletics*) enhanced as a distance or time by a **following wind**, and therefore ineligible for official records

wind-up (*baseball*) a coiled position assumed by a **pitcher** before throwing the **ball**

windcheater (*golf*) a **ball** struck low with strong **backspin** into the wind

Windies (*cricket*) colloquial name of the West Indies team

window (*angling*) the area of upward vision of a fish, taken into account when **fly fishing**, especially for trout

window jump (*skiing*) a stunt in which the skier supports himself on his **sticks**, swings the **skis** between them, then turns the skis in the air

Windsor (*horse racing*) a **flat racecourse** at Windsor, Berkshire, England

windsurfer (*windsurfing*) a person who takes part in **windsurfing**

windsurfing (*sport*) a blend of **surfing** and **sailing**, consisting in riding the waves on a **sailboard**

windward (*sailing*) toward the direction from which the wind is blowing, as distinct from **leeward**

wing (*general*) (1) another term for a **winger**; (2) the part of the **field** in which he plays; (*paragliding, paramotoring*) an equivalent to the **parachute** in the form of an inflatable elliptical **canopy** with small air pockets

wing attack (*netball*) an attacking player restricted to the attacking **third** and center third

wing defense (*netball*) a defensive player restricted to the defending **third** and center third

wing forward (*rugby union*) another term for a **flanker**

wingback (*association football*) a player on the **wing** with a greater attacking role than a conventional **fullback**

winger (*general*) in **field games**, a player on the right or left **wing**, who in **association football** has the prime task of sending **crosses** into the **penalty box** and in **rugby league** and **rugby union** tries to run fast with the **ball** down the side of the **pitch**

Wingfield Sculls (*rowing*) the **trophy** awarded to the winner of an annual **sculls race** over the **Boat Race** course in London [inaugurated in 1830 by Henry C. Wingfield, a lawyer]

winner (*tennis*) the **stroke** that ends a **rally**, so winning a **point**

winning gallery (*real tennis*) the last **gallery** on the **hazard side** of the **court**, a **shot** into which wins a **point**

winning hazard (*billiards, snooker*) a **stroke** in which the **object ball** goes into a **pocket**

winning line (*general*) another term for the **finishing line**

winning opening (*real tennis*) each of the three openings around the **court** into which the **ball** may be struck from the far side of the **net**, these being the **dedans**, the **grille**, and the **winning gallery**

winning post (*horse racing*) the post marking the **finishing line** on a racecourse

winter book (*horse racing*) the estimate made by a **bookmaker** of the **odds** for **races** in the coming season

winter football (*sport*) alternate name for **bandy**

Winter Olympics (*Olympics*) an international festival of **winter sports** introduced in 1924 as an independent extension of the **Olympic Games**

winter sports (*general*) open-air sports practiced mainly (but not exclusively) in winter on snow and ice, such as **ice hockey**, **ice skating**, and **skiing**

wipeout (*general*) a fall from a **surfboard**, **skateboard**, **skis**, or the like, especially when spectacular

wire (*croquet*) (1) the part of the **hoop** above the ground; (2) to play a **shot** in such a way that a **ball** is hampered by a **hoop**; (*greyhound racing, horse racing*) another term for the **finishing line** [formerly marked by a wire stretched across the **racetrack**]

wired (*croquet*) prevented from making an intended **shot** because a **ball**, or a proper swing of the **mallet**, is hampered by a **hoop**

Wisden (*cricket*) short title of *Wisden Cricketers' Almanack*, an annual comprehensive and definitive record of the sport [first published in 1864 by John Wisden (1826–1884)]

wishbone (*American football*) a variant of the **T-**

formation, in which the two **halfbacks** are set back from the **fullback** to form an inverted "V" or "wishbone"

with the darts (*darts*) winning a **leg** with the advantage of throwing first

Wizards (*basketball*) short name of the Washington Wizards team

WM (*association football*) a **formation** of five **defenders** (three **backs** and two **halves**) in the shape of a "W" and five **attackers** (five **forwards**) in the shape of an "M"

wobbler (*angling*) a **lure** that wobbles and does not spin

wobbly duck (*American football*) colloquial term for a badly-thrown **pass** [it wobbles instead of going straight]

Wolverhampton (*horse racing*) a **flat** and **National Hunt racecourse** at Wolverhampton, near Birmingham, England

Wolves (*association football*) nickname of the English **club** Wolverhampton Wanderers; (*rugby league*) short name of the English **club** Warrington Wolves

wood (*bowls*) another term for a **bowl** [originally made of wood, but now of a composite material]; (*golf*) a **club** with a bulky head [traditionally made of wood, but now usually of metal]

wood shot (*tennis*) a **shot** inadvertently played off the rim of the **racket** [formerly made of wood]

wooden spoon (*general*) the last place in a competition [originally a spoon made of wood presented to the candidate coming last in the mathematical tripos at Cambridge]

woodwork (*association football*) colloquial term for the **goalposts** and **crossbar**

Worcester (*horse racing*) a **National Hunt racecourse** at Worcester, Worcestershire, England

work (*cricket*) the manipulation of the **ball** by the **bowler** to give it a **swing** or **spin**; (*horse racing*) exercise in preparation for a **race**

work out (*boxing*) to fight a practice **bout**

worker (*golf*) colloquial term for a **shot**, especially a **putt**, that runs a long way

workout (*boxing*) a practice **bout**

world (*general*) shortening of **world championship**

World Bowl (*American football*) an annual contest first held in 1991 as the **championship game** of the World League of American Football but from 1995 that of **NFL** Europe

world champion (*general*) the **champion** of a sport in an international contest

world championship (*general*) an international sports contest whose winner will become **world champion**

World Cup (*general*) the **cup** awarded to the winner of an international **tournament** in a particular sport, the best-known being that first held in 1930 in **association football**, formerly known as the **Jules Rimet Trophy** [other sports with World Cup contests are (with year of inauguration) **athletics** (1977), **baseball** (1938), **cricket** (1975), **field hockey** (1971), **golf** (1953), **lacrosse** (1982), **polo** (1987), **rugby league** (1954), **rugby union** (1987), **skiing** (1967), **table tennis** (1980), **volleyball** (1965), **water polo** (1979)]

World Matchplay Championship (*golf*) an international **championship** with a valuable **prize** inaugurated in 1964 and until 2008 played at **Wentworth**

world record (*general*) an internationally unsurpassed **record**

World Road Race Championship (*cycling*) an annual international **road race** competition first held in 1927

World Series (*baseball*) a series of **games** contested annually since 1903 between the **champions** of the **National League** and the **American League**

world title (*general*) another term for a **world championship**

worm (*angling*) the **earthworm** used as **bait**

wormer (*angling*) a person who collects **worms** for **bait**

wrap (*gymnastics*) a twining around of the body during a **routine** on the **asymmetric bars**

wrestle down (*wrestling*) to bring an opponent to the ground

wrestler (*wrestling*) a person who participates in the main sport or in **sumo**

wrestling (*sport*) a **combat sport** in which two contestants grapple, each trying to throw his opponent to the ground and pinion him there

wrestling match (*wrestling*) a contest between two **wrestlers**

Wrigley Field (*American football*) the **home ground** of the Chicago Bears team in Chicago

wrist play (*cricket*) a technique in which a **batsman** scores **runs** by tipping the **ball** with a turn of the wrist rather than by wielding a full-on **stroke** with the **bat**

wrist wrestling (*wrestling*) a variant of **arm wrestling** in which the contenders lock right thumbs instead of hands in an attempt to force down each other's arm

wrong-foot (*general*) to destabilize an opponent by means of a deceptive **move** or **shot**

wrong 'un (*cricket*) another term for a **googly**; (*horse racing*) a horse dishonestly held back so as to lose a **race**

wushu (*general*) a term for the Chinese **martial arts** [Chinese *wu*, "military," and *shu*, "art"]

X Games (*Olympics*) an alternate form of **Olympic Games** devoted to **extreme sports**, held since 1995 in the United States, where they are controlled and arranged by the sports broadcaster ESPN [so named as designed for "Generation X," who became adults in the early 1990s]

XI (*cricket*) conventional designation of an **eleven**, especially in **fixtures** [Roman numerals]

Xs and Os (*American football*) a formula adopted by **coaches** when explaining tactical maneuvers to players by means of diagrams, "X" being an **attacker** and "O" a **defender**

XV (*rugby union*) conventional designation of a **fifteen**, especially in **fixtures** [Roman numerals]

yacht (*sailing*) a sailing vessel equipped for **racing** [Dutch *jacht*, formerly *jagt*, from *jagen*, "to chase"]

yacht club (*sailing*) a **club** for **yacht** owners or participants in **yacht races**

yacht race (*sailing*) a **race** among **yachts**

yacht racing (*sailing*) the competitive **racing** of **yachts**

yachting (*sport*) a former alternate term for **sailing**, officially dropped for competitions in 2000

yachtsman (*sailing*) a person who owns or sails a **yacht**

yachtswoman (*sailing*) a woman who sails in a **yacht**

yahoo (*cricket*) an exuberant (but not always successful) attempt to hit the **ball** hard

yakker (*baseball*) colloquial term for a **curveball**

Yankee (*horse racing*) a multiple **bet** on four horses in four **races**, consisting of six **doubles**. four **trebles**, and an **accumulator**

Yankee Stadium (*baseball*) the **home ground** of the New York Yankees team in the Bronx, New York City

Yankees (*baseball*) short name of the New York Yankees team

yard (*horse racing*) the **stables**, grounds, and facilities owned by a **trainer**; (*sailing*) a long beam on a **mast** for spreading **sails**

yard-on (*bowls*) a heavy **shot** to break up or disturb the **head**

yardage (*American football, golf*) a distance measured in yards

Yarmouth (*horse racing*) a **flat racecourse** near Great Yarmouth, Norfolk, England

yaw (*sailing*) to deviate temporarily from a **course**

yearling (*horse racing*) a **racehorse** that is officially one year old, as calculated from January 1 in its year of foaling

yell (*general*) a rhythmic cheer or chant, often containing nonsense words or syllables, used to encourage sports teams, as in **college football**

yellow (*snooker*) the yellow **ball**, worth two **points**

yellow card (*association football*) a card shown to a player by the **referee** as an official warning after an infringement; (*rugby league, rugby union*) a card shown to a player by the **referee** following

an infringement and sending him to the **sin bin**

yellow flag (*auto racing*) a **flag** waved to show that there is danger ahead and that there must be no overtaking

yellow jersey (*cycling*) (1) the jersey worn by the **leader** in the **general classification** at the end of particular day in the **Tour de France** [French *maillot jaune*, "yellow jersey"]; (2) a similar jersey in the **Tour of Britain**

yellow spot (*snooker*) the spot on the **billiard table** where the **yellow** is positioned, in the right corner of the **D** (viewed from the **balk** end)

yielding (*horse racing*) a category of **going**

yipper (*golf*) a golfer suffering from the **yips**

yips (*golf*) nervous twitching caused by tension before playing a **putt** [a word coined by Scottish **professional** Tommy Armour in the 1920s]

Yngling (*sailing*) a class of **keelboat** sailed by a crew of three [Norwegian *yngling*, "youngster"]

yoko-shiho-gatame (*judo*) a **hold** from the side in which a combatant pins his opponent's shoulders and hips to the ground [Japanese *yoko*, "side," "across," *shiho* (from *shi*, "four," and *ho*, "direction"), and *katame*, "to lock"]

yokozuna (*sumo*) a grand champion, as the highest rank of **wrestler** [Japanese *yoko*, "across," and *tsuna*, "rope," from the garland originally presented to a champion]

Yonkers Futurity (*horse racing*) an annual **harness race** for three-year-old **trotters**, first held in 1958 at Yonkers, New York

york (*cricket*) to **dismiss** a batsman by bowling a **yorker**

York (*archery*) a **round** of 72 **arrows** for men at 100yds (91m), 48 at 80yds (73m), and 24 at 60yds (55m); (*horse racing*) a **flat racecourse** at York, North Yorkshire, England

yorker (*cricket*) a **delivery** of the **ball** that pitches on the **popping crease** and passes under the **bat** of the **batsman** [said to have been introduced by Yorkshire players]

Yoyos (*association football*) nickname for the Scottish **club** Stirling Albion [from the team's alternating **promotions** and **relegations**, sending them up and down like a yoyo]

yuko (*judo*) a **score** of five points, awarded for a **throw** or **hold** not worthy of a **waza-ari** [Japanese]

yump (*auto racing*) in **rally driving**, to leave the ground when going over a ridge or crest [Norwegian *jump*, "jump"]

Yurchenko (*gymnastics*) a **routine** in the **vault** consisting of a **round-off** onto the **springboard**, then a **flic-flac** onto the vault, then a **dismount** by way of a **backflip** [first performed in competion in 1982 by the Soviet **gymnast** Natalya Yurchenko (1965–)]

Zamboni (*ice hockey*) proprietary name of a machine used to clean, resurface, and smooth the ice on a **rink** [invented in 1949 by Frank J. Zamboni (1901–1988)]

zebra (*American football*) colloquial term for a member of the officiating team [from their black-and-white striped shirts]

Zebras (*association football*) nickname of the Italian **club** Juventus [from the team's black-and-white striped shirts]

zero tackle (*rugby league*) an additional **tackle** awarded at the beginning of the standard set of six, awarded after a **knock-on** or a **forward pass**

zip (*general*) to beat a team without allowing them to score

zippers (*American football*) the permanent scars that disfigure the bodies of many players as a result of tough contact play

zonal marking (*general*) another term for **zone defense**

zone (*ice hockey*) one of the three equal parts of the playing area, as the center or neutral zone, attacking zone, and defending zone

zone defense (*American football, association football*) a method of **defense** in which a player patrols a particular area of the **field** rather than **mark** a specific opponent; (*basketball*) a method of **defense** in which a player patrols a particular area of the **court** rather than **mark** a specific opponent; (*ice hockey*) a method of **defense** in which a player patrols a particular area of the **rink** rather than **mark** a specific opponent

zoo (*surfing*) colloquial term for a crowded **line-up**

zooter (*cricket*) a **ball** bowled by a **leg spinner** that does not spin but dips late in flight to the **batsman** [apparently a random word]

zorb (*general*) a large transparent **ball** containing a smaller ball within which a person is secured and then rolled along the ground, down hills, and the like [apparently a random word, perhaps meant to evoke a science-fiction creation]

zorbing (*general*) the **extreme sport** of traveling in a **zorb**

Appendix:
Abbreviations of Ruling Bodies and Administrative Organizations

Below are some of the many abbreviations used for the various sports ruling bodies and administrative organizations, whether international or national. Abbreviations with their own entries in the book are printed in **bold** (e.g. **AFL**). Translations of foreign titles are provided.

AAA

AFC

AFL

AIBA (*boxing*) Association Internationale de Boxe Amateur (International Amateur Boxing Association)

ATP (*tennis*) Association of Tennis Professionals

BHA

BWF (*badminton*) Badminton World Federation

CFU (*Canadian football*) Canadian Football League

CIPS (*angling*) Confédération Internationale de Pêche Sportive (International Sport Fishing Confederation)

CMSB (*boules*) Confédération Mondiale de Sports Boules (World Boules Confederation)

ECB

FA

FAI (*ballooning, gliding, parachuting*) Fédération Aéronautique Internationale (International Aeronautical Association)

FEI (*equestrianism*) Fédération Équestre Internationale (International Equestrian Federation)

FFPB (*pelota*) Fédération Française de la Pelote Basque (International Pelota Federation)

FIA (*auto racing*) Fédération Internationale de l'Automobile (International Automobile Federation)

FIB (*bandy*) Federation of International Bandy

FIBA (*basketball*) Fédération Internationale de Basketball (International Basketball Federation)

FIBT (*bobsledding*) Fédération Internationale de Bobsleigh et Toboganning (International Bobsleigh and Toboganning Federation)

FIE (*fencing*) Fédération Internationale d'Escrime (International Fencing Federation)

FIFA

FIG (*gymnastics, trampolining*) Fédération Internationale de Gymnastique (International Gymnastics Federation)

FILA (*wrestling*) Fédération Internationale de Lutte Amateur (International Wrestling Federation)

FIM (*motorcycle racing*) Fédération Internationale de Motocyclisme (International Motorcycling Federation)

FINA (*swimming, water polo*) Fédération Internationale de Natation (International Swimming Federation)

FIP (*polo*) Federation of International Polo

FIPV (*pelota*) Federación Internacional de Pelota Vasca (International Pelota Federation)

FIQ (*tenpin bowling*) Fédération Internationale des Quilleurs (International Skittles Federation)

FIRS (*roller hockey, roller skating*) Fédération Internationale de Roller Sports (International Roller Sports Federation)

FIS (*skiing, snowboarding*) Fédération Internationale de Ski (International Ski Federation)

FISA (*rowing*) Fédération Internationale des Sociétés d'Aviron (International Rowing Federation)

FITA (*archery*) Fédération Internationale de Tir à l'Arc (International Archery Federation)

FIVB (*volleyball*) Fédération Internationale de Volley-ball (International Volleyball Federation)

GHA (*hurling*) Gaelic Athletic Association

IAAF (*athletics*) International Association of Athletics Associations

IAF (*aikido*) International Aikido Federation

IBAF (*baseball*) International Baseball Federation

IBF (*boxing*) International Boxing Federation

IBSF (*snooker*) International Billiards and Snooker Federation

ICC

ICF (*canoeing*) International Canoe Federation

IFNA (*netball*) International Federation of Netball Associations

IFWLA (*lacrosse*) International Federation of Women's Lacrosse Associations

IHF (1) (*field hockey*) International Hockey Federation; (2) (*handball*) International Handball Federation

IIHF (*ice hockey*) International Ice Hockey Federation

IJF (*judo*) International Judo Federation

IKF (1) (*kendo*) International Kendo Federation; (2) (*korfball*) International Korfball Federation

ILF (*lacrosse*) International Lacrosse Federation

IOC

IOF (*orienteering*) International Orienteering Federation

IRB (*rugby union*) International Rugby Board

IRF (*racquetball*) International Racquetball Federation

ISA (*surfing*) International Surfing Association

ISAF (*sailing, windsurfing*) International Sailing Federation

ISDRA (*sled dog racing*) International Sled Dog Racing Association

ISF (1) (*skateboarding*) International Skateboarding Federation; (2) (*softball*) International Softball Federation

ISJA (*ju-jitsu*) International Sport Ju-jitsu Association

ISSF (*shooting*) International Shooting Sport Federation

ISU (*ice skating*) International Skating Union

ITTF (*table tennis*) International Table Tennis Federation

IWF (*weightlifting*) International Weightlifting Federation

IWUF (*kung fu*) International Wushu Federation

JJIF (*ju-jitsu*) Ju-jitsu International Federation

JSA (*sumo*) Japan Sumo Association

MCC

MLB (*baseball*) Major League Baseball

NBA (*basketball*) National Basketball Association

NCAA (*American football*) National Collegiate Athletic Association

NFC

NFL

NHL

NPA (*paddleball*) National Paddleball Association

NRA (*rounders*) Natinal Rounders Association

PBA (*bowls*) Professional Bowls Association

R&A

RFL (*rugby league*) Rugby Football League

RFU (*rugby union*) Rugby Football Union

RORC (*sailing*) Royal Ocean Racing Club

RYA (*powerboat racing*) Royal Yachting Association

T&RA (*rackets, real tennis*) Tennis and Rackets Association

UCI (*cycling*) Union Cycliste Internationale (International Cycling Union)

UEFA

UIAA (*mountaineering*) Union Internationale des Associations d'Alpinisme (International Union of Mountaineering Associations)

UMB (*billiards*) Union Mondiale de Billard (World Billiards Union)

USGA (*golf*) United States Golf Association

USPTA (*paddle tennis*) United States Paddle Tennis Association

WAKO (*kickboxing*) World Association of Kickboxing Associations

WBA (*boxing*) World Boxing Association

WBC (*boxing*) World Boxing Council

WBO (*boxing*) World Boxing Organization

WCBS (*billiards*) World Confederation of Billiard Sports

WCF (1) (*croquet*) World Croquet Federation; (2) (*curling*) World Curling Federation

WDF (*darts*) World Darts Federation

WGRF (*greyhound racing*) World Greyhound Racing Federation

WIBC (*bowls*) World Indoor Bowls Council

WKF (1) (*kabaddi*) World Kabaddi Federation; (2) (*karate*) World Karate Federation

WPA (*billiards, pool*) World Pool-Billiards Association

WPBSA (*snooker*) World Professional Billiards and Snooker Association

WSF (1) (*snooker*) World Snooker Federation; (*squash*) World Squash Federation

WTF (*tae kwon do*) World Taekwondo Federation

Select Bibliography

Arlott, John, ed. *The Oxford Companion to Sports and Games*. London: Oxford University Press, 1975. [Comprehensive coverage of the rules and terminology of sports worldwide, including bullfighting, but omitting blood sports (and fishing) and board and table games.]

The Badminton Library of Sports and Pastimes. [A set of 23 volumes by various authors published in London from 1887 and originally planned in 1882 by Henry Somerset Beaufort, 8th duke of Beaufort (whose family estate is at Badminton) and Alfred Watson as "a series of books that would attempt to highlight, examine and explain all of the many great sports that this nation enjoys." Coverage includes not only hunting, "a subject always very close to my family's heart," but "Fishing; Racing and Steeplechasing; Lawn Tennis; Shooting; Driving; Athletics; Football, and even Cycling and Motor Driving" (11th duke of Beaufort, Introductory Note to 1985 reprint of *Hunting*, 7th ed., 1894).]

Ballard, John, and Paul Suff. *The Dictionary of Football*. London: Boxtree, 1999. [An innovatory guide to the world of Association Football.]

Bloodgood, Lida Fleitmann, and Piero Santini. *The Horseman's Dictionary*. London: Pelham, 1963. ["Including over 3,500 words used on the Turf, in the Hunting field, Show-ring, Manège, on the Road, Trotting-track, Polo field, Ranch, and in the Stable or Stud."]

Brasch, Rudolph. *How Did Sports Begin?* New York: David McKay, 1970. [A readable account of the origins of well-known sports and their distinctive vocabulary.]

Brooks, Katie, ed. *Chambers Sports Factfinder*. 2d ed. Edinburgh: Chambers, 2008. [Covers results and key figures in over 100 sports with selective glossaries of their jargon.]

Dale, Rodney, and Steve Puttick. *The Wordsworth Dictionary of Abbreviations and Acronyms*. 2d ed. Ware: Wordsworth, 1999. [Contains general and special categories of abbreviations including sports, with ball games individually represented.]

Darton, Mike, and John O.E. Clark. *The Dent Dictionary of Measurement*. London: J.M. Dent, 1994. [Contains detailed information on the measurements, units, and playing positions of most sports, as well as plans of the area of play in American football, archery, association football, badminton, bandy, baseball, basketball, billiards, cricket, curling, field hockey, Gaelic football, ice hockey, lacrosse, polo, pool, rugby league, rugby union, table tennis, and tennis.]

Davies, Christopher. *Divided by a Common Language: A British/American Dictionary Plus*. Rev ed. Sarasota, FL: Mayflower, 1998. [Includes a small but interesting selection of baseball terms that have taken on a metaphorical sense.]

Encyclopædia Britannica. 15th ed. Chicago: Encyclopædia Britannica, 2002. [Vol. 28, pp. 100–166, has a good section "Major Team and Individual Sports," the former comprising association football, U.S. football, Canadian football, rugby, cricket, basketball, and ice hockey; the latter comprising tennis, golf, athletics, and surfing.]

Foley, Keith. *A Dictionary of Cricketing Terminology*. Lampeter: Edwin Mellen Press, 1998. [A timely key to many of the sometimes baffling terms, formal and informal, encountered in the game, with examples of usage.]

Galitsky, Aleksey, and Leonid Pereplyotchikov. *Puteshestviye v strany igr* ("A journey into the land of [sports and] games"). Moscow: Fizkul'tura i sport, 1971. [For Russian readers, an informative and entertaining insight into the history and rules of a range of sports and games, from internationally known baseball, cricket, American football, association football, golf, lacrosse, and pelota to the more esoteric national games of Russia and the countries of the former Soviet Union, such as lapta, lelo, tskhenburti, and aymtskachare.]

Green, Jonathon. *Dictionary of Jargon*. London: Routledge and Kegan Paul, 1987. [A collection of some 21,000 words and phrases including several from the world of sport.]

Hammond, Gerald. *Horse Racing: A Book of Words*. Manchester: Carcanet, 1992. [A useful guide to the sometimes arcane jargon of the sport.]

Heatley, Michael. *Football Club Origins and Nicknames*. Hershey: Ian Allan, 2008. [An informed study of the history and names of British football clubs.]

Lewin, Esther, and Albert E. Lewin. *The Thesaurus of Slang*. New York: Facts on File, 1994. [An American-oriented reference that includes terms and definitions relating to sports such as baseball, basketball, (American) football, (ice) hockey, and racing, but omits all major British sports, including cricket, (association) football, rugby, and (field) hockey.]

Meadows, Chris, with Allen F. Richardson. *The Encyclopedia of Golf*. Bath: Parragon, 2007. [A practical guide to the game, with a brief summary of the rules and a short glossary.]

Montague, Trevor, comp. *A to Z of Everything*. 4th ed. London: Little, Brown, 2007. [A regularly revised general knowledge compendium first published in 2001, with a major section Sport and Leisure, pp. 1256–1340.]

_____. *A to Z of Sport: The Compendium of Sporting Knowledge*. London: Little, Brown, 2004. [Main emphasis is on sports results, awards, and personalities, but includes selective definitions of sporting terms.]

The New Encyclopædia Britannica. 30 vols. 15th ed. Chicago: Encyclopædia Britannica, 2002. [The main entry "Sports" (vol. 28, pp. 100–166) is devoted to the history and sociology of sports, with accounts of major team and individual sports (association, American, and Canadian football, rugby, cricket, basketball, ice hockey; tennis, golf, athletics, surfing), while separate articles on other sports and games appear elsewhere.]

Norridge, Julian. *Can We Have Our Balls Back, Please? How the British Invented Sport*. London: Allen Lane, 2008. [An account of the sports professedly invented by the British. The 15 chapters are titled: 1. Boxing, 2. Horse Racing, 3. Cricket, 4. Golf, 5. Sailing or Yacht Racing, 6. Football (Soccer), 7. Rugby (and Rugby League, Australian Rules and American Football), 8. Rowing, 9. Baseball, 10. Lawn Tennis (and assorted games), 11. Hockey (and maybe even Ice Hockey), 12. Athletics (and the Modern Olympics), 13. Swimming, 14. Pub Games, 15. The Ones That Got Away. The final chapter includes motor racing, basketball, fencing, gymnastics, shooting, weightlifting, wrestling, equestrian sports, winter sports (skiing, ice skating, bobsleigh, curling), and cycling.]

Pavlov, S.P., ed.-in-chief. *Olimpiyskaya entsiklopediya* ("Olympic encyclopedia"). Moscow: Sovetskaya Entsikopediya, 1980. [A Russian reference guide to the Olympic Games, their history, results, and performers, including descriptions of the Olympic sports themselves.]

Pick, J.B., comp. *The Phoenix Dictionary of Games*. London: Phoenix House, 1952. [Divided into five sections: Full-Dress Outdoor Games, Informal Outdoor Games, Covered Court Games, Gymnasium Games, and Indoor Games.]

Visual Dictionary. rev. ed. London: Dorling Kindersley, 2002. [A valuable resource that includes (pp. 522–563) pictures of sports equipment and playing areas, including those of football, rugby, basketball, volleyball, baseball, cricket, hockey, athletics, tennis, golf, archery, judo, skiing, equestrianism, fencing, swimming, rowing, sailing, and fishing.]

Willock, Colin. *The Angler's Encyclopaedia*. London: Odhams, 1960. [A popular alphabetical guide to coarse, sea, and game fishing, *Achill* to *zander*.]

_____, ed. *The New ABC of Fishing: A Revised Guide to Angling for Coarse, Sea and Game Fish*. Rev. ed. London: Andre Deutsch, 2003. [A new edition of a book first published in 1992 and itself a revised edition of *The ABC of Fishing*, published in 1964.]

Wilson, Bob. *Bob Wilson's Ultimate Collection of Peculiar Sporting Lingo*. Cambridge: Icon, 2008. [Gives origins and meanings of 335 sporting terms, from *Addicks* to *zooter*.]

Woo, Suzanne. *On Course for Business: Women and Golf*. New York: John Wiley, 2002. [Has a useful glossary of golfing terms, pp. 209–223.]

As well as the titles listed above, the following general dictionaries were also consulted:

Brookes, Ian, ed.-in-chief. *The Chambers Dictionary*. 11th ed. Edinburgh: Chambers Harrap, 2008.

Brown, Lesley, ed.-in-chief. *Shorter Oxford English Dictionary*. 5th ed. Oxford: Oxford University Press, 2002. 2 vols.

Gove, Philip Babcock, ed.-in-chief. *Webster's Third New International Dictionary of the English Language*. Springfield, MA: Merriam-Webster, 1961.

The Sunday Times Sport Calendar 2009 was used for the names, dates, and venues of scheduled world sporting events.